"This book is the most thorough, systematic treatment of Software Reuse published to date. The authors have extensive experience in this field, and they support their conclusions with a wealth of empirical results. Their data show that effective reuse really can be achieved, with major reductions in cost, defects, and time to market. But these same data also show that reuse isn't free — it doesn't happen automatically with the adoption of objects, nor can it be achieved without investment, planning, and deep organizational support. This book offers a proven, workable program for achieving reuse and reaping its rewards. I predict that it will quickly become the primary reference on this important subject."

David Taylor, President, Enterprise Engines Inc.

"This book tells it as it is: reuse is a business as well as a technical decision that requires engineering discipline and management support. If you are serious about improving your software development productivity and reducing your time to market by making OO work for you, then read this book. You won't be disappointed!"

Will Tracz, Senior Programmer in Advanced Technology, Lockheed Martin Federal Systems.

"Certainly this book is overdue. Achieving serious reuse is hard — we need all the codified expertise we can get."

David Redmond-Pyle, Chief Methodologist, LBMS Inc.

"This book clears up the controversy about whether object-oriented software reuse can really pay off, providing not only many successful examples from the authors' work at Hewlett-Packard and Ericsson, but also an experience-based approach for repeating the success. The approach requires not just a class-library silver bullet, but a strategy integrating business-case analysis, domain engineering, product line architecting, people and process management, and life-cycle software asset management. A particularly nice feature is a reuse-oriented tailoring of the Unified Modeling Language."

Barry Boehm, TRW Professor of Software Engineering,
Director of Center for Software Engineering, University of Southern California.

"This book is comprehensive in its coverage of the fundamentals of software reuse, the subject that is catalyzing the transformation of our industry from a craft to an engineering discipline. I commend Jacobson, Griss and Jonsson for their important contribution to the field."

Paul Bassett, Senior Vice President Research, Netron Inc.

Ivar Jacobson is the inventor of the Objectory OO method and founded Objectory AB, Sweden. He is currently Vice President of Business Engineering at Rational Software Corporation where he is intimately involved with the development of UML and a leader in the OO community. He is well known for his pioneering work and close to 30 years experience using object methods for the design of large, real-time systems. His work on large-scale, architected reuse was a key element of the success of Ericsson's AXE telecommunications switch. He is principal author of two influential books, *Object-Oriented Software Engineering – A Use Case Driven Approach* and *The Object Advantage: Business Process Reengineering with Object Technology*.

Martin Griss is a Senior Laboratory Scientist at Hewlett Packard Laboratories. For the last 23 years, 14 at HP and 9 as a Professor at the University of Utah, he has carried out research in the fields of software engineering processes, tools and environments, object-oriented technology, component-based software engineering and software reuse. As HP's "Reuse Rabbi", he created the Corporate Reuse Program and led the systematic introduction of software reuse into HP's divisions. He led HP's technical contributions as co-submittor of UML to the OMG. He also writes a reuse column for *Object Magazine* and is active on several reuse program and steering committees.

Patrik Jonsson works for Rational Software Corporation in Sweden as a Senior Consultant. He has been involved in specifying the requirements for Objectory's CASE tool and has been developing the architecture and method of the Objectory process with a current focus on reuse and user interface development. He is a co-author of *Object-Oriented Software Engineering – A Use Case Driven Approach*.

SOFTWARE REUSE

ARCHITECTURE
PROCESS AND
ORGANIZATION FOR
BUSINESS SUCCESS

Selected ACM titles

The Object Advantage: Business Process Reengineering with Object Technology
(2nd edn) *Ivar Jacobson, Maria Ericsson, Agneta Jacobson, Gunnar Magnusson*

Object-Oriented Software Engineering: A Use Case Driven Approach *Ivar Jacobson,
Magnus Christerson, Patrik Jonsson, Gunnar Övergaard*

Software for Use: A Practical Guide to the Models and Methods of Usage Centered
Design *Larry L Constantine & Lucy A D Lockwood*

Bringing Design to Software: Expanding Software Development to Include Design
Terry Winograd, John Bennett, Laura de Young, Bradley Hartfield

CORBA Distributed Objects: Using Orbix *Sean Baker*

Software Requirements and Specifications: A Lexicon of Software Practice, Principles and
Prejudices *Michael Jackson*

Business Process Implementation: Building Workflow Systems *Michael Jackson &
Graham Twaddle*

New Community Networks: Wired for Change *Douglas Schuler*

Civilizing Cyberspace: Policy, Power and the Information Superhighway *Steve E Miller*

Computer-Related Risks *Peter G Neumann*

Interacting Processes: A Multiparty Approach to Coordinated Distributed Programming
Nissim Francez & Ira Forman

Design Patterns for Object-Oriented Software Development *Wolfgang Pree*

Intelligent Database Systems *Elisa Bertino, Gian Piero Zarri*

Modern Database Systems: The Object Model, Interoperability and Beyond *Wom Kim*

Database Security *Silvana Castano, Giancarlo Martella, Pierangela Samarati,
Mariagrazia Fugini*

Internet Security *Dorothy E Denning & Peter J Denning*

SOFTWARE REUSE

ARCHITECTURE
PROCESS AND
ORGANIZATION FOR
BUSINESS SUCCESS

IVAR JACOBSON

MARTIN GRISS

PATRIK JONSSON

ACM Press

New York, New York

Addison-Wesley

Harlow, England • Reading, Massachusetts
Menlo Park, California • New York
Don Mills, Ontario • Amsterdam • Bonn
Sydney • Singapore Tokyo • Madrid
San Juan • Milan • Mexico City • Seoul • Taipei

ACM PRESS BOOKS

This book is published as part of ACM Press Books — a collaboration between the Association for Computing (ACM) and Addison Wesley Longman Limited. ACM is the oldest and largest educational and scientific society in the information technology field. Through its high-quality publications and services, ACM is a major force in advancing the skills and knowledge of IT professionals throughout the world. For further information about ACM, contact:

ACM Member Services
1515 Broadway, 17th Floor
New York, NY 10036-5701
Phone: 1-212-626-0500
Fax: 1-212-944-1318
E-mail: acmhelp@acm.org

ACM European Service Center
108 Cowley Road
Oxford OX4 1JF
United Kingdom
Phone: +44-1865-382388
Fax: +44-1865-381388
E-mail: acm_europe@acm.org
URL: http://www.acm.org

Library of Congress Cataloging-in-Publication Data is available

Cover designed by Designers & Partners, Oxford, UK
Typeset in 10/12pt Palatino by 43
Printed and bound in The United States of America

First printed 1997. Reprinted 1997 and 1998.

ISBN 0–201–92476–5

The publishers wish to thank the following for permission to reproduce the material cited. For Figure 7.4, thanks to Object Management Group, Framingham, MA, USA. For Figure 9.4, thanks to P Kruchten and *CrossTalk — The Journal of Defense Software Engineering*.

FOREWORD

By Björn Svedberg

Information technology is playing an ever increasing role in the effective execution of the fast-paced global business that characterizes our industrial world of today. In developing these IT systems, software design is critical for the creation of mission-critical enterprise systems. These systems enable rapid information flow and support decision making across the enterprise.

The success of a company is very often coupled with how well it manages its software assets. Efficient software truly is a means of competition and has proven to be the reason why some companies succeed, rising to the top of their industries, while others sink into oblivion. As chairman of Ericsson and president of Skandinaviska Enskilda Banken, I have seen the critical impact an effective software strategy has on two such different companies as a multi-international telecommunication company and a bank.

Today, banks and telecommunication companies both compete on the rapid development and deployment of new services. This would not be possible without a well-designed, well-managed set of software components.

At Ericsson in the mid 1970s we developed the AXE system, which was a new generation of switching systems. At that time I was personally responsible for the development work and was able to see fully the importance of the software element.

With Ericsson working in a competitive, worldwide arena, we knew we had to be able to give every telecom operator a tailor-made product. This meant that the foremost requirement we placed on the development effort was to create a highly adaptable product. We designed a core system that could be reused all over the world. We worked hard to ensure that the extra work needed to adapt and extend AXE for each new market could be minimized.

Thanks to a component-based design approach, developed by a core team where Ivar Jacobson played a most important role, we were able to develop a product that made us superior from our customer's point of view to our competition. The AXE system had a software architecture that was unique. It was built up from components on different levels, interconnected by well-defined interfaces. This structure allowed us to swap in new components as the functional requirements of the system had to be enhanced. We could configure a particular customer system by selecting a specific subset of our components and adding some new customer-specific components.

Without a doubt, this component reuse approach has been an essential element in the success of Ericsson.

A modern bank like the Skandinaviska Enskilda Banken is also critically dependent on software. Rapid flow of information is absolutely crucial. Customers want new capabilities as the pace of business accelerates and the world changes. New kinds of accounts, new services, new trading policies, and on-line banking are simple examples. These exist almost entirely in the software domain. To provide value, and to compete effectively, banks must design, develop and deploy these new services in a short time period, often of only a few months. Software must be developed quickly, but without loss of quality or excessive costs.

At the same time, we must respond to new technologies, and gracefully replace the huge investment in legacy software as we move from mainframe computing to distributed computing based on the Intranet and reach out to customers over the Internet. To meet these challenges and satisfy our customers needs, we depend on an effective, flexible system architecture and a component software strategy.

Knowing what I know about the experience that underlies this book and about the impact Ivar has already had on software development at Ericsson and at other companies, I am convinced that the lessons and insight provided here will be of crucial value to any company dependent on software.

In writing this book Ivar paired up with Martin Griss, the leading reuse expert from Hewlett-Packard. Hewlett-Packard is a world-leader in platforms, measurement systems and manufacturing. The combined and complementary experience from Ericsson and Hewlett-Packard in component-based design and reuse makes me truly believe that this book is a seminal contribution to the software industry.

Björn Svedberg

Dr Björn Svedberg started his professional career at Ericsson after graduating from the Royal Institute of Technology in Stockholm, department of Electrical Engineering. He moved quickly up the ranks of the company, to more and more responsible positions, all with a strong technical content: memory design, computer architecture, software design and implementation, software architecture, development process. At the age of forty Dr Svedberg became president of the world-leader in telecommunications, Ericsson, a position he held for more than a decade. In 1990 Dr Svedberg was appointed chairman of the board of Ericsson. At about the same time he accepted a new challenge as president for Skandinaviska Enskilda Banken, one of the largest banks in Sweden.

Dr Svedberg was awarded an honorary doctorate from the Lund Institute of Technology in 1984.

FOREWORD

By Joel Birnbaum

I feel privileged to be asked to write a foreword to a book that I think every senior manager with responsibility for software use or development should read. It will surely become a classic work in the evolution of software engineering, theory and practice, because it can be helpful at many levels: for general understanding of the challenges and the nature of the best solutions we have today, for detailed insight into techniques for the preparation of reusable code, and for an architectural framework to customize the processes which are a critical element of competitive advantage in these information technology dependent times.

For over thirty years I have been working, first as a researcher, and then as a manager/sponsor of industrial and university research, on the deceptively difficult problem of bringing the design, development, and modification of software to the same high levels of engineering discipline that characterize the enormous progress the information industry has made in hardware systems. For fifteen years at IBM Research, and now for sixteen at Hewlett-Packard, I have considered our inability to reduce software development to a predictable, repeatable procedure as the single greatest impediment to the transformation of computing to a truly pervasive technology. For example, at HP, which many think of as mostly a computing hardware platform, measurement instrument and computer peripheral manufacturer, an informal survey a few years ago revealed that well over 70% of our R&D expenses were software and firmware. A conservative estimate today would probably show an increase to almost 80% of the $3 billion that we expect to spend in 1997 on R&D, as more and more of our revenue becomes dependent on providing full solutions, systems integration, and services to our customers.

As the senior technologist at HP, I am deeply involved on a daily basis with those ideas, methods, processes or tools that will make a substantial, long-term difference to the success of our company, and the work of Martin Griss and his colleagues in Software Reuse is beginning to make a big difference at HP. The nature of my job as head of R&D causes me to meet with many customers from very diverse industries to try to understand their needs and major challenges. I have never met one who didn't have software at or near the top of the list.

I have known Martin Griss since he joined HP in 1983 and from the beginning I thought he had the right blend of talents, experience and interests to lead our research efforts in this area. For one thing, he had a rigorous training in physics, and a very good feeling for how to conduct scientific experiments. Many academically trained computer scientists and software managers lack the experience to design, execute, and statistically analyze the results of studies which must systematically isolate variables and search for non-obvious correlations. Martin had already had great success as a Professor of Computer Science at Utah as well, where, among other things, he distinguished himself as an usually creative language designer by leading the team that produced Portable Standard Lisp, a very innovative language for its time. At HP Labs, he added organizational and managerial skills to his already broad areas of expertise. I had been looking for a creative leader who combined breadth of knowledge, vision and tenacity with expertise in topics as far ranging as programming language design, development of software engineering tools, software process design and modeling, and organization design and transformation. Martin seemed made to order and I set about convincing him to devote the next decade of his career in pursuit of this elusive goal. We both knew it would not be easy, or glamorous, and that there would be no single tool or silver bullet. We also knew that managers who came from hardware backgrounds would neither understand nor have patience with the need to make progress methodically, and therefore slowly. Martin accepted the challenge, and neither of us has been sorry since. Today almost all sectors of our company practice systematic reuse, and the results have gone straight to the bottom line.

As software has become a critical enabler not only for us, but for most of our customers as well, Martin's originally little-understood work has gained acceptance and adherence in and out of our company. Many have come to realize that a reuse architecture is almost certainly the most effective path towards dramatic improvement of both development costs and time. In a world where the majority of programmers are still involved in the repair or modification of code, usually written by someone else, the ability to add software-based features in an efficient and timely way often emerges as the key differentiator.

For the important work described in this book, Martin has teamed up with the distinguished object-oriented methodologist and industrial software engineer, Ivar Jacobson, who had so much influence on the theory and practice of software design and development practice in the software industry and particularly at Ericsson. I have heard that much of the success of the pioneering AXE telecommunications system can be traced to the successful application of Ivar's ideas, and Dr Svedberg makes it clear in his foreword the key role that Ivar's vision and drive, coupled with the consistent support of his management, played in this landmark system for the communications industry. With Ivar and Martin working closely together, we have here the dream team of Software Reuse. As the authors state, the successful practice of component-based software engineering requires the commitment of senior management, who need to be informed about the essence and practice of building families of complex software systems from well-designed, architected software components. Digesting the wisdom of this book is a wonderful way to begin.

Joel Birnbaum PhD
Senior Vice President, R&D and Director, HP Laboratories.

PREFACE

This is a book for software engineering practitioners and their managers, interested in dramatically improving their software development performance. For many industrial and commercial enterprises, accomplishing key business goals, such as satisfying the customer, achieving time to market with products and services, or controlling costs, has direct implications on the way they choose to develop and use information technology and software systems for competitive advantage. In most of these cases, objects, component-based development, and software reuse are key parts of their software engineering strategy. Succeeding with industrial-strength object-oriented software engineering requires that the promise of large-scale software reuse be realized in a practical way. This book provides a pragmatic framework for success.

Systematic software reuse

Ever since libraries of shared components were first proposed by Doug McIlroy in 1968, software reuse has been recognized as an attractive idea with an obvious payoff. Building software systems from previously developed, high-quality components certainly saves the cost and time of redundant work and improves systems. For many years, obtaining high levels of reuse has been elusive. Many different technical, process, and organizational issues have blocked progress. But despite pursuit of a variety of other "silver bullets" to improve software development, it remains clear that systematic software reuse and component-based development is still one of the most promising ways to significantly improve the software development process.

Most software development organizations move to object technology because engineering managers believe that this will lead to significant reuse. Unfortunately, without an explicit reuse agenda and a systematic reuse-directed software process, most of these object adoption efforts do not lead to successful large-scale reuse.

Why do we use the term "reuse"? No other engineering field uses this term. Instead, the systematic design and use of standard components is accepted practice; many handbooks of hardware components, ranging from motors and gears to chips, are produced annually and studied daily by design engineers. Despite the use of the term "Software-IC" coined by Brad Cox, and component-based development as encouraged by Microsoft and others, a software components industry with an associated widespread use of components is still in its infancy. In the future, component-based software engineering will be taught as a standard part of the software engineering curriculum and the word "reuse" will become obsolete; today, we use the term "reuse" to describe the goals of this still emerging area of software engineering.

Over the past ten years, the software reuse and software engineering communities have come to better understand component-based software engineering. In almost all cases of successful reuse, the keys were management support, system and component architecture, a dedicated component group, a stable application domain, standards, and organizational support. Many software engineering books and conferences focus specifically on systematic software reuse and on object technology. Many mention reuse, architecture, and process- and domain-specific application development, but they differ in their approach to reuse. Some object technology books, including Jacobson *et al.*'s 1992 Object-Oriented Software Engineering (OOSE) book, address certain object reuse issues directly or have significant sections on reuse. Appendix B provides an annotated bibliography of pertinent work.

What is this book about?

This book is directed at bringing us significantly closer to a future in which object-oriented component-based software engineering will become the norm. There is a growing belief that systematic, large-scale reuse, coupled with object technology, is the only way to radically improve the process of software development. Based on our experience with reuse at Hewlett-Packard and Objectory (now Rational), and with our many customers, we believe that substantial degrees of reuse can be achieved only by radically changing traditional software architectures and development processes. First, we are convinced that substantial reuse requires that software must be architected, designed, packaged, and supported for reuse. Architecture here means that systems and components must be structured to support independent development, and later integration and evolution, of components and systems. Second, the software engineering processes, involving specific software development steps, the supporting management and organizational structures, and even the mode of interaction with customers, must be adapted to allow the organization to work effectively with these reusable components. Finally, processes and tools must be integrated into an infrastructure to support the key activities.

Introducing effective reuse into a software engineering business requires a concerted and systematic effort by both management and software developers in order to overcome the business, process, organizational, and technical impediments that often hinder effective reuse. Effort must also be directed at involving customers, users, and maintainers early on. While many of these issues and possible solutions are by now well known in the reuse community, their existence still comes as a surprise to those who adopt object technology and expect it to yield reuse automatically. Without an explicit reuse agenda and a systematic approach to design and process, the desired levels of object reuse will not be achieved.

In this book we develop a coherent model and a set of guidelines that help ensure success with large-scale, object-oriented reuse. Our framework, which we call the Reuse-driven Software Engineering Business (abbreviated as Reuse Business), deals systematically with these key business, process, architecture, and organization issues.

We believe that both the theory and practice of systematic software reuse and the theory and practice of systematic, model-based, object-oriented software development and business engineering have matured sufficiently for us to develop this new, consistent approach. Our coherent solution merges the best ideas of both fields with our own contributions in the areas of systematic methods, architectures, domain-specific software engineering, and reuse adoption. We base our work on Jacobson's use case driven architecture and process modeling fundamentals – Object-Oriented Software Engineering (OOSE) (Jacobson *et al.*, 1992), Object-Oriented Business Engineering, described in *The Object Advantage* (TOA) (Jacobson *et al.*, 1994) and the Unified Modeling Language (UML) (Booch *et al.*, 1997).

Who needs a Reuse-driven Software Engineering Business?

Any software-producing organization can benefit from the ideas presented in this book. After many years of cautiously viewing object technology as interesting but still emerging, many large organizations have increased their commitment to objects and are investing substantial resources in reengineering their businesses and reimplementing their supporting information systems. For many businesses, an effective software engineering development strategy is an essential part of their use of information technology to accomplish key business objectives, such as effective use of resources, improved time to market, and agile response to market change. They are looking to objects and reuse to provide them flexible, cost-effective implementations, which are based on commercial and their own application frameworks, reusable business components, and distributed object-oriented middleware.

To help them achieve their strategic software goals, we provide a clear statement of how large-scale, architected object reuse can help improve the software process. Our reuse business model describes how these software organizations can transition to a reuse-driven business. The full benefits will only be obtained if the software organization:

- produces related applications (or significant subsystems) that are members of a product line or product family;

- is willing to make a significant investment to build up reusable architectures, components, processes, and tools; and

- is willing to make certain process and organizational changes.

Such an organization is usually feeling increasing pressure to deliver more applications in shorter time-scales, in order to meet more complex customer needs.

The Reuse Business approach is targeted pricipally to organizations in which the development of mission-critical information systems and software products is key to their success. However, we also address how the Reuse Business may be specialized to a range of organizations that are able to benefit from many aspects of our systematic approach to reuse, even if they are not able or do not choose to operate fully in accord with our model. In the optimal case, the software development organization is run as a software engineering business. By business, we mean both that the information technology and software engineering goals are key to accomplishing the enterprise business goals, and that as a consequence, the software organization itself is operated as a business, with well-defined customer and financial objectives. As a reuse-driven software organization, this organization is engaged in producing multiple, related applications (a product line or product family), centered and optimized on the production and reuse of components. As a business, this organization must understand its customers, and serve their needs, while at the same time effectively achieving its profit and expense objectives. Such business trade-offs are managed using economic, product and process measures.

Our experience

Since mid-1993, when the principal authors of this book first became familiar with each other's work, we have worked closely together on panels, at conferences, at workshops, and in joint research in order to integrate our skills and experiences into the shared vision described in this book. Together, we are uniquely positioned with a wealth of complementary skills. Ivar Jacobson brings the strong architectural perspective and large systems experience of developing the AXE Telecom switching system at Ericsson, and the experience gained with OOSE development and Objectory clients. Martin Griss has broad experience with reuse organization, adoption, and technology. Both have extensive experience with systematic software process definition and improvement. Patrik Jonsson joined the work in May 1994, bringing his process experience to the project, when we decided to make our efforts into a formal collaboration leading to this book.

This collaboration had each of us playing different roles, and doing different amounts of work at different times. We have unanimously chosen to list the authors in the order that best reflects our relative contributions to the technical substance of the book, the most important criterion in a work of this kind.

Ivar Jacobson is inventor of the OOSE method and founder of Objectory AB, Sweden. He is currently VP of Business Engineering at Rational Software Corporation, and was before that VP of Technology at Objectory Corporation. He is a leader in the object-oriented community. He is well known for his pioneering work and more than 20 years of experience using object methods for the design of large real-time systems. He spent 25 years at Ericsson working on the AXE switching system, where he developed an architecture and software engineering process to support extensive reuse. His early object-based design technique has evolved into the international CCITT/SDL Telecom standard. He is the principal author of two influential books: *Object-Oriented Software Engineering – A Use Case Driven Approach* and *The Object Advantage – Business Process Reengineering with Object Technology*, as well as several widely referenced papers on object technology. His work on use case engineering has influenced almost all of the OO methods in use today. He has served on the OOPSLA, ECOOP, and TOOLS program committees.

Martin L. Griss is a senior Laboratory Scientist at Hewlett-Packard Laboratories, Palo Alto, California where for the past 14 years he has researched software engineering processes and systems, systematic software reuse, object-oriented reuse, and measurement system kits. He has a defining role as senior reuse consultant within HP's Professional Services Organization, working with the Object-Oriented Solutions Center. As HP's "reuse rabbi," he led research on software reuse process, tools, and software factories; the creation of an HP Corporate Reuse program; and the systematic introduction of software reuse into HP's divisions. He was director of the Software Technology Laboratory at Hewlett-Packard Laboratories, and has over 25 years of experience in software engineering research. He was previously an associate professor of computer science at the University of Utah, where he is currently an adjunct professor. He has authored numerous papers and reports on software engineering and reuse, writes a reuse column for *Object Magazine*, and is active on several reuse program committees.

Patrik Jonsson was one of the first people to join Objectory AB, and has been working closely with Ivar for many years. He has been involved in several different activities, including customer projects, process and method development, specifying the requirements for the Objectory CASE tool, and teaching. He is a co-author of the Addison-Wesley bestseller *Object-Oriented Software Engineering – A Use Case Driven Approach*. He now works at Rational as a senior consultant. Patrik joined Ivar and Martin to help capture and formulate their ideas. He has been a main driver in integrating the concept of a Reuse-driven Software Engineering Business into the OOSE software engineering framework, and has added many ideas of his own.

How this book is organized

The book consists of four parts.

Part I: Introducing the Reuse-driven Software Engineering Business provides motivation, background and an overview of our systematic reuse-driven approach, abbreviated as the Reuse Business. Chapter 1 surveys software reuse experiences and key management, architecture, process, and organizational principles that motivate the approach we have taken. Chapter 2 describes the overall concepts and goals of the Reuse Business. We define application systems and component systems, and describe the key processes of Application System Engineering, which utilizes component systems to build applications, and Component System Engineering, which creates reusable component systems.

Part II: Architectural Style describes the architectural concepts and notation that underlie the Reuse Business. These architectural building blocks, connectors, and composition rules enable us to describe a variety of architectures. Chapter 3 introduces

Object-Oriented Software Engineering (OOSE) and the Unified Modeling Language (UML), including models, actors, use cases, objects, types, classes and systems. Chapter 4 describes application systems, components, and component systems. We define the concept of facade as a generalized interface, and describe variability mechanisms that provide manageable, yet flexible reuse. Chapters 5 and 6 provide much more detail on use case and object components. Chapter 7 addresses layered architectures and systems of interoperating systems to support large-scale, controlled reuse.

Part III: Processes addresses the reuse-oriented software engineering processes needed to systematically create, use, and manage the architectural elements described in Part II. Chapter 8 describes Object-Oriented Business Engineering, including the modeling of business systems, business processes, and workers. Business models are connected to information systems and human resources. Object-Oriented Business Engineering and OOSE can be used together to develop and precisely describe the processes, organization models, and tools underlying the Reuse Business. Chapter 9 describes a high-level business model for the Reuse Business, which provides a framework for the more detailed treatment of the key processes and organizations in the following chapters. We define and relate Component System Engineering, Application System Engineering, Application Family Engineering, and managing reuse. Chapter 10 applies business engineering to the customer business to define the suite of applications that supports their business processes. Application Family Engineering then analyses these applications which then leads to the overall layered architecture and decomposition into reusable component systems. The incorporation of legacy systems is also addressed. Chapter 11 describes Component System Engineering, showing how to analyze sets of requirements to produce high-quality components and their facades. Chapter 12 describes Application System Engineering, showing how to construct applications by selecting, customizing, and reusing components drawn from one or more component systems.

Part IV: Organizing a Reuse Business provides advice on establishing a specific reuse business that conforms to the Reuse Business model. Chapter 13 describes a systematic transition to a reuse business, combining business engineering techniques with change management and reuse-specific guidelines. This leads to an incremental adoption process, with several process and organization changes. The basic Reuse Business model can be adapted to a variety of software development scenarios. Business engineering techniques are used to partition the reuse roles and departments to create organizational structures for a specific reuse business. Several tools and technologies help manage the process, and create and package the component systems. Chapter 14 describes how instances of the various processes are created and managed, what techniques and economic, process, and product measures are used to manage trade-offs and progress flow, and what organizational and technical infrastructure is needed to support a reuse business. Chapter 15 provides a summary of the key architectural, process, and organizational principles, and the critical role senior management must play in directing your next steps.

The appendices provide detailed reference material. Appendix A is a complete glossary of terms. Appendix B is an annotated bibliography of key readings and online resources, Appendix C summarizes the Unified Modeling Language notation and extensions used, while Appendix D lists all references used in the book.

What this book offers

This book on industrial object-oriented software engineering with substantial reuse has as its main purpose the explanation of the key issues involved in building a Reuse-driven Software Engineering Business. The reader does not need any object or reuse experience in order to understand the book.

The book is not a complete handbook and therefore does not provide all the detailed information necessary to implement and run a reuse business. More detailed process guides, training, and practical experience will be needed to ensure success. Just as OOSE and Object-Oriented Business Engineering are simplifications of the more detailed and precise Rational Objectory SE and BE processes, the work presented in this book is the simplification of a more complex process.

It is important that all readers, potential participants in the reuse business, have a shared understanding of the key concepts, as covered in Chapters 1 and 2, and the introductions to Parts I–IV. In addition:

- Upper managers, responsible for authorizing and funding the move to a reuse business, should also read Chapters 13, 14 and 15 carefully.

- Reuse managers responsible for the day-to-day running of a reuse business should read all chapters.

- Project managers should read Chapters 3, 4 and 7 in Part II and the processes described in Part III.

- Software engineers, system architects, component developers, reusers, and component system maintainers should be familiar with all of Part II and the particular processes described in Part III that are most relevant to their role.

These readers might expect to gain the following benefits.

Upper managers want to understand the economic, political, and organizational consequences as well as the time-to-market, quality, and cost benefits.

Reuse managers want to establish, run, and improve a large-scale reuse organization.

Project managers want to learn how to run application projects, and what process changes are needed to take advantage of reuse.

System architects want to design an architecture that allows for substantial reuse and evolution.

Component developers want to learn how to design and build reusable component systems.

Reusers want to learn how to build applications from component systems.

Maintainers of component systems want to package and support component systems, and to deliver associated services.

While we have designed the book for managers and practitioners who have not much practical experience with object-oriented software or systematic software reuse, readers who have experience in one or both of these areas should still find considerable material of value. In particular:

- Readers already familiar with the concepts of systematic software reuse, such as domain engineering and creator/utilizer reuse-oriented process and organization, will see how we have integrated these concepts into a significant object-oriented method, OOSE, and how we have taken advantage of object-oriented business engineering.

- Readers who already have experience with an object-oriented analysis and design method will see how we have adapted and extended the architecture and process of OOSE to incorporate an agenda of large-scale, systematic reuse.

- Readers who already know OOSE will see how it has been extended to take advantage of the new Unified Modeling Language (UML), software architecture, and reuse process and technology.

When we started this work, we imagined that we would simply combine what we each knew about object-oriented software engineering, business engineering and systematic software reuse, based on our many years of experience. But as the work progressed, we discovered that we needed to make numerous technical innovations, synthesizing, extending, and inventing many ideas. These included:

- Re-expressing OOSE using the Unified Modeling Language (UML). As we did this, several of our architectural, process, and reuse extensions provided useful input to the evolving UML design.

- Extending and exploiting UML, OOSE and Object-Oriented Business Engineering in order to support the key technical, process, and incremental adoption aspects of systematic software reuse. New constructs for components, facades, layered architectures, and variability were devised.

- Discovering how to use and extend OOSE and Object-Oriented Business Engineering to do a systematic form of reuse domain-engineering and architecture development.

- Discovering how the business processes, the software engineering processes, and the organization needed to change to optimize the development of enterprise information systems based on substantial reuse.

We have worked hard to keep the notation in this book consistent with the Unified Modeling Language, which was still evolving as we revised the final draft of the book. Some last minute changes were made during proof reading to ensure that we are almost 100% compatible with UML 1.0, released in January 1997, and we hope no changes have been missed.

Acknowledgments

Many people provided inspiration and encouragement that led to the creation of this book. Some helped by commenting on the form and content of the book, some by participating in tutorials and providing feedback, and some by open discussion of the ideas.

We particularly thank Ramesh Balasubramanian, Per Björk, Stefan Bylund, Patricia Cornwell, Nathan Dykman, Håkan Dyrhage, Christian Ehrenborg, John Favaro, Daryl Foy, Steven Fraser, Agneta Jacobson, Sten Jacobson, Per Kröll, Philippe Kruchten, Reed Letsinger, Mary Loomis, Ruth Malan, Patricia Markee, Vered Marash, Susan McBain, Ware Myers, Keith Moore, Karin Palmkvist, Joe Podolsky, Jeff Poulin, Mats Rahm, David Redmond-Pyle, Mark Simos, Mike Short, Greg Siu, Kevin Wentzel, and Lorna Zorman for their detailed comments, and commitment.

We are highly indebted to Karin Palmkvist, Susanne Dyrhage, and Staffan Ehnebom, who, together with Ivar Jacobson, developed the concept of System of Interconnected Systems. We are grateful to Stefan Bylund, Christian Ehrenborg, Magnus Christerson, Staffan Ehnebom, and Gunnar Övergaard, for their participation in the development of the notion of interfaces, processes, and physical devices as they appear in this book. We are grateful to Gunnar Magnusson and Håkan Dyrhage for their helpful suggestions and comments on applying Object-Oriented Business Engineering to a software development organization. Patricia Cornwell was a key partner in the development of Hewlett-Packard's reuse maturity model and incremental transition strategy which significantly influenced our treatment in Chapter 13.

John Favaro, Intecs Sistemi, provided valuable feedback as he applied a preliminary version of the Reuse Business to reuse in the Italian telecommunications industry. He particularly found the concepts of component systems, layered architectures, explicit extension points, variants and variation points, and use case components to be powerful additions to a domain analysis methodology derived from FODA. His input was very helpful in clarifying and sharpening our explanation of several concepts.

We particularly appreciate the extensive efforts of Ware Myers who commented on all chapters, and helped us rewrite several chapters of this book numerous times to make them more effective. Without his help, we would not have completed the book on schedule, nor as well. We are also grateful to Lorna Zorman who carefully read and suggested improvements to many drafts of many chapters.

We are grateful to Hewlett-Packard and Rational for supporting this project, and to Mary Loomis for providing encouragement and support that enabled us to start and complete this work.

Finally, we thank our family members and partners for their patience during the many weekends and evenings that we worked on the book.

Ivar Jacobson
Stockholm, Sweden
ivar@rational.com

Martin Griss
Palo Alto, California
griss@hpl.hp.com

Patrik Jonsson
Stockholm, Sweden
patrik@rational.com

DEDICATIONS

"To my mother, Edith, who helped me with my homework as a child, and taught me a pattern of thinking that led to the framework behind this book." IJ

"To the memory of my father, Isaac, who would have been so proud, and to my mother, Win, who is. To my wife P'nina, and my children Doron and Shelli, for their love and encouragement." MG

"To my beloved wife Katarina, and my two wonderful sons Gabriel and Samuel." PJ

CONTENTS

PART I
INTRODUCING THE REUSE-DRIVEN SOFTWARE ENGINEERING BUSINESS

A consistent message emerges from many years of experience with software reuse: it can help to dramatically cut lead times, improve quality, and reduce costs. Equally clear, however, is that software reuse only works when it is applied with a systematic approach, optimized to achieving business goals. To be effective, such an approach must focus on software architecture, development processes, and how the developers are organized.

Part I introduces the concepts of systematic reuse and our approach to architecture, processes, and organization for successful reuse.

The Reuse-driven Software Engineering Business is our full name for the organization it takes to make an economically viable "business" of the software development function. On the organization level the Reuse Business consists of several elements.

- An architectural group studies the planned set of applications and creates an architecture and high-level design for reusable components.

- Other engineers, the component developers, develop the components. The development process consists of a series of object-oriented models covering analysis, design, code, and test.

- Project groups reuse these components, using a similar development process to build application systems.

- A support group performs the functions linking the component developers with the project groups.

- The fifth organizational element is the reuse manager, making it all work together.

The organization of the Reuse Business requires taking a longer and broader view than the single project, for the reuse manager is concerned with many projects and looks forward to reusing components over the time span of many successive projects. This is a step-up in organizational complexity compared to the software development manager supervising a set of project managers, each working independently. This step-up necessitates greater managerial involvement in the coordination of component-system creators and reusers.

As a business, executive management holds the reuse business responsible for return on investment. But that return has now moved up from the single project to a group of concurrent projects and a series of projects over time, all developing software of improved quality at less cost in a shorter time. Executives expect these three factors to more than offset the cost of creating and then operating the reuse business.

Successful operation of a reuse business involves managing the complex interaction of advanced technology, organization structure, development process, and financing. This part introduces these principles.

Chapter 1 summarizes the body of knowledge known as Systematic Software Reuse. This information includes experiences, concepts, and reuse management, architecture, process, organization, adoption, and technology guidelines.

Chapter 2 describes the overall concept of the Reuse-driven Software Engineering Business (abbreviated Reuse Business), and its goals. We introduce the concepts of application systems and component systems, and the key processes of Application System Engineering, which utilizes component systems to build applications, and

Component System Engineering, which creates reusable component systems. Object-oriented business and systems engineering techniques provide a systematic framework for our approach.

1

SOFTWARE REUSE SUCCESS FACTORS

Software is intruding further and further into the operation of the modern world. Cyberspace depends on it. So does the banking system, the electrical utility grid, and telecommunications. The automobile looks like a standalone system, but its power train depends upon several dozen small microprocessors. Software drives them.

Competition is becoming both more intense and more widespread. More and more companies depend on mission-critical business information systems to manage customer interactions, speed goods to their destinations, and manage finances in an ever more complex, global business environment. Often companies compete on small differences in quickly introduced, innovative services.

For many industrial and commercial enterprises, accomplishing key business goals, such as satisfying the customer, achieving time to market with products and services, or controlling costs, have direct implications on the way these organizations choose to develop and use information technology and software systems for competitive advantage. Improving business performance often means they must dramatically improve their software development performance.

In all these cases, success means that products and services that rest upon a software base must get their software "faster, better, and cheaper."

Faster The software has to meet a market window. Competitive organizations set that time.

Better The software has to serve the requirements of the process it is to support and later, when serving its process, it has to do so with few failures.

Cheaper The software has to be less expensive to produce and maintain.

Let us consider two main paths to these goals. Either the software must be produced more efficiently or large portions must be reused.

The first path is to increase the effectiveness of the organization that produces the software. The software community has accomplished wonders along this path in the past half century. For example, it has advanced through a series of increasingly efficient language generations. It has transferred many activities difficult for people to do into software tools, from editors to debuggers.

This path can be effective. Organizations producing business systems have improved by 10% per year; engineering systems, by 8%; real-time systems, by 6% (Putnam and Myers, 1996). The best record — 16% per year, sustained over 15 years — was made by the business-software division of a large telecommunications company. In all these cases the improvement was in "process productivity," a concept measuring the effectiveness of the whole software process — management, facilities, tools, and people.

This record of improvement is not universal. A measurement of improvement must be based on software organizations that keep data. Many do not. They presumably are faring worse. The point is that this record of process improvement is an existence proof that the means for software organizations to improve do exist.

The second path is reuse. Fifty years ago there was no software. When there was little or no software available, everyone had to develop the programs they needed from scratch. Now there are some 100 billion lines of code at work in the world. Many functions have been written thousands of times. Actually much code is reused — if you count all the operating systems, compilers, word processors, spreadsheets and so on — the shrinkwrapped products. And if you count the outsourcing contractors who are increasingly substituting their own products for the idiosyncratic programs of their clients. And if you count the libraries of mathematical, statistical, and other specialized programs. Nevertheless, in spite of this quite decent record, the problem still remains: how to get the word to software developers.

For most companies trying to improve their software development performance, objects and software reuse must become key parts of their software engineering strategy. Succeeding with industrial-strength object-oriented software engineering requires that the promise of large-scale software reuse be realized in a practical way. In this chapter we will describe some of the experiences and principles that underlie practical reuse today. These pragmatic success factors and guidelines provide the motivation and basis for the systematic Reuse-driven Software-Engineering Business that we introduce in the next chapter. A variety of architecture, process, and organization elements must be combined in a coherent and systematic way.

1.1 Software reuse is a simple idea

The basic concept of systematic software reuse is simple (McIlroy, 1969): Develop systems of components of a reasonable size and reuse them. Then extend the idea of "component systems" beyond code alone to requirements, analysis models, design, and test. All the stages of the software development process are subject to "reuse."

Developers can save problem-solving effort all along the development chain. They can minimize redundant work. They can enhance the reliability of their work because each reused component system has already been reviewed and inspected in the course of its original development. Code components have passed unit and system test elsewhere and often have stood the test of use in the field. By these means developers can reduce development time from years to months, or to weeks instead of months.

Experience at companies such as AT&T, Brooklyn Union Gas, Ericsson, GTE, Hewlett-Packard, IBM, Motorola, NEC, and Toshiba show that significant cost and time savings result from systematic reuse. Other companies, those that are doing nothing in particular about reuse, provide a baseline. In these organizations, which Ed Yourdon labeled "passive" reusers, individual programmers informally reuse code at the 15–20% level, taking it from their own desk drawers or those of nearby associates (Yourdon, 1996a).

The major Japanese software factories, perhaps because they rose out of engineering organizations accustomed to standard parts, have been pursuing more formal reuse for several decades. By the mid-1980s they had reached levels in the vicinity of 50%, according to Michael A. Cusumano (1991). A recent report set the rate in Hitachi's Eagle environment between 60 and 98%. This environment "lets software engineers reuse standard program patterns (or 'skeletons') and functional procedures (about 1600 data items and routines for I/O data conversion and validation) to write business applications in COBOL or PL/I" (Isoda, 1994).

Starting from early experiments in 1984, in the next 10 years Hewlett-Packard reached 25–50% reuse levels in firmware for its instrument and printer products. One instrument line attained 83%.

Several organizations have obtained reuse levels around 90% in certain projects or areas:

- AT&T: 40–92% in Telecoms operation support system software

- Brooklyn Union Gas: 90–95% in a process layer, and 67% in a user interface and business object layer

- Ericsson AXE: 90% in hundreds of customer-specific configurations

- Motorola: 85% reuse and a 10:1 productivity savings ratio in compiler and compiler-tool test suites

- A statewide school system: 93%, as reported by Netron.

Our experience and our knowledge of what many organizations have achieved through reuse persuades us that management may expect substantial gains:

- Time to market: reductions of 2 to 5 times

- Defect density: reductions of 5 to 10 times

- Maintenance cost: reductions of 5 to 10 times

- Overall software development cost: reduction of around 15% to as much as 75% for long-term projects (this includes the overhead cost of developing reusable assets and supporting their use).

The examples on which these estimates are based are not yet widespread, but again they constitute an existence proof of what is possible.

There are many other examples of more intangible, yet possibly even more strategic benefits. These include highly customizable products, increased market agility, and consistent families of related products that provide familiar, compatible interfaces to many customers.

Components are sometimes referred to as *assets* or *workproducts*. While the three terms refer to the same underlying reality, they carry somewhat different connotations. "Component" suggests interfaces and packaging. "Asset" brings to mind matters of ownership and management. "Workproduct" highlights the fact that a component is a unit in a cycle of work, the software life cycle.

1.2 Components are fueling a revolution in application development

The growing popularity and availability of component-based software technologies is fueling a change in the habits and expectations of millions of programmers. New application development tools and technologies have made "components" the key to reusing larger-grained "objects" to build applications rapidly. These technologies include Microsoft's Visual Basic, ActiveX and OLE, SUN's Java, and OMG's CORBA Interface Definition Language (IDL). Internet computing using applets and scripting languages such as VBScript and JavaScript make it easy to develop and quickly deploy novel interactive applications across the enterprise. Component Object Models and distributed computing infrastructure in the form of OMG's CORBA middleware technologies or Microsoft's operating system support for the Distributed Component Object Model (DCOM) and OLE technology enable more complex distributed, large-grain objects and components to be used. These technologies define and manage component interfaces separately from component implementations.

Practical reuse has also been quite successful with non-object-oriented languages such as COBOL and Fortran. These non-object-oriented component-based technologies reinforce the fact that successful reuse is not really about object-oriented languages or class libraries. While object-oriented languages have many of the qualities sought when developing components, they are not sufficient in themselves. There is a growing commercial market for components providing larger chunks of functionality than typical object classes do, called ActiveX components or OLE components (OCXs). As an increasing number of these component-based applications are constructed and deployed by independent developers, we will see even more importance placed on the careful definition of architecture and mechanisms that enable reusable components. Business objects and components will be defined and constructed by separate groups, yet must work together to meet business information system needs. Component-oriented modeling methods and supporting CASE tools will become increasingly important (Yourdon, 1996b).

1.3 A systematic approach makes pragmatic reuse work

Despite such examples of the promise of reuse, its actual achievement has been an elusive target. The obstacles blocking progress are fourfold: engineering, process, organizational, and business-oriented.

Engineering   The technology and method deficiencies include:

- Means to identify clearly elements of the models that describe requirements, architecture, analysis, design, test, and implementation along the development stream. Clear identification underlies the ability either to reuse them or to allow them to be candidates for replacement by reusable component systems.

- Lack of components to reuse. This category covers a host of obstacles: failure to select and strengthen components for reuse in the first place; lack of techniques to package, document, classify, and identify components; inadequate design and implementation of library systems; poor access to component libraries for potential reusers.

- Lack of flexibility in potentially reusable components. If a component is rigid, it fits few or sometimes no reuse opportunities. In the past our methods for designing a flexible, layered architecture have been immature. Our ability to adapt a component to fit a new need or a new architecture has been limited.

- Lack of tools to carry out reuse procedures. A number of new tools are needed — tools that can be integrated into reuse-oriented support environments.

Process   Above the engineering and technology level, the traditional process of software development is itself deficient in opportunities to encourage reuse. Nowhere in most of the processes that are used today is there a point where developers sit down and ask themselves, "What can we separate out that has been done before and replace with reusable component systems?"

The potential role of the architect in reuse has not been defined. Similarly, the role of a reuse engineer — or a reusable component engineer — has not been worked out.

The places in the process at which developers might consider inserting component systems have not been built in. After analysis, design, or code components have been blocked out, review, inspection, and walkthrough procedures fail to contemplate reuse.

Organizational   Very few organizations systematically practice reuse as an established best practice. One reason is that they focus on one project at a time. Reuse requires a broader focus. The management group has to look ahead, focusing on a set of projects that cover an application area, that is, that they believe possess some characteristics in common. This area is a "domain." From this domain someone — a domain engineer — has to identify the reusable elements and carry on from there.

One difficulty is at once apparent — the conflict between those in the management group focused on single projects and those with a broader product portfolio or application domain view. Few organizations, yet, have a management structure that can accommodate these two views. Behind this difficulty stand others: the culture, often found, of not trusting others in the organization; the attitude of fearing dependency on others. Along with this distrust goes failure to share information with others. This failure, of course, is poison to reuse, for the very essence of reuse is sharing reusable component systems. To share, one must trust.

Underlying these organizational difficulties is lack of knowledge. Managers lack knowledge of how to organize for reuse. Developers lack knowledge of how to implement this process. Sometimes they fear loss of their own creativity if they depend upon components produced by others. Some developers, lacking faith in management-initiated reuse programs, prefer to place their faith in technology, such as languages and tools, alone.

Business Reuse takes capital and funding. It takes capital to finance domain engineering, the building of components and component systems strong enough to justify reuse, and the creation of in-house libraries of components. These operations tie up capital until projects that reuse the components pay for them. It takes funding to provide education, training, and access to vendor-supplied components. It takes money to cope with an unstable domain — as when the initial domain is poorly defined, or when similar domains in different organizations must be merged. It may take money to penetrate the legal and social reasons for sharing or not sharing software.

Furthermore, solving just a few of these issues does not provide enough impetus to overcome the inertia of doing things the same old way. Simply announcing a library of "donated" components will not change the behavior of most engineers. Rather, they must adjust their desire to build perfect systems to the realistic hope of building very good systems much more cost-effectively.

At the same time, individual developers can do little about reuse on their own. Management must institute the mechanisms needed, provide organizational support for them, and money to finance them. In other words, some simple-sounding step, like instituting object-oriented design and programming, will not by itself automatically yield reuse.

1.4 Ericsson and Hewlett-Packard reuse experience reveals common principles

We have been deeply involved with major reuse efforts at Ericsson and Hewlett-Packard, and have closely examined the experience of a number of other large organizations with software reuse programs. Several common features appeared time after time. The role of senior management in making and sustaining change, the criticality of product line architecture, and the importance of reuse-enabling process and organization are repeating themes. Not all reuse efforts have exactly the same experiences, but the essence of reuse success is clear. We use several examples of organizational reuse to explain and motivate reuse to colleagues and customers. They are a representative set, and are by no means a comprehensive sample. Many more reuse case studies have been documented and analyzed. The 1994 *IEEE Software* special issue on software reuse (Frakes and Isoda, 1994) provides a good starting point for more information.

Ericsson   The AXE 10 telecommunications switching systems product is the largest commercial success story in Sweden, having been adapted for use in over 100 countries. AXE has been customized to the needs of thousands of separately operating and managed installations. It is believed to be the largest product ever built using OO technology (Jacobson, 1996a).

The development of a precursor to the AXE telecom switching system was begun in 1967. Because Ericsson wanted to supply telephone systems worldwide, it faced the necessity of adapting them to the needs of many different countries. To meet these requirements and also to meet anticipated competitive pressures, a strategic decision was made early on to architect and implement the product for substantial reuse and evolution. This required the use of new technology and design methods, previously untried in Ericsson.

This 30-year experience demonstrated the importance of several key architecture, process, and organizational principles (Jacobson, 1996b).

The first was the need for extensive initial investment and long-term organizational commitment. That need, of course, can be met only with early and unwavering top-management support, and it was forthcoming. The historic decision to use new technology and methods was not easy, and required many months of staunch advocacy by a technical champion. Ultimately, the decision could not have been made without the vision and support of a senior manager. Ivar Jacobson was the technical product manager, and was able to convince a senior manager to accept the novel approach. This manager ultimately had to overrule the objections of many other managers and technical advisors. This led to the development of a first product, successfully sold in about 10 countries. Experience with this product encouraged the development, starting in the early 1970s, of a much more flexible and maintainable product base which became the AXE system. It took nearly 10 years from the original decision before it was clear to everyone involved that the principles behind the reuse-oriented architecture and development process were key to success.

The second was the importance of a well-designed architecture — an architecture aimed at flexibility and adaptation for reuse and customization from the beginning. The system architecture was carefully articulated so that even salespeople were able to use it to explain the functioning of a system to a prospective customer, and to specify appropriate configurations. AXE implemented this architecture in terms of independent telephony services to produce a flexible, understandable switching-system framework, adaptable to the needs of many customers.

The third was to enable the support of various configurations by implementing the system in terms of carefully designed small subsystems, called service packages. Each service package implemented a well-understood telephony service, such as "establish a call" and "call waiting," with well-defined interfaces to other service packages. Each customer-specific AXE configuration is created by assembling service packages drawn from this single source system. Each configuration consists of an appropriate set of mandatory and optional service packages. Close to 90% of the service packages were completely reusable, while the remaining 10% were customer specific, and had to be specifically developed for a particular sale. A lot of effort was devoted to identifying and designing excellent standard, mandatory service packages, so that most customers would choose the services provided by these reusable packages, rather than specifying unique components.

The fourth was to structure the development organization to match the system architecture. Service packages were treated as atomic pieces of work, and not split between developers. Sets of service packages were grouped into subsystems, each assigned to a manager responsible for the developers who produced those service packages. The interfaces between services packages were also treated as managed products, and were an essential part of allowing independent developers to create optional service packages for reuse in different configurations.

The basic concepts have been refined and widely publicized in the OOSE book (Jacobson *et al.*, 1992) and the more comprehensive Objectory process product from Rational. This experience and these methods underlie the approach developed in this book.

Hewlett-Packard Reuse efforts date back to 1984 when some divisions began to develop reusable components in Instrument Basic, Objective-C, and C++ (Griss 1993, 1995a). The company developed a simple guidebook and the beginnings of a corporate reuse library by 1987. These efforts influenced several major divisions – Microwave and Electronic Instruments, Medical Instruments and Systems, Printers and Plotters, Analytic Instrument Systems, and Networking Systems – to begin reuse programs. In 1990 HP corporate began a reuse program, initiated and led originally by Martin Griss, to collect best practices in architecture, process, organization, and adoption in order to facilitate their spread to other divisions. It sponsored several workshops, training in reuse concepts and domain analysis, and workbooks. It urged that reuse objectives be incorporated in technical reviews. In 1992 research directed by Griss in HP Laboratories focused on the concepts and methods for basing reuse on object-oriented technology. The laboratory began to develop kits specific to a domain.

During this period an important principle emerged. It became clear that concerted pilot-driven adoption was the best idea. A company such as Hewlett-Packard cannot simply order reuse, nor install it all at once. Rather, it must encourage reuse adoption by a wide variety of means, and employ systematic techniques to introduce and institutionalize this new technology (Griss and Wosser, 1995).

The Microwave Instrument firmware reuse program is one example of a divisional pilot program guided by the corporate reuse program. The need for such a program became clear when managers realized that the nature of the business had changed. Pressure to decrease time to market was rapidly increasing. If this pressure was to be accommodated, the division had to develop software more rapidly. At the same time, customers were demanding a greater variety of products that "mixed and matched" features. That meant still more software, and more structure in the software to enhance customization and reuse.

The effort had begun in 1989 when six instrument divisions participated in a common firmware council for about a year. One of the outcomes of the council's deliberations was the appointment of a full-time reuse program manager. He, in turn, gained financing from upper management to support a nine-month architecture effort. Five lead architects worked at a common site. They produced an architecture based on large-grain components. Initially this architecture covered about 30% of a typical firmware software product, typically about 75 000 or more source lines of C code.

A novel feature of the architectural effort was the "tour." The entire team of architects toured the instrument divisions, going from site to site. One purpose was to ensure that the component creators, who were in the divisions, would understand what was involved. The other purpose was to encourage the many developers who would ultimately reuse these components to buy in.

In 1991 the instrument divisions set up a multi-site "barter" organization. Each site was to produce one of five large components, each about 8000 to 10 000 source lines. Each site, of course, had to have confidence in the work of the other sites. To aid this effort, the reuse organization established an instrument specification language and defined a system generator. By 1993 the reuse effort had participated in the production of the first two products. Using the reuse components in "pushed pilot" mode, the division had cut time to market from 18 months to five months. By 1995 it had produced another 15 products using the assets. They showed 25–50% reuse. Ten more products are under way. These components and the architecture into which they fit became part of two new C++ firmware platforms, modeled using Fusion (Coleman *et al.*, 1994) with reuse extensions (Malan and Dicolen, 1996). In 1995 the Microwave divisions created a shared Software Technology Center to "own" and support the components and architecture.

In 1994 Wayne C. Lim exhaustively analyzed the effect of early reuse efforts on two other Hewlett-Packard projects, one in the Manufacturing Productivity section of the Software Technology Division, the other in the San Diego Technical Graphics Division (Lim, 1994). The defect density of the reused code was less than a quarter of the defect density of new code. Productivity (as measured in lines of code per person-month) doubled. Time to market was reduced 42%. A return-on-investment analysis, using the net-present-value method, demonstrated a return of 410% on one project and 215% on the other.

AT&T   As we developed the reuse program at HP, we carefully studied several of the AT&T reuse efforts started in its divisions over the years. Here we describe the essence of one started in 1987 by a senior manager (Ryan, 1991; Beck *et al.*, 1992). The domain in question was telephone operation support systems. The senior manager knew from long experience that the division had implemented many variants of these systems over and over again. He was, at the same time, senior enough to be a "corporate angel" (a committed management sponsor) and technically knowledgeable enough to be an architecture champion. As a sponsor, he established the funding model, helped set up the support organization, and instituted a reuse-oriented review process. His technical influence enabled him to involve senior architects and the first pilot groups, and to maintain commitment over the difficult initial period.

The architects spent the first two years developing a large-grain architecture based on a software bus. They and the developers reengineered and repackaged several large-scale components to conform to this bus. They identified key components that seemed subject to reuse by means of an informal domain analysis. The applications included online transaction processing (OLTP) and network management. They based the system on client—server principles. Components included a database management system, a user interface, and a forms package. They provided each component with a new variable-length, self-identifying record structure adapted to communication over the new software bus.

Starting in 1989, the core group (of about 10 people) began to "push" the reusable assets onto two pilot projects. Both were developing fairly large projects — around 400 000 source lines of code. The architects and component developers from the core group supported both pilot projects. At the same time, accepting feedback from the pilot projects, they improved their own architecture and components.

That leads us to a point of emphasis. *Do not develop reusable components in an ivory tower. Try them out on real systems and modify them, if necessary, to fit that reality.*

As more projects started to use the components, managers realized that a distinct support organization, separate from both the component creators (core group) and the reusers, was needed. They set it up in 1990 and it grew to about 30 people. It had development and/or maintenance responsibility for most of the reusable components. It did some component development in its own group, but it also contracted out to developers well suited to producing others. The support group provided training and a help desk for the reusers. Overseeing the technical aspects of the entire process was an architectural review board, responsible for gathering information on reuse and evolving the architecture.

The results were impressive. As of 1993, the assets were being used by over 70 projects. AT&T named the system BaseWorX and productized it for still wider use. The projects using the assets achieved reuse levels of 40–92%. The programs varied in size from 75 000 to 550 000 source lines of C code. Development time dropped from 12–20 months to 6–12 months. The project with 92% reuse, for instance, put out 487 000 source lines of code in six months. Quality improved. Overall, the division estimated a cost saving of at least 12%, after allowing for the cost of developing and supporting the reusable components.

Microsoft   The use of shrink-wrapped PC products – languages, operating systems, and applications – is enormous. In a sense, this distribution to millions of buyers represents a form of service reuse. However, Microsoft also develops products, such as Visual Basic, ActiveX, and OLE (Object Linking and Embedding), that enable its own application development groups, as well as those of thousands of external application developers, to reuse already developed features. Following the idea of a standardized user interface tookit first developed at Xerox and popularized by Apple, the user interface on most Windows applications, for instance, looks and behaves the same because menus, toolbars, icons, and window frames are reused.

Since its introduction in 1990, the component-based Visual Basic environment has significantly affected the way people think about developing component software (Udell, 1994). The model is that of a layered system, built by a layered organization. The components were initially called VBXs, Visual Basic Custom Controls, then OCXs, OLE Custom Controls, and now ActiveX components for the World Wide Web (WWW). Built in C++ or C by experienced programmers, they are customized and glued together by end users and application integrators, using an interpretive Basic language in a powerful, easy-to-use visual environment. Generative wizards simplify the customization of connected objects.

Microsoft and many third parties provide components and tools. They spread the word with newsletters, journals, and online help. As Windows 95 and its successors have spread, these component technologies have become major forces, resulting in thousands of available components. In addition, many organizations are developing their own domain-specific components. Some organizations have announced that they will support the Microsoft standards on UNIX. VBA (Visual Basic for Applications) and a simpler version for the WWW, VBScript, are becoming standard glue and customization languages.

The flexible, medium-grain, reusable components use an open, extensible packaging based on Microsoft's Component Object Model (COM) architecture. While initially targeted to graphics user interfaces and databases, these packages have been extended to other domains, such as communications, speech processing, instrument control, account-ing, scheduling, multimedia, report writing, graphics, security, credit-card handlers, and statistics.

Behind the graphic interfaces are programs such as word processors, spreadsheets, or calculators that used to be written separately for each product. "At one time, for example, Microsoft managers determined they had fourteen different collections of text-processing code in their products," Michael Cusumano and Richard Selby discovered (Cusumano and Selby, 1995). The company has been establishing linkages between product development groups to reduce this duplication. Focusing on one implementation of a feature across its many application products did more than provide the economies of reuse. More importantly, to a company selling millions of units, it provided a consistent pattern of use to millions of users.

In its early days Microsoft was focused on projects, not potential similarities between systems being produced by different project groups. As Cusumano and Selby put it: "Microsoft in the past has not always paid a lot of attention to defining a high-level architecture that is separate from the source code in its products." However, that indifference is changing. The need for consistency across a line of products, as well as efficiency in producing those products, is leading to a principle that we have noted in other settings. "Microsoft's development groups (including those for OLE, Office, and Cairo, among others)," Cusumano and Selby said, "are increasingly thinking in terms of divisible product architectures and shared components." Planning for reuse has to begin at the architecture stage.

Netron, Inc.   The nearly two-decade experience of Paul G. Bassett with the introduc-tion and commercial use of frame technology – a means of software reuse – confirms the validity of the principles we have been setting forth. "Reuse technology is a necessary but far from sufficient element of effective reuse," Bassett asserts. "In my experience technology gets us at best a quarter of the way. The other three-quarters involve processes and people, for after all, reusing other people's software requires trusting and sharing" (Bassett, 1996).

The goal of frame technology is to provide a flexible software development environment in which customized versions of large information systems can be rapidly constructed by small changes in a few selected places. These changes then configure a complete application system. Each application system is described with a hierarchical set of frames. Each frame is an object-like template that references lower-level frames, and inherits from upper frames. The references are explicit "editing" instructions that may optionally include, exclude, or modify features at distinct points in the lower-level frames. Frames also inherit default behavior and parameters from higher-level frames. After a few changes in an upper frame, the frames are processed by a special generator to quickly create appropriately customized target workproducts, such as code, data, or documents, to build the application.

Each frame may contain new material or — here is where reuse comes in — it may pick up, by use of appropriate frame commands, existing material. This "existing material," such as code, classes, or scripts, may be supplied by vendors, such as Netron, or by other parts of a company. The existing material may even be legacy code that is still doing the job, and has an interface described by a frame.

The ability that frame technology provides its users — the ability to flexibly reuse and customize code or other development materials from other sources — leads to substantial increases in the effectiveness of software development. In fact, Bassett's organization, Netron, Inc., retained QSM Associates of Pittsfield, Massachusetts, an independent metrics company, to verify this assertion. Essentially, QSM Associates compared the experience of 15 projects executed with frame technology with the experience tabulated regarding "ordinary projects" in the 4000-project database accumulated by Quantitative Software Management, Inc.

- Time to market was reduced by 70%.

- Project costs were reduced by 84%.

- Effectiveness of the project teams, as measured by QSM's process productivity metric, improved by a factor of 9.4. Process productivity includes not only the code production of programmers, but the effectiveness of management, organization, methods, and tools.

The percentage of reuse among Netron's clients varies from about 50% to the upper nineties, depending on the degree of sophistication of their practice of frame technology.

1.5 Reuse requires changes in process

The reuse community has come to understand — on the basis of its experience — that making systematic reuse effective requires major changes in the way organizations develop software. In the past the software process has focused on developing each application from scratch. At most, individual developers have shared code on an *ad hoc* basis.

The new way links many application development projects with processes that identify and create reusable assets. To do so means they must overhaul their business and organizational structures. We have come to understand that this significant organizational change can be thought of in terms of business process reengineering. It is a rethinking of everything pertaining to software from the standpoint of those who ultimately benefit from good software obtained quickly, reliably, and inexpensively.

What are we seeking to achieve? Substantial reuse requires, first of all, that reusable assets be identified in terms of a system architecture. Then the assets must be created and appropriately packaged and stocked. Potential users must have confidence in the components' integrity. Secondly, an organization must refashion its systems engineering processes so that developers can identify opportunities for reuse and work selected components into the process.

> Systematic software reuse is thus the purposeful creation, management, support, and reuse of assets.

As illustrated in Figure 1.1, this can be expressed in terms of four concurrent processes. We call the people in the reusable asset processes, *creators*, and those in the development projects, *reusers*.

Create   This process identifies and provides reusable assets appropriate to the needs of the reusers. These assets may be new, reengineered, or purchased, of various kinds, such as code, interfaces, architectures, tests, tools and so on. This process may include activities such as inventory and analysis of existing applications and assets, domain analysis, architecture definition, assessment of reuser needs, technology evolution, reusable asset testing and packaging.

Reuse   This process uses the reusable assets to produce applications or products. Activities include the examination of domain models and reusable assets, the collection

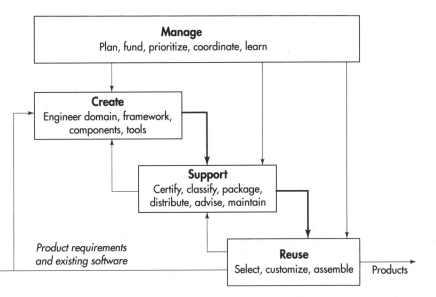

Figure 1.1   *Systematic reuse involves four concurrent processes.*

and analysis of end-user needs, the design and implementation of additional components, adaptation of provided assets, and the construction and testing of complete applications.

Support This process supports the overall set of processes and manages and maintains the reusable asset collection. Activities may include the certification of submitted reusable assets, classification and indexing in some library, announcing and distributing the asset, providing additional documentation, collecting feedback and defect reports from reusers.

Manage This process plans, initiates, resources, tracks, and coordinates the other processes. Activities include setting priorities and schedules for new asset construction, analyzing the impact and resolving conflicts concerning alternative routes when a needed asset is not available, establishing training, and setting direction.

Collectively — because they are financially valuable — we use the term *asset* to refer to high-quality software workproducts (code, designs, architectures, interfaces, and tests) as well as documents, tools, processes, and compiled knowledge (guidelines, models, formulas) that can be reused by the business.

Domain engineering In most reuse programs to date, a key activity associated with the create process is a fairly systematic way of identifying potentially reusable assets, and an architecture to enable their reuse. This activity is called domain engineering in the systematic reuse community. The development or reuse process is also sometimes called application system engineering. The essence of systematic software reuse is that initial investment by the creator to identify and carefully structure reusable assets will enable reusers to build applications rapidly and cost-effectively.

Domain engineering reflects the idea that sharing between related applications occurs in one or more application domains — or problem domains or solution domains. Reuse of the assets then occurs during a subsequent application system engineering phase.

Sometimes domain engineering has been loosely described as "just like ordinary systems engineering, such as Structured Analysis/Structured Design or Object-Oriented Analysis/Object-Oriented Design, except that it applies to a family of systems, rather than just one." True, it is like systems engineering, but it is also more than "one of a kind" systems engineering. It looks beyond a single system. It seeks the family of similar systems that can inhabit a domain. As a result, domain engineering is more complex than established systems engineering. So far, it is less well understood. Therefore, management should not turn to it without forethought, and should establish domain engineering only when it foresees a business benefit in reuse.

These domain and application system engineering activities, summarized in Figure 1.2, identify an application or subsystem "domain," a design space for a family of related systems. The domain engineering process identifies commonality and variability in the chosen problem domain, defines an architecture for applications and components, and develops a set of appropriately generalized components. Its intent is to find the reusable assets that can be cost-effectively exploited in subsequent application system engineering.

A half-dozen different methods for carrying out domain engineering have arisen (Arango, 1994; Prieto-Diaz and Arango, 1991; Lung and Urban, 1995). Each tends to highlight a different aspect of the subject. Some focus on how to identify the domain effectively. They make use of the available domain, architecture, and systems expertise.

Define and scope domain

Analyze examples, needs, trends

Develop domain model and architecture

Structure commonality and variability

Engineer reusable component systems,
languages, and tools

Do delta analysis and design relative to
domain model and architecture

Use component systems as starting point

Find, specialize, and integrate components

Exploit variability mechanisms,
languages, generators, ...

Figure 1.2 *Domain engineering prepares reusable assets for subsequent assembly into applications.*

Others focus on how to select existing examples from the domain, and how they analyze needs and trends. Still others concern themselves with how to collect, represent, and cluster feature sets.

The various methods differ in how they identify and scope the domain and how well they match to the target software processes and technology. Most applications consist of several recognizable or distinct subsystems or sub-problems, only some of which are worth addressing from a reuse perspective.

Once the appropriate domain is selected, the key features are modeled and then grouped into common and variant clusters. The activity then develops a domain architecture relating mechanisms, features, subsystems, and variants. The variability is described using appropriate variability mechanisms, such as inheritance or templates. Finally, the "most important" subsets of the assets are implemented and released as certified, reusable component systems.

We might label some of the methods rather lightweight – their originators describe them in only a few pages. Others come with extensive documentation, such as guidelines, handbooks, role definitions, and checklists. Some of the methods show how they apply object-oriented technology. Some explain how to integrate domain analysis into the complete software engineering life cycle.

Since the creation of reusable components is typically more expensive than "ordinary" system development, we should only develop components when an economic or business reason for reuse exists. Thus, create components only when they *will be reused multiple times*. An important issue is how "proactive" or "reactive" to be in deciding which domains, and subsequently which components, to develop. A set of reusable components must anticipate future needs, but since this is difficult and expensive to do reliably, the process must help engineers to identify and prioritize the most important features to find essential commonality and variability. This relates in part to the reliability with which we can anticipate which applications will be built, and which components will in fact be needed. It also depends on how much risk we are willing to take, either of having too many components, or too few.

In the approach we develop in this book, we do not have an explicit domain engineering activity. Instead, we have integrated several domain-engineering-like steps into our reuse-oriented processes. We use an object-oriented business engineering approach to identify an anticipated application suite, and to develop an architecture against which reusable components are developed. An object-oriented business engineering of a target business guides us to the applications, the architecture, and the high-payoff components. In our judgment, one cannot simply guess that some components may be reusable. Engineers must use a disciplined process to define the components, otherwise the result will be components that do not work well together, and do not effectively support the follow-on application engineering.

Architects and component developers need a systematic approach to prioritize future needs. The details of how we approach these activities and integrate them with the object-oriented systems engineering (OOSE) model-driven techniques will be detailed in subsequent chapters.

Application system engineering   This activity has long existed in the form of building applications from scratch, possibly with the aid of a few "back pocket" programs. The goal now is to make use of the extensive set of reusable assets that have been provided. The intent is to build the application much more rapidly and cost-effectively.

Application system engineering specializes and assembles these components into applications. These applications are largely constrained to "fit" the architecture and the components. Typical applications usually consist of components from several different sets of components. The appropriate steps are summarized in Figure 1.2.

Starting from the models of the architecture and reusable components, the reuser puts together available reusable assets to meet at least the bulk of the new set of requirements. This is sometimes called a "delta" implementation, because it is an outgrowth of what already exists. The reuser has to find and specialize components by exploiting the variability mechanisms provided. If it is not possible to meet all the new requirements with the available reusable components, additional programming will be needed. This programming may be done by the creators, producing new reusable components, or by the reusers. Finally, the components are integrated and the application tested.

1.6   Reuse requires changes in organization

The traditional software organization was a senior manager over a number of project managers. The senior manager allocated resources, such as people coming off projects that were completing, to projects that were building up. Each project manager ran his or her own project. There was no organized source of reusable components. An organization geared for reuse is different.

A systematic reuse process is different because it involves two primary functions, which usually find expression as two organizations. One is the creator, or domain engineering organization. The second is the reuser, or application engineering organization. The latter may cover a number of projects. Companies with experience in systematic reuse generally find that a third function evolves: that of support. It, in turn, finds expression in organizational form, as shown in Figure 1.3.

Experience shows some problems with other organizational structures. For example, if creators are put into the project organizations under project managers focused (quite rightly) on getting something out the door, that objective often results in delaying, or even forgetting, the creator objectives. This pressure explains why setting goals on how much software is to be contributed to a library (reuse deposition ratios) and establishing financial rewards for reuse (reuse creator incentives) have not worked well.

However, if creator and reuser functions are totally separated, as happens when a reuse repository is set up in a geographically separate area, the creators tend to be working in a vacuum. That is, the reusable components do not meet the practical needs of the reusers, or they may appear too late to meet schedule needs.

Experience demonstrates that the answer is the happy medium. The creators must be close enough to the reusers to keep reusable components practical. At the same time they must be insulated from daily project pressures if they are to get reusable components designed and built. The result is the three-function organization diagrammed in Figure 1.3.

Even with this organization structure, the pressures are still present. The creator and reuser functions have distinct goals. Creators need to build high-quality assets that will serve the needs of many reusers over years of product cycles. Reusers have the usual business goals: more, faster, cheaper. For example, a project manager facing tight deadlines and a highly challenging problem might "kill" to get a highly qualified creator on his or her team. That would interfere with the more long-range goals of the creator organization. There is no "right" answer to issues such as this one. That is why the diagram shows a senior manager over all three functions. He or she has to adjudicate the interests of creators and reusers. Some organizations have labeled this post the "reuse manager." That title has the advantage of focusing attention on the overall goal.

One variation of this organizational arrangement replaces the senior manager with a reuse management council. The council will include architects as well as managers. All the conflicting interests are represented in the council. This form of organization is often found in very large companies which are trying to promote reuse across organizational and geographic boundaries. Here the time-scale may be long enough to permit the council sufficient time to resolve conflicts. For such companies, it may take the organizational weight of a council to make decisions. In the more limited framework of a

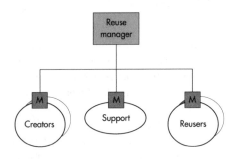

Figure 1.3 *A standard reuse organization. (The "M" in the box represents a local manager.)*

In the approach developed in this book, we will describe several different variations of an incremental route to a fully functional reuse-driven software engineering business, depending on business need and organizational readiness. In some cases, going directly to architected reuse is a strategic necessity. For example, Ericsson as a whole could not meet its business objectives at all without high levels of architected reuse. In this case, a major effort was committed and managed. Not all details of the architecture nor all components were developed in the first increment, but these were evolved rapidly as the architecture and matching organization was created. In other situations, a company such as Hewlett-Packard has many more independent product lines, facing different business issues. Each can adopt a different incremental route to match the needs of the existing product line with some degree of proactive and managed reuse.

Measure progress   Midnight hackers may play with their programs as long as they like, paying no heed to time or cost. Here, however, we are talking about software development as a business. A business runs on measurements. So, too, must a reuse program. We have observed that over the years, management has used a variety of measurements to gauge the progress of reuse programs. Fundamentally, they appear to fall into three categories.

The first category measures levels of reuse within an application area; for example, each completed system employs 75% of reused components. A second measures the properties of reusable components for the purpose of assessing their intrinsic reusability. These include measures of size, complexity, cohesion, and coupling to other components. The third category measures process efficiency and savings in development time and cost, as QSM reported in the case of Netron's clients. Some of these metrics are also useful for estimating new projects.

Use economic guidelines   From such metrics, previous reusers have evolved some rules of thumb:

1   A component has to be used three to five times in application projects to recover the initial cost of creating it and the ongoing cost of supporting it.

2   It costs 1.5 to 3.0 times as much to create and support a reusable component as it does to implement a similar component for a single application.

3   It costs only one quarter as much to utilize a reusable component as it does to develop a new one from scratch.

4   It takes two or three product cycles, usually about three years, before the benefits of reuse become significant. It takes time for the accumulating benefits to pay off the start-up costs.

Even after the domain engineers have created reusable components, there are continuing costs for support and for the training of reusers. Numerically, there has to be enough reuse of components under economic guidelines of this sort to at least offset these running costs, assuming that earlier instances of reuse have paid off the start-up costs. With few or no metrics, it would be easy for an organization to be happy with a little reuse, even though more adequate measurements would show it was running the reuse program at a loss. The lesson: the reuse program has to be good and it has to stay good. To find that out we keep metrics.

Object-oriented technology plus   One of the basic tenets of object-oriented technology is inheritance. That is, one object can inherit an attribute from another object in its hierarchy. This inheritance appears to be a form of reuse. Indeed it is, but it is not all there is to reuse. As a result, those who adopted object-oriented programming languages — without implementing the other steps involved in a reuse program — have often been disappointed. As an African proverb says, "It takes a village to raise a child," not just a single mother. Similarly, it takes a specific reuse agenda, involving the process and organizational steps, to raise a reuse program, not just a single programming language or narrow methodology (Pitman, 1993).

Furthermore, inheritance alone is not rich enough or flexible enough to express the kinds of commonality and variability found necessary to support good domain engineering (Griss, 1995d). For example, Netron frames and Microsoft generative wizards all depend on richer generative templates and scripting languages to express variations and alternatives more flexibly than is possible with inheritance alone.

Domain-specific kits are one technique for delivering richer and more flexible components in a particular application area (Griss, 1995c; Griss and Kessler, 1996). A kit is a set of compatible, reusable parts that work well together. These are a framework, components, languages, and tools. An application framework implements the core functionality of the domain architecture, and provides services and mechanisms to shape all applications developed with the kit. Also provided is a set of reusable components that fit within the framework, and a scripting or glue language for customizing and assembling the components. Furthermore, a variety of domain-specific tools, such as generators and visual environments, make it easy to build a family of related applications in the domain.

Typically, when there are many components and a large framework, developers find it hard to select and customize components quickly (Laubsch, 1996). Domain-specific tools such as generators and domain-specific languages help hide the complexity from the application developer.

As we will see in later chapters, we will build on the rich object-oriented method (OOSE) and UML in our systematic approach, but will add extensions, processes, and guidelines to ensure effective reuse using these more flexible techniques.

1.8   Input from other reuse programs

Several other reuse programs and reuse process and technology developments have been funded by governments, corporations, and consortia. These have developed and documented a variety of reuse guidelines and processes, verified reuse metrics, and developed reuse tools.

REBOOT Consortium   REBOOT is an acronym for REuse Based on Object-Oriented Techniques. Established in 1990, it was funded by ESPRIT and initially consisted of nine partner companies in western Europe. The work is documented in an excellent book,

Software Reuse: A Holistic Approach (Karlsson, 1995). REBOOT developed two process models to support reuse: development for reuse and development with reuse, and a set of tools, called the REBOOT environment.

One of the principles the project emphasized was the need for potential reusers to have confidence in reusable components. Developers tend to reject reuse because they lack this confidence. To offset this attitude, REBOOT recommended a documentation structure that included test information and reusers' experience (Morel and Faget, 1993).

They also emphasized that reuse does not necessarily mean code alone. Components can also come from the analysis and design phases. Nor must components be limited to the small and simple, such as a class. Components may range in size up to a whole system, such as personnel administration.

STARS   The Software Technology for Adaptable, Reliable Software is a long-running program of the US Department of Defense. A significant focus has been on the integration of process, architecture, and reuse. Its vision of the software cycle for product-line development comprises four concepts:

- Process-driven: The production of reliable software within management constraints depends in the first instance on a repeatable process. If an organization never knows what is going to come out of its process, well − it never knows!

- Architecture-centric: Reuse begins at the architecture level by sorting out objects or components that are potentially reusable.

- Domain-specific: Reuse is most likely to be profitable within a domain, not between domains.

- Library-based: Reusable components are stored in organized repositories that can be easily accessed by application programmers seeking to reuse.

STARS and the Department of Defense have funded the development of reuse technology either directly or through prime contractors such as Boeing, IBM, Loral, and Unisys. The technology includes a conceptual framework for reuse processes, CFRP (STARS, 1993), organizational domain engineering methods, ODM (Simos, 1995b; STARS, 1995), feature-oriented domain analysis, FODA (Kang, 1990), several handbooks and guides as part of a comprehensive approach to reusable defense software, CARDS (Gregory, 1995), domain-specific software architecture, DSSA (Tracz *et al.*, 1993), and a model for reuse library interoperability.

A project at the Boeing Defense and Space Group applied STARS product-line development principles to a flight dynamics simulation of an instrument trainer. Because the project was reusing previous software to a considerable extent, it was able to iterate the design half a dozen times. Among other benefits, the final defect rate was down to a low 0.7 defects per thousand lines of code. On the economic front the project demonstrated that product-line reuse will demonstrate a return on investment at three or more systems (Macala *et al.*, 1996).

Motorola   This company's experience of introducing software reuse shows the importance of several of the principles. One is the importance of top-management support. According to Rebecca Joos, the software reuse champion at Motorola, the company's "culture dictates that major changes be driven from the bottom up rather than the top down, for example, from the production engineers up through management." Yet several times the chief executive officer had to refocus management attention on the program. In one of these refocusings, he assigned two senior executives to the challenge. "Unlike the grass-roots groups," Joos pointed out, "this level of management has the resources to implement programs" (Joos, 1994).

The second principle is the necessity for both education and training to support a new activity such as reuse. In this case the reuse working group, the spark plug for the program, worked closely with Motorola University in developing the education courses.

Brooklyn Union Gas The developers combined a well-planned architecture and object-oriented methods in a new mainframe customer-support system (Davis and Morgan, 1993). The architecture was in three layers: interface, process, and business objects. The framework consisted of 650 classes, 8600 methods, and many small objects. The company integrated tools such as a screen generator, report writer, code generator, and ERA (Entity–Requirements–Attributes) dictionary into the development environment.

A small core staff of object-oriented experts managed the architecture and created the objects. The application developers – less experienced in object-oriented technology – were constrained by the framework, layers, and tools. The result was that the company implemented new applications with as much as 90–95% reuse of code in the process layer. In the user-interface and business-object layers, it achieved better than 67% reuse.

IBM A corporate reuse council oversees and coordinates reuse activities across the company. It has provided financial incentives for creators and reusers, funded several reuse support centers, and funded work in the areas of component development, reuse handbooks, reuse metrics, and domain engineering. The reuse support centers maintain libraries of reusable parts, such as 500 zero-defect Ada, PL/X, and C++ components. They identify and train reuse champions. Initially focused on generic components, the centers are now emphasizing domain-specific software architectures (Tirso, 1991b).

Jesus R. Tirso told the 1992 Workshop on Software Reuse of becoming the first IBM site champion for reuse at the Mid-Hudson Valley Programming Laboratory in 1988 (Tirso, 1991a, 1992). He described one program where, under the leadership of a champion, the site went "from no program at all to being one of the leaders in less than one year." His experience and that of other champions emphasize this role as a key one in introducing reuse to a complicated organization.

At the same workshop, Jeffrey S. Poulin outlined three reuse metrics: (1) the percentage of reuse in a product, (2) the reduction in product cost as a result of reuse, and (3) the value added. In the course of discussing reuse metrics, he enunciated an important principle. Good design and management, he had observed, were common within development organizations, but were less common between organizations. Yet exchange of information across organizational boundaries is fundamental to the practice of reuse. "Therefore," he concluded, "measurements must encourage reuse across these organizational boundaries." At IBM and subsequently at Loral, Poulin has developed compelling analyses of reuse and economic models underlying the business case for reuse

(Poulin *et al.*, 1993; Poulin, 1996). Malan and Wentzel (1993) and Lim (1994) similarly analyzed reuse at HP.

University of Maryland and NASA Software Engineering Laboratory   Victor Basili, colleagues and students stressed the organizational aspects of software reuse and domain engineering in their pioneering work on spacecraft software reuse at a NASA laboratory. Basili's group developed the concepts of a "component factory" (Basili *et al.*, 1992) and an "experience factory" (Basili, 1993) and have articulated key architecture and software development processes to support the creation and reuse of software components and also more general domain knowledge.

1.9 It takes a set of principles

In recounting the experience of many organizations with reuse in this chapter, we encountered a number of principles that appeared to be common to most of them. To achieve systematic software reuse, an organization must keep this set of principles in mind:

1   Maintain top-management leadership and financial backing over the long term.

2   Plan and adapt the system architecture, the development processes, and the organization to the necessities of reuse in a systematic but incremental fashion. Start with small pilot projects, and then scale up.

3   Plan for reuse beginning with the architecture and an incremental architecting process.

4   Move to an explicitly managed reuse organization which separates the creation of reusable components from their reuse in application systems, and provides an explicit support function.

5   Create and evolve reusable components in a real working environment.

6   Manage application systems and reusable components as a product portfolio of financial value, focusing reuse on common components in high-payoff application and subsystem domains.

7   Realize that object or component technology alone is not sufficient.

8   Directly address organization culture and change, using champions and change agents.

9   Invest in and continuously improve infrastructure, reuse education, and skills.

10   Measure reuse progress with metrics, and optimize the reuse program.

As we design the Reuse-driven Software Engineering Business, we take great care to ensure that the architecture, process, and organizational models we define support and enhance these principles.

1.10 Summary

Practical reuse experience shows that effective management of architecture, process, and organization is key. Levels of reuse close to 90% are achievable, and lead to dramatic improvements in time to market, quality, maintenance costs, and development costs. Reuse works best when business goals strongly motivate a reuse approach to product line development. A key activity is to systematically identify high-payoff common and variable features, using a combination of business engineering and domain engineering techniques. This leads to a robust application family architecture and set of reusable assets. The most effective reuse organizations have an explicit separation between creators and reusers, and explicit management and support functions.

1.11 Additional reading

The September 1994 *IEEE Software* special issue on software reuse, edited by Frakes and Isoda (1994), provides a superb starting point for more information on systematic reuse. It includes a literature survey, a history of reuse, and several articles describing a variety of reuse programs.

Two papers by Jacobson (1996a, 1996b) in the May and July 1996 issues of *Object Magazine* provide compelling details on the strategic importance and technical details of the Ericsson AXE experience, and how OO architecture, process, and reuse were key to success.

A paper by Griss (1993), "Software reuse: From library to factory," in the *IBM Systems Journal* describes the early history of reuse at HP, the concepts of domain-specific kits, and provides an extensive set of references to other reuse experiences. Two 1995 columns provide more recent details on reuse at HP (Griss, 1995a; Griss and Wosser, 1995).

Several excellent books on software reuse provide a variety of reuse examples and guidelines, descriptions of domain engineering, reuse process, and reuse organization. Many are described in Appendix B. Of particular note are *Software Reusability*, edited by Schaefer *et al.* (1994) and *Software Reuse: A Holistic Approach*, edited by E.-A. Karlsson (1995).

REUSE-DRIVEN SOFTWARE ENGINEERING IS A BUSINESS

While many organizations have made impressive gains in several software development projects using a variety of software reuse principles, it is time to move from software development as a one-of-a-kind *project* to software development as a repeatable, many-of-a-kind *business*. In order to accomplish key business goals and improve business performance, these organizations have to dramatically improve their software development process. This means that industrial-strength object-oriented software engineering and software reuse must become key parts of their software engineering strategy – in fact, a key part of their business strategy.

It has been possible to develop single systems in a rather unbusiness-like way. For example, around 70% of the over 435 software organizations assessed up to December 1994 under the guidelines established by the Software Engineering Institute of Carnegie Mellon University fell in Capability Maturity Level 1.

An organization on Level 1, according to Watts Humphrey, the principal developer of the levels, "typically operates without formalized procedures, cost estimates, and project plans. Tools are neither well integrated with the process nor uniformly applied. Change control is lax, and there is little senior management exposure or understanding of the problems and issues. Since many problems are deferred or even forgotten, software installation and maintenance often present serious problems" (Humphrey, 1989).

That certainly sounds grim, but it is consistent with Tom DeMarco's charge that "Fifteen percent of all software projects never deliver anything; that is, they fail utterly to achieve their established goals" (DeMarco, 1982). Of course, despite the deficiencies of many organizations, the software community as a whole has managed to deliver over 100 billion lines of code. A great portion of the world's activities operates on it.

Despite the many benefits of reuse, moving from single-project development into development on a reuse scale greatly increases the complications the organization faces. The new organization has to be *driven* by the necessities of software reuse. It has to be operated as a *business*. We call it the Reuse-driven Software Engineering Business (RSEB). For short, we call it the Reuse Business.

2.1   Is it a business for you?

Yes, reuse can be critical to the success of your software development effort. If you are a developer in a software organization of some size, with a goal of significantly increasing your competitive position, and are producing some form of product line or sets of related systems, then the RSEB may be a business for you. Reuse is becoming increasingly necessary for competitive reasons. Treating software as a business operation is necessary for the same reason. However, there are several situations in which it will not be feasible to invest in establishing a reuse business. A reuse business may not be for you if you only construct small programs, or programs with limited similarity to other programs in your organization. Or, if you are buried in an organization without much hope of significant process improvement. While improving beyond Level 1 is crucial to long-term survival of most businesses dependent on software, some organizations simply cannot mount the necessary commitment. But business pressures will drive the need to change.

Increasingly, software organizations are facing simultaneous pressures:

- to reduce time to market;

- to reduce the cost of the product;

- to improve the productivity of the organization;

- to improve the predictability of the process;

- to increase the reliability of the product; and

- to increase the quality of the product.

Quality has long meant, in a broad sense, meeting the requirements of the ultimate users, and it still does. In recent years, however, the term has come to include a number of new goals. One is the ability of the software to operate in heterogeneous environments, such as a distributed environment. This category includes systems such as DCE (Distributed Computing Environment), WWW (World Wide Web), Java, and CORBA (Common Object Request Broker Architecture).

Another quality goal is the ability to customize software easily for a particular environment, or to adapt it to fit a new application, or to globalize it, that is, to deliver it in many local languages and styles. Some software needs "openness," a quality that permits other vendors to provide add-on capability. So far as current knowledge permits, software should be flexible; it should be adaptable to a yet unknown future.

Example

As an example to be used throughout the book, we consider a hypothetical financial institution, the XYB banking consortium. XYB is facing major changes due to deregulation and to new competition and capabilities enabled by the World Wide Web. This example will be developed further as we proceed. The XYB plans to develop a suite of new applications to support the rapidly changing home-banking and finance markets. It has directed its software development subsidiary, XYBsoft, to develop these applications, and an appropriate software development strategy, architecture, and infrastructure to meet the business challenges.

The financial market is changing rapidly. Banks have to compete with each other and other financial institutions in the rapid delivery of innovative services both to end-customers and to other service providers. XYB and XYBsoft believe that, to accommodate this changing environment, their application suite should be delivered as a set of interoperable, customizable, configurable components and applets, rather than as a monolithic structure.

XYBsoft expects the architecture to follow a distributed, client—server or peer-to-peer model. It anticipates that client components and applets will have to run on a variety of personal computers and be accessible via the World Wide Web. Server components will run on personal computers, as well as other machines. The client components will have to work with office and financial tools already running on personal computers and the Internet. XYB also wants to make sure its components will be consistent with the new Microsoft Open Financial Connectivity (OFC) standards, and can take advantage of customizable components such as Microsoft Money'97, Secure Netscape, and Cybercash CyberCoin components for small payments over the Internet.

XYBsoft also thinks there might be a long-term business opportunity in selling a home-banking framework to other non-competitive financial institutions. That will initially be a low-priority issue until XYB can see a clear market for such frameworks, and has tested the concept with its own new home-banking services. XYBsoft believes that customizable home-banking business components, or applets, should be attractive to the credit unions, insurance companies, and telephone companies it expects to enter this field.

At the same time that quality is becoming a more complex objective, the size of software projects is increasing. That is to be expected, of course. As software does more, it grows in size. But that size growth means that the business side of software – development time, number of staff, cost – grows as well. That growth adds to the pressure for more business-like organization and processes. A Reuse Business is naturally business-like by definition. And it substitutes reuse for developing ever-growing volumes of single-system software.

2.2 Make reuse cost-effective

The Reuse-driven Software Engineering Business (RSEB) is a concept of four interlocking dimensions. The first is its *business orientation*. It has to be both cost-effective and effective in terms of time to market, or there is no point to immersing your organization in its intricacies. For example, a project may be so unique, at least to your company, that there are no comparable projects with which it may share components. Of course, that is an extreme situation. More commonly, a project may fall short of uniqueness, yet still promise little economic gain from an attempt at reuse. Management implements this first dimension, business orientation, through organization. Not just any organization will do. It needs a clear business reason for reuse and should be producing a reasonable family of related applications. Its processes have to be measured and controlled. That is how management can know if it has a "reuse business," not just a collection of wonderful-sounding phrases.

The second dimension is the RSEB's *engineering orientation*. Experienced architects and developers have to architect the family of applications they expect to develop, and identify a domain of interest within the company's sphere for which reuse looks economically promising. Using an architecture and model-driven process, they structure this domain to break out components and component systems that are likely to be used again. Creators, called component engineers, build these elements, using methods based on the Object-Oriented Software Engineering (OOSE) approach devised by Ivar Jacobson (Jacobson *et al.*, 1992). These components are later incorporated in many application systems by developers we call reusers, again using OOSE-based methods.

The third dimension is *technical sequence*. The RSEB methods involve a series of OOSE models: architecture, analysis, design, test, and code. A structure is traceable through these models, both forward and backward, so that a change can be reflected throughout the whole series. The models prime component-based development by allowing reuse, not only of code, but of upstream elements as well. "Effective reuse includes much more than just code," Capers Jones (1994) explained. "Efforts to reuse only source code do not have a particularly good return on investment. Coding is only the fourth most expensive activity when building large software applications." Maintenance, testing and defect repair, documentation, and even meetings and communications can be more expensive.

The fourth dimension is *business process reengineering*. This activity was championed by Michael Hammer and James Champy (1993). Under the name Object-Oriented Business Engineering in *The Object Advantage* (TOA), Ivar Jacobson applied object-oriented techniques to the modeling and transformation of these business processes, so that a more systematic engineering approach could be applied (Jacobson *et al.*, 1994). These models of the business processes then lead to a more natural and effective implementation of the business information systems using OOSE. It is worth noting that since the rapid development of new mission-critical business information systems may be a key part of the reengineering of a company, not only will key business processes be reengineered, but in fact the software development process that creates these business information systems may itself be reengineered. This might mean that the business and technical activities of the RSEB may be working with the dynamically changing processes of a company being reengineered.

Wits (or half-wits) used to say of a prominent American politician, now happily retired, that "he couldn't walk and chew gum at the same time." Well, those are two rather easy "dimensions." How much more difficult it is to keep these four interlocked dimensions in the air simultaneously! Yet that is what an organization hoping to become an effective RSEB has to do.

This is why we need Object-Oriented Business Engineering techniques to provide a systematic, incremental approach to improve an organization and the information systems on which it depends. This systematic, incremental approach helps manage the risks and costs of change in a dynamic environment. Then, using this business engineering approach, a Reuse Business must address the interlocked dimensions of architecture, process, and organization in a concerted way. The effectiveness of approaches such as layered architecture, incremental architecting, concurrent reuse-oriented processes, and model-driven development depends on a consistent integration of these dimensions. By bringing these dimensions together, an RSEB enables an organization to work through a complicated effort successfully.

Remember however, the concept of architected, process-driven, software reuse will yield benefits only if the business situation warrants reuse and if reuse is practiced well. At best, the creation of a full-scale reuse business is complex, since each of the activities that we integrate has innate complexity.

This may sound too complex to achieve. However, the methods we outline will reduce the burden of integrating the dimensions of reuse. By using object-oriented methods to describe components, architecture, and the processes that create and reuse components, you can keep these interlocking dimensions operating in concert, and achieve business success.

2.3   A Reuse Business has business characteristics

In our discussion, we distinguish the term "the Reuse Business," referring to the generic model or conceptual framework we develop in this book, from the term "a reuse business," referring to a particular software organization that is trying to conform to the Reuse Business model.

A reuse business conforming to the Reuse Business model is run as a software engineering business. By business, we mean both that the information technology and software engineering goals are key to accomplishing the enterprise business goals, and that as a consequence, the software organization itself is operated as a business, with well-defined customer and financial objectives. As a reuse-driven software organization, this organization is engaged in producing multiple, related applications, centered and optimized on the production and reuse of components. These applications commonly form a product line or product family. As a business, this organization must understand its customers and serve their needs, while at the same time effectively achieving its profit and expense objectives. Such business trade-offs are managed using a variety of economic, product, and process measures.

To live up to its name, a reuse business must be subject to control by upper management in regular business terms. Like other business activities, it must provide a return on the investment put into it. Benefits must offset costs. Ordinarily, in the early years the costs expended will be greater than the benefits received. The chart in Figure 2.1 illustrates a scenario in which a typical product cycle takes about 18 months. In the first year the investment and cost is high; the return in terms of improved application development is nil. In the second year the first benefit (above the line) reduces the accumulated cost. By the fourth year the costs have been offset by the benefits, and the organization goes into the black. In other scenarios, with shorter product and component cycles or many more applications built, break-even can occur as early as the third year.

Why is this so? And why would management commit to such a program? It is because relative to the cost and effort of one team building a single application from scratch, there is significant extra work in the initial design and adoption of the architecture, processes, and organization to support the concurrent development of many component systems that will be reused across a suite of applications. The payoff comes after several years when numerous applications are built more cost-effectively and more quickly using the reusable components. This payoff of reduced time to market and reduced cost builds up over time as the components are reused repeatedly and as more components are developed.

Cost recovery is not the only, nor even the most important reason to mount a large-scale, architected reuse effort. In many cases, without the additional up-front work to architect the family of applications and component systems, and to become an appropriate organization, it would not be possible to meet the business objectives at all. For example, in the case of Ericsson, and many other companies who see architected reuse

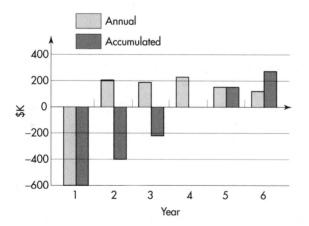

Figure 2.1 *A running chart of investment and costs (below the line) and benefits (above the line) shows upper management that the costs of getting started begin to be recovered by benefits in the second year.*

as the key to competitiveness or even survival, management is able to focus in a straightforward way on building their reuse business. It was critical to do so, and so Ericsson management invested the resources and drove the change. Management did not consider avoiding costs in year 1 or 2 by simply avoiding the task of creating a reuse business. It would simply not be feasible to develop the thousands of customized AXE installations without the careful management of architecture and service packages.

The capital commitment committee of a corporation is ordinarily beset with requests for investment funds. All promise a handsome return on investment after a year, or two or three. The proponents of an RSEB have to operate in this financial environment. They have to organize their reuse business to make the measurements that provide the cost and benefit figures that upper management expects. A nice return on investment not only assuages the nervous strain that managers responsible for results feel, but keeps the money coming for extensions of the concept. One can design and install a reuse business in 1–2 years. While this will cost more than not installing a reuse business, management can expect to see significant cost and time-to-market benefits starting in year 3, and ramping up steadily.

There is, however, an alternative path, with much smaller long-term benefits but with smaller initial investments. The alternative can be stated very simply: Do not develop any architecture and components, but integrate what others have done. Then develop each application system by reusing existing architectures and components. This alternative works when the number of related application systems are relatively small and the potential for reuse of application-specific or business-specific functionality is limited. But it does not work as well when there is a large family of application systems that have many similarities. Then the cost of doing and maintaining the same thing over and over again in different application systems without introducing new reusable components gets overwhelming and allows competitors to do things faster and better. In practice, the best path for most organizations may lie somewhere between the low-impact approach and the radical full-scale organization change. We will show how to take some steps on the alternative path as we discuss the processes in more detail in Part III.

In order to decide what sort of reuse business to propose, and how to follow a path that leads to timely success, proponents of a reuse-driven approach must understand the Reuse Business model. This model integrates essential ideas and pragmatic guidelines from our knowledge of systematic software reuse as described in Chapter 1. We have used as a major input our personal experience with the architecture and the development processes used to develop the AXE Telecom switching system at Ericsson, and with reuse architecture, process, adoption and organization experience gained with Hewlett-Packard's Corporate Reuse Program.

Reuse-driven characteristics   The Reuse Business treats predicted market needs with risk-management techniques, requiring careful motivation of new requirements that cannot be met by reuse of existing assets. The RSEB carefully evaluates and acquires available products and tools such as Object Request Brokers and components such as Microsoft ActiveX Components. Business objects, architectures, and components are found systematically using Object-Oriented Business Engineering and OOSE methods. The RSEB establishes a reuse-oriented organization, separating application and component engineering into distinct organizations and concurrent processes.

Applied engineering discipline   The Reuse Business uses systematic techniques to establish the "right" system architecture to help managers and engineers control the complexity of the system. An evolutionary or incremental software life cycle builds up new functionality in a series of increments and releases. This integrates all cross-life-cycle activities, such as version control, metrics, reviews and inspections, and quality assurance. This requires specialists in the scores of occupations found in large-scale software engineering, such as project managers, configuration managers, user-interface experts, or testers.

Our overall engineering approach is based on Jacobson's use case driven architecture and process modeling frameworks – Object-Oriented System Engineering (OOSE) (Jacobson *et al.*, 1992) and Object-Oriented Business Engineering described in *The Object Advantage* (TOA) (Jacobson *et al.*, 1994). We use the modeling concepts and notations of the Unified Modeling Language (UML) (Booch *et al.*, 1998; Jacobson *et al.*, 1998; Rumbaugher *et al.*, 1998) as a basis to ensure that all developers have a common language for understanding, developing, and sharing models within their own organization, and with others. With these system and process modeling techniques, we can relate and optimize all processes (activities and supporting infrastructure) and products (architecture and components) to the business goals of a reuse business.

2.4   Architect components and applications

Most important is the architecture of the components and applications. One approach to understanding this architecture is to view it from the standpoint of engineering application systems from component systems, as illustrated in Figure 2.2. Here, a number of component systems (rectangles at the bottom of the diagram) are combined by various software engineering processes (ellipses in the middle of the diagram) into a number of application systems (rectangles at the top). Our use of ellipses to represent software

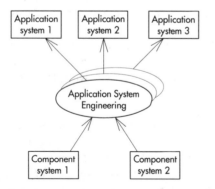

Figure 2.2   *At each stage of software development, from requirements to code, developers engineer application systems from component systems. This is an informal diagram with a mixture of UML notation from several models.*

engineering processes as business use cases and rectangles to represent software systems is a very informal use of the UML and OOSE modeling notation we shall introduce and use more precisely later in the book. In other words, employing software engineering processes, developers construct application systems by assembling reusable components drawn from component systems. At an early stage of software development, they would work with reusable information system use cases. At later stages, they work with reusable design components or actual code.

Another way to visualize the architecture is illustrated in Figure 2.3, as a set of layers. A reuse business systematically engineers a layer of related application systems, at the top. Behind the front row of applications are related versions of the applications. The application-specific software is engineered by extensively reusing component systems, which we imagine as existing on three lower layers. Below the application layer are components reusable only for the specific business or application domain area, such as insurance applications, banking systems, human resources and personnel information systems, telecoms switches, or microwave instruments. This layer includes components usable in more than a single application. The third layer of middleware components provides interfaces to other established entities, such as graphical user interfaces. The lowest layer of system software components provides interfaces to hardware, such as an operating system interfacing to the computer (or to its built-in instruction set).

The Reuse Business uses an extended OOSE modeling notation and process to provide support for architecting reuse-oriented applications and components. New constructs support layered, modular architectures, in which application systems are built from a combination of concrete and abstract components. Modular here relates to large-grain components such as OCXs. Related components are grouped into component systems, which can be frameworks or collections of components such as use cases or Java classes. New mechanisms make explicit the commonality and variability crucial to effective engineering of components for families of systems. These variability mechanisms facilitate the use of problem-oriented scripting languages, component generators, and system builders to produce domain-specific application construction kits. Object-Oriented Business Engineering techniques are applied to the target organization to identify business objects and application families that support customer business processes.

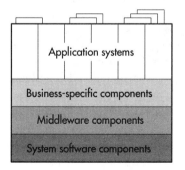

Figure 2.3 *A typical architecture on which a Reuse Business rests is three layers of components that go into the application systems at the top of the diagram.*

2.4.1 Applications and application systems

Reusers construct an application system by selecting component systems and integrating them together into an application system. They may specialize or augment the component systems to adapt them to the new application. Thus, a component system is a set of customizable and configurable software elements. In some cases reusers may have to supplement the reusable components with newly developed software. While they are usually traditional developers, reusers could also be installers, a production department, or even end users. In addition to code modules, the application system may include configuration scripts, customization capabilities, and installation and maintenance documents.

In many situations applications come in families. One example is a suite of applications that work together, such as Microsoft Office, which includes a word processor, spreadsheet, database management, and presentation program. Another example is the suite of applications that supports customers and workers in a bank; this suite deals with accounts, loans, audits, and fund transfers.

In other situations, applications come in variants. Here different versions of the same application might be used by different people, countries, or situations. For example, the Ericsson AXE switch is delivered in different forms for a large installation, a small installation, or different countries. Similarly, different models of the Hewlett-Packard Laser printer require different versions of firmware.

Still another situation is where the applications are fairly independent, but can be treated as a family because they are built from the same set of components, such as the Microsoft Foundation Classes or a user interface library. Larger systems such as database management systems, for example, are also typically implemented from a set of components based on the specialized database architecture that has evolved from building many systems of this type.

These families of related applications possess a commonality that is exploitable by reusable components. They can be implemented from a set of lower-level components. At the same time, the applications, while related, also have differences. These differences mean that the components must have the capability of being varied to accommodate the differences.

As we discussed in Chapter 1, the application families or domains to be analyzed and the components to be built have to be chosen carefully. The cost of breaking application systems into component systems and building them up from component systems has to make business sense in a Reuse Business. The cost of creating and maintaining a suitable set of component systems has to be offset by the gains resulting from using them to create and maintain application systems. The prospective number of application systems has to be sufficient to provide enough gains to offset the initial and continuing cost of the component systems.

2.4.2 Components and component systems

The three lower layers of the layered architecture shown in Figure 2.3 are each composed of components, grouped into sets called component systems. Let us explain these further.

Reusers employ components to put together application systems. When we look at this operation more closely, we see that it makes sense to have something larger than small components to work with. We need a larger aggregation of components that can be more easily handled by reusers. That "something larger" is a component system. Also, looking closely, we see that reusers don't need complete information about a component system. Complete information might be overwhelming. Reusers need only the subset of the information necessary to assemble the component systems into an application system.

Stepping back, let us clarify and expand on our terminology. We use the term *component* to refer to an element of a development model that meets two criteria: It is loosely coupled to other elements and it promises to be reusable. All software life-cycle workproducts are potentially components or sources of components. These workproducts include not only any of the models we use, but also interfaces, tests, manuals, and the source code itself. In our conception, a component is very general, and includes OCXs, Ada packages, C++ components, and use cases. Some components are fairly formal and structured; some are operational code or tools; others are process descriptions or even less formal documents.

We use the term *component system* to refer to a set of related components that accomplishes some function larger than that accomplished by a single component. Instead of tracking thousands of elements, a reuser can restrict his or her scope to a few hundred components, packaged into a relatively small number of component systems.

In order to manage the interfaces between component systems, we export only a subset of the information for use by reusers. This is done by publicizing subsets of components through one or more *facades*. Each facade exports to a reuser only those aspects of the entire component system that he or she needs to reuse it. We think of it as a simplified model of the component system, revealing only those parts that need to be directly visible or that need to be understood by the reuser.

Some components or component systems are used "as is". They do not need to be specialized and consequently, when they match the problem, they are easy to reuse. More abstract components or component systems contain at least one of a variety of specialization mechanisms. A reuser exploits this mechanism to adapt the component to the particular application. This adaptation effort, of course, imposes a little work on the reuser, but it greatly expands the number of applications to which he or she can apply the component system. If we made no provision for variance, we would have to resign ourselves to the burden of a very large number of "concrete" component systems.

2.4.3 Layered architecture

In general, we build the larger applications as layered systems with a modular, layered architecture. Each layer in the system is constructed from an appropriate (set of) components drawn from several component systems in lower layers. An application explicitly imports components from the component-system facade. Exports, imports, and facades work together to support both layering and modular pluggability.

We implement traditional object-oriented frameworks as component systems. These systems have "slots" into which a reuser may plug components to augment their abilities. Or, they may be specialized by using inheritance or several other mechanisms.

In this layered architecture, each application is represented as a separate system. Each is constructed from components organized as component systems. Each component system, in turn, may be constructed from other, lower-level component systems, as illustrated in Figure 2.3. The reuser constructs each application, which is distinct, but related, from a set of application domain, business-specific components or component systems in the top layer. They can also directly reuse some components from lower layers, such as utility classes defined in the middleware or system software layers. The business-specific components, in turn, use components from lower layers.

This layered architecture is a mental model that enables each person in the reuse business to understand the practice of engineering application systems from component systems. By having distinct layers and clear interfaces between them, this architecture allows developers to work effectively in parallel. The middleware layer, for example, provides platform-independent *interfaces* to distribution and interoperability mechanisms. Well-defined, stable *interlayer interfaces* provide openness and flexibility. The architecture, therefore, allows component systems to evolve independently, as new technologies and opportunities arise.

2.5 Software engineering processes

Developers employ a number of software engineering processes and support environments (tools) to create application systems and families from component systems. We group these processes into three categories: *Component System Engineering*, *Application System Engineering*, and *Application Family Engineering*, each shown as an ellipse in Figure 2.4. The engineering of component systems and application systems consists largely of traditional software engineering processes, augmented as appropriate for reuse. The overall system architecture is created by the application family engineering process. A key goal of this process is to identify the architecture and a set of component systems that will support the suite of applications to be built. The overall management of the reuse business is also shown as a process, *Managing the Reuse Business*.

Object-Oriented Business Engineering is used to model these software development processes. Business actors and use cases model the interaction of persons with the software organization. These models are then refined to define the responsibilities of reuse workers, and customized to produce a reuse-oriented software organization structure that meets the needs of specific software development organizations. A business reengineering transition framework and change management techniques are used to systematically restructure a software development organization into a reuse business.

2.5.1 People and processes interact

People are involved in two ways in the software engineering processes. One way is when they act as a worker within a software engineering organization as managers, software engineers, librarians, and testers, for example. Workers perform the software engineering processes, or support those who do.

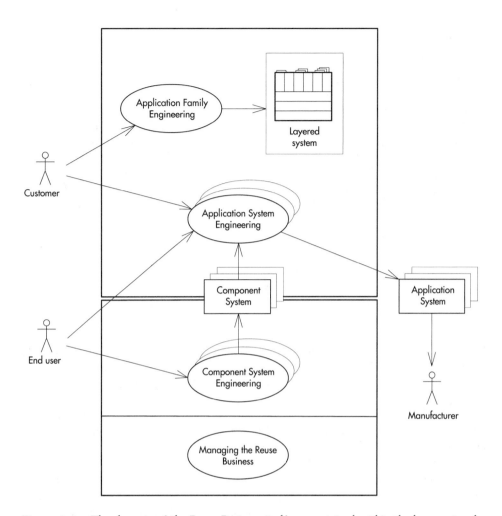

Figure 2.4 *The elements of the Reuse Business itself are contained within the large rectangle. The stick figures outside the big rectangle represent the environment within which the Reuse Business functions. The arrows indicate the major interactions.*

The other way is as people outside the organization, either as an *end user* of the application systems produced or as a *customer* of the RSEB. End users and customers should get benefits from the reuse business. A reuse business must be useful to its customers, to organizations outside it, and to its end users.

Therefore, to present a complete picture of the Reuse Business, we include people. We use stick figures to represent them on diagrams, as shown in Figure 2.4. More precisely, a stick figure is a *business actor,* a term we use to represent a class of people or roles interacting with a process.

Customer   These are people who order, specify, and typically pay for an application system. They do more than issue paperwork. They are the focal point for requirements.

Customers are also involved as a source of information when developing new versions of component systems.

End user These are the people who will use an application system when it is installed in the target organization, as contrasted with people involved in the acquisition process who will not actually use the system. It is desirable to find ways to enable end users to participate in the engineering of application systems. Some end users are also involved as a source of information in the development of new versions of component systems.

Manufacturer The manufacturer receives a new version of an application system when it has been developed, then produces and delivers complete applications to customers and users.

2.5.2 Application Family Engineering

This process determines how to decompose the overall set of applications into a suite of application systems and supporting component systems. The process architects the layers, facades, and interfaces of the subsystems and component systems that support the complete family of related applications.

We call the designer of a family of application systems an architect. The architect faces a larger task of understanding requirements than the designer of a single system. He or she has to find out not only what current users of similar systems now know they need, but also what potential users and customers now think they might want in the not entirely known future.

The architect then develops the layered architecture, introducing structure to make the architecture robust enough to survive the inevitable changes that systems undergo. Individual application and component systems become visible.

Existing software, such as large legacy systems, often millions of lines of code, and vendor systems must be considered. The architect has to include these existing elements within his or her plans. Developers incorporate legacy systems and purchased systems with the components and component systems that together make up the sources from which application engineers can put together a family of application systems.

In other approaches to reuse, effective component system engineering relies on an activity historically called "domain engineering," described in Chapter 1, to determine an architecture and set of components. The RSEB does not have an explicit domain engineering process, but distributes key domain engineering-like activities between the Application Family Engineering and Component System Engineering processes.

2.5.3 Application System Engineering

This process selects, specializes, and assembles components from one or more component systems into complete application systems. It uses appropriate tools, methods, processes, and instructions provided explicitly with the component system.

Application system engineering begins when a customer requests a new version of an application system. Developers first elicit and capture the requirements from a few sources, primarily the customers and the end users. Then the developers try to express the requirements in terms of available *architecture* and *component models*. Certain requirements are met by directly reusing some components or specializing others. If the overall systems architecture is well designed, and if a comprehensive set of component systems has been made available, developers should usually be able to find an appropriate component to reuse. In the (hopefully less common) case where no appropriate component is available, they may have to seek a new component or even develop a model and software to meet the requirement themselves.

The next step is to design and implement an increment of the eventual application system. The increment should be large enough to be workable. In the case of models early in the development stages, "workable" may be a matter of judgment. In the case of code, "workable" means a portion of the eventual system that developers can run and test.

The final step comes, in some cases, during the life of the application system. User complaints or infrastructure changes may send the system back for improvement.

2.5.4 Component System Engineering

This process designs, constructs, and packages components into component systems. The process will use appropriate code, templates, models, dictionary, documents, and perhaps custom tools. In many respects the actual process of component system engineering is similar to that of application system engineering. The process begins when a reuse business needs to create a new component system. The first step is to collect and analyze the requirements about both needs and trends from a wide range of sources. The sources include business models, architects, domain experts, and application users. The goal is a consistent model that explicitly expresses commonality and variability across the suite of applications that will reuse these components. Using techniques for cost–benefit estimation, developers decide what functionality should be incorporated in the component system.

In addition to concrete components that will be reused as is, many components must be designed to be specialized. In addition to inheritance, other mechanisms based on problem-oriented languages, parameterized templates, generators, and domain-specific kits (Griss, 1995d) can be used. Components can range from a very simple set of code elements and interface models to a very complex set of code elements, templates, tests, and scripts.

Next, the component engineers architect, and incrementally design, implement, and test the component system. The process concludes with the certification and packaging of the component system for retrieval by reusers.

Later, there may be further steps. Users or reusers may complain. The infrastructure may change. New types of application systems may appear. All these bring the component system back to the component engineers to rework.

2.6 Establishing and managing a reuse business

If you choose to run your software engineering activities as a Reuse-driven Software Engineering Business, then questions arise: How best can you transition to it? How do you run it day to day? In our experience the best way is to reengineer your existing software development function by systematically employing the methods of business process reengineering and specifically those of Object-Oriented Business Engineering (Jacobson *et al.*, 1994). Organizational structures and management policies and plans are developed as the reuse business is established. Once established, the reuse business needs to be managed and optimized.

To deal with the complexity and scale of organization and systems, the RSEB has to manage risks in a systematic way. A primary way of dealing with scale is incremental adoption – successively scaling up different parts of the system, process, and organization.

The management of a reuse business as a whole involves a level of responsibility over and above the management of individual projects and processes. This kind of management is not very different from the overall management of other major business segments. Perhaps first among these responsibilities is making sure that plans for the future are made and that these plans are followed and communicated to upper management. Close behind and, in fact, related to the plans are decisions on the investment of resources, not only of money, but of people and time. In particular, how much should the organization invest in the construction of component systems, especially in anticipation of upcoming needs.

Other overall management functions an RSEB needs include:

- determining who shall own and maintain a particular component system;

- collecting metrics data to manage and optimize the reuse business;

- determining how many workers are needed over the future period in the light of the work planned, and arranging hiring, training, and salary;

- trading off the management variables such as time to market, cost, functionality, and quality, and resolving conflicts over resources and schedule.

There are two extreme ways to look at adoption of a reuse business. One extreme would be to move the entire present organization, process, and people in small steps to the new mode. The other would be to build an entirely new reuse business organization, while letting the existing software development organization carry on day-to-day activities. While it does control risk, the small-increment approach can easily get lost in the necessities of carrying on current business. Moreover, it might take far more years than competition promises to allow to get there in tiny steps.

As to building an entirely new organization, few companies can afford the added cost. Some companies have been successful, however, in choosing a single focus for an entirely new organization to work in. Then the company incrementally adds new domains and people to the new organization, letting the old organization fade away. That new organization is an instance of an RSEB and it grows as rapidly as the company can manage to make it grow. The transition happens incrementally across the organization, affecting different parts at different times.

We can't tell you in general where to place your transition plan. What we can tell you, because we have seen it happen time after time, is that the road to large-scale reuse holds many obstacles and risks. Companies have succeeded in traversing that road only if they address these obstacles as challenges, only if they have a vision of where the road leads, and only if they move from point to point in a systematic, incremental and concerted way.

As we stated in Figure 2.1, the multi-year cost–benefit trade-off chart, transitioning to a reuse business takes a significant investment over a time period of two to three years, or even longer. Carrying on any program over a period of years is difficult in modern business, beset as it is by technological and market turbulence. That is why creating a reuse business is a strategic decision that looks ahead to where the business has to go. That vision, of course, has to be backed by a strong upper-management commitment. It has to be consistently supported over a period of years. Otherwise, there is great risk that the company will not reach the point where the benefits surpass the investment. Difficult as we make this path appear, the other path – the path of not reducing software costs, of not reducing time to market – is even darker. We leave its demons to your imagination.

We approach the *systematic transition to an RSEB* as a process of business reengineering. Our RSEB approach combines concepts from three areas and our own experience: business process reengineering, change management, and incremental systematic reuse adoption. Together, these provide a path to overcome the many anticipated and numerous unexpected difficulties as they arise. This approach enables you to take the successful, but fragmentary reuse efforts deployed by some today and integrate them into a coherent approach to reuse.

Some people say every organization is different. Each has seemingly unique markets, technology, people, and processes. Others say organizations are fundamentally the same. This supports the idea that a good manager can manage any organization. For the purpose of installing a reuse business, however, we identify four types of organization:

1   Those where the RSEB improves the internal business processes of the organization, such as customer interaction, management information systems, or manufacturing processes.

2   Those in which the RSEB is to engineer software into a hardware product, such as a telecommunications switch, a defense product, a printer, or an instrument.

3   Those in which the RSEB develops application systems for outsourcing customers, such as Andersen Consulting or EDS.

4   Those in which the RSEB develops software products, such as Microsoft.

2.6.1 Improving internal processes

In this type of organization the proposed reuse business exists entirely within one organization, such as a bank or insurance company. Its mission may be, at a minimum, to understand the company's present processes better in order to implement them in software more effectively. At a maximum, it may be to participate in a business reengineering effort. In either case the rapid and effective development of a set of integrated and related application systems offers a competitive advantage.

For example, Hewlett-Packard's Corporate Information Systems produces a variety of human resource, manufacturing, and financial application software systems for all of the divisions serving the corporation's 90 000 worldwide employees. Many of these systems are customized to local divisional and country needs. Yet they must support HP-wide policies and conform to HP-wide standards. To accomplish these dual goals, Corporate Information Systems must identify the commonalities that extend across the entire corporation. At the same time it must seek out the variabilities that different lines of business and different country cultures impose upon HP's far-flung units. Then it must engineer component systems that accommodate these two objectives.

2.6.2 Embedded software

In this type of organization, the proposed reuse business again exists wholly within one business, usually large. The business produces products for external users, such as HP producing Laser printers and instruments, Ericsson producing the AXE switching system, or a defense contractor producing weapons systems for armies, navies, and air forces. The product is typically based on special purpose hardware, operated and specialized by software. For example, electronic telephone switches, such as the ESS5 produced by AT&T and the AXE by Ericsson, contain both electronic parts and many millions of lines of software to tell the transistors what to do. Constructed and maintained over generations by large teams combining hardware and software skills, these systems must be designed for customization. The software must adapt the switching systems to the practices of different telephone companies and the cultures and regulations of different countries. Moreover, it must be adaptable to successive generations of hardware. Telephone switching systems have a long life span.

In fact, the physical products in which software engineers embed programs typically have a long lifetime. Generally there is an architectural group for the product (or product line) responsible for maintaining an architectural model embracing both hardware and software over the product line's lifetime. This model defines the interface between the hardware and software. The architectural group has major responsibility for planning the evolution of the architecture in response to anticipated and actual changes in product features and technology.

These plans are inputs to the software engineers in the reuse business. It is then their task to develop component systems from which application engineers can produce application systems adaptable to what may come.

2.6.3 Software house

In this type of organization, the reuse business exists as an organization separate from the user of the software. We may discern two patterns here. One is an outsourcing vendor, such as Andersen Consulting or EDS, that contracts to develop and operate the information services of a client. Another way is for the software house to take full responsibility for building systems or subsystems under contract to a client, but the client will operate the system.

If an outsourcing vendor has many clients, it has the opportunity over time to adapt essentially the same system to the somewhat different requirements of its clients. Actually carrying out such a program requires the vendor to build business models of the common needs of many clients. Beyond modeling clients' existing practices lies the opportunity to assist them in reengineering their businesses, resulting in still more effective models. Then the reuse business looks for the commonalities and variabilities in these models. They, in turn, provide the basis for appropriate component systems. The component systems, of course, lead to application systems appropriate to each client.

Software houses operating in the second pattern often confine their efforts to clients in one industry segment, such as power utilities, financial services, or manufacturing. Clients in the same industry have similar software needs. Once the vendor becomes familiar with these needs, it can build business models to reflect them. Then, as before, it can build suitable component systems, with variability enabling the vendor to adapt them to the different circumstances of different clients.

Initially the software house will probably sell application systems that it has put together from its own component systems. One can envisage component systems and business models delineated so clearly that client personnel can themselves create the application systems.

2.6.4 Software product vendor

In this type of organization, software products are sold to customers either off the shelf in retail establishments or through direct sales channels. Many of these products are marketed ready-to-use. We can envisage products that are essentially what we have been calling component systems. Users themselves have the task of adapting them to their particular application. Obviously, the product must include user instructions so foolproof that the vendor's help lines are not deluged. Alternately, if the user instructions are so complex as not to be foolproof, the vendor must offer training or even on-site consulting assistance.

For example, vendors of utility software, multimedia software, and frameworks fall within this category. Microsoft Office is an example of a suite of interoperable application systems, largely built from common components. Other examples include the banking application frameworks such as Quartz offered by TCS, or software utility frameworks, such as CommonPoint by Taligent, or Orbix by Iona.

A reuse business in this class, as before, must identify what is common and what varies across the several application systems that it plans to sell. The reuse business may itself develop these application systems or it may develop component systems for the user to adapt. A systematic approach for the reuse business is to prepare business models of anticipated end-user requirements as its basis for engineering an appropriate set of component systems. Developing business models is a crucial task, requiring a good sense of where the market is heading and where new opportunities may occur.

2.7 Summary

The Reuse-driven Software Engineering Business (RSEB), or Reuse Business, is a systematic approach to running a software development organization. Its goal is to develop a family of related *application systems* that meet customer needs as effectively as possible. Architected reuse is the key engineering strategy. The RSEB is managed in strict business terms, using economic and process metrics to optimize investment and performance. Key to ensuring success are software processes and an organization optimized to the layered architecture.

The RSEB structures the software development organization around a *layered system architecture* and model-driven software development *processes* that ensure large amounts of reuse. The RSEB develops a suite of related application systems for customers and end users. These application systems are built from reusable *components*, packaged into groups called *component systems*.

A reuse business analyzes the software activities within its scope, both inside its own company and within its market horizon. The reuse business must understand the class of application systems it will build, and how future technologies and market needs will change these in the future. The key RSEB processes in a running reuse business are *Application Family Engineering, Application System Engineering, Component System Engineering* and *Managing The Reuse Business*.

Quite often, the RSEB exists to create the application systems needed to support the reengineered business processes as an enterprise or business organization reengineers itself to dramatically improve business performance. Business process reengineering of the enterprise then defines the needed applications and helps drive the RSEB.

A systematic *transition to a reuse business* uses a business process reengineering framework to incrementally reshape an existing software development organization into a customized reuse business. This reengineering may result in a substantial overhaul of the existing software development organization or even, in some cases, the creation of a new organization. Reengineering is based on Jacobson's Object-Oriented Business Engineering approach (Jacobson *et al.*, 1994).

2.8 Additional reading

Ivar Jacobson's *Object Magazine* columns describe the development of Ericsson's AXE (Jacobson, 1996a, 1996b) in more detail, and explain the principles of architecture, process, and organization change needed for success with AXE. These motivate several aspects of our approach (Jacobson, 1996b).

Martin Griss' *Object Magazine* columns describe reuse adoption and processes at HP (Griss, 1995a, 1995b; Griss and Collins, 1995), experience with domain-specific kits (Griss, 1995c; Griss and Kessler, 1996), and how application domain commonality and variability are represented (Griss, 1996).

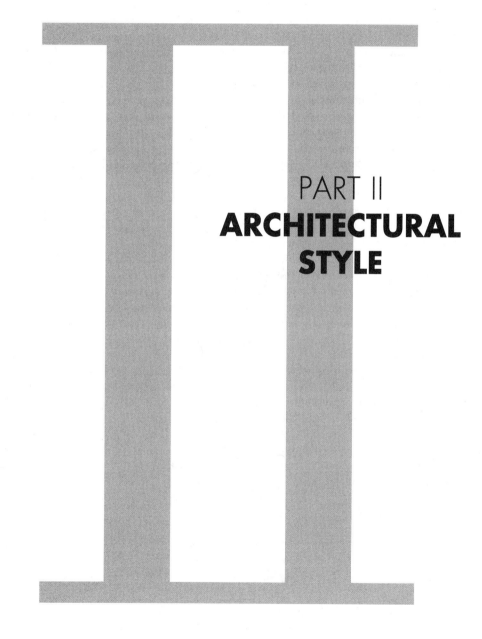

PART II
ARCHITECTURAL STYLE

The business of a software engineering organization is to produce software systems, usually called applications, that satisfy its customers' needs. The goal of a Reuse-driven Software Engineering Business is to engineer these applications as effectively as possible, using reuse. Significant levels of software reuse can only be achieved with an investment in the architecture and careful design of software systems and the reusable components from which they are built.

Software engineering is a process that builds software in the form of applications and supporting systems by systematically transforming requirements related to a problem in the real world into code that will execute on one or more machines. This process proceeds in stages by building a series of models, each represented by several diagrams and documents. Each model describes important aspects of the problem or of the software systems that will realize the solution. Each participant in this process works with different subsets of the models, which aim to present views of the systems appropriate to the issues the participants must address. When they are dealing with several related systems, they often find it useful to first develop a common set of components that they can specialize and reuse in each application.

The right modeling constructs and notation are crucial to making these participants effective. It is the principles, mechanisms, and patterns that do this — that define and communicate the structure of a system — that we call architecture. Getting it right is the key engineering task. The architecture then allows applications and components to evolve gracefully. It enables software engineers to achieve significant levels of reuse, enables components to work well together, and allows software engineers to develop under-standable systems which are easier to maintain.

Our modeling notation is object-oriented and graphical. Object-oriented systems are engineered using types, classes and objects. A system's structure and design are defined by its types and classes and the relationships between them. As will become clearer in the following chapters, objects provide a very convenient and flexible way of dealing uniformly with system design and implementation at many levels of detail. But objects alone are not enough! There is a need for some constructs that allow engineers, users, and the customer ordering the system to define what the system should do. This is what use cases are used for. Each distinct way of using the system is defined by a distinct *use case*.

We start by treating each application as a separate complete system, an *application system*. Each application system offers a coherent set of use cases. It can be ordered by customers, developed by software engineers, and installed independently of other application systems. Each application system is described by its own set of models and documents. We loosely use the term "system" to refer to the set of models describing the software system. Each model defines a different aspect of the system. Use case models define what the system should do for a user. Several kinds of object models define the system's structure and design. Test models help confirm that the system performs as expected.

When we build several application systems, we can reuse *components*. A component is a piece of software that has been engineered to be reusable. Usually, a single component is not used alone but in conjunction with related components. We group these related components into systems, called *component systems*. Each component system is carefully designed, packaged, and managed to be as reusable as possible. By using these larger groups of components as units, we overcome many of the problems associated with the reuse of lots of small objects.

Systems that share a similar high-level structure and key mechanisms are said to have a similar architectural style. We have chosen an architectural style and notation that will ensure that our systems will have common characteristics, described using common elements, according to well-understood principles. Approaching software reuse without understanding the architectural style of the envisioned system is like starting to construct a building without knowing if it will be a skyscraper or a garage!

The developers of components can also reuse lower-level components. Thus both application systems and component systems can be built from other reusable component systems. We can see this as a kind of layering with the application systems on the top and the component systems underneath, as shown in Figure II.1. We call this a *layered system*, with a *layered architecture*.

A layered architecture is an architectural style that simplifies system evolution and enables substantial reuse of components. Our approach is targeted to building systems in a layered, modular, object-oriented style, which we believe greatly enhances systematic reuse. Using our object-oriented modeling notation, mechanisms, and architectural style, engineers can become accustomed to building systems effectively using objects.

An architectural style is defined by the type of *constructs* that can be used to engineer a system. In an object-oriented approach the constructs include different kinds of types and classes, use cases, interfaces and groups of constructs as subsystems. A particular architectural style restricts the way in which modeling constructs are used, and how they may be related. Its rules define how to engineer architectures and systems that conform to the style.

Let us give a more precise definition of architectural style. It is the reflection of the system structure in a model or series of models. Software engineers, in the model-driven approach outlined in this book, construct a series of models using successive *modeling languages*. The modeling languages define the constructs that can be used to define the system and how the constructs relate. Then we say:

> The **architectural style** of a system is the denotation of the modeling languages used when modeling that system (Jacobson *et al.*, 1992).

We can think of the architectural style as the set of all (good) models that can be built using the modeling languages.

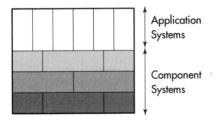

Application
Systems

Component
Systems

Figure II.1   *A layered architecture of application and component systems.*

The following five chapters successively develop the details of a layered architectural style that supports high levels of reuse.

Chapter 3 defines a basic object-oriented modeling notation. Object-oriented software engineering defines systems in terms of several object-oriented models. We follow Jacobson's use-case-driven object-oriented software approach (OOSE) (Jacobson *et al.*, 1992) which exploits systems modeling constructs such as use cases, objects, and relationships between use cases and objects. We use the Unified Modeling Language (UML) (Booch *et al.*, 1997) as a base.

Chapter 4 explains how application systems can systematically reuse components. Selected model elements can be structured and packaged as reusable components when building applications. Components are grouped into component systems. Explicit variability and packaging constructs are needed to build and use flexible reusable components.

Chapter 5 provides more detail on use case components and component systems, and how variability is expressed. Chapter 6 describes object components, frameworks, and patterns, and how to relate sets of object components to corresponding use case components.

Chapter 7 defines layered systems and architectures, and discusses the different layers of a prototypical layered architecture. Layered systems can be modeled in terms of its constituent subsystems. We also describe how legacy systems can be integrated into a layered system.

OBJECT-ORIENTED SOFTWARE ENGINEERING

3.1 Software engineering transforms requirements into code

Software development starts with a problem in the real world, a world filled with complexity and continuous change. The task of the software engineering process is to turn an informal statement of a problem in the real world (the requirements) into a limited amount of code (the system) that correctly models the aspect of the real world that concerns the user, and solves the stated problem.

In very small systems, or even smaller systems coded by the user alone, there may be only one outward step between the real world and the code representation of the solution. More steps may be implicit in the developer's mind, though not outwardly documented. In larger systems, experience indicates that a series of models, constructed by people with talents appropriate to the particular level of each model, stand between the real-world problem and the eventual code solution.

Object-oriented software engineering is the process of systematically building software systems using objects, types and classes. A system's structure and design are defined by its types and classes and the relationships between them. The process proceeds in stages by systematically building a series of object models, each represented by several diagrams and documents. Each model describes important aspects of the real world or of the software systems that will realize the desired solution.

A key enabler of object-oriented software engineering is an object-oriented, graphical modeling notation that provides a clear and precise modeling language that allows us to describe an architecture and components that will ensure the development of robust, reuse-supporting systems. Several object-oriented software engineering notations and methods for implementing this series of models have been developed by many authors, including Ivar Jacobson (Jacobson *et al.*, 1992), James Rumbaugh (Rumbaugh *et al.*, 1991), and Grady Booch (1994).

Since 1995 the notations underlying these and other object-oriented methods have been brought together by the three originators in the Unified Modeling Language (UML) (Booch *et al.*, 1997). The approach we develop in this book is based on Ivar Jacobson's Object-Oriented Software Engineering (OOSE) modeling notation and method (Jacobson *et al.*, 1992). We have updated the OOSE notation to conform to UML, and to take advantage of several new UML features.

3.2 Software engineering is a team process

The process of industrial software engineering typically involves large projects, of a size that requires many people. Many different skills are involved in requirements capture, specification, architecting, high- and low-level design, coding, test planning, testing, and debugging. Many different kinds of people participate. The skills discussed in this book require a team in order to provide all of them.

Software engineering is a process in which a team of people build software systems using systematic engineering principles and techniques, such as model building, simulation, estimation, and measurement. We will often refer to these people as software engineers, even though many different skills and specialties are involved, and some developers or other team members may not have full software engineering training. Figure 3.1 shows several of these team members as well as other key stakeholders such as customers and end users. We have not shown all the roles. For example, user interface designers, documentors, and librarians are also important team members.

The development of most software systems involves the creation and evolution of several software artifacts or *workproducts*, such as diagrams, source code files, test files, installation scripts, design documents, and user documents. Each of these workproducts describes a different aspect of the system, of interest to different members of the software engineering team, customers, or users.

A complete, well-defined software engineering process will describe in detail which workproducts to build, the steps to follow in order to build them, who should build them, and the inspections, standards, metrics, and tests that should be used to control quality and certify system correctness. To be an effective member of the software engineering team, each person must be trained in the principles and activities he or she needs, and also have the process sophistication and experience to apply the methods and tools well.

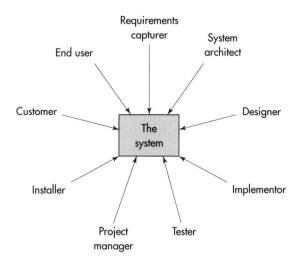

Figure 3.1 *A system has many facets, defined by models, each viewed by different stakeholders through a variety of tools and documents.*

3.3 Software engineering is systematic model building

More formally, software engineering is a process of building several related models. Each *model* defines a specific aspect of the system, and is described using several diagrams and documents that have a prescribed format. Each model is examined or manipulated by different people with different specific interests, roles, or tasks. We define a *stakeholder* as someone who is interested in using the system, understanding the system, placing requirements on the system, or developing some part of the system. A stakeholder may be a *worker* within the software development organization, such as an engineer or manager, or someone outside the organization such as a customer, installer, or end user as shown in Figure 3.1. Each of these people may need to see a different aspect of the system. Thus the software development team needs to build several different, but related models. Each worker manipulates his or her models through a variety of different tools and documents.

We treat each application as a separate complete system, an *application system*. Each application system can be specified, ordered, and paid for by customers, developed by software engineers, and installed more or less independently of other application systems. Each application system is described by its own set of models and documents. We loosely use the term "system" to refer to the set of models describing the software system.

There are five main software engineering activities (sometimes called phases or subprocesses), shown in Figure 3.2. These are requirements capture, robustness analysis, design, implementation, and testing. During each activity, the team refines its under-standing of the system and describes its function and the structure of the desired system in increasing levels of detail. During each activity, several team members are involved, and several models are used.

Requirements capture	Robustness analysis	Design	Implementation	Testing

Figure 3.2 *The five main activities of a single software development cycle are requirements capture, robustness analysis, design, implementation, and testing.*

As shown in Figure 3.3, the requirements capture activity deals with more abstract, high-level views of the system, starting with requirements, while the design and implementation activities deal with more concrete, lower-level details, ending with code that matches the target hardware, operating systems, and other constraints. Two of the most important external stakeholders of a system are its *customers* and *end users*. They are primarily interested in what the system will be able to do and how they can use it. During requirements capture they work with the *requirements capturer* to specify the different *use scenarios* of the system. These use scenarios are first captured informally, and then expressed more formally as a *use case model* of the system. The analysts may also develop a model or prototype of the graphical user interface.

The *analysts* then develop an *analysis model* that helps to build a structure that is reusable and robust when faced with changing requirements. This analysis model does not deal with low-level details of the implementation, but concentrates on the high-level static structure of the system, which constitute the first steps towards the system architecture. Informally, the architecture is the high-level design showing structure, interfaces, and dependencies. The most important step during robustness analysis is to carefully allocate parts of the use cases to responsibilities undertaken by separate parts of the system, such as different subsystems. This separation is done so that changes in the design of one part of the system may occur without requiring too many changes in other parts.

During design, the *designers* develop the *design model* which expresses how the system is to be implemented. The design model provides details of the structure, interfaces, and behavior of the code to be written, and its organization into subsystems. The designers first transform the high-level model as expressed in the use case and analysis models into the more detailed, lower-level design model to define how the use

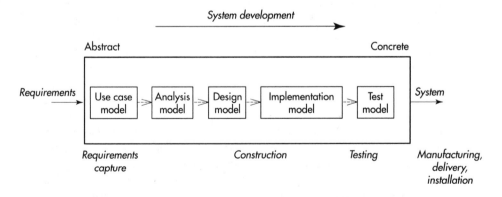

Figure 3.3 *Software engineering is a process of building models for different stakeholders. Each activity uses several different models, transforming and refining them from activity to activity.*

cases will be performed by the system. They define the specific interfaces, data structures, and methods to be performed by the code. They also define implementation mechanisms and provide additional details on how to solve different kinds of implementation problems, such as mapping to a particular language, operating system, or distributed execution environment. Then the *implementors* implement this detailed design in some programming language, filling in the remaining details to produce the *implementation model* of the system. This consists of the source code in the selected programming language, many documents and annotations that describe the code, and various scripts to produce executable code.

The *testers* develop a *test model* that describes how the resulting system should be inspected and tested, to verify that all requirements are fulfilled and that an appropriate level of quality is met. Their goal is to make sure that the end users can use the system as specified. The use case model provides a starting point for developing test specifications. Each possible "execution" of a use case, described as a scenario, will correspond to one test case. There are several other types of tests, such as unit tests and system tests. In addition, engineers and other stakeholders will review and inspect each model to identify defects as early as is feasible. They define mappings between one model and the next to ensure consistency.

The different models, and the elements defined in the different models, are seamlessly connected with each other by *traces*. These links allow the engineers to track changes from requirements through the different models all the way to the code. This will help them to analyze the impact of any changes they contemplate making, or to understand why certain decisions were made.

Throughout all of the above discussion, we have consciously deferred detailed discussion of the many opportunities for reuse to later chapters, since this chapter is mostly about single system construction; reuse will be dealt with in much greater detail and is the main focus of the book. Suffice it to say that as developers create models during each activity, the process should enable them to take advantage of available reusable model elements.

3.3.1 The incremental, iterative software engineering life cycle

It is the rule, rather than the exception, that all the system requirements are not fully known at the outset of a project. The process of defining and constructing the system will uncover many requirements that might be too difficult, or even impossible, to articulate at the outset. Instead, knowledge of the system and the requirements will grow as work progresses. In many situations, the requirements actually change over time, in response to unavoidable and unforeseen changes in the real world, or in other systems with which the system under construction interacts. The whole software engineering process is designed to systematically uncover details and incompatibilities in the requirements that may not have been obvious to the customers at the outset.

Because of this inevitable evolution, we almost always develop systems incrementally. A system is developed step by step and released in a series of versions, releases, cycles, or increments, as shown in Figures 3.4 and 3.5. Within each increment, we iterate over the various models and overlap the activities until we are satisfied with the models

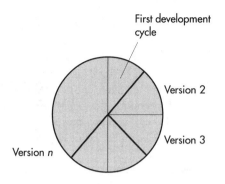

Figure 3.4 System development is a cycle that starts with "greenfield" engineering of the first version, and then proceeds to deliver successive versions over time.

and the connections between them. We begin the series of cycles by identifying some of the most important use cases, and develop a plan to produce first those that are most risky to develop, or perhaps those that are most useful to early users. These are then analyzed, designed, implemented, tested, and delivered. Later, additional use cases will be considered, built, and delivered in successive increments. If we have done the analysis and design well to produce a good system architecture, and if the number of changed requirements and the extent of technology evolution is not too large, adding new functionality or making small changes after the first few increments will only cause isolated changes to the models, and require relatively small changes to existing parts of the system.

Since a system normally evolves as we deliver successive new versions, the development of the first version from scratch (called greenfield development) is only a special case of incremental development, as shown in Figure 3.4. Nevertheless, the development of the first few increments is a very important activity, since it is then that we establish the architectural base that must last for the whole of the system's lifetime. As we see it, a good architecture is the key to managing effective system evolution.

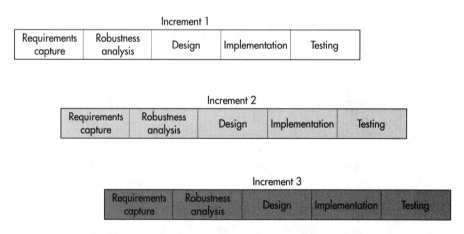

Figure 3.5 Several cycles, or increments, of software development. In the first few increments, we plan the overall series of increments and develop the base architecture.

3.4   Objects unify the modeling process

The concept of an *object* has turned out to be ideal for representing most elements within the various software models. An *object* is a modeling and programming construct that effectively represents things in the real world as well as in the models of the system. The object construct differs from other analytical approaches by containing both information (data, state) and methods (behavior).

In the real world objects have a state (for example, they are somewhere) and they operate (for example, they are in motion from here to there). In the several levels of models, too, they have a state and they operate. Hence, the object concept is a construct that carries from things in the real world through things in the series of models to "objects" in the code itself. Thus the use of object-oriented models makes it much easier to create sets of related models, moving smoothly from the high-level analysis phase to the concrete code.

Since an object is an abstraction of a thing in the real world, or in the running system, an object model is an abstraction of a system design, consisting of many related objects. Views of the objects and their relationships are shown on several diagrams and documents, where each view displays some interesting aspects of the objects.

3.4.1   Objects contain both behavior and data

Objects *encapsulate* data and behavior, hiding details from view outside the object. An object's data can be examined or manipulated only by sending a *message* or *stimulus* to the object. When an object receives a message that corresponds to one of its operation definitions, it displays specific behavior that might lead to changes in the internal data, and to new messages being sent to other objects. An operation is a service that may be requested from an object to effect behavior. We represent a particular object, sometimes also called an *instance*, by a rectangular shape, shown in Figure 3.6. Objects may be referred to by name, such as **My Checks** for an object of the **Account** type. Encapsulation and messaging are the key features that allow us to structure object-oriented systems, and their models, into relatively independent parts. Each part hides details that other parts do not need to do their job. The same encapsulation principles are true also for other approaches to component-based development, such as Microsoft OCX/ActiveX and the Ada programming language.

An object is an instance of a type. A type is a description of a set of instances that share the same operations, abstract attributes, and relationships, and semantics. A type may define an operation specification (such as a signature) but not an operation implementation (a method). An object belongs to a *type* that defines a structure and behavior template for all objects conforming to the type. A type is also shown by a bold rectangular shape, with several variations showing more details, as indicated in Figure 3.7

MyChecks		MyChecks:Account

Figure 3.6   *Two alternative notations for an object instance,* **My Checks***, of a type,* **Account***. The instance is shown by underlining the object instance name; the type name may also be included.*

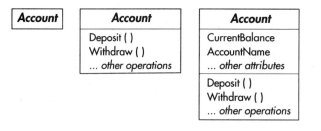

Figure 3.7 *Three alternative notations for a type (or class). The first shows only the name. The second shows the name and a list of operations. The third shows the name, list of attributes, and list of operations.*

for an **Account** type. As shown in Figure 3.6, we might choose to include the name of the object type when naming an instance.

A class is the realization of a type. A class defines the methods that implement the operations of the types that the class realizes. The process of creating an object of some class is called *instantiation* of that class. In this book we primarily use classes rather than types in the design and implementation models, while types are used in the analysis models.

Data is represented by *attributes*, and behavior by *operations* and *methods* An *operation* specifies a method, procedure, or function to be performed by an object when it receives a certain message. A *method* is the concrete implementation or realization of the operation. An *attribute* represents a property of the object. Attributes are owned by the object and are local to it; that is, they are not shared with other objects, but they may be public so that other objects may read or set them.

UML 1.0 carefully distinguishes types and classes, as well as instances. A type is essentially a specification, capturing the essence of an abstraction, while a class also includes a realization, or implementation, of the abstraction defined by the type. An instance is a concrete manifestation of a type or class. For example, the type might define operations, while the class will also define method bodies corresponding to the operations of the types. Thus use case, analysis and design models are mostly concerned about types, while the implementation model is mostly concerned about classes.

3.4.2 Stereotypes define different kinds of types, classes and other elements

One of the motivations for using the Unified Modeling Language (UML) (Booch *et al.*, 1997), is to take advantage of its extension mechanisms. UML provides the concept of *stereotype*, to allow the definition of new kinds of types, classes and other UML constructs used in the various models. This turns out to be very useful in providing a natural notation for the RSEB approach. The stereotype is a "tag," or symbol, used to mark the type (or meta-classification) of an object or other construct so that it can be distinguished and treated differently from other types of constructs.

There are three formats for showing stereotypes. A stereotype is sometimes shown on the type rectangle using the «*stereotype*» notation, or may be shown by a distinguished icon on the rectangle, or by a different shape or notation for the type or class instead of the rectangle when using a more collapsed notation. As an example, Figure 3.8 shows a *boundary type*, indicated by the stereotype «*boundary*», a special type of type used to

Figure 3.8 *The standard, the expanded and the collapsed view of a «boundary» stereotype of a type.*

represent a certain type of type in analysis models. The expanded view shows the boundary type icon in the type rectangle, while the collapsed view shows only the icon and the type name. We will show some additional examples below when we describe use cases and analysis types. Different kinds of types or classes may have additional properties, as well as attributes and operations. The «stereotype» tag is also used to distinguish various kinds of relationships between objects, types and classes.

3.4.3 Relationships connect objects

Objects may have one or more *relationships* with other objects, which are shown by different kinds (UML stereotypes) of connecting lines on diagrams. These relationships are used to depict the various ways that the system's responsibilities and structure are partitioned among the various objects and how these objects are interrelated. Some classes and types are "similar to other classes and types"; some objects send messages to other objects; and some objects make use of other objects in different ways.

A *relationship* is a semantic connection among model elements, such as among types, classes, or use cases. A relationship also may have a defined direction, either bi-directional or uni-directional. Different relationships are shown on diagrams using solid or dashed lines, usually with one or several kinds of arrowheads, and perhaps a label or a *«stereotype»* tag attached to the line to indicate the kind of relationship. The direction of an arrowhead usually indicates which of the two objects or classes initiates or owns the relationship. The most important relationships are *generalizations, associations,* and *dependencies.*

A *generalization* is a taxonomic relationship between a more general element and a more specific element. The more specific element is fully consistent with the more general element and contains additional information. An instance of the more specific element may be used where the more general element is allowed. The most common form of generalization is *inheritance,* shown in Figure 3.9 as a solid arrow line with a closed, unfilled arrowhead; other kinds of generalization will be shown using the stereotype mechanism. Since inheritance is the default, we may omit the *«inherits».* For class

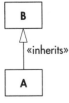

Figure 3.9 *Generalization between two types or classes, showing type or class **A** inheriting from type or class **B**. (Strictly speaking, the «inherits» is not needed, since it is the default.)*

Figure 3.10   *A communicates association from type (or class)* **A** *to type (or class)* **B**.

inheritance (*subclassing*), class A is called the *subclass*, and it inherits many of its operations and attributes from class B, called the *superclass*. For type inheritance (*subtyping*), the type A is called the the *subtype*, and B the *supertype*. A is sometimes also called a *specialization* of B, while B will conversely be called a *generalization* of A.

Classes and types can be either abstract or concrete. An *abstract* class or type cannot be instantiated as-is, but exists only to be specialized, while a *concrete* class or type, such as A, can be instantiated as-is. Abstract classes and types have their names written in italics, for example **Account**.

Sometimes, it is important to distinguish type inheritance and class inheritance, as distinct stereotypes of generalization.

An *association* is shown with a solid line, with zero, one or two open arrowheads (Figure 3.10), and is used to show that object A can access or refer to object B, perhaps to express communication between the objects, or that B is "part" of object A, or that A has a pointer to object B. Since «communicates» is the default, we may omit the tag.

A *dependency* is a relationship between two modeling elements, in which a change to one modeling element (the independent element) will affect the other modeling element (the dependent element). A *dependency* is shown with a dashed line (Figure 3.11), and is typically used to show that class A has some historical, implementation, or other connection to class B. For example, A «becomes» B, or A «imports» from B. We can also use this to show how subsystems are dependent on other subsystems. Traces are also shown with a dashed «trace» arrow.

3.4.4   Packages and subsystems group classes, types and other elements

The system may be structured by collecting or grouping related classes, types and other elements into *packages*, shown using a folder-like notation. A package is a general purpose mechanism for organizing elements into groups. Packages may be nested within other packages. Different stereotypes of package are used for a variety of grouping purposes. A system may be thought of as a single high-level package, with everything else in the system contained in it. Packages typically contain packages, types and classes that belong together according to some criterion, perhaps because they offer a particular service, or should be used together, or will be implemented for execution on a particular machine. Packages can be treated as configuration or management units to be owned by a particular development group.

A *subsystem* is a kind of package, marked using the «subsystem» stereotype, used to divide the system into smaller parts. Subsystems may in turn contain other subsystems. The

Figure 3.11   *An imports dependency from class* **A'** *to class* **A**.

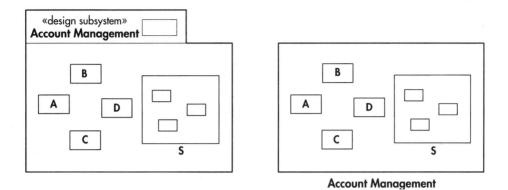

Account Management

Figure 3.12 *The expanded and collapsed views of a design subsystem,* **Account Management***, a package that contains design types* **A**, **B**, **C**, **D** *and a design subsystem,* **S**.

lowest level of subsystem is called a *service package*, and is viewed as a change unit, that is, a set of classes representing the smallest unit of optional functionality that must be installed together. Each subsystem and service package should offer a coherent unit of functionality.

Figure 3.12 shows two views of a *«design subsystem»* package, **Account Management**. The expanded view uses the standard rectangular folder form of a package, while the collapsed view uses a plain rectangular format. This subsystem contains four types, **A**, **B**, **C**, and **D**, and another design subsystem, **S**.

Figure 3.13 similarly shows two views of an *«analysis subsystem»* package, **Account Management**. The expanded view uses the standard rectangular folder form of a package, while the collapsed view uses a rounded corner format. This subsystem contains four analysis types, **A**, **B**, **C**, and **D**, and another analysis subsystem, **S**.

Subsystems and service packages also can be used to represent components that may not be implemented using object-oriented programming languages, such as some Microsoft OCX/ActiveX components – as long as each service package or subsystem offers an explicit interface it can still be reused easily.

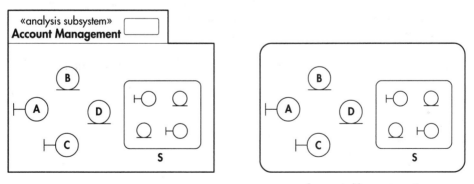

Account Management

Figure 3.13 *The expanded and collapsed views of an analysis subsystem, a package that contains analysis types* **A**, **B**, **C**, **D** *and an analysis subsystem,* **S**.

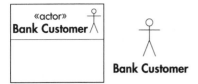

Figure 3.14 *The expanded and collapsed views of the* **Bank Customer** *actor, showing the iconic stick figure for actor.*

3.5 The use case model captures system requirements

At each stage of modeling, it is useful to have models at different levels of detail, with different kinds of objects, to meet the different needs of different workers. The model closest to the requirements, and with the least amount of detail, is the *use case model*.

The main purposes of the use case model are to define *what* the system should do, and to allow the software engineers and the customers to agree on this (Jacobson, 1994a). The use case model is used to drive the rest of the development work; that is, it is the starting point for the object modeling activities.

The use case model consists of *«actor»* types and *«use case»* types.

The users and any other systems that may interact with the system under construction are represented as actors. Because they represent users of the system and hence are outside the system, actors help us to delimit the system and get a clear picture of what it is supposed to do. Actors are drawn as stick figures, as shown in two views of the actor **Bank Customer** in Figure 3.14.

The behavior of the system is represented by use cases, and use cases are developed according to the actor's needs. This ensures that the system will turn out to be what the users expected. The execution of a use case is an instance of the use case, which the system obeys during the flow of events of the execution. When we use the term "use case" we mean a use case type, and we refer to use case instances as instances of a use case. Instances of use cases can be described by scenario descriptions.

Use cases are drawn as ellipses, like the use case **Deposit Money** shown in two views in Figure 3.15.

A use case model shows a set of actors and use cases, and the relationships between them.

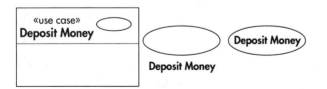

Figure 3.15 *The expanded and collapsed views of the* **Deposit Money** *use case, showing the ellipse icon.*

Example

An **ATM Cashier** application system for walk-up banking offers the use cases **Withdraw Money**, **Deposit Money**, and **Transfer Between Accounts**. (In later chapters the same use cases will be generalized to allow bank transactions using other types of interfaces such as an Internet home-bank. The use cases that we talk about here will then be renamed **Withdraw Cash** and **Deposit Cash** while **Transfer Between Accounts** will keep the same name.) The possible communications between the actor and use case instances are shown as bi-directional «communicates» associations. **Withdraw Money**, for example, lets a **Bank Customer** withdraw money from an ATM or similar interface. The use case model is shown in Figure 3.16.

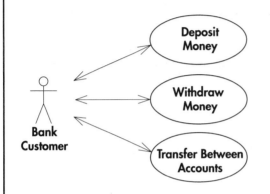

Figure 3.16 *An example of a use case model with an actor and several use cases.*

During analysis, design, and testing, the same use case model is mapped to the analysis, design, and test models.

3.5.1 Actors model roles

An **actor** is anything that interacts, that is, exchanges data and events, with the system.

Hence, an actor can be a human user, external hardware, or another system. The difference between an actor and a user of the system is that an actor represents a particular *type of user* rather than a real physical user. Several different physical users of a system can play the same role in relation to the system. These are instances of the same actor. A single user can also have several roles, and so act as several different actors.

Actors communicate with the system by sending and receiving messages. An actor can send a message to the system and the system can send a message to an actor. To fully understand the role of an actor, we must know which use cases the actor is involved in. We show this by «communicates» associations between the actor and the use cases. Figure 3.16 depicts a **Bank Customer** actor instance communicating with instances of the use cases **Withdraw Money**, **Deposit Money**, and **Transfer Between Accounts**.

Instances of several actors can interact similarly with instances of a particular use case. Thus, a **Private Customer** and a **Corporate Customer**, both of whom transfer money between accounts, can be seen as variants of **Bank Customer** by the use case instance that does the transfer. The shared task definitions are modeled as an inherited actor, **Bank Customer**, as shown in Figure 3.17.

3.5.2 Use cases model system transactions

A **use case** is a sequence of transactions performed by a system, which yields an observable result of value for a particular actor.

Let us look more closely at some of the key words in the above definition:

Use case   The definition given above is really an instance. There are many possible instances, many of them similar. In order to make a use case model understandable, it is important to carefully select the use case types that can offer those instances. When we say that we identify and describe a use case, we really mean that we identify and describe the use case type.

By a system   When we say transactions performed by a system, we mean that the system provides the use case. An actor instance communicates with a use case instance offered by the system.

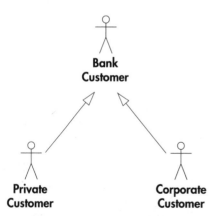

Figure 3.17   *The actors* **Private Customer** *and* **Corporate Customer** *inherit all the properties of a* **Bank Customer** *actor.*

An observable result of value It is very important to make sure that a use case is not too small. A use case should be chosen so that an actor can perform a task that has an identifiable value. It must be possible to put a price or a value on a successfully performed use case instance.

Transaction A transaction is invoked either by a message from an actor to the system or by a timed trigger within the system. A transaction consists of a set of actions, decisions, and messages to the invoking actor instance or other actors. It is an atomic set of activities, which is performed either entirely or not at all.

A particular actor The actor is perhaps most important when finding the correct use cases, especially because focusing on the actor helps us avoid use cases that do not offer a result of observable value. It is important to begin with individual actors, that is, instances of actors. It is a good idea to name at least two different people or systems who would be able to perform the role of the actor.

Example

The **Withdraw Money** use case involves the following flow of events:

1. The **Bank Customer** identifies himself or herself.
2. The **Bank Customer** chooses how much to withdraw and from which account. The system responds with how much can be withdrawn from that account.
3. The system dispenses the amount and deducts the amount from the account.

We describe the functions of the system by means of a number of different use cases, each of which has a task of its own to perform. The collected use cases constitute all the possible ways of using the system, though in practice we choose not to *describe* all use case variants.

3.5.3 Use case generalization

There are two important use case generalization mechanisms, *«uses»* and *«extends»*.

While we are identifying and outlining the transactions of each use case in the system, we will find behavior that is common to several use cases. To avoid describing the same flow of events several times, we can define the common behavior in a use case of its own. This new use case can then be reused by the original use cases. We show this relation with a *«uses»* (Jacobson, 1994b) generalization. Uses can be thought of as a kind of inheritance, since instances of the "using" use cases can perform all behavior described in the "used" use case.

A *«uses»* generalization from a use case A to a use case B indicates that A inherits B, which means that an instance of A can perform all behavior described for B.

Example

The **ATM Cashier** application system offers the use cases **Withdraw Money**, **Deposit Money**, and **Transfer Between Accounts**. All these use cases involve the movement of money between monetary holders. Monetary holders here include accounts, and other containers such as Smartcards. This commonality can be exploited and represented as an abstract use case **Monetary Transfer**. Figure 3.18 illustrates this.

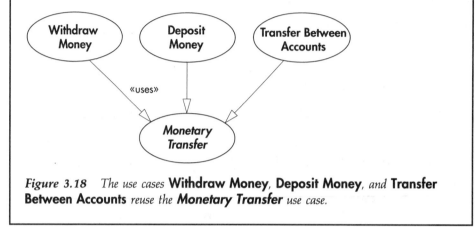

Figure 3.18 *The use cases* **Withdraw Money**, **Deposit Money**, *and* **Transfer Between Accounts** *reuse the* **Monetary Transfer** *use case.*

A *concrete use case* is a use case initiated by an actor; its instances constitute a complete flow of events in the system. Some use cases exist only for other use cases to reuse. These are called *abstract use cases*.

An *abstract use case* will never be instantiated by itself. Like other abstract classes, no separate instances are created. When a concrete use case is initiated, an instance of the use case is created. This instance also exhibits the behavior that is specified by the abstract use cases that it (re-)uses.

The other generalization is *«extends»* (Jacobson, 1994b). Extends models additions to a use case's flow of events. An extension behaves as if it is something that is added into the original description of a use case type. This is quite similar to the way inheritance is used to define a new class that adds behavior to an existing class. When the original use case is instantiated, the extension is also performed as if it had been written in-line in the original use case.

An *«extends»* from a use case B to a use case A indicates that an instance obeying the use case A may at some time discontinue obeying that use case and instead begin obeying use case B. When the instance has finished obeying B it will resume obeying A. Thus A and B together act as a specialization of the use case A.

Example

A **Bank Customer** withdrawing money may cause an overdraft. This is handled
by a use case **Overdraft Management** which extends the use case **Withdraw
Money** to handle account overdrafts (Figure 3.19). The **Overdraft Management**
extension may, for example, deduct an appropriate fee.

Figure 3.19 **Overdraft Management** *is performed when an account is overdrawn
in the* **Withdraw Money** *use case.*

3.6 The analysis model shapes system architecture

Architecture deals with the principles, mechanisms, patterns, and structures that clearly
define and communicate the structure of a system. The architecture is first considered
during *robustness analysis*, in which the high-level type structure is first defined. It is then
developed in increasing detail during design. Most important is the high-level static
structure, showing types, their grouping, and relationships with other types. The analysis
model consists of analysis types and subsystems plus their relationships.

The *analysis model* is a model of the system design at a high level, ignoring the specific
low-level details of the target implementation environment. Analysis objects thus represent
a situation where objects are executed in an ideal system. Many factors such as the database
management system, distribution, specific programming language, existing products,
performance, and storage specifications will not be addressed in the analysis model, but
deferred to the design model.

To do the mapping from the use cases to the analysis model during robustness
analysis, the analyst searches through the descriptions of the requirements and use cases,
looking for the elements that can become the types in the analysis model. OOSE
provides three standard stereotypes, «boundary» types, «entity» types, and «control» types,
to help in this search. Figure 3.20 shows an example from an analysis model.

The different icons correspond to different types of analysis types, described in more
detail in Section 3.6.1. For example, **Cashier Interface** is a «boundary» type defining a
user interface to an actor.

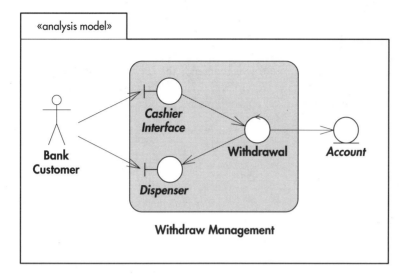

Figure 3.20 *A partial analysis model, shown as a class diagram. This model corresponds to the* **Withdraw Money** *use case, showing types of communicating analysis objects and a* **Withdraw Management** *subsystem.*

It is useful to recast the use case description in terms of analysis objects, moving closer to the specification of analysis types, responsibilities, and operations.

Example

We now rephrase the **Withdraw Money** use case in terms of interacting analysis objects and actors, shown in Figure 3.20 using a class diagram.

Withdraw Money Use Case Description: Analysis model

The **Bank Customer** chooses to withdraw money. The *Cashier Interface* first asks the **Bank Customer** to identify himself or herself.

If the identification is successful, the *Cashier Interface* asks the **Bank Customer** to choose how much to withdraw and from which *Account*. The *Cashier Interface* orders the **Withdrawal** object to confirm that the **Bank Customer** has the right to withdraw that amount from the *Account*. The **Withdrawal** object validates the request.

If the **Bank Customer** can withdraw that amount, the **Withdrawal** object asks the *Dispenser* to dispense the amount and deducts the amount from the *Account*.

3.6.1 Different analysis stereotypes capture standard system structure

An **analysis type** represents an abstraction of classes in the system's implementation. This abstraction assumes an ideal implementation environment.

Since they are higher-level abstractions of design types and implementation classes, the analysis types form useful concepts when discussing system architecture on a logical level. Developers can model essential concepts of the problem domain in terms of analysis types. They can decide on the allocation of responsibilities, how the types relate to each other, and how the types will be structured to allow the system to evolve. With an analysis model as a starting point, it is easier to decide on a suitable design and implementation by adding constraints and exploiting opportunities offered by the implementation environment.

OOSE provides three analysis stereotypes to help: «boundary», «control», and «entity», shown in Figure 3.21. The expanded form highlights the connection with later implementation classes, while the collapsed form is more compact for diagramming. Having these three distinct stereotypes helps develop a robust structure when identifying and specifying types. Each stereotype has a special significance in the analysis model.

An **«entity» object** is in general a long-lived object in the system.

That is, they outlast the use case instances in which they participate. Entity types are often used to model business objects that represent "things," such as accounts and loans, dealt with in many of the use cases. Thus they are typically generic to many use cases.

A **«boundary» object** handles communication between the system and its surroundings.

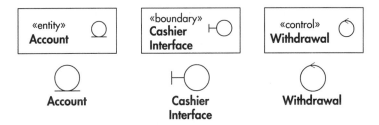

Figure 3.21 *Three different kinds of analysis types, showing the expanded format above and the corresponding more compact collapsed format below.*

This involves transforming events and objects from the system's representation to a representation suitable for its surroundings, and vice versa. Boundary types constitute the presentation-dependent part of the system, whereas control and entity types are surroundings-independent. Windows, communication protocols, sensors, and printer interfaces are all examples of boundary types.

A **«control» object** performs use-case-specific behavior.

Control objects often control or coordinate other objects. A control type offers behavior that does not belong to an entity or interface type. The behavior is surroundings-independent because it should not be sensitive to how the surroundings communicate with the system. Control types should be independent of whether this communication occurs via electric signals, processor stops, keyboards, menu selections, or procedure calls.

Like other types, analysis types have operations, attributes, and relationships to other types or classes. Relationships include «communication» associations from one type to another, which indicate that their instances interact, and «acquaintance» associations, which indicate that instances of one type hold a reference to instances of some other class. Other relationships include generalizations and traces.

3.6.2 Diagrams show relationships between analysis types

Analysis objects interact in performing the use case instances. The primary modeling activity during analysis is to identify the various types and relationships, and to allocate responsibilities to these types. Each analysis object plays one or more roles in at least one use case. The responsibilities need to be allocated so that all the steps in instances of the use case are performed by some interactions between the objects. Several different kinds of *interaction diagrams* can be used to show how the analysis objects interact in performing the use case instance. Figure 3.22 shows a *collaboration diagram*, which can be drawn for each individual use case or for each group of use cases. A *sequence diagram*,

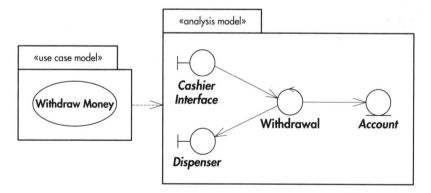

Figure 3.22 *For each use case, there is a collaboration diagram that illustrates how objects perform the use case. The dashed line is a trace between the use case and the analysis types.*

such as Figure 3.23, shows more detailed message flow and operation details. The sequence diagram is more commonly used with the design model. Analysts also may create a modified use case description, used to textually explain the collaboration diagram, Figure 3.22.

Example

During the **Withdraw Money** use case the detailed flow may be something like the following, shown also in the sequence diagram in Figure 3.23.

Withdraw Money Use Case Description: Analysis model

The **Bank Customer** chooses to withdraw money. The *Cashier Interface* first asks the **Bank Customer** to identify himself or herself and verifies the identity with the **Withdrawal** object. (There should probably be another object responsible for verifying the identity of the customer, since this behavior is common to several use cases, including **Transfer Between Accounts**. The flow shown here is a simplification made for the purpose of illustrating the concept of a sequence diagram.)

If the identification is successful, the *Cashier Interface* asks the **Bank Customer** to choose how much to withdraw and from which *Account*. The *Cashier Interface* sends the **Withdraw** message to the **Withdrawal** object. By sending the **Withdraw** message, the **Withdrawal** object asks the *Account* object to validate the request and if possible withdraw the amount from the *Account*. Then the **Withdrawal** object asks the *Dispenser* to **Dispense** the amount.

Note that this example only deals with simple cases where everything runs without any problems. A problem would occur, for example, when the balance on the **Account** is too low to allow a withdrawal.

We have also shown *class diagrams*, such as Figure 3.20, which indicate the generalization and association relationships between types or classes. Other diagrams, such as *state diagrams*, are used to show the detailed dynamic behavior of types, classes or instances.

Let us explain sequence diagrams in more detail. Sequence diagrams are used to show the details of object interactions during a use case instance. The diagram shows the messages sent from one object to another.

In a sequence diagram an object is represented by a vertical column (Figure 3.23). The time axis is directed downwards. At the left-hand side, the behavior that the objects will carry out is described; this behavior is called *activities*. Activities are represented by rectangular sections on the object columns. Later on, the activities provide the input for the identification and description of the types' operations and the subsequent method implementation.

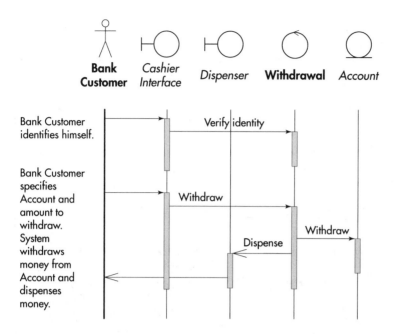

Bank
Customer

Cashier
Interface

Dispenser

Withdrawal

Account

Bank Customer
identifies himself.

Verify identity

Bank Customer
specifies
Account and
amount to
withdraw.
System
withdraws
money from
Account and
dispenses
money.

Withdraw

Withdraw

Dispense

Figure 3.23 *A sequence diagram describes how the objects perform a use case instance.*

Since an object may participate in several use cases, it will be present in several interaction diagrams. All of these views taken together illustrate the different roles the class has in the model. Several of these diagrams might be combined, to show how objects of each class contribute to several use cases, as shown in Figure 3.24.

Example

The **Withdraw Money** use case is invoked through the **Cashier Interface** boundary object, and then controlled by the **Withdrawal** control object, see Figure 3.24. The **Withdrawal** object updates the **Account** object and then dispenses money through the **Dispenser** boundary object.

The **Transfer Between Accounts** use case is invoked through the **Cashier Interface** boundary object, and then controlled by the **Transfer** control object. The **Transfer** object updates the **Account** objects involved.

The **Deposit Money** use case is invoked through the **Cashier Interface** object, and then controlled by the **Deposit** control object. The **Deposit** object accepts money through the **Money Receptor** boundary object and then updates the **Account** object.

Note that the same instances of **Account, Cashier Interface, Money Receptor**, and **Dispenser** participate in several use case instances, while the instances of the «control» types **Deposit, Transfer**, and **Withdrawal** participate in one use case instance only.

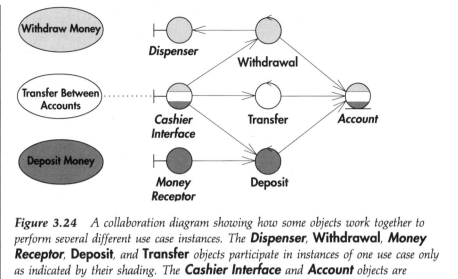

Figure 3.24 *A collaboration diagram showing how some objects work together to perform several different use case instances. The **Dispenser**, **Withdrawal**, **Money Receptor**, **Deposit**, and **Transfer** objects participate in instances of one use case only as indicated by their shading. The **Cashier Interface** and **Account** objects are involved in all three use cases.*

3.7 The design model defines the implementation

The design model serves as a higher-level view of the source code – a "blueprint" of how the source code is organized, and some of its key features. Similar to the analysis model, the design model consists of design classes (and types) and design subsystems. In the transition from the analysis types to the design classes, more details related to the target language and execution environment will be incorporated.

A *design class* represents a class at a more detailed, but still high level in the system's implementation. Each design object plays one or more roles in the use cases. Design classes are drawn as rectangles. Exactly what each design class corresponds to in the code depends on the implementation language. The design classes can be found by using the use case descriptions and the analysis model and by considering the implementation environment. Which design classes have to be created depends on, for instance, choice of programming language, process structure, available Commercial Off The Shelf (COTS) software, and legacy systems.

As a starting point, each analysis type will be mapped and have a trace to a similar design class. Then additional design classes may be added, other classes split, combined, or removed, and some relationships added or changed. For example, new classes may be needed to define attribute types, to provide support or inheritable superclasses, or to wrap legacy systems. Likewise, analysis subsystems will be mapped (and have a trace) to corresponding design subsystems, and others will be added, or changed. Some relationships, such as extends or even inheritance, may be difficult to implement in some languages, and so should be replaced by associations, such as communicates, aggregation, or delegation.

Like the analysis model, the design model is organized into subsystems, in which lower-level subsystems and design classes (and types) are grouped. The design classes (and types) have much the same properties as the analysis types, but tend to match the intended implementation more closely.

Example

During analysis, the developers of the **ATM Cashier** application system decide to divide the analysis types between several analysis subsystems, as shown in Figure 3.25.

Later, during design they consider allocation to several distributed processes, initially to one client process and one server process. They expand the analysis types and subsystems into design classes, changing some classes and adding others. They also create different design subsystems, as shown in Figure 3.26. The **Account, Money Receptor, Dispenser**, and **Cashier Interface** types will be completely allocated to corresponding design classes and will be mapped to one process each. But the control objects will be distributed over the two processes.

In the design model, this is dealt with by dividing each "distributed" control type into two design classes, one to be allocated to the **Bank Server** process and one to the **ATM Client**. The **Withdrawal** control types would, for example, be divided into a **Withdrawal Server** and a **Withdrawal Client**.

A different design decision for distribution might be to use an object request broker (ORB), leading to a different decomposition into multiple classes.

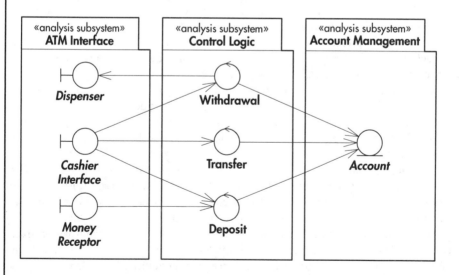

Figure 3.25   *The analysis model with three subsystems, showing some types that will need to be split before mapping to design classes.*

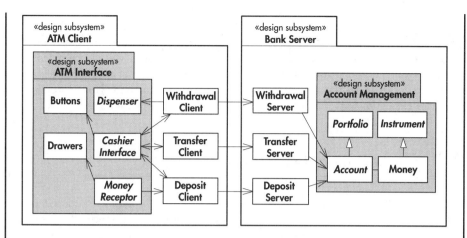

Figure 3.26 *The corresponding design classes will be allocated to two design subsystems, in preparation for allocation to either a client or a server process. Certain analysis types might be split into two design classes, such as* **Withdrawal***. Additional support classes, such as* **Buttons***,* **Drawers***,* **Instrument***,* **Money***, and* **Portfolio***, might be added or reused.*

3.8 The implementation model is the code

The implementation model consists of the source code, classes, and also necessary documents and annotations to make the code readable. Classes are types, with the addition of implementation details, such as method bodies. It also includes scripts and

---

Example

The following is part of the definition of the operations for the **Account** class, using OMG IDL to define the interfaces; we could just as easily have used C++ header files. Use of IDL for interfaces will be discussed further in Chapter 6.

```
module AccountManagement{
interface Account : Portfolio{
    Account create(
        in Customer owner, in String title, in AccountNumber account_id);
    void Deposit (in Money amount, in String reason);
    void Withdraw (in Money amount, in String reason);
    };
}
```

instructions to produce the final code and supporting files. It is not necessary to use an object-oriented programming language. While programmers can map the object-oriented design models to any programming language, the mapping will typically be much easier if the programming languages used are object-oriented. C++, Java, or Smalltalk makes the transition to code much more direct. The most important principle is to define the interfaces explicitly, since this simplifies reuse and component-based development.

3.9 The test model validates the system

The *test model* is used to confirm the validity of the other models produced during software engineering. Simply stated, the test model consists of the specifications of tests, and the expected results of the testing. A test − like a use case instance − may be viewed as an instance. By doing this, we can view the test specification as the test's type, and thus we can also inherit common parts or compose tests from several test specifications. Thus a test execution is an instance of a test specification. The instance is an object − it has behavior and also state. The outcome of a test execution is a test result.

Use cases provide an excellent instrument for test planning − the test specifications can be identified from the use cases as soon as the requirements are reasonably stable. There are other tests as well: system tests, subsystem tests, and unit tests. Inspections and reviews should also be scheduled as part of the test plan to validate the consistency of each model, and its mapping to other models.

3.10 Summary

Software engineering is a process in which several people build different models of a system. Stakeholders include customers, end users, and workers within a software engineering organization, such as requirements analysts, analysts, designers, implementers, testers, and managers. The system is defined by use case, analysis, design, implementation, and test models. Each model is described by several documents and diagrams.

In most cases, it is best to develop the system step by step, beginning with some of its most important or risky use cases. Later, new use cases can be considered as the system is designed in increments, growing in stages.

Objects encapsulate data (attributes) and behavior (operations and methods). An object's data can be examined or manipulated only by sending messages or stimuli to the object. The behavior of an object is defined by the object type. Types have relationships to one another, which are shown by different kinds of generalizations, associations, and dependencies. A class is the realization or implementation of a type.

The use case model consists of actors and use cases. Actors define the roles of people or other systems that interact with the system. A use case instance is a sequence of transactions performed by a system, which yields an observable result of value for a particular actor. Each execution scenario of system use is an instance of one of the use cases.

The analysis model is a high-level abstraction of the system implementation. There are three different kinds of analysis type stereotypes: boundary, entity, and control classes. Analysis objects interact in performing the use case instances. Each object plays one or more roles in at least one use case instance. The objects that perform the use case instances are presented in collaboration or sequence diagrams which are prepared for each individual use case, or for each group of use cases.

The design model consists of detailed design object classes (and types), which correspond more closely to the final system implementation and source code in the implementation model.

The system may be structured by grouping analysis types and design classes (and types) into subsystems that reveal the system architecture. A subsystem divides the system into smaller parts. Subsystems contain types, classes, and other model elements that belong together according to some criteria. Subsystems may in turn contain other subsystems.

Using the UML package notation, an OOSE system can be expressed as a set of related models, packaged together as shown in Figure 3.27, where each model packages several OOSE constructs, diagrams, and associated documents. There are traces between the various models.

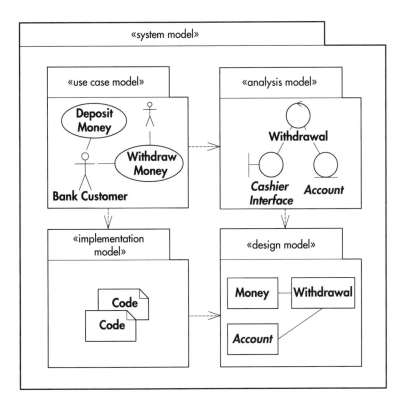

Figure 3.27 *An OOSE system as a set of models, packaged together, and connected with trace links.*

3.11 Additional reading

Much more motivation and details about the role of objects, and the specific constructs and approach used in OOSE, can be found in *Object-Oriented Software Engineering: A Use Case Driven Approach* (Jacobson *et al.*, 1992).

For a lighter introduction to the concepts of objects and their importance to software engineering, we recommend Taylor's (1990) book, *Object Oriented Technology: A Manager's Guide*.

Information on the Unified Modeling Language, UML, can be obtained from the UML Report, issued by Rational Software Corporation (Version 1.0, January 1997), and the forthcoming books: Booch (1998), Jacobson (1998) and Rumbaugh (1998). See also http://www.rational.com/uml/.

Ivar Jacobson describes the concepts of models and the role of stereotypes in modeling languages in several papers in *ROAD* and the *Object Magazine*.

4

APPLICATION
AND
COMPONENT
SYSTEMS

4.1 Application developers can reuse OOSE model components

The object-oriented software engineering process, OOSE, described in Chapter 3, is used to develop independent application systems, without explicitly considering the reuse of software or models between systems. However, if we are developing several related applications, it often makes sense to create a set of reusable components that developers of any of the models can systematically reuse. To introduce reuse in a systematic and manageable way, we need to extend our modeling language to directly support reuse. A reuse-driven software engineering organization will then engineer both sets of applications and sets of reusable components. The reuse-oriented process will be seen to be an extension of the OOSE incremental, iterative development approach. In this approach, we still treat each application as a separate, complete system, an *application system*, delivering a coherent set of use cases to an end user, but we will emphasize commonality and variability of the model components.

A *system* is a well-documented workproduct owned by an organization unit, such as a group. Each application system is a system consisting of a set of related models and associated documents. These systems are engineered using types, classes and other modeling constructs. The various models and documents support different participants in the software engineering process. In general, each application system can be ordered, developed, and installed independently of other application systems. However, reuse will connect these otherwise independent systems together, and the organization will have to manage sets of related application systems.

We can view systems as organizational assets that:

- require investment, version control, configuration management, development, certification, testing, packaging, maintenance, and release management;

- are generally configurable and have attached user, installation, and maintenance documents, tools, and processes for installers to follow.

Systems can be developed by breaking them into pieces or workproducts. A *workproduct* is a unit of code, a document or piece of software model that can be independently managed within a software engineering organization. Individual types, classes and other model elements from the various models, diagrams, and related documents are typical workproducts. Complete models, subsystems, and test models are also workproducts. Some workproducts are abstract, management-oriented entities and not always specific pieces of software. For example, a workproduct can be a configuration file, listing the names and versions of other software workproducts that are intended to be used together. Typically, each workproduct has a unique identity and a person assigned to be responsible for it. This means that each individual type or class, or a group of types, classes and documents, could have its own documentation, be configured, and so on, as shown in Figure 4.1.

Application systems are delivered to someone outside the Reuse Business. This characteristic distinguishes an application system from reusable components which are intended for use within the organization to engineer application systems. (Some reuse-driven software engineering businesses develop components for sale or for use by others. In this case, they do in fact deliver components outside the RSEB.)

We use the term *application system* instead of the looser term *application*, because we want to stress that application systems are software system products, and are defined by

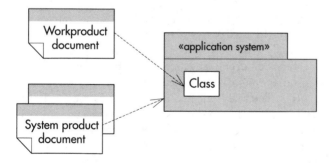

Figure 4.1 *Systems are products and types and classes are workproducts. Each has associated documents that describe purpose and usage.*

system models. We will sometimes also use the term *system product* to further stress the product-like nature.

We can thus define an application system:

> An **application system** is a system product delivered outside of the Reuse Business. When installed, an application system offers a coherent set of use cases to an end user.

4.2 Application families allow significant reuse

Many application systems share common features.

> An **application system family** is a set of application systems with common features.

This commonality can be exploited by building a set of common reusable components from which to build members of the application family.

Note that it must still be possible to develop and maintain each application system as a separate system product. Each application system should therefore have minimal, well-understood dependencies on other application systems.

We can distinguish several different kinds of application system families:

- An *application system suite* is a set of different application systems that are intended to work together to help some actors accomplish their work. For example, the Microsoft Office suite includes an editor (Word), a database (Access), and a presentation package (PowerPoint) that work together within Windows to provide a fairly complete office environment. In general, an application system suite should help an organization with people in several different roles to perform its processes (Jacobson *et al.*, 1994).

- *Application system variants* are useful when essentially the same application systems need to be configured, packaged, and installed differently for different users. For example, the Ericsson AXE family of telecommunications switching systems is customized to different countries and customers (Jacobson, 1996a). Sometimes, different variants can be achieved by simply installing and adapting application systems differently. At other times, the variability is achieved by engineering different application systems from common components.

- Some sets of otherwise *fairly independent application systems* can be treated as members of a family, by building them from the same sets of lower-level reusable components. For example, several application systems with similar Windows behavior can be built from the Microsoft Foundation Classes.

Example

The XYB banking consortium is developing a set of new financial applications for the rapidly growing electronic home-banking market. Since the market is changing rapidly, banks and financial service organizations must compete in providing rapidly delivered new and innovative services to end users, commercial customers, and other service providers. In order to accommodate this rapidly growing family of related applications, XYBSoft believes that the new services should be delivered as a suite of many relatively independent, interoperable applications.

As illustrated in Figure 4.2, a **Seller** of some goods or services can use XYB to send an electronic invoice to the **Buyer**. The **Buyer** can then pay that invoice. We think of this as a business process **Sales From Order To Delivery**, which the **Buyer** invokes. XYB provides supporting information systems, perhaps to the **Seller**'s organization, to enable this to happen electronically. In this process a **Buyer** first orders some goods or services, the **Seller** invoices the **Buyer**, the **Buyer** pays, and finally the **Seller** delivers the goods or services. It is becoming more common for a **Buyer** and a **Seller** to prefer doing this using the Internet, particularly to simplify the issuing and payment of invoices.

To manage rapid change, and meet the demands of a variety of different customers, XYB will design the applications as small, customizable, configurable components called *applets*, rather than larger, monolithic applications. Furthermore, there will be several variants of certain services and applets, to meet the needs of different customers in different countries. The issuing and payment of invoices in this business process uses a small application suite, consisting of two application systems, **Payment** and **Invoicing**. **Invoicing** is used by a **Seller** to request payment for some service or goods and later to follow up the payment of invoices. **Payment** is used by a **Buyer** to pay received invoices. Different legal restrictions and banking conventions in different countries will result in several variants of these applications.

XYBSoft decides to consider flexible application construction based on components, and plans to construct the applets systematically from a set of reusable components.

Figure 4.2   *The business process* **Sales From Order To Delivery**.

4.3 Application systems are built from reusable components

When we build several related application systems, we create several different models. As we do this, we can reuse use case types, object types and classes, interfaces, and other constructs such as test cases, rather than developing each model from scratch. In order to produce the desired set of manageable, relatively independent application systems, we cannot reuse just any model element. Instead, model elements intended for reuse must be carefully designed and packaged specifically to be reusable components. A significant part of the component design process will consider how to minimize dependencies, and how to break models into reusable components of the right size and structure.

> A **component** is a type, class or any other workproduct that has been specifically engineered to be reusable.

Components include use case, analysis, design, and implementation model elements. They include interface specifications, subsystems, and attribute types. Components also include other workproducts, such as templates, documents or test case specifications, OCX/ActiveX components, CORBA-based components, and other types of components. We will use the standard class rectangle in figures to indicate a component of unspecified type. When referring to components of a specific type, we use UML notation as appropriate to the component type, such as an ellipse for use case components, or rectangles for design classes.

A component is designed, packaged, and documented to be reusable. A component is cohesive and has a relatively stable public interface. A component may be very general and reusable in many types of application system, or it may be limited and specific to only a certain business area.

Example

A **Buyer** may use the application system **Payment** to pay invoices. Within this application system, a **Pay And Schedule Invoices** use case lets the **Buyer** pay invoices electronically by deducting money from one of the **Buyer**'s accounts at the XYB (or corresponding financial institution).

The **Buyer** will also use other application systems. **ATM Cashier** is a general application system to support money deposit, withdrawal, and transfer from ATMs, while **Payment** has a more specialized function.

Several components can be reused to implement these key application systems. The **Account** type, shown in Figure 4.3, is an «entity» component that is useful in many XYB application systems such as **Payment** and **ATM Cashier**.

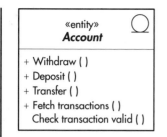

| «entity» |
| **Account** |
| + Withdraw ( ) |
| + Deposit ( ) |
| + Transfer ( ) |
| + Fetch transactions ( ) |
| Check transaction valid ( ) |

Figure 4.3   *An entity type component,* **Account***, with some of its operations.*

The **Account** component supports a private operation, **Check transaction valid**, and several public operations:

- **Withdraw**, which transfers money from the account
- **Deposit**, which transfers money to the account
- **Transfer**, which handles transfers between accounts
- **Fetch transactions**, which returns a list of the transactions done to the account.

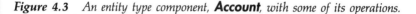

The term "component" is also used in several different ways by other authors. REBOOT uses a broad definition as a collection of related workproducts (Karlsson, 1995). Barnes and Bollinger (1991) advocate broad-spectrum reuse, treating all kinds of workproducts (for example, documents, guidelines, plans, tests, and code) as reusable components. Microsoft, UML and OMG use the term "component" to mean an encapsulated module of code, or large-grained, run-time object, providing several services implemented in some technology – which is compatible with our approach but not as general as we suggest.

Object orientation has many characteristics that simplify developing good components, such as encapsulation and polymorphism. But there are also mechanisms that, when used unwisely, can harm the goal of component-based development. One such mechanism is inheritance. Inheritance introduces strong dependencies between a class and its superclass, or a type and its supertype, which complicates the maintenance of components.

4.4   Group components into component systems

Most often, a single component is not useful alone but is reused in conjunction with many other components. Such related components are organized together into *component systems*. Like application systems, component systems are managed by the software organization as system products. A component system can range in size from only a few

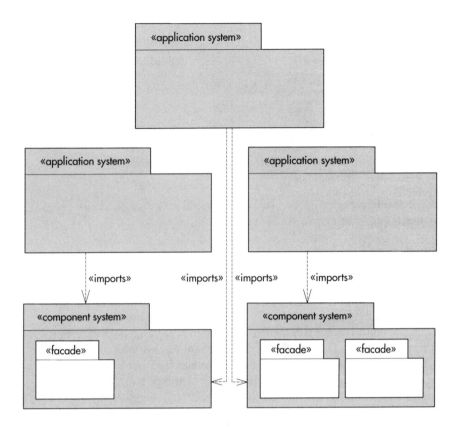

Figure 4.4 *Several application systems reusing components from two component systems. Each component system has at least one facade to export reusable components.*

components and supporting documentation, to a large number of components, developed by a team of engineers.

Application systems reuse common components by *importing* reusable components from the component systems, as shown in Figure 4.4. The «imports» dependency is used to show the reuse relationships. The component systems include a special type of package called a *facade*, to be described in more detail in Section 4.5.

Typically, the components in a component system have several relationships with each other, as shown in Figure 4.5. Components may inherit functionality from other components, send messages to other components, or have other associations to support collaboration.

Component systems can range from collections of relatively independent classes (essentially a packaged class library), to frameworks of collaborating classes, to collections of Java classes and OCXs, to more complex and sophisticated component systems from which complete application systems can be generated. For a component system to be more than just a class library, it should include sets of related components that work together to produce a society of interacting objects. These components then can be combined by reusers to offer some coherent use cases to end users.

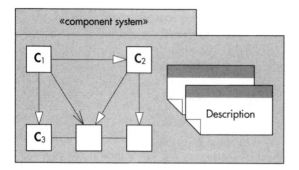

Figure 4.5 *A small component system, consisting of several related design classes and attached documents which describe the component system.*

Example

A well-engineered mathematical or graphical code or class library can be viewed as a simple component system. A component system is *not* a random collection of reusable components. These well-designed software systems typically include an organized set of related source code and header files, and carefully structured documentation for each component and for the set of components. Other documents suggest how to use the components effectively together to solve different problems. The components in the set are carefully engineered to work together, with common naming conventions, standard error handling mechanisms, and uniform interfaces. Each consistent set of compatible components is expected to be under version control together and to be released as a complete system product. In many cases, analysis and design models accompany the code components as a form of documentation.

Both application and component systems are system products. They are defined using the same type of models and constructs. The main difference is in how application and component systems are engineered, managed, and used. Component systems are more generic, reusable, and specializable than application systems, but on the other hand require more effort to engineer. (We might think of an application system as a kind of simplified component system, which would be customized and installed by people outside the reuse business who are not application developers, including installers or end users.) Component systems are used to engineer application systems and also other component systems. A component system is a well-packaged and certified set of components. Component systems are generally not (in contrast to an application system) delivered outside the Reuse Business. Each component system is treated as a separate product, carefully designed and packaged, and often developed, owned, and managed by separate organizational units.

> A **component system** is a system product that offers a set of reusable features. Features are implemented as related and interconnected sets of components of various types, associated packages, and descriptive documents.

A well-designed component system will enable reusers to develop high-quality systems cost-effectively and rapidly. Each component within the component system will be implemented efficiently yet retain appropriate flexibility. Each component will be designed to work well with other components, and with other component systems, to provide an appropriate level of functionality to the reuser. The component system will be easy to understand and use. Individual component types, classes, interfaces, and interactions with other components will be well documented and will use consistent terminology. Components should be carefully modeled, implemented, documented, and tested, to allow effective future maintenance and evolution.

A component system may be accompanied by related process and tool products, which support the reuse of its components. This often leads to the development of a component system kit (Griss, 1995c), in which components, tools, problem-specific customization languages, and custom development processes are packaged together.

4.5 Facades control access to component system internals

A component system exports only a subset of its types, classes and other workproducts to reusers. The remaining workproducts are hidden. This separation insulates a reuser from the specific details of how a component system is implemented, and allows internal changes without necessarily impacting the reuser. To support this separation, the component system presents the reusable components through one or more component system *facades*.

> A **facade** is a packaged subset of components, or references to components, selected from the component system. Each facade provides public access to only those parts of the component system that have been chosen to be available for reuse.

The facades thus encapsulate the internals of the component system in order to minimize dependencies and rippling change as the component system evolves. Each facade acts as a kind of public interface to the component system. We use the distinct term "facade" to stress that the subset exported can include *all types* of constructs such as use cases, and not just object types, classes or interfaces, as might be suggested by the UML term *interface* or the related concept of a contract. An interface is different in that there might be many alternative implementations behind the same interface, while a facade explicitly refers to and exports type and class elements from within the component system.

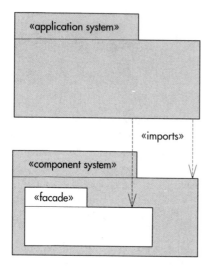

Figure 4.6 *An application system that «imports» from a component system through a facade.*

A facade is a reuser's view of a component system. It simplifies the job for reusers who wish to use the components of various types included in the facade. The facade, and the components it includes, should be selected and documented so that reusers need to understand only the components and documents included in the facade, and not others.

The number of facades and the content of each will be carefully designed. They must conform to appropriate architecture and industry standards, meet appropriate reuser needs, yet not expose too much of the component system internals to permit future evolution. The facade creation process may involve extensive negotiation between architects, component engineers, and reusers.

Figure 4.6 illustrates how application systems, component systems, and facades are related. We use several special stereotypes of package to indicate the parts: *«application system»*, *«component system»*, and *«facade»*. The application system is dependent on the component system, shown with an *«imports»* stereotype of the dependency relationship. In fact, if a component system has multiple facades, we need to show the dependency of the application system on the specific facade, as well as on the whole component system.

4.6 Facades and component systems are special kinds of packages

Here we present a facade in more detail. A facade is a special kind of UML package, shown in Figure 4.7 as a UML stereotype «facade». The facade package may have some components directly defined within it, and will import other components from the internal OOSE system, shown as a separate package, **Internals**. This **Internals** package is not strictly needed, but helps highlight the naming and importing, using the UML reference notation, ***Account'=Internals::Account***, as shown in Figure 4.7. We could instead have

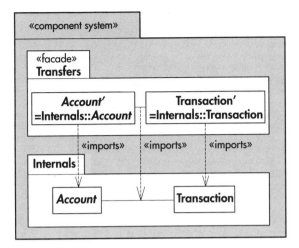

Figure 4.7 *A more precise notation for a* **Transfers** *facade as a special kind of package, importing references to the* **Account** *and* **Transaction** *classes in the* **Internals** *part of the component system. The association between the classes is also imported.*

chosen to copy the **Account** component directly into the facade. We would then use a «trace» or «copied» dependency to help manage subsequent change.

While the use of, and reference to, the **Internals** package in Figure 4.7 is not strictly necessary, the example gets more interesting if there are two internal packages, as shown in Figure 4.8. Now the package name is crucial to distinguish which of the classes is intended.

The internals of a component system are themselves constructed from several UML packages, representing the different models, as illustrated in Figure 4.9.

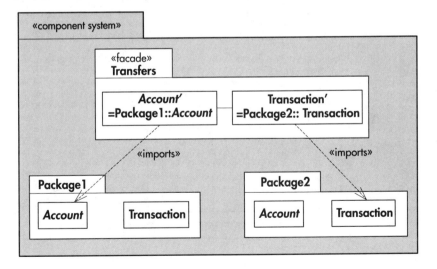

Figure 4.8 *A facade importing classes from two different internal packages,* **Account** *from* **Package1** *and* **Transaction** *from* **Package2**.

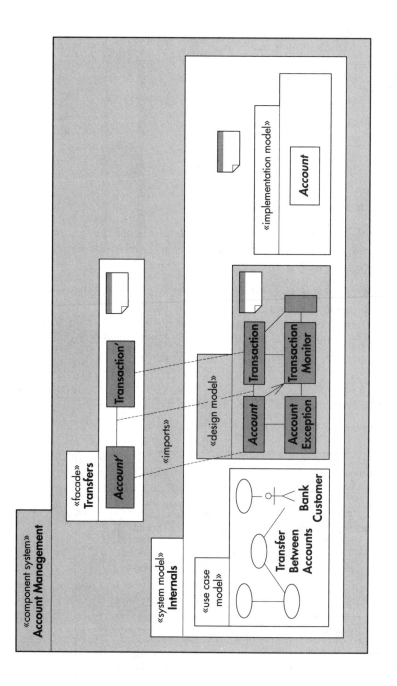

Figure 4.9 *A partial view of the internal structure of the **Account Management** component system, showing the **Transfers** facade, as well as the internal system models as separate packages of different kinds.*

4.7 Component systems export components via facades

Each component system *exports* a set of reusable components; that is, makes them publicly accessible for reuse. Only those elements that application engineers need to "connect to" directly are exported via a facade. The other elements are considered component system internals and are hidden as private elements.

"Exported" means that selected types, classes, relationships, and attached documents become available to reusers in one or more facades. Types and classes include all kinds of constructs such as: actor, use case, analysis, and design objects and templates; subsystems and service packages; interfaces; implementation classes; and attribute types. Classes, types and packages can here also include other types of components such as Java applets, Microsoft OCXs and DLLs. Selected generalization, association, and dependency relationships between elements in one model are also exported. Exported constructs from different models may also be connected to each other by traces.

Only those elements that reusers directly need to see are exported. More specifically, these are the public elements with which reusers need to create relationships. Often, these are simply UML references to the internal elements. The other hidden or private types and classes provide the necessary machinery that enables the exported elements to do their work, as shown in Figure 4.10. This encapsulation is essential in

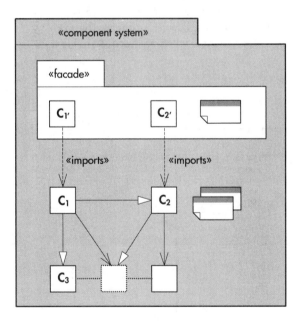

Figure 4.10 *More detail on the component system shown in Figure 4.5. The component system exports some types or classes, C_1 and C_2, and documents via a facade, while the other types or classes, C_3, . . . are hidden in the internals of the component system. We show C_1 and C_2 in the internals of the component system, with imported C_1' and C_2' in the facade connected by «imports» to C_1 and C_2.*

order to control facade changes as the component system evolves, since the stability of facades is crucial to all reusers.

In general, each component system can have several facades. Each facade defines an alternative exported set of related components offering an independent and consistent way of reusing the component system. This is compatible with COM, CORBA, and Java components, which can provide multiple alternative interfaces. These alternative interfaces are provided for backward compatibility, to offer multiple kinds of services, or to divide a large interface into manageable pieces. A change in a component should affect only the facades where the component is exported and thus only the reusers of those (possibly new) facades. Older facades should continue to exist for backward compatibility as component systems evolve. This is one advantage of having several distinct facades for each component system.

Example

The XYB **Account Management** component system offers a range of types, classes and packages that work together to support customer accounts. As shown in Figure 4.11, the types include **Account, Transaction, Account Exception**, and **Risk**. Each instance of the **Transaction** class records one **Account** transaction. Whenever there is a problem with an **Account** transaction, an instance of **Account Exception** is created to indicate what the problem was and to support recovery. The **Risk** type is used to allow bank customers to estimate the risk they are exposed to on their accounts; for instance, when an **Account** holds a foreign currency.

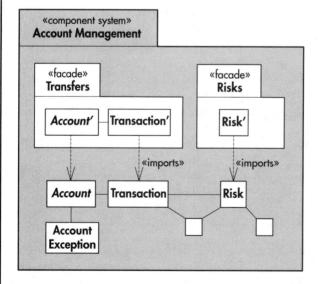

Figure 4.11 The **Account Management** *component system exports components organized into two separate facades,* **Transfers** *and* **Risks**.

Only the types **Account**, **Transaction**, and **Risk** are exported to facades. The imported copies or references are shown as **Account'**, **Transaction'**, and **Risk'**. These public types are organized into two different facades: **Transfers** for the **Account** and **Transaction** types which are used together by almost all application systems, and a separate **Risks** facade for **Risk** and related types, since it is used mostly independently of **Transfers**.

Each separate facade groups related functionality, so that a reuser implementing, for example, a new kind of checking account need only look at the **Account** component and a few documents in the **Transfers** facade, rather than looking at all exported components together.

The **Account Exception** type together with other internal types that are not shown, such as **Account Identity Verifier**, **Transaction Monitor**, and **Fee Grabber**, are private, hidden types.

Some components are intended only to be reused locally within an application *class* or *type*, such as a reference to an attribute type. To ensure this, such a component is exported only for use as an attribute type. This limits the visibility of the component within the reusing system to being part of the internal design of an application class or type.

When an application system imports a component from a facade, a UML reference to the component is included in the appropriate model of the application system. Figure 4.12 shows an application system, **Payment**, reusing several imported components. We show the imported type as a type named **Account''** in the application system, suggesting that it is related to **Account** or **Account'**. In UML, we use the importing clause, **Account''=Transfers::Account'** to reference the imported type. The component is defined in the component system, but it can now be used in the models of the application system. An imported component behaves much like a class or type defined in the importing system, with the exception that it cannot be changed by reusers. As shown, types defined in the application system may have several relationships to the imported components, but no new relationships should originate from the imported component. A relationship from the component would be, in effect, a change to the component, and not a reuse of it. An imports dependency connects **Account''** to **Account'**, and **Transaction''** to **Transaction'**. An imports dependency also connects the application system to the **Transfers** facade and to the component system itself.

4.8 Specialize some components before reuse

To make component reuse practical and effective, many of the components exported by a component system need to offer some degree of *variability* in order to be useful. To accommodate the differences between individual application systems, either we might need a large number of similar, but distinct *as-is* components, or we can build a smaller

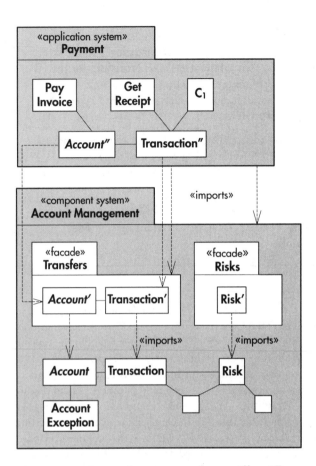

Figure 4.12 *Imported components,* **Account"** *and* **Transaction"**, *are included in the models of the* **Payment** *application system. New classes in the application system, such as* **Pay Invoice** *and* **Get Receipt**, *can have relationships to* **Account"** *and* **Transaction"**, *but not directly to* **Account'** *and* **Transaction'**.

number of more flexible, general components. These more general components will then need to be specialized in some way before reuse. Several kinds of *variability mechanisms* provide different ways of specializing reusable components.

Several kinds of variability mechanism are needed to cost-effectively match the different patterns of variation that are encountered when building practical systems. In the past, object-oriented system developers have primarily used only inheritance for variability. While the use of hierarchical class structures and inheritance has reduced the total number of components that would otherwise be needed, the use of inheritance alone has limited flexibility, resulting in some rather complex, brittle systems. Bassett (1996) stresses the importance of engineering systems for increased "softness". He says that the ease of software customization is one of the fundamental differences between software engineering and other disciplines, such as hardware engineering.

The following examples of variability drawn from experience with Ericsson AXE, Netron CAP, and Visual Basic show why it is important to have a variety of component types and variability mechanisms.

Netron CAP/Fusion   This technology describes an application system with a hierarchical set of *frames,* each of which references lower-level frames and inherits features from higher-level frames. Each frame looks likes a class or code file, but is in fact a template containing parameters and explicit editing instructions that optionally include, exclude, or modify features at distinct points in lower-level frames. In this way, like object classes, frames can inherit default behavior and parameters from higher-level frames. But in addition, a special generator, called a frame processor, processes the edited frames, generating customized workproducts. If the frame processor is processing documents, for example, it generates a new document. If it is processing source code, it generates rearranged source code in a form acceptable to a compiler. Thus a frame processor is a mechanism for variability.

Ericsson AXE   A development department creates source system products, such as component systems and preconfigured application systems. A component-based production process customizes them into final application systems. To do so, the production department uses special configuration languages, tools, and scripts, and follows detailed instructions. The development department builds source systems out of products of several types: systems, subsystems, and service packages. Each system product has a specific format consisting of instances of code, configuration templates, and documents. The documents explain how to use and customize the code and templates, and how to reference subproducts "used" (or reused) by this product. Thus configuration languages and careful partitioning into selectable *as-is* components are two kinds of variability mechanisms.

Visual Basic   An OCX or ActiveX component is a packaging of several related workproducts. These workproducts may be code, OLE interfaces, property-sheet templates, palette icons, form icons, help files, or example files. When loaded into the development environment, the component extends each part of the environment appropriately. For example, certain design-time tools might be added to the component palette or toolbar. These include wizards, generators, builders, problem-oriented languages, and environment add-ins. These elements are application-, domain-, or component-specific tools that help create, customize, or integrate components. They often start with a general template of the component with some default parameter values. For example, clicking on a component icon in the palette might bring up a custom wizard dialog, rather than simply adding an as-is component to the program being developed. The wizard will ask questions and suggest alternative settings of the parameter values. This dialog helps the reuser generate a specific component. The reuser might then further customize the component by using the normal Visual Basic editing, property-sheet, and event-routine development tools.

Imported components can be either abstract or concrete. *Concrete* components can be reused directly (as is) without change. All we need to do with a concrete component is to import it and all other components that it depends on. Then we can create relationships to it as shown in Figure 4.12. *Abstract* components are generic or incomplete in some way and must be specialized before use. Examples are supertypes, superclasses and templates with parameters. Since there are so many different types of techniques, we will first address specialization in general.

Different application systems and component systems can be distinguished from similar systems on the basis of the functionality, services, and many other features that they offer. When discussing variability, we find it a convenient shorthand to use the term "feature." In this book, we will mostly talk of features related to use cases and requirements. In our presentation we focus almost entirely on responsibilities (or features) related to functionality requirements. We capture such responsibilities using use case models. There are certainly other types of system features that are best represented in other models — these, however crucial, we do not discuss in any detail.

> A **feature** is a use case, part of a use case or a responsibility of a use case.

These can be informally stated, like "handles deposits," "handles transfers," "uses a calendar to schedule payments," or "uses tree form of account browser." They can also be more formally expressed. Generally, it is also convenient to use the term "feature" to refer to implementation details or operating constraints, such as target operating system, choice of window system, size, and performance. Thus a feature is *any* distinguishing characteristic of a component, component system, or application system that customers or reusers can use to select between available options. (Our use of the term "feature," and its relationship to variability, is similar in spirit to the use of the term in Kang's FODA (Feature Oriented Domain Analysis) method (Kang, 1990). The essence of domain analysis, as described in Chapter 1, is to identify and represent common and variable features effectively.)

As we shall see, it helps when each feature is implemented as a coherent set of related use case and object type or class components. Related components from different models that support a common set of features are linked to each other by «trace» links. In Chapter 5 we will discuss the concept of a collaboration and several additional «trace» and «participates» links.

Abstract components provide some common features or responsibilities that all reusers need. Abstract components also have variable features and responsibilities where the reusers need to choose or provide a certain variant. Variable features and reuser-extensible features are among the most essential characteristics of reusable component software.

4.9 Variability occurs at variation points

We can discuss variability mechanisms quite generally. We say that variable features are exploited at *variation points* in a component. Note that specific variations and variation points are actually implemented by a variety of different mechanisms. As shown in Figure 4.13,

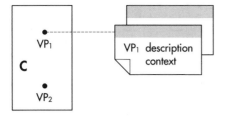

Figure 4.13 *A component* **C** *with two variation points,* **VP₁**, *and* **VP₂**, *each indicated as a* ●. *Each* **VPᵢ** *is described with an attached document that explains the context and mode of specialization needed.*

> A **variation point** identifies one or more locations at which the variation will occur.

An abstract component is specialized by attaching one or several *variants* to its variation points. *Attaching* roughly means integrating the variant into the component, but the exact semantics depends on the specific variability mechanism. Sometimes special tools are provided to handle the variability, such as template fillers or generators. We consider the various variability mechanisms in the next section. Variant types include subclasses, extensions, template instances, bound parameters, generator language files, and scripts.

Example

The different countries where XYB will offer its services have different requirements on the **Account** component. The **Account** identity will have a different format in different countries. In the United States, WFB-6912-182267 may be a legitimate account number, while 2340-667987-4 may be viable in Sweden.

Different types of **Account** also have different approaches to handling account overdrafts. Some accounts will charge a fee when an overdraft occurs, like **Checking Account**, others will not charge a fee if an appropriate credit card or saving account is linked, while still others do not permit overdrafts at all.

These two variable features are represented as variation points, **VP₁** and **VP₂**, in the generic **Account** component.

The design of facades and variants is related, since most facades contain both concrete and abstract components. Many facades also contain a number of predefined variants that can be reused by attaching them to the appropriate variation points for which they were engineered. As shown in Figure 4.14, this means that each variation point (**VP₁** and **VP₃** in the figure) may have a set of associated predefined variants, such as (v_1, v_2, v_3) and (v_4, v_5). In some cases, such as variation point **VP₂**, only the variation point itself has been defined, and it is not accompanied by any predefined variants. Each variation point

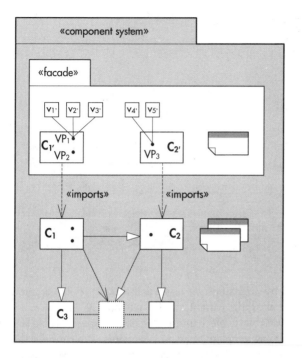

Figure 4.14   *A component system exports two components, C_1 and C_2, and several component variants $v_1 \ldots v_5$. The components have several variation points, $VP_1 \ldots VP_3$, shown as ●.*

and variant should be accompanied by documentation that explains how to use it and how to choose among the variants. Not all variation points and variants need to be visible in all facades to a given component system.

Each variable feature, such as a use case responsibility, of a component system may be implemented by one or more variation points in some components. It is simplest to have as few variation points as possible corresponding to each single variable feature. Each alternative version of the feature is similarly associated with one or more variants. This means that when a variant is chosen for one variation point, some corresponding variants may need to be chosen at other related variation points for the feature to be complete. Dependency links may also be used, as well as constraints, to establish these relationships. The attached documents describing the variation point need to make these constraints clear. This will be discussed further in connection with use case and object components in Chapters 5 and 6.

4.10   Use several kinds of variability mechanisms

Abstract components can be specialized using a wide range of generalization and specialization techniques, the *variability mechanisms* (Jacobson *et al.*, 1992; Griss, 1995d). We treat all such mechanisms as a form of «generalization». A partial list of typical variability mechanisms will be discussed in more detail in the following sections. These include the following.

Inheritance   This is used to create subtypes or subclasses that specialize abstract types or classes at their variation points. A virtual operation can be thought of as a variation point that can be specialized with inheritance.

Uses   This is a use case inheritance mechanism.

Extensions and extension points   These are particular small type-like attachments that can be used to express variants (extensions) attached at variation points (extension points) in use case and object components.

Parameterization   This is used for types and classes using templates, frames, and macros.

In addition, several languages and tools can be used to implement variability.

Configuration and module-interconnection languages   These are used to declaratively or procedurally connect optional or alternative components and variants into complete configurations.

Generation of derived components and various relationships from languages or templates. The generator is often a conversational or language-driven tool, as illustrated in the following example.

Example

Microsoft Wizards, used in many Microsoft office and programming tools, are a simple example of a generator. The Wizards help a user to create a presentation, document, or initial program by asking a number of questions, and then creating the output for further editing and processing by the tools. Such a Wizard is based on a domain-specific language that can be used to define a presentation or document, consisting of text, formatting, graphs, figures, structure, and a program, consisting of Visual Basic or C++ text. The Wizards are "conversational" in the sense that they ask a series of questions that are answered by typing in text or selecting options. The result is a derived component or application.

Other generators are language driven, rather than conversational. A script is written in a problem-oriented language or 4GL of some form, and this is preprocessed to produce the resulting specialized component or connect a set of components. Netron frames (Bassett, 1996) and system generators (Batory, 1993, 1994) use such languages.

These variability mechanisms are not entirely distinct. Several can often be used in conjunction with each other. For example, the Netron frames described above (Bassett, 1996) use a combination of parameters, inheritance, an editing language, and a generator to specialize a set of component frames.

Each variability mechanism affords a different trade-off. The component engineer needs to choose the mechanism that provides support for the right type of variability and possible range of variation. It is also important to consider ease of use and the complexity of the mechanism for the reuser. Each of the mechanisms described above has been shown in practice to provide a powerful way of making components more generic, and thus enhancing reusability.

Table 4.1 provides an overview of how variation points and variants are expressed for each of the suggested mechanisms. There are also brief suggestions as to when the mechanism works best.

Choosing the right mechanism for each component helps build a small, coherent set of appropriately generic components. These components can then be combined in a variety of ways to produce the desired application systems quickly and efficiently. In the past, software engineers have tended to think only of inheritance as the mechanism to use when producing generalized components. Unfortunately, in many situations, this leads to brittle component systems that are hard to reuse and hard to maintain, requiring frequent reorganization of the inheritance tree.

Table 4.1 *Variability mechanisms.*

Mechanism	Type of variation point	Type of variant	Use particularly when
inheritance	virtual operation	subclass or subtype	specializing and adding selected operations, while keeping others
extensions	extension point	extension	it must be possible to attach several variants at each variation point at the same time
uses	use point	use case	reusing an abstract use case to create a specialized use case
configuration	configuration item slot	configuration item	choosing alternative functions and implementations
parameters	parameter	bound parameter	there are several small variation points for each variable feature
template instantiation	template parameter	template instance	doing type adaptation or selecting alternate pieces of code
generation	parameter or language script	bound parameter or expression	doing large-scale creation of one or more types or classes from a problem-specific language

4.10.1 Using inheritance

The exact semantics of inheritance depends on the modeling language or programming language. Different programming languages typically allow different types of properties, such as operations, attributes, and associations, to be inherited. In some implementations of inheritance, only a subset of the properties can be inherited (such as only public and protected operations in C++).

Inheritance at the design level is most useful for subtyping. Subtyping can be used when an application class has the same interface as a component class, except for a number of additions to or variations of the interface. The interface is defined as a type, essentially the specification of a set of "virtual" or "dummy" operations in the superclass. Specialized variant interfaces are obtained by redefining operations in the subclasses.

Class (or type) inheritance can sometimes be a problem for manageable reuse. Inheritance reduces the encapsulation and opens up the internals of the class to its subclasses. This is often desirable for flexibility, but the reduced encapsulation can cause problems if the subclass designers misuse the operations or the attributes of the superclass. Deep class hierarchies often cause another problem, the "YoYo problem" (Taenzer et al., 1989b). It can become difficult to understand which operations are invoked, when an instance calls several internal operations at different levels in the class hierarchy. It is also hard to localize changes. Other problems arise during testing, since it is difficult to test abstract classes and to decide what to test and retest when adding a subclass. One possible way around some of these problems is to consider the protected operations of abstract classes as a kind of interface. (Protected in UML implies operations that can be accessed by operations declared in the class and its subclasses.) However, these interfaces must be designed as thoroughly as public interfaces, using, for instance, sequence diagrams.

Example

There are several ways of handling **Account** overdrafts. Here, the variability in handling overdrafts is implemented as a virtual operation, that is, an operation that should be reimplemented by another method in **Account** subclasses. Different ways of handling overdrafts are implemented as distinct subclasses.

The **Overdraft** operation is furthermore a protected operation (indicated by the UML # token).

```
Account
+ Identity: {Type};    //Account type implemented as parameter
  Current Balance:     Float;
+ Transfer (amount: Float, Destination: Account)
# virtual Overdraft (transaction: Transaction Type)
# virtual Exception (transaction: Transaction Type)
```

4.10.2 Using extensions

A use case type or object type or class **extension** is a use case type or object type or class that adds new responsibilities or behavior (extends) another use case type or object type or class.

An instance that obeys the extended type or class will also obey the extension. The extension is a variant that is attached at a variation point called an *extension point*. Extensions are most effective when several variants must be attached to one variation point.

An extension is usually a small type or class that cannot be used by itself. Instead, an extension is relevant only as an attachment to another type or class at the extension points. Each use case or class can have extension points, that is, places in the type or class where an extension may be inserted. Extensions are used to improve the structure of a type, class or system, and also can be used to add additional behavior, associations, and attributes to the extended type or class. Extension points indicate places where the addition may occur.

An extension point may be *implicit*, which means that it is not directly visible at all in the component, or *explicit*, which means that it is explicitly visible and documented in the component.

Implicit extensions should be used by component engineers whenever reusers first need to understand the component without seeing its variability displayed explicitly. Implicit extension points are described in a separate template or table prepared by the component engineers. This separate document refers to the locations in the component where the extension points apply. The component may need to be carefully written (or rewritten) so that the implicit extension points can easily be referred to without explicit in-lined extension points. It is the responsibility of the component engineers to identify all places where implicit extensions will occur. Sometimes a tool could be used to optionally display or suppress the connection between the implicit extension points described in the table and the associated component that is being extended.

In Figure 4.15, we show a component with two implicit extension points, **VP₁** and **VP₂**, where extensions **v₁**, **v₂**, and **v₃** are designed to be inserted at **VP₁**. Notice that the variation points are not marked directly in the class body, **C**.

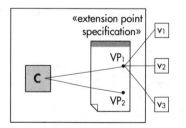

Figure 4.15 *Implicit extension points are not directly visible in the component* **C** *itself, but instead are described in the attached extension point specification table or template, owned by the component. There could also be a separate section in the type or class description for extensions.*

Explicit extension points will show up as some appropriate in-line syntax in the component, and be visible to a reuser examining the component. While explicit extension points may sometimes clutter the description of the main purpose of the component and distract first reading, the reuser can directly study the definition of the component type or class to determine its intended variability.

4.10.3 Using parameterization, templates, and macros

Parameterization is a simple but powerful technique that can be used to express component variability. A component is parameterized by inserting unbound parameters or macro expressions at appropriate variation points within a component. Parameterization can be used in the description of a use case, in the name of a type or class, within the operation definition, or within the body of a method. The parameterized component can then be specialized by binding or macro-expanding the parameters with actual parameter values, as shown in Figure 4.16. Here, the parameter **Type** appears in the body of the Identity operation, using the variation point notation, **{Type}**.

Example

The following is a sketch of the **Account** class that provides variability in the format of **Account** identities as a parameterized template. **{Type}** and **{Limit}** are parameters. Limit determines the minimum balance needed for this class of account.

Account
+ Identity: *{Type}*;   //Account type implemented as parameter
   Current Balance: Money;
      If Current Balance <= *{Limit}* then No Interest Added.
+ Transfer (amount: Float, Destination: Account)
# **virtual** Overdraft (transaction: Transaction Type)
# **virtual** Exception (transaction: Transaction Type)

Public operations and attributes are preceded by a + token. Protected operations and attributes are preceded by a # token.

Parameterization is most suitable when the feature variants are small (for example, smaller than one sentence — often a numerical value, phrase, or expression). Parameterization shows its greatest strength when the same variation point is used at several places within the same component or even distributed across several components; one parameter can then control compatible choices in several places. Parameters can also be used to choose among different implementations using conditional expansion, common to many programming language tools.

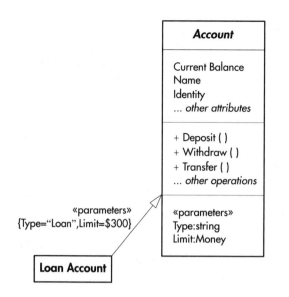

Figure 4.16 A **Loan Account** *type (or class) created by specializing a parameterized* **Account** *component, using parameter generalization, and binding the parameters* **Type** *and* **Limit**.

4.11 Reuse variable components to build application systems

The models of each application system are engineered by first deciding which reusable features are desirable. Then the components and reusable variants that implement these features can be imported, as shown in the transition from Figure 4.17 to Figure 4.18. Once it has been decided to import a component system, the first step is to decide which components and variants to import, shown as C_1' and v_2'. These are then imported into the application system, shown as C_1'' and v_2'' in Figure 4.18.

As shown in Figure 4.18, additional application-specific classes and variants, such as C_3, C_4, and v_6, can be created in order to meet application-specific requirements. Notice how the application system itself defines the variant v_6 for the variability point VP_2. Several «import» dependencies show the various reuses.

Example

As shown in Figure 4.19, the **Account Management** component system offers the **Account** component together with two variants, **Deduct Fee** and **Overdraft Not Allowed**, with different strategies to handle account overdrafts.

Because one of the XYBsoft customers wants a special overdraft handling process, neither of the supplied variants is directly feasible for reuse by the **Payment**

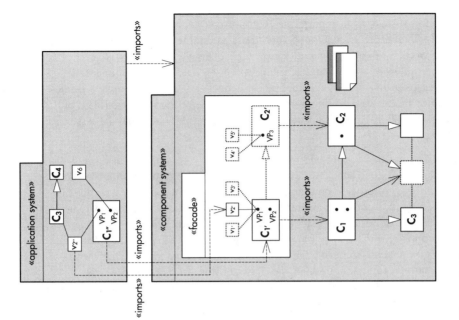

Figure 4.18 *The application system imports the component C_1' and the variant v_2' as C_1'' and v_2''.*

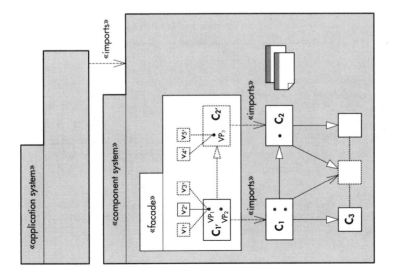

Figure 4.17 *A specific component, C_1, and a variant, v_2, are selected for import (non-dotted). The variants are attached at the variability points (black circles) in C_1 and C_2.*

application system, as it imports the **Account** component. Instead another type, **Flexible Overdraft**, is developed specifically as another variant to be used with the **Payment** application system (Figure 4.20). This variant allows a bank customer to select which types of invoices will be paid despite an overdraft. When an overdraft occurs, the application deducts a fee. For example, a **Bank Customer** might want to pay mortgage and insurance invoices regardless of whether or not that creates an overdraft, while other invoices may be less pressing.

Let us see how this variant and variation point can be expressed using a UML-like notation. Let us think of the variation point as an extension point in the **Account** type. Another type that extends the **Account** type is attached at the extension point. In order to maintain the encapsulation of the **Account** type it would be unwise to let the extending classes "look into" the internal design of the **Account** type. Therefore the extension point is published in the interface specification of the **Account** type but its precise location within the internals of the **Account** type is not specified. To illustrate this we might add a new construct. **Extension Point** is used in a type interface specification to indicate that a type has an extension point that can be triggered during the execution of its operations:

> **Extension Point Specification:** *Account* **type**
> **+ Extension Point** Overdrawn: Transaction Type **(catch Exception** = Overdraft)

Each operation in the **Account** type that can result in an overdraft, such as **Withdraw**, checks for an overdraft and signals an overdraft if one occurs. Then all extensions attached at the Overdrawn extension point in the **Account** type are executed. The extensions take as an argument the transaction that caused the overdraft. The **Flexible Overdraft** variant would be implemented as an extension that will be attached at the overdraft extension point: **Account.Overdrawn** (Figure 4.21). The **Flexible Overdraft** variant could be specified as follows:

> **Extension** Flexible Overdraft: *Account* **class**   // Extends *Account*
> **Extend at** Account.Overdrawn (Transaction: Transaction Type)
>   // at the Account.Overdrawn extension point
> **begin**
>   **If** (Transaction **is** Critical Payment)   // A critical payment such as Mortgage,…
>   **Then** Log Overdraft;   // Transaction will proceed after logging Overdraft
>   **Else Raise** Overdraft;   // Transaction is aborted, signal exception
> **end**;

Note that not all extensions can be implemented as elegantly as this. Some extension points may need to refer to individual method statements in the extended class. These will be numbered or labeled.

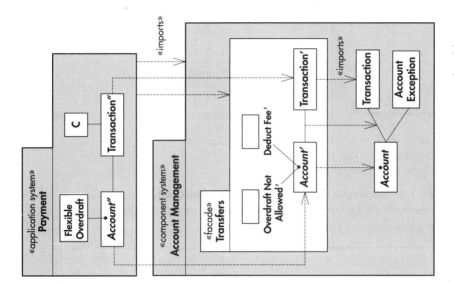
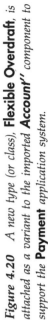

Figure 4.20 *A new type (or class),* **Flexible Overdraft***, is attached as a variant to the imported* **Account***″ component to support the* **Payment** *application system.*

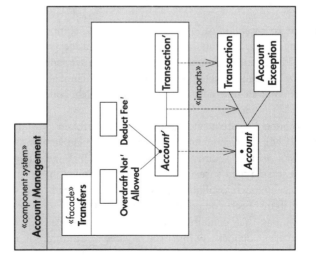
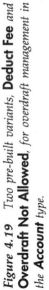

Figure 4.19 *Two pre-built variants,* **Deduct Fee** *and* **Overdraft Not Allowed***, for overdraft management in the* **Account** *type.*

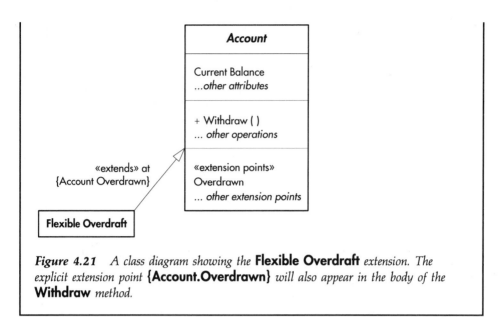

Figure 4.21 *A class diagram showing the* **Flexible Overdraft** *extension. The explicit extension point* **{Account.Overdrawn}** *will also appear in the body of the* **Withdraw** *method.*

As we shall discuss in Chapter 5, the use case model of an application system can be largely engineered from actor and use case components, together with pre-built variants. Similarly, in Chapter 6, we will discuss how the object models can be built from analysis and design components, interfaces, attribute-type components, and object and subsystem components, together with pre-built variants.

4.12 Package and document component systems for reuse

It is important to carefully package and document a component system in terms of its exported components, variants, and facades. The facades must make clear to intended reusers how the various components and pre-built variants should be used and how they should be specialized. The facade must also document how the components relate to each other and include any restrictions on which components may be used with others.

The component system and facades will be broken into pieces for configuration management (CM). A *configuration* consists of particular versions of configuration items. A *configuration item* is a segment of a model that may be subject to version control, such as a use case type, a service package containing analysis types, or some code modules. Typically, each configuration item is represented as a stereotype of package, «configuration item». Each component system can thus be divided into non-overlapping configuration items that contain all the types, classes, variants, documents, and even alternative facades defined within the system. Configuration items have several characteristics:

- A configuration item may exist in several versions.

- A configuration item containing several component types also contains all attributes, operation definitions, relationships, and documents for the types in the configuration item.

- Each configuration item should be fashioned to contain more or less independent sets of components and variants that work together. This approach simplifies reuse of optional features, by packaging the corresponding use cases, object types and classes, and variants into independent units.

- A configuration item corresponds to some construct in a configuration management system, such as a file.

The purpose of a configuration item is to be a unit of configuration management, as shown in Figure 4.22. This means that from the project management's perspective, a configuration item is the smallest piece of a model that can be assigned to separate parts of the organization. From production management's perspective, a configuration item is the smallest piece of the finished system product that can be installed. Sometimes configuration items also can be used to support the implementation of a simple form of

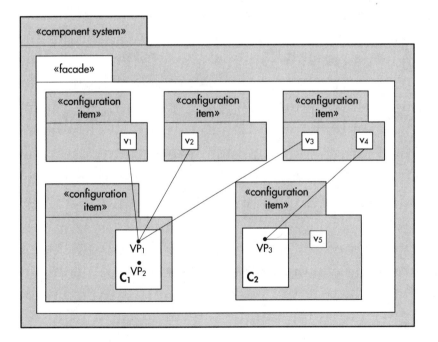

Figure 4.22 *Configuration items (packages) slice parts of a component system into non-overlapping segments. For example, variants* **v₃** *and* **v₄** *should always be used together, variant* **v₅** *should always be used with* **C₂**, *but all other parts, including the components* **C₁** *and* **(C₂ + v₅)**, *should be managed separately.*

variability, by selecting alternate configuration items to import the alternate components for *as-is* reuse.

Packaging related components and variants as independent features organized into configuration items allows reusers to quickly find and use them. The reusers can look for a desired feature or use case, and then find the corresponding analysis types and

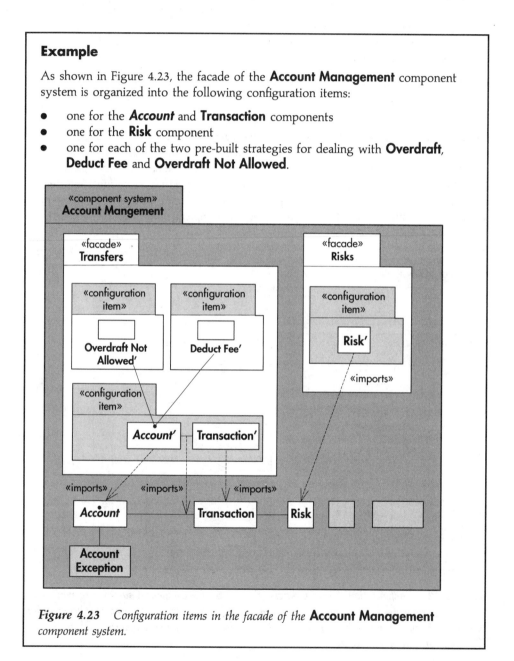

Example

As shown in Figure 4.23, the facade of the **Account Management** component system is organized into the following configuration items:

- one for the *Account* and **Transaction** components
- one for the **Risk** component
- one for each of the two pre-built strategies for dealing with **Overdraft**, **Deduct Fee** and **Overdraft Not Allowed**.

Figure 4.23 *Configuration items in the facade of the* **Account Management** *component system.*

design classes, and implementation classes that offer the feature bundled into a related configuration item.

4.13 Summary

Application systems are constructed by importing reusable components. Related components are grouped together into packages called component systems. Component system facades reveal the public or exported components, while the body of the component encapsulates the private, hidden internals. Reusable components can be of many different types, including use cases, types, classes, attributes, subsystems, interfaces, and documents.

Concrete components are reused as-is, while abstract components are specialized before use. Components can be specialized by selecting a variant and attaching it at a variation point in the component, using one of several different variability mechanisms. The major variability mechanisms include parameters, templates, inheritance, extensions, and generation.

Groups of related components and variants may be bundled together into configuration items or configurations, allowing independent management of features.

It is important to document clearly how components are specialized and used, how they depend on each other, and what restrictions exist on how they may be used together.

4.14 Additional reading

A discussion of the concept of many kinds of components and broad-spectrum reuse can be found in the paper by Bruce Barnes and Terry B. Bollinger, "Making reuse cost-effective," *IEEE Software*, **8**(1), 13–24, January 1991, and in the book by E.-A. Karlsson (ed), *Software Reuse: A Holistic Approach*, Wiley, Chichester, 1995.

A comprehensive discussion of variability and how this is exploited by Netron frames to enhance reuse can be found in the paper and book by Paul G. Bassett, "Software engineering for softness," *American Programmer*, **4**(3), 24–38, March 1991, and *Framing Software Reuse: Lessons from the Real World*, Prentice-Hall, 1996.

The concepts of domain-specific kits and how variability and domain-specificity are allocated across components with different kinds of variability mechanism can be found in the paper by Martin L. Griss and Kevin Wentzel, "Hybrid domain-specific kits," *Journal of Software and Systems*, 30, 213–30, September 1995.

More information on extensions and their role in variability can be found in Ivar Jacobson, Magnus Christerson, Patrik Jonsson, and Gunnar Övergaard, *Object-Oriented Software Engineering: A Use Case Driven Approach*, Addison-Wesley, 1992 (Revised 4th printing, 1993).

5

USE CASE
COMPONENTS

5.1 Structure the use case model to ensure component reuse

The first step in using OOSE to engineer a particular application is to transform the specific requirements into a use case model, as described in Chapter 3. If we want to reuse components, we should start by expressing the specific use cases and features of the application system in terms of the more generic use cases offered by the reusable component systems. Selected use case components can then be specialized and augmented to create the use case model.

Furthermore, to ensure component-based development at all stages, from requirements capture to implementation, it is critical to identify the most feasible components to reuse early in the software development process. If we want to get high levels of reuse, we want the requirements to match the available use case components well. This may sometimes require us to change the application requirements in small ways, or to negotiate more substantial changes.

We will also need to structure the application use case model carefully to match the use case components. If we delay considering reuse to the design or implementation stage, we may find our design is incompatible with the features offered by the component systems. Without great care, we will inevitably use terminology and make so many architectural and design decisions that are incompatible with the available component systems that it will be hard, if not impossible, to find and reuse appropriate components.

One of the main reasons that most code and class libraries are so hard to reuse and yield disappointing levels of reuse is because they are often searched too late, after the major design decisions have been established. The available code components most likely will not match the design decisions we have already made. Frameworks can improve the reuse situation somewhat. An application framework can be informally thought of as a skeletal application that can be readily augmented to produce a complete application. It is usually delivered as a set of concrete and abstract components that are architected and designed to work together to provide most of the functionality needed by a set of related applications. In principle, a developer can easily reuse the framework by subclassing some classes, directly reusing other classes, or adding some new classes. Because many architectural and design decisions explicitly reveal themselves in the class structure, frameworks provide conceptual models and terminology that constrain a developer to express requirements and design decisions in terms that are largely compatible with the supplied reusable classes and code. Even so, developers often still find it hard to directly express problem-level requirements in terms of the potentially large number of solution-space features offered by a framework and its supporting class libraries.

The sooner we can identify a component and integrate it into an appropriate model of the application system, the faster and more accurately we can build the target system. The Reuse Business does this by providing reusable use case components within the component systems that then naturally guide the developers to reusable analysis, design, and implementation components through traces. We stress that if we start by reusing use case components to build the use case model, we set the stage for later being able to more easily express analysis, design, and implementation models in terms of corresponding components that are known to work together. On the other hand, if we do not express our specific use case model in terms of the use case components, we will find it harder to reuse object components in the later models.

5.2 The use case model shapes the rest of the system

As stressed in Chapter 3, the use case model defines *what* a system should do for its users. The use case model is used during requirements capture by the customers, end users, software engineers, and other stakeholders as they decide what the system should do.

In the use case model, users of the system are called *actors*. Each actor defines a distinct role assumed by a person or a machine interacting with the system. Each way an actor uses the system is a distinct use case. Each *use case* defines a set of interactions with the system. The use case model consists of actors and use cases, together with descriptions of their interactions and connections.

The model must precisely define how *responsibilities* are allocated to actors and use cases.

A **responsibility** here is something that an actor or use case needs to do or keep track of as the system is used. More generally a responsibility is a contract or an obligation of a class or a type.

A use case **User Login** may, for example, have the responsibilities: **wait for user login attempt, validate user login attempt, acknowledge correct user login attempt**, and **disconnect user**.

The use case model is described in a number of documents, the most important being the *use case description* which defines the responsibilities of one use case, and also defines the responsibilities of the actors as they interact with instances of that use case.

The use case model is used as an important input when developing the various object models, such as the analysis and design models, which describe *how* the system is architected and designed. The use case model is related to the analysis and design models via several *mappings* which show which analysis types contribute to which use cases. Instances of several analysis types collaborate to perform instances of a use case, segment of a use case, or a use case responsibility. These collaborations are described using collaboration diagrams or sequence diagrams, collectively called interaction diagrams, by restating use case descriptions in terms of analysis types. The most direct way of showing the traceability from a use case to the analysis model is to introduce a corresponding collaboration, shown as a dashed ellipse in Figure 5.1, which is connected to the use case by a «trace» relationship. The collaboration is connected to the analysis types by «participates» dependencies. So if a reuser can reuse the **Withdraw Money** use case, the trace then points to corresponding analysis components.

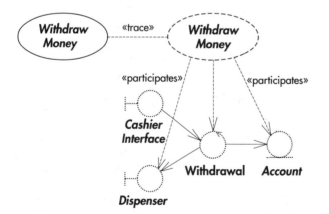

Figure 5.1 *Traceability between a use case model and later object model. The* **Withdraw Money** *use case is traceable to the collaboration,* **Withdraw Money**. *Instances of the various analysis types are participants in the collaboration.*

5.3 Reusing components to build the use case model

Use case components can be reused during requirements capture by treating the component systems as a toolbox of reusable model elements. Each use case component defines some system responsibilities in problem-oriented terms. As shown in the example in Figure 5.1, and more schematically in Figure 5.2, each use case component in the component system is traceable to corresponding reusable type and class components. If a particular use case component is reused, then its corresponding type and class components (if any) should be considered for reuse in later development phases.

There are several reasons to reuse use case components. A stakeholder (customer, end user, requirements analyst, developer, or other interested party) will gain a number of benefits.

Effectiveness The use case components can be used as a toolbox expressing known system functionality. Stakeholders can capture requirements faster and more accurately by picking and choosing among predefined use case components.

Quality Stakeholders can improve the quality of the requirements capture by reusing certified use case components. They will also not miss some less obvious requirements since as they are choosing from a "complete" set of use cases, they get an opportunity to see all requirements.

Predictability Project estimates can be improved by reusing use cases, since more will be known about how to implement them. Most use case components come with mappings to the analysis, design, and implementation models.

Uniformity By reusing the same use case components in several application systems the engineers will design systems in a uniform way. The use case components provide a common shape and set of functionality for each application system. Reusing use case components ensures consistency of terminology and systems.

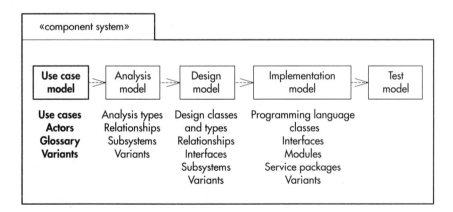

Figure 5.2 *A component system has a use case model and also a number of object models linked through traces.*

When developing analysis, design, implementation, or testing models of an application system, designers will gain two benefits if they reuse use case components.

Design reuse Most use case components have mappings to the object models and the implementation. Reusing a use case component makes it possible to reuse also the design and the implementation of that use case.

Rapid learning The use cases provide usage-oriented documentation of the component system. This documentation allows new engineers to learn more quickly how to design applications from the component system. They can see how the component system is intended to be used by looking at the use cases.

5.4 Design the use case components for effective reuse

When we engineer a component system, we must ensure that we really meet the needs of the component reusers. By identifying use case components the component engineers can build the right object models for the component system. An easy-to-use set of use case components is thus critical to the (re-)usability of the entire component system.

The terminology used to describe the actors and use cases is very important. A common and consistent *glossary* of terms used to describe the problem requirements and features should be developed as component systems are created, and also used as application systems are engineered. This is particularly important for the use case model of the component system and for use case components, so that the stakeholders can communicate effectively and avoid many misunderstandings by using standard and well-thought-out terms.

In the XYB, there are many terms such as: **Customer, Buyer, Payer, Cash, Digicash, Money, Instrument, Check, Loan, Mortgage, Stock, Portfolio, Account, Borrow, Overdraft, Invoice, Withdraw, Deposit, Transfer, Exchange, Monitor**. These terms have subtle relationships to each other, and are used in combinations to name use cases, variants, and other components. If the correct terms are used to name and describe components, reusers will be led most rapidly from requirements to use cases, and then to the appropriate components and variants in the other models.

Careful use of the terms helps reusers distinguish and relate variants. Using the phrases **Withdraw Money, Withdraw Cash Variant**, and **Withdraw Digicash Variant** makes the connections, differences, and roles of the components quite obvious.

Each component system should have its own glossary of terms. Some of those terms will be used to describe the components exported from the component system, and will help reusers understand how to use it. Note that terms like **Instrument, Transfer, Monitor, Exchange,** and **Stock** mean different things in the banking domain, the networking domain, and other domains that the XYB needs to deal with. Thus a subset of the glossary will be described in one of the documents attached to the facade (this glossary would be called the domain dictionary if we were doing conventional domain engineering, for example). In the case of multiple facades, each facade might provide a separate document of key terms. The terms associated with each facade need to be carefully chosen and standardized, since they are used by the reusers to understand what the components do and to help select between alternative variants.

This glossary is also useful later when developing object models of a system. The use of standard terms to name components and variants will help reusers relate the components to the use case models and requirements. For system-level component systems, the terms in the glossary might also reference key implementation features that reusers might need to understand.

When developing the analysis, design, implementation, or testing models of a component system, use cases serve just as they do for application systems. They help us improve the usability and coherence of the component system, and simplify the work needed to design and test the component system against the most frequent ways of using it. It is important to realize that some use cases are used only inside the component system, to ensure its coherence and reliability, while others are explicitly exported for reuse.

5.5 Not all use cases should be reusable components

Different types of use case components are appropriate to export for reuse in varying degrees. Concrete use case components are generally economic to design and reuse. Abstract use case components can often be used to implement common mechanisms, such as **Monetary Transfer** in the example below. These use case components can be generic to a greater or lesser extent. The more generic the use case component, the more useful it is, but also potentially more expensive to develop, understand, and reuse.

Example

The **Monetary Transfer** use case component can itself be designed as a specialization of the abstract use case component **Instrument Transfer**, which moves an arbitrary type of **Instrument**, such as **Money**, from one **Portfolio** to another. **Portfolio**, while not shown in Figure 5.3, is an abstract use case type which includes accounts, loans, and stock portfolios.

There may not be a need for both the **Monetary Transfer** and **Instrument Transfer** use cases to be components. Perhaps the **Monetary Transfer** use case adds little reusable value compared with **Instrument Transfer**. In this case, it is best that only the abstract use case **Instrument Transfer** be implemented as a component. Then the use cases **Withdraw Money**, **Deposit Money**, and **Transfer Between Accounts** can reuse directly from **Instrument Transfer**.

Alternatively, it might be too hard to give such a general use case as **Instrument Transfer** an effective and sufficiently understandable implementation to be useful. **Instrument Transfer** is then an abstract use case expressed at a high level, essentially a template written in terms of several variation points. This can be thought of informally as a form of pattern, described further in Chapter 6.

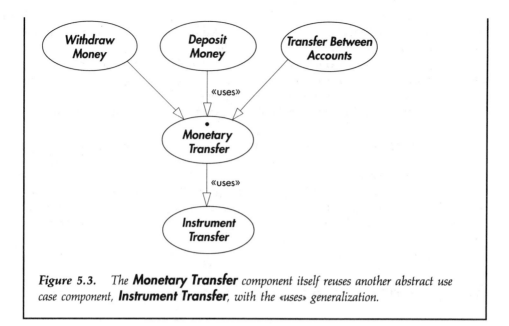

Figure 5.3. The **Monetary Transfer** component itself reuses another abstract use case component, **Instrument Transfer**, with the «uses» generalization.

Sometimes abstract use cases are too small in size or too oriented towards technology to be relevant for reuse during requirements capture. Instead they provide useful mechanisms to reuse only later as application use cases are *designed* and *implemented*. This might be true for the abstract use case **Instrument Transfer**. However, a use case like **Monetary Transfer** is probably relevant to reuse during both requirements capture and robustness analysis, and should be implemented as a use case component.

5.6 Reusing concrete or abstract actor and use case components

The general approach to reusable components described in Chapter 4 applies to the use case model and to its use case and actor components, which are exported from component systems via facades. Application systems or other component systems can import these components from the facades. (An *actor component* is an actor designed and packaged to be reusable in several systems. A *use case component* is likewise a use case intended to be reusable in several systems.)

Actor and use case components can be either concrete and reused *as-is*, as common components without change, or *abstract*, meaning that they need to be *specialized* before reuse. For instance, a use case component for **User Login** might be reused as-is if several systems require precisely the same user login procedure.

There are several situations when abstract use case and actor components will need to be specialized. One example is when several application use cases have almost the same description, but with variations in how user or system errors are dealt with.

Variation points define varying responsibilities and features in the use case component. When such use case components are later reused, they have to be specialized by attaching use case *variants* at the variation points. Recall from Chapter 4 that "attaching a variant" here means doing what is appropriate to the specific situation, such as subtyping or subclassing when the variability mechanism is inheritance.

When several application systems have the same actor with the same characteristics, it is feasible to define a *concrete actor component* which can be reused *as-is*. When several application systems have similar actors, it may be feasible to define an *abstract actor component*. Each application system actor can then inherit the component actor, adding to or specializing its role. Inheritance can thus be used as the variability mechanism.

Example

The actor **Bank Customer** represents a class of individuals who interact with the XYB for all kinds of purposes. This actor performs many of the use cases offered by the XYB, such as **Withdraw Money** and **Deposit Money**. When buying goods or services, and when paying an invoice, a person who is a **Bank Customer** would also have a more specialized role of **Buyer**. The **Buyer** actor inherits from **Bank Customer** many properties which are relevant for interaction with the **Pay And Schedule Invoices** use case.

Similarly, when several application systems need to offer the same use case, it can be represented as a *concrete use case component*. These use case components can be reused as-is, which means that the use case type does not have to be specialized to be of value to an actor.

Example

All application systems in the XYB suite require that users first log in to verify their authority. This can be represented with a concrete use case component, **User Login**, reused as-is in all XYB application systems.

When application systems need to offer similar use cases, the common aspects can often be represented as abstract use cases. *Abstract use case components* offer both common responsibilities and variation points, and are appropriate when several use cases offer the "same behavior in essence" but have one or more responsibilities or features that distinguish them. In this case, we structure the use case to display one or more variation points, and pick an appropriate variability mechanism. When abstract use case components are reused, they have to be specialized by attaching use case variants at the variation points.

Example

As the developers work with the use cases **Withdraw Money**, **Deposit Money**, and **Transfer Between Accounts** they realize that all of these use cases can be generalized to support banking transactions at both ATMs and Internet home-banks. They therefore change the use cases so that they contain only what is general for both ATMs and Internet home-banks, and place the generalized use cases in the component system **Money Management** as shown in Figure 5.4. Later in this chapter we will see the structure of the generalized use cases and how, as part of **Money Management**, they are reused in two application systems: **ATM Cashier** and **Digicash Cashier** (for Internet home-banks).

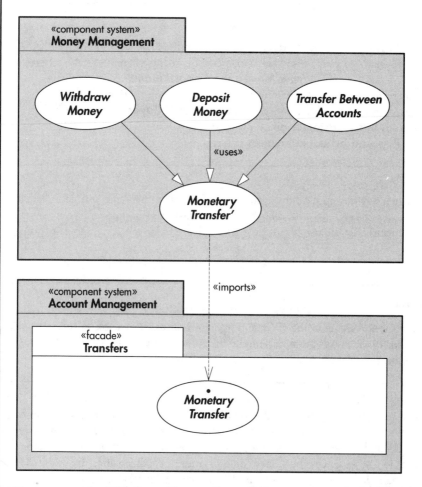

Figure 5.4 The **Withdraw Money**, **Deposit Money**, *and* **Transfer Money** *use cases use the «uses» generalization to reuse the use case component* **Monetary Transfer** *from the* **Account Management** *component system.*

All these use cases involve the movement of money between monetary holders. Monetary holders here include accounts and other money containers operated on by the bank, such as Smartcards or cashier checks. This commonality can be exploited and represented as an abstract use case **Monetary Transfer**, imported from the **Account Management** component system (Figure 5.4). One benefit of reusing the abstract use case **Monetary Transfer** is that it is possible to define and maintain a common procedure for all types of monetary transfers.

5.7 Expressing use case variability

Abstract use case components often have associated variants exported along with them. These act as pre-built specializations of the component. A reuser may then import the abstract component, select among the provided variants, and import the chosen variant for immediate attachment.

Example

As shown in Figure 5.5, the **Account Management** component system offers the **Monetary Transfer** use case component. Along with the use case there are also two component variants with different strategies to handle potential account overdrafts. One variant deducts a fee for each overdraft. The other variant does not permit overdrafts at all. These variants are associated with the variation point **{Account Overdrawn}**.

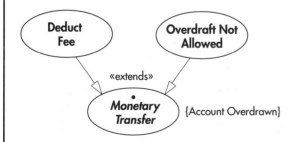

Figure 5.5   *The abstract use case component* **Monetary Transfer**, *together with two variants for handling account overdrafts to be inserted at the* **{Account Overdrawn}** *variation point, using extends as the mechanism.*

There are several ways of expressing commonality and variability of use case components, and several different types of variability mechanisms that are useful. These include use case templates, macros and parameters, use case inheritance (uses), and use case extensions. Each mechanism has different advantages, some already discussed in Chapter 4.

Variability is used to allow for variations in functional requirements and also in non-functional requirements. It is easier to understand the need for variability when looking at different categories of variability to see how they can be represented and implemented. Some typical reasons to exploit variability in a use case component are illustrated below.

Varying user or **system interfaces**   Different kinds of users, or different specializations of use cases, might specify a different user interface. Likewise, different installations of a system or different operating environments may require different system interfaces or customized device drivers for different kinds of ATMs, home-banking stations, or E-cash methods.

Different entity types referenced   For instance, an **Account** may be either a checking or a joint account. Such variations often correspond directly to entity-type variants in the object models.

Example

The use case component **Instrument Transfer** can be expressed in terms of types **Portfolio** and **Instrument**. Just as the use case **Instrument Transfer** is specialized to **Monetary Transfer**, as shown in Figure 5.3, a **Portfolio** and an **Instrument** is specialized to an **Account** and **Money**, illustrated previously in Figure 3.26.

Alternative and optional functionality   Different variants of the use case might offer optional or alternative behavior.

Example

A **Bank Customer**, acting in the role of **Buyer**, may desire to get confirmation when the **Seller** actor has received payment for an invoice. But only some installations of the **Pay And Schedule Invoices** use case will give the **Buyer** such confirmation, since this might require additional processing power at the installation. There might be several alternative variants of the **Pay And Schedule Invoices** use case component to support the alternatives.

Varying constraints and business rules   Different variants of a use case may have different restrictions on the order in which tasks may be performed. They may have different pre-conditions or constraints on whether the use case is allowed to execute, and there may be different business rules that apply.

> **Example**
>
> In some installations the **Pay And Schedule Invoices** use case component must check that the **_Account_** will not be overdrawn when paying an invoice.
>
> In other installations, each instance of the **Pay And Schedule Invoices** use case must be checked for possible fraud before approval. This is done by comparing invoices against the normal pattern of invoice payments associated with the **Bank Customer** and **_Account_** used.

Error-detection   The best strategy for error-detection and recovery during a use case often depends on the type of user interface, or the type of account or other related objects.

> **Example**
>
> Some installations may avoid **_Account_** overdrafts during the **Pay And Schedule Invoices** use case by instead paying an invoice from a different account than the default account.

Performance and scalability differences   Differences in performance requirements, timing constraints, or number of active instances may vary among different installations of a system.

> **Example**
>
> Different installations of the **ATM Cashier** application system may be allowed to tolerate different response times in the **_Withdraw Money_** use case before treating a delay as an error. Likewise, the amount of time to try to connect to another bank before timing out probably depends on the quality of the telecommunication network.
>
> Finally, some installations of the Internet home-bank application system **Digicash Cashier** may need to be able to simultaneously serve 100 customer requests. In other installations 20 may suffice.

Requirements capture in terms of the use case model can be used as the starting point to identify the variation points discussed above. (This analysis of commonality and variability of use cases, requirements, and other features in the use case model is an example of how domain engineering steps are integrated, as discussed in Chapter 1.) The stakeholders can go through the set of provided use cases and decide which responsibilities and features need to be expressed as something that might be varied during reuse and which are common to all reusers. Sometimes it is useful to describe such variability with explicit variation points in the use case descriptions. Other times it may be preferable to express such variability in a separate document, as implicit variation points, so that it is easier to understand the use case model structure and the descriptions without getting obstructed by the variation points. This would be true if very complex variability needs to be expressed.

We use the following example to illustrate several different types of use case variability mechanisms, with variation points shown as **{Variation point}** in text, and as a solid dot in diagrams.

Example

In Figure 5.6, we show a simplified use case description. A more typical use case description might be 3–20 pages long. We have greatly simplified the flow of events section, which in this example contains no mechanisms for recovery of user errors, but does handle some other errors.

There is one variation point for handling different ways of dispensing money **{Dispenses The Money}**, such as dispensing cash or Digicash. This variation point might most easily be specialized using the «uses» generalization, as discussed in Section 5.7.2.

Withdraw Money Use Case Description: Use case model

1. Introduction
Withdraw Money lets a **Bank Customer** withdraw money from an ATM, home-banker, or similar banking interface.

2. Flow of events
First the **Bank Customer** is identified.
Then the **Bank Customer** chooses how much to withdraw and from which {**Account**}.
The system responds with how much can be withdrawn from that {**Account**}, which depends on type of {**Account**}.
Then the system {**Dispenses The Money**} and deducts the amount from the {**Account**}.
If the deduction results in an overdraft, it is handled according to {**Account Overdrawn**}.

3. Special requirements
The following are maximum response times as the system:
- verifies the identity of the **Bank Customer**: {**Identification time**}
- presents the balance of {**Account**} that the **Bank Customer** has chosen: {**Balance time**}
- dispenses the amount and deducts the amount from the {**Account**}: {**Dispense time**}.

Whenever the server does not respond within {**Time out**} seconds, the client considers the server to be down and cancels the use case.
There may be no more than {**Instances**} instances of use case *Withdraw Money* executing in parallel on this server.

Figure 5.6 *A simplified use case description, showing several variation points.*

There is a second variation point that deals with error recovery in the case of overdrawn accounts, which has been indicated with **{Account Overdrawn}**.

It is not obvious which mechanism to choose for dealing with overdrawn accounts, since it depends on the different ways reusers might need to deal with overdrafts. Simple solutions can be done with inheritance. More sophisticated business rules might require extensions, or even a template-based generator or business rule language. We leave that decision open for the moment.

Several other variation points are shown as **{Account}**, **{Dispense Time}**, and so on, which are intended to be replaced by parameters.

5.7.1 Using use case parameters and templates

A parameterized use case contains *use case parameters*. A parameter, **Parameter**, will be indicated by the variation point **{Parameter}** in the body of the use case description, and perhaps also be listed in a special **Parameters** section. When the use case is specialized and reused, these parameters will be replaced by some other text or references. Parameters are mostly used to define relatively simple and well-defined variability that is often to be replaced in multiple places.

Example

The example shown in Figure 5.6 contains four different types of parameters representing response times, time-out, and number of active instances. Parameters have been represented using the variation point marker: **{Parameter}**: **{Identification time}**, **{Balance time}**, **{Dispense time}**, **{Time out}** and **{Instances}.**

A more complex form of parameterization is to treat the use case as a template. In this case, a generator tool would process the use case description or an attached template specification. The "text" associated with each variation point is treated as a procedure invocation or an executable expression in some scripting language, such as Visual Basic Script. The replacement "text" will be used to generate a completely new concrete use case, or to create a set of interacting types as a starting point for reuse in the analysis model.

5.7.2 Using use case inheritance

The uses generalization implies that a use case inherits another. This can be used to represent commonalities among several use cases.

Example

As shown in Figure 5.7, the use case **Withdraw Digicash** inherits («uses») the use case component **Withdraw Money**. The subtype use case defines behavior that is unique to the withdrawal of the Digicash form of electronic cash over the Internet. There is a similar variant **Withdraw Cash** for withdrawal of money in the form of cash or checks from an ATM.

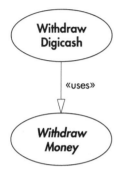

Figure 5.7 The use case **Withdraw Digicash** uses the use case **Withdraw Money**.

This could particularly affect the last part of the flow of events section of Figure 5.6. We replace the variation point **{Dispenses The Money}** with the specific binding **{Dispenses Digicash Using Secure Web Browser}**:

Then the system **{Dispenses Digicash Using Secure Web Browser}** and deducts the amount from the **{Account}** . . .

5.7.3 Using use case extensions

A use case *extension* is a use case that *extends* another use case. The extension specializes the extended use case, in that a use case instance that obeys the original use case will now also obey the additional behavior of the extension. Extensions are best used when it is necessary to attach several variants at one variation point in a use case.

Example

Along with the **Monetary Transfer** use case component, there are also two variants with different strategies to handle potential account overdrafts.

One variant, **Deduct Fee**, charges for each overdraft, and can be represented as an extension that applies at the extension point, **{Account Overdrawn}**. This extension point could also be documented in a special Extensions section of the use case description. This variant is then defined as:

Deduct Fee:

Extension at {Account Overdrawn}: Deduct a fee from the account and then perform the transaction even if it would result in an overdraft.

5.7.4 Choosing between uses and extends for variability

It is sometimes difficult to decide when to select the uses generalization and when to select the extends generalization to represent variability in a use case component.

Extends can be used in two different ways. One is to add a flow to a use case which is already "complete" in itself. In Chapter 4 we discussed this as an "ad hoc" extension. The other is to add some variant at a carefully selected and designated extension point in a use case component. The extension provides some specialized behavior that is executed when an instance of the extended use case is executed. The abstract use case component behaves as a kind of "template" or "frame" into which the extension is inserted.

Uses is instead simply used to reuse or inherit common behavior definitions, which can then be augmented. Typically, this is employed when there is a sequence of common behavior that can be reused by several other use cases.

5.8 Packaging and documenting use case components

The actors, use case components, variants, facades, and glossary need to be carefully packaged and documented for effective reuse. One aspect of this is that independent components and variants need to be organized into an independent configuration. Stereotypes of package, «configuration item» and «configuration», are used to represent *configuration items (CI)*, or items grouped into a *configuration*. Reusers can then look for a desired piece of functionality, and find the corresponding actors, use cases, and variants that offer it, all bundled into a single configuration package.

Figure 5.8 illustrates how the XYB component system **Money Management** is packaged into configuration items, for reuse to develop either **ATM Cashier** or **Digicash Cashier**.

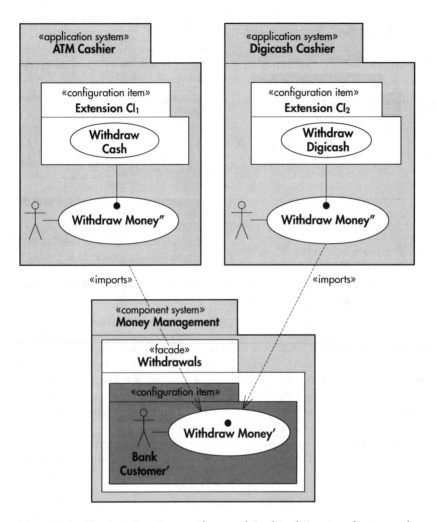

Figure 5.8 *Configuration items as they are defined in different application and component systems.*

Example

The following set of «configuration item»s (CI) are suggested for the **Withdraw Money** use case in the **Money Management** component system and the variants **Withdraw Cash** and **Withdraw Digicash** for the **ATM Cashier** and **Digicash Cashier** application systems:

Withdraw Money Use Case CI:

A single «configuration item» containing:

- the **Bank Customer** actor,
- the abstract *Withdraw Money* use case component with variation points using extends as the variation mechanism.

Withdraw Cash Use Case Extension CI$_1$:

A single «configuration item» for the ATM interface variant of the {**Dispenses The Money**} variation point, containing the use case variant **Withdraw Cash**.

Withdraw Digicash Use Case Extension CI$_2$:

A single «configuration item» for the home-banking interface variant of the {**Dispenses The Money**} variation point, containing the use case variant **Withdraw Digicash**.

The **Digicash Cashier** application system thus defines a new configuration item and imports one from the component system **Money Management**, and combines them in the following configuration:

Withdraw Digicash Use Case Configuration$_A$:

A «configuration» containing all the configuration items that make up a complete configured **Withdraw Digicash**:

- **Withdraw Money Use Case CI**
- **Withdraw Digicash Use Case Extension CI$_2$** ...

It is also important to carefully document use case components and their role in each facade, so that potential reusers can easily understand them and discriminate among them. While it is important to document all reusable model components properly, this is particularly crucial for actor and use case components, since these will perhaps be used in discussion with customers and other stakeholders, not just software engineers. Careful use of the glossary terminology and a standardized document format can highlight the situations in which a certain component or variant should be selected. For example, the document could have several standard sections which explain under which circumstances a certain variant might be preferred, and how to specialize the component using the variant. Together, the set of documents for the component system should explain what each component or variant does, when to use it, and how it compares and relates to other components and variants.

5.9 Summary

To ensure high levels of reuse, it is important to shape the requirements description and use case model for an application system at an early stage, in order to match the terminology and features provided by the available component systems.

Actor and use case components can either be reused *as-is*, without change, or reused after they are *specialized*. *Variation points* are used to define locations of variability in the use case component. When later reused, the components will be specialized by attaching use case *variants* at the variation points.

Each component system and facade should have a *glossary* of the terms used to describe the concepts, components, and variants. These terms help the reuser to understand, relate, and select among the various components and variants.

There are different mechanisms that can be used for expressing use case variability. These include simple *parameters*, more complex *templates*, *inheritance*, and *extensions*. Use case inheritance (*uses*) and *extends* structure use case models to enhance clarity and sharing. Parameters and templates allow specialized use cases to be easily generated from a more generic description.

Use case components help the reusers both as a catalog of reusable system specifications to pick and choose from, and as an entry point into the subsequent object models and implementation.

5.10 Additional reading

The OOSE book, *Object-Oriented Software Engineering: A Use Case Driven Approach*, by Ivar Jacobson, Magnus Christerson, Patrik Jonsson, and Gunnar Övergaard, Addison-Wesley, 1992 (Revised fourth printing, 1993) discusses criteria for writing good use case models and provides extensive examples.

The patterns book, *Design Patterns — Elements of Reusable Object-Oriented Software*, by Erich Gamma, Richard Helm, Ralph Johnson, and John Vlissides, Addison-Wesley, 1994 (ISBN 0-201-63361-2) suggests templates for documenting patterns, relevant to the way use cases might be documented to better display their reusable aspects.

The paper by Ivar Jacobson, "Basic Use Case Modeling (continued)," *ROAD*, July—August, **1**(2), 1994 describes how to use extends effectively.

OBJECT
COMPONENTS

6.1 Object models define system architecture and design

At this point, we have used OOSE to transform the requirements for our application system into a use case model, and we have reused appropriate use case components from the available component systems to build it. By so doing, we have begun the process of shaping our requirements and application system to take maximum advantage of the reusable component systems at our disposal.

Starting from this use case model, we now develop the object models, containing the various model elements shown in Figure 6.1. The use case model is one of the most important inputs when developing these analysis and design object models. The reusable use case components will guide us to appropriate object components that will be reused when building the object models.

While the use cases describe *what* the system is supposed to do from each user's perspective (more precisely, each actor's perspective), the various object models describe *how* the system is architected, designed, and implemented to meet these user requirements.

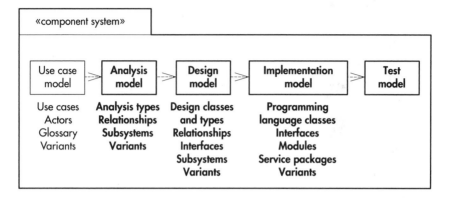

Figure 6.1 *A component system includes several object models, including analysis and design models, each consisting of types or classes, subsystems, and variants.*

The **use case model** is primarily used to express what the system should do. The analysis and design **(object) models** are primarily used to express system structure and design.

As we explained in Chapter 3, each object model describes the design of a system at some level of abstraction. Each object model consists of types or classes, usually organized into subsystems. In general, each object model defines how responsibilities are allocated to types or classes, indicating what responsibilities each type or class has in relation to others.

Responsibility here means something that an object needs to do or keep track of as the system is in use.

For example, a type **Account** may have the responsibilities **monitor overdrafts, validate customer access rights, log transactions, transfer money correctly,** and **compute interest**. Each model is described by several diagrams and documents showing relationships, collaborations, and mappings between types or classes.

The analysis model is more abstract and closer to the application domain, while the design model is closer to the implementation. The analysis model defines an architecture that should be reusable and robust in the face of new and changed requirements. It tries to be as independent as possible of specific implementation issues. The design model is derived from the analysis model and serves as a blueprint of the implementation, taking into account various programming language and execution environment constraints. The design model should map fairly directly onto the implementation model. While most of our discussion applies equally well to both the analysis and design model, some programming language and execution environment concerns show up more directly in the design model. These will influence how we manage to map various relationships.

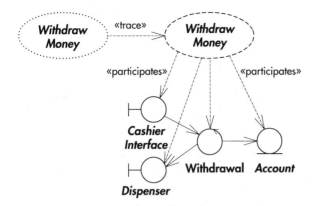

Figure 6.2 Traceability between a use case, **Withdraw Money**, and related object model components. The use case is realized by, and is traceable to, the collaboration, **Withdraw Money**, shown as a dashed ellipse to emphasize its connection to the use case. The various analysis types are participants in the collaboration.

OOSE uses distinct analysis and design models, to provide an opportunity to explicitly structure a robust architecture during the analysis (or robustness) activity, before becoming too focused on specific implementation language or infrastructure concerns. This separation of concerns helps us develop a system structure that enhances reuse, and avoids making too many decisions that bind us to implementation specifics.

The object models are seamlessly connected to the use case model. *Trace* relationships from use case to analysis model, and from analysis model to design and implementation models, lead the reuser from reusable use components to related object components. Several analysis types interact to perform a use case, segment of a use case, or a use case responsibility. These collaborations are described using collaboration diagrams or sequence diagrams, collectively called interaction diagrams, by restating use case descriptions in terms of these types. The most direct way of showing the traceability from a use case to the object model is to introduce a corresponding collaboration, shown as a dashed ellipse in Figure 6.2 (repeated from Chapter 5, but with the analysis model emphasized), which is connected to the use case by a «trace» relationship. The collaboration is connected to the other types by «participates» dependencies.

Collaborations are similar to patterns, which are small standard architectural designs that connect a number of types or classes in a distinctive way. The connections to use cases, and the use of collaborations, patterns, and other reuse structuring guidelines will help us architect systems to increase the achievable levels of component reuse. We will discuss architecture and design patterns in more detail in Section 6.5.1.

6.2 Reusing analysis and design components

The reuse constructs described in Chapter 4, such as component systems, facades, variation points, and variants, can be directly applied to types, classes and subsystems in the various object models. Reusable object components, consisting of types, classes and subsystems in analysis, design, and implementation models, will be exported from the component systems via facades.

> An **object component** is a type or class which is reusable in several systems. A **subsystem component** is a set of object components organized as a subsystem.

Subsystems can also be used to represent components such as OCXs and Java applets. When we are engineering an application system we will want to reuse and specialize individual types or classes, as well as complete subsystems.

Figure 6.3 illustrates several of these elements and relationships in the XYB **Account Management** component system which provides components for many of the application systems such as **ATM Cashier**. Components of various types in the different models are imported into the **Transfers** facade as shown by the «imports» dependency. Recall

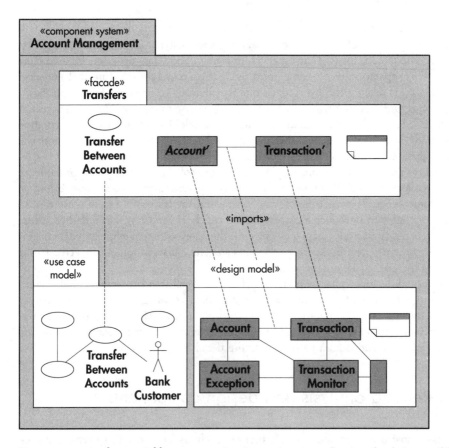

Figure 6.3 An **Account Management** *component system, showing the design model and the use case model. Several components are exported via the* **Transfers** *facade.*

that the ellipses represent use cases, the various kinds of circles present analysis types, and the rectangles represent design classes.

Note that some types might appear as components in several facades, although that is not the case in the above example where only one facade has been shown. Usually, the graphical notion with explicit dashed «imports» dependencies will suffice to show the connections. If we need to be more precise in certain documents or configuration scripts, we would use the UML importing statement to write

Account'=Account Management::Analysis::Account

to explicitly import the **Account** type into the **Transfers** facade.

Components in the facades can then be imported into the models in the systems we are building. Again, this will be shown graphically using the «imports» dependency. The more precise notation to import the component from the **Transfers** facade into an application is:

Account''=Account Management:: Transfers::Account'

Often, unambiguous context will allow us to simply say **Account''=Account'**, or even to use **Account** directly as if it were in the facade.

6.3 Expressing variability in object model components

When several application systems need exactly the same type, class or subsystem, the element can be represented as a concrete object component. Concrete object components can be reused as-is, which means that the component does not have to be specialized before incorporation into a model by a reuser. For example, the design class **Login** could be reused as-is if several application systems, such as **ATM Cashier** or **Payment**, offer precisely the same procedure and interface for **Bank Customer**s to identify themselves to the system. The **Withdrawal** analysis type, in the **Money Management** component system shown in Figure 6.5, is used as-is, but **Cashier Interface**, **Dispenser**, and **Account** are intended to be specialized.

Several types of variability mechanism can be used for specialization. The most frequent reason to define object components that need to be specialized is when these components offer both common and varying responsibilities, as when several application classes behave almost the same but offer variations in how user or system errors are dealt with. Another common occurrence is for different implementation situations to demand different treatment of essentially the same features, such as device drivers and GUI classes. First the object component is assigned those responsibilities that are common to the application types and classes, and then the responsibilities that vary are defined.

Variation points are used to define varying responsibilities in the object component. When such object components are later reused, they have to be specialized at their variation points, which is done by attaching variants at the variation points. A variant provides a specialization of an object component at one or more of its variation points.

Component systems often provide concrete components, abstract components, and associated variants. A system that reuses the component system can then import the components and some of the variants that fit with the abstract components, using either the graphical notation with «imports» or the explicit UML import operator, ::, as shown above.

The variability mechanisms most appropriate to type and class specialization are inheritance, extension, parameters, templates, and generation. Each of these has been discussed in some depth in Chapter 4, and they have distinctly different advantages and characteristics. Some of the structural commonality and variability of type, class and subsystem components can also be expressed in terms of patterns. In this chapter we will focus on architecture and mechanisms, and also on the implications of the mechanisms on design and implementation.

6.4 Tracing use case variability to the object models

As we implement our use cases in terms of analysis types and design classes, we will reuse appropriate analysis and design components. Some of the reused use case components have *variation points* that express some variability in the requirements, and in the way the system built from these use components will be used. These use case components will have been specialized by attaching use case variants at the variation points. Similarly, abstract object components have variation points that support the variability needed to specialize components that are not directly reused as-is. If the use cases express variability, corresponding variability must be offered by the object components since they will be reused to build object models that offer the functionality of the use case model.

Each use case variation point therefore needs to be traceable to one or more variation points in an object model. Likewise, the object models need to offer the same variant features as the use case model, and so each use case variant needs to be traceable to one or several variants in an object model.

As we implement our object models, we will map use case variation points and variants to corresponding analysis, design, and implementation constructs. In a well-constructed component system, traces from the use case components and variants that we reused to build the use case model will often link us to corresponding candidate analysis object components and variants.

The seamless traceability between models and corresponding variability in each model helps achieve maximum reuse. It is of course possible to reuse only a use case component, without having to reuse the corresponding object, implementation, and test components (if any). However, we would then have to design and implement some additional software that we might otherwise have been able to reuse. Likewise, we may choose to have some reusable, specializable analysis, design, or implementation components that might not have corresponding use case components. For example, the implementation may be provided by purchased class libraries, in which case reusers may not get the help of use cases that guide them to object components.

Example

The following description of the **Withdraw Money** use case in the **Money Management** component system is based on that in Chapter 5. We will then show a rewritten version that includes the analysis model.

Withdraw Money Use Case Description: Use case model

First the **Bank Customer** identifies him/herself.

Then the **Bank Customer** chooses how much to withdraw and from which {**Account**}. The system responds with how much can be withdrawn from that {**Account**}, which depends on type of {**Account**}.

Then the system {**Dispenses The Money**} and deducts the amount from the {**Account**}. If the deduction results in an overdraft, it is handled according to {**Account Overdrawn**}.

We will describe how the three explicit variation points, {**Account**}, {**Dispenses The Money**} and {**Account Overdrawn**}, are handled.

Now the use case description is rephrased in terms of interacting analysis types and actors shown in Figure 6.4. Notice that the {**Account**} variation point in the use case has been mapped to an analysis component, **Account**, and that a variation point mentioned several times in the use case model description may appear a different number of times in the analysis model. While not explicitly shown, there will be a trace from variation point {**Account**} in the use case model to the analysis object **Account**.

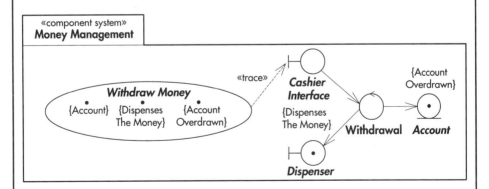

Figure 6.4 *The **Withdraw Money** use case has three variation points that are traceable to the types in the analysis model. The* {**Account**} *variation point maps directly to an abstract type,* **Account**.

Withdraw Money Use Case Description: Analysis model

The **Bank Customer** chooses to withdraw money. The **Cashier Interface** boundary object first asks the **Bank Customer** to identify him/herself.

If the identification is successful, the **Cashier Interface** asks the **Bank Customer** to choose how much to withdraw and from which *Account* entity object. The **Cashier Interface** orders the **Withdrawal** control object to confirm that the **Bank Customer** has the right to withdraw that amount from the *Account*. The **Withdrawal** object validates the request.

If the **Bank Customer** can withdraw that amount, then the **Withdrawal** object asks the *Dispenser* control object to ensure that it {Dispenses The Money} and deducts the amount from the *Account*. If the deduction results in an overdraft, it is handled according to {Account Overdrawn} as defined in the *Account* object.

The {Dispenses The Money} variation point has been allocated to the abstract analysis type *Dispenser*. The variation point {Account}, used to allow for different types of accounts with different restrictions on transactions, has been mapped to the abstract analysis entity type *Account*. The {Account Overdrawn} variation point is also allocated to the *Account* type.

Note that variability can be expressed in different ways in different models. For example, the variability of dealing with account overdrafts can be represented as an extension point in the use case component **Withdraw Money** and also as an extension point in the analysis type *Account*. In the design model, however, the same variability may be represented using an exception **Overdraft** in the class *Account* together with some variant component that handles the overdraft.

When the **Withdraw Money** use case is subsequently reused and specialized, the corresponding object models might be specialized in several ways. For example:

- The account type can be changed by creating a subtype to the *Account* type.
- The type of money to dispense, such as DigiCash or Cash, can be defined by attaching an appropriate variant at the {Dispenses The Money} variation point in the *Dispenser* type.
- The strategy for handling the {Account Overdrawn} variation point can be defined by attaching the appropriate variant to the variation point in the *Account* type.

As illustrated in the example above, the use case description for robustness analysis and the corresponding collaboration diagrams are used for tracing the variation points in the use cases to corresponding variation points in the types.

6.4.1 Reusing compatible use case and object components

Component reusers typically reuse corresponding use case and object components and variants together. By doing this they can more quickly build consistent models of their application system.

Example

As shown in Figure 6.5, the **Money Management** component system exports the use case component *Withdraw Money* and also two use case variants, **Deduct Fee** and **Overdraft Not Allowed**, with different strategies to handle potential account overdrafts. One variant deducts a fee for each overdraft, while the other does not allow overdrafts to take place at all.

The **Money Management** component system also exports several analysis model components corresponding to *Withdraw Money*: *Cashier Interface*, *Account*, *Withdrawal*, and *Dispenser*. Along with the *Account* component there are also two variants with different strategies to handle potential account overdrafts: **Deduct Fee** and **Overdraft Not Allowed**.

In the use case *Withdraw Money* we are using «extends» as the variability mechanism, but in the analysis model we have chosen to express this variability using a kind of «template» generalization. We will also use several other techniques of representing the same variability in the object models to illustrate several possible ways of doing it.

A developer reusing the **Money Management** component system to build the **ATM Cashier** application system might decide to use the fee-deduction strategy,

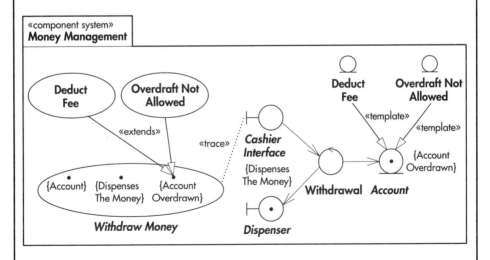

Figure 6.5 *Variation points in, and two variants of, the use case component map to corresponding types, variation points, and variants in the analysis components.*

and hence will reuse the corresponding variants in both the use case model and the object model.

Note that the **Account** type, together with the chosen «template» variant **Deduct Fee** at the {**Account Overdrawn**} variation point, is imported from the **Money Management** component system into the analysis model for the **ATM Cashier** application system.

Sometimes, as the reusers work on their application systems they will need to develop their own variants, both in the use case model and in the object model.

Example

Instead of reusing the fee-deduction strategy, the reusers building a different **ATM Cashier** may decide to devise their own strategy, for example one that allows overdrafts by some family members. This variation would then be represented by its own use case variant and corresponding analysis type and design class (or type) variants. This variant is not provided as a pre-built part of the component system, but is developed as part of the application system.

In general, the mapping of variation points and variants is not necessarily one-to-one between the models. A single variation point in a use case component may for instance correspond to several coordinated variation points in a corresponding object model. Figure 6.6 shows a component system that offers several use case and analysis components with variation points and pre-built variants to attach at these points. The facade exports use case components UC_X and UC_Y with three variation points, and several pre-built variants, v_1, v_2, v_3, and v_4. Related to these use cases are several analysis classes that also have corresponding variation points. Notice how the single variation point VP_1 in the use case UC_X is traceable to two variation points, VP_{1a} in component C_5 and VP_{1b} in component C_3 in the object model. Likewise, the use case variants are traceable to the exported type variants. For example, the variant v_1 at variation point VP_1 is traceable to the variants v_{1a} and v_{1b}.

It is not necessary to use the same variability mechanism to express variability in two different models, but two different models of the same system must express the same variability. That is, if some model component has a variation point, then it must be possible to trace it to corresponding variation points or optional types or classes in the other models of the same system. Likewise, if there is a variant in a model, then it must be possible to trace it to corresponding variants in the other models of the same system. Also, when several variants must be used together in the use case model, the corresponding object model variants should be used in a compatible coordinated manner.

Sometimes a variation point or variant is not relevant to a certain model. For instance, if some variation points address specific implementation issues, they should appear not in the analysis model, but in the design or implementation models.

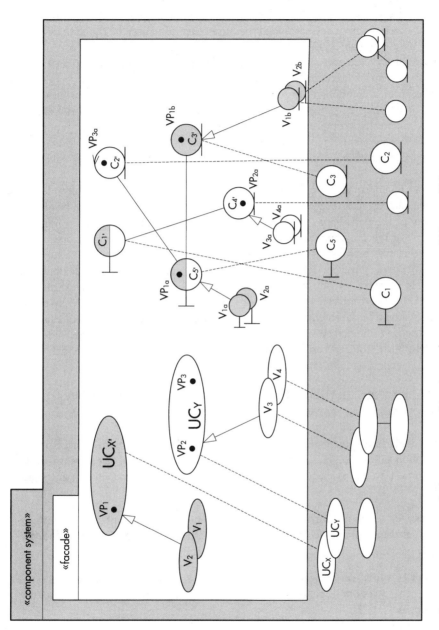

Figure 6.6 A component system which exports variable, abstract use case components **UC**$_X$ and **UC**$_Y$ and corresponding analysis type components **C**$_1$..**C**$_5$. There are three use case variation points, **VP**$_1$..**VP**$_3$, and associated variants, **v**$_1$..**v**$_4$, and also corresponding analysis variation points and variants.

6.4.2 Designing a component system to be reusable

When an application system is constructed by reusing components from a component system, some of the new use cases will be easy to design and implement in terms of the use case and object components provided, because these use cases fit the structure and purpose of the component system. Other use cases may be more difficult to construct through reuse of use case and object components, because they may not map as well to the design and intent of the component system.

The design of a component system thus affects its reusability. The reusability of a component or a group of components depends on how they are connected to other components. Generally, components are not reused individually, but as groups of interconnected components. A component system can be thought of as a framework that provides the underlying "boilerplate" design, key mechanisms, and object collaboration patterns.

One way to improve the reusability of a component system is to carefully identify and document the key variability of the component types and classes. We will be able to identify many of the variability requirements directly from the component use cases. We can also improve the usefulness and accessibility of a component system by organizing the types and classes as subsystems and frameworks.

The component object models should be designed to offer the required flexibility. It is not possible to make an object design flexible "in all directions" without sacrificing something, such as performance or understandability. Instead a trade-off has to be made. Great caution should be taken when designing component systems for flexibility to avoid building "unneeded" flexibility. Only required variability should be designed into the object models. Such required variability can be identified from the use case model.

6.4.3 Mapping use case variability to an appropriate object variability mechanism

Below we provide some guidelines on how to design variable object models based on the kind of variation points the use case model offers. For each type of use case variation point, we suggest an approach to expressing the corresponding variability in an object model.

Varying user or **system interface** Represent each variation point by an abstract boundary type, using inheritance. For example, the **Dispenser** type in the **Withdraw Money** example.

Different entity types referenced Represent each variation point by an entity type. For example, the **Account** type for the {**Account**} variation point in the **Withdraw Money** example.

Alternative and optional functionality Represent each variation point by a corresponding variation point in the object model, perhaps using «inherits», «extends», or «template». For example, the {**Account Overdraft**} variation point in the **Account** type in the **Withdraw Money** example.

Varying constraints and business rules, or **checking that some pre-conditions hold** Allocate the variation point to one control type and implement the variability using the Strategy pattern (Gamma *et al.*, 1994), which represents each specialized computation in terms of a uniform interface and several "algorithm" variants. See also the discussion of design patterns in Section 6.5.1.

Example

Checking a requested invoice payment against the normal payment pattern for a **Bank Customer** is usually done to detect certain kinds of fraud. If this functionality is relevant only to invoice payment, then the variation point should be implemented in the control type **Pay Invoice**. If the functionality is relevant to all use cases that effect deductions from an account, then the variation point should be located in the *Account* entity type instead.

Error-detection Some errors signaled by an object can be captured by an encapsulating wrapper object using an exception handling mechanism. These exceptions can then be dealt with in a customizable fashion using extensions or the Strategy pattern (Gamma *et al.*, 1994).

Example

Some installations may avoid account overdrafts by paying an invoice or a check from a different account. Such an exception can be captured in the *Account* type, by an extension that triggers on the overdraft exception. The extension is then responsible for executing the right procedure.

Performance and scalability differences Design these as parameters or information stored in tables or files. For example, we could set as a parameter the amount of time that should elapse before timing out on trying to connect to another bank.

Limit on number of simultaneous instances should be represented as a parameter or variable in a boundary or control type.

Example

Some installations of the **ATM Cashier** application may need to be able to serve 100 customer requests simultaneously. In other installations 20 may suffice. This can be implemented by having the *Cashier Interface* type keep track of the number of active instances, and compare it against the parameter or variable.

When possible, a good design heuristic is to let one type realize each individual variation point. This makes it easier to understand and easier to introduce variants in the object model since each variant then specializes only one type.

6.5 Reusable analysis components

When several application systems need to reuse similar analysis types, the common characteristics can often be represented by abstract types, using inheritance as the default generalization mechanism. In this case, we structure the types to display variation points as virtual operations. We specialize by "attaching" the variants (subtypes) at the variation points (virtual operations), using the «inherits» generalization. Figure 6.7 illustrates the **Account** type, which is a component that is useful in many banking application systems. It has several public operations, indicated by a UML visibility marker, +. Some of these may be purely virtual, intended to be specialized as described.

Example

The variability in handling account overdrafts can be implemented as a virtual operation that should be replaced in subtypes of **Account**. The idea here is that different ways of handling overdrafts are implemented as different subtypes that override the virtual operation, **Overdraft**, used in the **Withdraw** operation.

As discussed in Chapter 4, there are several other variability mechanisms that can be used with analysis components. Apart from inheritance, extensions and parameters are the most common ways of mapping from corresponding variability in the use case components. We could have defined a different form of **Account** component, using a different variability mechanism. Instead of «inherits», with variation points being virtual operations, we could have used «extends» with extension points as the variation points, or perhaps «parameters» with **{Parameter}** markers in some responsibility or operation

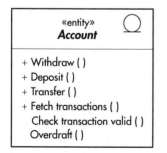

Figure 6.7 *The **Account** component with the operations it supports.*

descriptions. A generator could be also used to create a variety of very specialized account types from a template with several «template» markers.

6.5.1 Architecture and design patterns correspond to abstract use cases

A technique for building good object architectures and designs is the use of architectural and design patterns.

Patterns are defined as standard object-oriented designs for standard problems, described in a standard way (Coad, 1992; Gamma *et al.*, 1994; Coplien and Schmidt, 1995). In UML a pattern is defined as a template collaboration.

These are generally expressed informally, using simple documentation templates, perhaps with some design model diagrams and sample implementations in C++ or other language. The key idea is that software engineers equipped with pattern catalogs and familiar with the use of patterns should be able to design robust systems that meet the requirements more quickly and with a minimum of effort and a maximum of flexibility. Furthermore, they can improve the sharing of ideas among designers by extending their vocabulary and document their own designs in terms of the nomenclature established in the pattern catalogs.

Rather than solving each design problem from scratch, our reuse-oriented robustness analysis and design process includes specific steps in which engineers try to match requirements or design problems to known, reusable design patterns. OOSE offers several built-in fine-grained architecture patterns that are applied as we construct and refine the analysis model. These patterns are expressed in terms of several stereotypes of analysis types, with specific association and generalization relationships to create clusters of types from the patterns. Using additional guidelines, the analysis model is then easily transformed into an initial design model (Jacobson *et al.*, 1994). The patterns include the following:

- Robustness analysis explicitly uses three different analysis stereotypes: «boundary», «control», and «entity» types. These are typically used in a "boundary-control-entity" pattern in which the control type acts as a central manager of interactions with several boundary and entity types. This separates user interface concerns from application functionality concerns and structure and also use-case-specific behavior from entity types, and resembles the well-known Model-View-Controller pattern (Krasner and Pope, 1988). These three stereotypes lead to a more robust object model architecture which simplifies three-tier partitioning.

- Responsibilities that are specific to a specific use case are placed in distinct «control» types, while more general responsibilities common to several use cases are placed in shared «entity» classes. Likewise, «control» classes are used to represent use-case-specific and task-related behavior, typically coordination of other objects, similar to the Mediator pattern (Gamma *et al.*, 1994).

- Object extensions, using the «extends» generalization, can be expressed using the Decorator pattern (Gamma *et al.*, 1994). A large use case with many optional transactions will be broken into a smaller use case, with several use case extensions that may be individually chosen and attached to allow more understandable, behavior.

- An aggregation pattern is represented using the «consists of» association, similar to the Composite pattern (Gamma *et al.*, 1994). A publish-subscribe pattern is represented using a special «subscribes to» association, similar to the Observer pattern (Gamma *et al.*, 1994).

Example

Several of these patterns are illustrated in the **Withdraw Money** example shown in Figure 6.4. This shows how a single use case has been designed according to the "boundary-control-entity" pattern.

This basic "boundary-control-entity" pattern could be represented as shown in Figure 6.8.

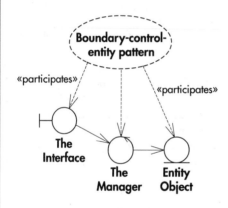

Figure 6.8 *A simple analysis micro-architecture pattern, which corresponds to a typical abstract use case.*

There are many other patterns that can be used when building the object models. These include both published patterns (Gamma *et al.*, 1994; Coplien and Schmidt, 1995; Buschman *et al.*, 1996) and problem- and solution-specific patterns we can develop to deal with common design situations. Some patterns describe small groups of classes or types, essentially micro-architectures or mechanisms, while other patterns describe larger groups or subsystems, essentially frameworks. In addition to architectural (analysis) patterns useful in mapping use cases to analysis models, there are many design patterns that are useful in mapping the analysis model to feasible design models and implementations. Some patterns introduce additional classes or types to help separate concerns, encapsulate mechanisms and decisions, or enable more flexible systems to be built. Other patterns explain the best way to implement a mechanism that is not directly built into the programming language, such as extensions.

Gamma *et al.* (1994) provide a good discussion of design patterns and their relationship to designing classes for more effective reuse. They discuss inheritance versus composition, and inheritance versus delegation. They suggest that inheritance is often over-used, and results in less flexible designs. They favor composition over inheritance, because this is more flexible than use of static inheritance. They stress that delegation can always be used instead of inheritance, and will lead to systems with fewer distinct classes. Many of their patterns deal with introducing patterns of flexible association, rather than more rigid inheritance. They briefly discuss parameterized types, but do not use it much with their patterns. They suggest that several patterns help design more robust systems, by overcoming rigidity introduced by practices such as specifying explicit class names or operation names, rather than having one class handle all accesses to classes that encapsulate fixed algorithms or business rules. Finally, they also discuss how patterns can be applied to increase design reuse in toolkits such as class libraries and frameworks, defined as sets of cooperating classes. Patterns can make interfaces more flexible, are used to document required collaborations, and help decouple classes.

Most sound design patterns can be identified as collaborations that implement an abstract use case. Some of these abstract use cases are domain-specific while others are more generic or solution-specific, such as access to distributed objects, or event-broadcast mechanisms. There are several reasons to represent design patterns as collaborations that implement abstract use cases:

- Each abstract use case has a well-defined purpose – a collaboration (or design pattern) based on an abstract use case will thus serve that purpose in the design.

- Abstract use cases can be seamlessly mapped to a collaboration in which several types ("a society of objects") collaborate in the analysis or design models. Explicitly naming the collaboration and showing which classes and types participate will enhance understandability, traceability, and maintainability.

- The (abstract) use case construct has well-defined semantics, which means that the mechanisms involved in the reuse of an abstract use case are well defined.

- Abstract use cases can be documented much the same way as suggested for design patterns in Gamma *et al.* (1994).

- Sets of abstract use cases can be used as a catalog to pick and choose from when building application systems, in much the same way as pattern catalogs can be used.

Sometimes abstract use cases are too small in size or too oriented towards technology to be directly useful for reuse during requirements capture. Instead they can act as useful documentation of a *collaboration*, a set of interacting analysis types or design classes. This can enhance the reuse of these standard, multi-class mechanisms as the analysis types or design classes are constructed.

Note that it is not sufficient to simply inherit from some or each of the classes and types that participate in the collaboration to create the concrete set of interacting classes and types. In addition, one has arrange for a comparable set of associations and other relations to be set up. It is in this sense that patterns are sometimes referred to as "generative"; applying such a pattern requires the creation of a society of collaborating types and classes, including appropriate linkages. This can be done informally, by following design notes or guidelines accompanying the pattern, or more formally, by using some sort of tool (a generator) that uses a template or script to produce the collaboration mechanically.

Example

In Chapter 5 we discussed the abstract use case **Instrument Transfer** as part of the **Portfolio Management** component system. This use case moves an arbitrary instrument type, such as money or stock, from one **Portfolio** to another. As shown in Figure 6.9, this use case is realized by a collaboration that corresponds to a piece of analysis model, a collaboration, in which the boundary type **Transferer** is responsible for the transaction and creates a **Transaction** entity object to document the transfer. It also moves each of the various **Instrument** objects from one **Portfolio** to another and updates the **Portfolio**. A **Portfolio** is an abstract financial collection, such as accounts, loans, or stock portfolios, each of which is a collection of instruments of an appropriate type. This pattern will be applied separately to each specific combination.

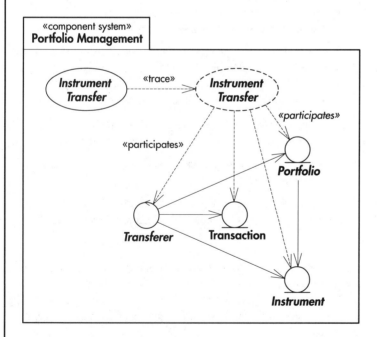

Figure 6.9 *A banking-specific collaboration, related to an abstract use case,* **Instrument Transfer**.

Notice that applying this pattern to some specific type of **Portfolio** and **Instrument**, such as **Account** and **Money**, means more than just specializing **Account** from **Portfolio**, and **Money** from **Instrument**. The associations from a **Transferer** to **Account** and **Money** will need to be established.

6.6 Subsystem components group related types and classes

Components with high coupling are grouped in the same component system. Sometimes it is useful to divide each component system into smaller groups of components. For analysis types and design classes this is done by organizing them into subsystems.

> A **component subsystem** is a subsystem that is exported through facades, and contains types, classes and other elements that are intended to be reused all together.

Some subsystems can be reused *as-is* since they offer a complete prepackaged set of functionality. Such concrete component subsystems are simply imported into the reusing system together with their contained classes and types.

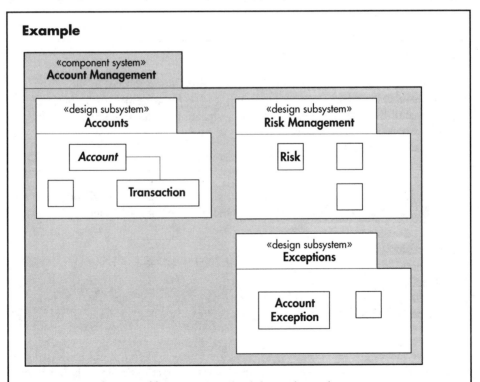

Figure 6.10 **Account Management** *divided into three subsystems.*

The **Account Management** component system described in Chapters 4 and 5 offers a range of types, including **Account**, **Transaction**, **Account Exception**, and **Risk** (Figure 6.10). These types can be organized in three subsystems: subsystem **Accounts** which contains the **Account** and **Transaction** types, subsystem **Exceptions** which contains the **Account Exception** type, and subsystem **Risk Management**, which contains the **Risk** type.

A subsystem normally conceals its internal structure, and only provides a limited number of interface types. A subsystem that is reused *as-is* should only be used through the public interfaces it supplies through its containing component system facade, as we will discuss in Section 6.6.2.

Service packages are a special type of subsystem used to represent the lowest-level grouping of common or optional services and features. Each service package offers a coherent unit of functionality, managed and installed as a unit.

Service packages contain component types, classes and variants that together make up common or optional sets of functionality.

A service package should reside in one configuration item that contains only the service package and its contents.

Example

We previously described a separate subsystem **Risk Management** in the component system **Account Management**. If **Risk Management** is an optional functionality that is reused only in certain installations of an application system, then it is probably better to use a service package instead of a subsystem to model and package **Risk Management**.

Service packages and subsystems can also be used to represent acquired components or components developed using non-object-oriented programming languages.

6.6.1 Frameworks are abstract subsystems

An **abstract subsystem** is a subsystem that contains abstract and concrete types and classes designed for reuse.

An abstract subsystem needs to be specialized in some way before it can be reused. The most common specialization mechanism used with abstract subsystems is inheritance. When one subsystem inherits another, some otherwise internal structure of the inherited subsystem becomes visible to the descendant. This means that the types and classes defined within the descendant subsystem may have relationships, not only to the interfaces explicitly supplied by the ancestor subsystem, but also to other details of types or classes within the ancestor.

Example

The **Accounts** subsystem within the **Account Management** component system contains **Account** and **Transaction** (Figure 6.11). This subsystem inherits from the **Portfolios** subsystem in the component system **Portfolio Management**. This allows the **Account** type to specialize the **Portfolio** type defined in the **Portfolios** subsystem.

To keep the diagrams simple, we have not shown the facades in **Portfolio Management**, nor the importing of **Portfolio** and **Transaction** into that facade, nor the other parts of **Account Management**.

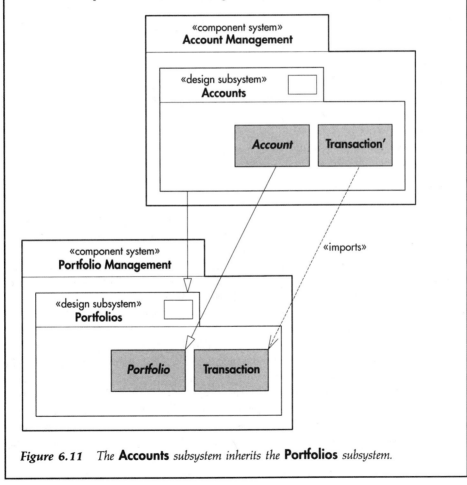

Figure 6.11 *The **Accounts** subsystem inherits the **Portfolios** subsystem.*

> An abstract implementation model subsystem is essentially a traditional
> subclassing **framework** (Johnson and Foote, 1988).

The code for the abstract types and classes within the framework defines virtual operations that will be redefined concretely in the subsystems. The corresponding analysis and design model subsystems act as models of the implementation framework. A well-designed abstract subsystem has several distinct patterns of collaboration between its types and classes. The design model, some use cases, and some collaborations can help define and document these collaborations. The abstract analysis model shows its architecture, and the abstract use case model shows the end-to-end services provided to reusers of the framework (and of applications built with the framework). Some of the use cases are realized by collaborations that help identify and define the object interactions.

The abstract design model subsystem corresponding to a framework is effectively a set of collaborations or patterns. Each abstract (sub)system should be traceable to a set of abstract use cases. This will simplify its reuse and ensure the integrity of the intended class collaborations.

Example

There are many different types of framework. These range from low-level application frameworks, such as MVC (Model-View Controller) and HotDraw, to sets of closely related frameworks such as Taligent's CommonPoint environment (Taligent, 1995), to high-level business-area specific frameworks, such as ET++ for finance, Quartz for banking, or Andersen's Utility/1 framework for power companies.

Ideally, a good framework is designed so that specializations can be constructed from its abstract types and classes with ease. Each specialization is added as a subclass or subtype of some abstract class or type in the framework. The ideal is when a reuser can add specializations to an abstract type or class without knowing the details of how the abstract subsystem works, or having to worry too much about interactions with other subclasses or subtypes added to specialize other abstract classes or types in the subsystem.

While a component system can define and export several independent abstract subsystems (frameworks), it is sometimes practical to think of a whole component system itself as a single framework. This is particularly relevant when the component system consists of several highly interconnected abstract subsystems which cannot be reused individually, but instead are reused and specialized together.

The Taligent CommonPoint system was designed as a family of many compatible frameworks, each intended to work together in groups. Since acquiring Taligent, IBM has been unbundling the CommonPoint system to produce sets of class libraries and smaller frameworks that can be used with VisualAge. From an RSEB perspective, each such group of closely related frameworks would be packaged into a single component system, with several facades providing independent access to appropriate parts of each framework.

6.6.2 Interfaces constrain interactions between systems

We use an interface type to specify more precisely how types and subsystems in a component system should be reused.

> An **interface** is the use of a type to describe the externally visible behavior of a class, object, or other entity, such as a subsystem. In the case of a class or object, the interface includes the signatures of the operations.

Each client of a subsystem conforms to the interface supplied by the subsystem, as shown in Figure 6.12.

Each interface is implemented by a type or class in the supplying subsystem. UML defines a stereotype «interface» as the legal pattern of interaction between two types or classes. An interface defines two roles, **client** and **supplier**. The relationship between the interacting subsystems is shown as a «conforms» (dashed line) dependency on the interface, rather than a direct relationship between the types or classes. This means that we can replace the client or the supplier by any other type, class or subsystem that conforms to the same interface.

Interfaces are commonly developed during design and implementation, but can also be used with the use case and analysis models. At its simplest, an interface consists only of a design type or implementation class definition, containing just the public operation prototypes and type definitions that define the interface. UML interfaces focus primarily on specifying compatible operation signatures. The operation prototypes could be defined in OMG CORBA IDL, for example, or implemented as a C++ header file.

More generally, the interface will also contain some constraints, such as pre- and post-conditions, or a specification of the ordering of the operations to ensure a consistent interaction. A state machine description can quite precisely specify how several operations should work together to supply the interface.

As we discussed in Section 6.5.1, we can employ use cases and actors to provide a high-level model of the requirements and services offered by a set of types or classes participating in a collaboration. We also can use a collaboration to describe how subsystems interact across an interface. We can associate an (abstract) use case with the collaboration and the actors with the clients of the services provided by the classes. This collaboration, or

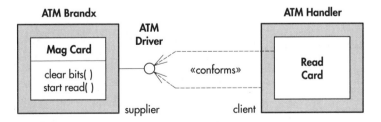

Figure 6.12 An interface, **ATM Driver**, between a **Read Card** class in the **ATM Handler** subsystem and hardware-specific firmware that controls magnetic card reading in a particular brand ("brandx") of ATM hardware.

pattern, connects the various types or classes that participate in the collaboration. The use case description can be provided informally, as a list of transactions, as a sequence diagram, or as a state machine. This description can provide a precise, high-level description of the interactions with the interface and its implementing classes. Because of the similarity of use cases and collaborations with patterns, the kind of interaction expected from an interface can often be described concisely as a known, documented pattern. This is also relevant to understanding and using frameworks (described above) effectively.

One can also think of the interface as specifying a contract that the implementing classes should supply. The clients of the interface should be consistent with this contract. In Figure 6.12, **ATM Driver** defines the interfaces that any ATM should provide, such as operations to read a magnetic card. Each ATM will implement these differently, and may have other commands. The **ATM Driver** interface allows the **ATM Handler** software, and the class **Read Card**, to be written without depending on these details.

The idea of using interfaces is to achieve implementation independence and pluggability; that is, the client should not be dependent on the implementation of the server. It should depend only on the interface. One way to ensure this is to include only the interfaces in the facade, and not to export any of the types, classes and subsystems from the component systems. Some types, classes and subsystems will need multiple interfaces, and these could be placed together in one facade, or spread across multiple facades, depending on how they will be used. For example, a system might need to support interaction with both CORBA and OLE/COM.

Both CORBA and OLE/COM use different kinds of Interface Definition Language (IDL) that can be used to define interfaces to components and component systems. CORBA IDL is a language-neutral interface description capability that supports multiple inheritance, C++-like types, and operation definitions. OLE/COM IDL is one of several interface definition or type definition languages used with OLE and COM. OLE/COM does not support multiple inheritance, but that is not critical; the important thing is that both CORBA and OLE/COM support component-based development through the explicit interface specifications.

Example

Consider the interface to an **Account** type, which has attributes of type **Money**, **Number**, **String** and an association with a **Bank Customer**, the owner.

In IDL these interfaces might be expressed in a file called Account.idl as something like:

```
module AccountManagment
{
#include "financialtypes.idl"
interface Account : Portfolio
    {
        exception Overdraft{Money amount}
        Account Create(
            in Customer owner, in String title,
            in IdNumber account_id);
```

```
    void Deposit (in Money amount, in String reason);
    void Withdraw (in Money amount, in String reason)
      raises (Overdraft);

  . . .
  };
};
```

The file "financialtypes.idl" would contain common definitions such as:

```
typedef number Money;
typedef number IdNumber;
typedef . . .
```

Example

A different example of an abstract subsystem as a kind of framework is an instrument or XYB banking communication network system that takes different kinds of lower-level instrument or network drivers. Each driver has an idiosyncratic behavior for the instrument or network it controls, but each has a common interface and standard defined protocol for use by the higher-level system of which it is part. Here, we would define the standard driver interface as an interface in a driver management subsystem. Each driver plugged in would have to conform to this interface.

In the XYB banking communication network, there may be several different banking interchange protocols for use when communicating with other banks. Each protocol could be implemented as yet another plug-in class with an interface that conforms to a protocol interface, while each specific network driver component will conform to the standard network interface.

6.7 Reusable design and implementation components

Once we have developed an analysis model by mapping from the use case model and by reusing analysis components, we move to the construction of the design and implementation models. Since the design model is a "blueprint" of the code, the mapping from the design model to the implementation should be straightforward and seamless.

The OOSE book (Jacobson *et al.*, 1992) and several other books (Booch, 1994; Goldberg and Rubin, 1995; Meyer, 1994; Lorenz, 1993) include a variety of discussions on component library design, and techniques for structuring class libraries. These books also give advice on effective use and control of inheritance, explicit separation of interface, body, and environment implementation, exception handling, and parameter passing. There is some discussion of reuse-oriented coding standards, naming conventions, program and library structuring guidelines, and documentation guidelines. Other guidelines include the appropriate size for components and modules, and heuristic measures of cohesion and coupling.

We will focus our discussion on variability mechanisms, and how these are expressed and transformed from model to model. In particular, we are interested in how various programming languages support the variability needs, and how their constraints reflect back to the design model.

6.7.1 Implications of programming language features

In general, various programming languages offer some features that match our recommended approach. At the same time, some of them lack features desirable for effective use of our approach. Smalltalk, for example, does not support private method definition. Nor does it support type templates, but that is somewhat offset by the fact that templates are not so important when there is no compile-time type-checking. Some even have features that we recommend you do not use. In this section, we briefly cover these features for only a few languages.

The OOSE book (Jacobson *et al.*, 1992) provides more details on how to use C++ and Smalltalk effectively to implement classes and object relationships. Other popular programming, scripting, and integration languages, such as Java and Visual Basic, have similar strengths and limitations.

C++ The OOSE book also gives some guidelines on how to map operations, attributes, and relationships onto C++ members such as class data, functions, objects, and pointers. Additional classes might be introduced to implement complex types for attributes. C++ access control keywords such as **public, protected, private,** and **virtual** aid in the encapsulation.

C++ provides separate header (.h) files, and private, protected, and public methods that support encapsulation, separate compilation, and the facade. C++ has inheritance and templates that support variability. C++ does not directly support extensions, so we need some other mechanism or convention to associate additional pieces of functionality with classes. Techniques we discuss below include the use of delegation of an operation to other classes, the interception of an operation using a wrapper class, and the C++ exception handling mechanism (try-recover).

Java Java is a full-fledged object-oriented language that supports encapsulation, classes, messaging, and single inheritance, but does not support multiple inheritance of classes. It supports superclass method overriding, explicit access to superclass methods via the **super.method**. Java uses the keyword **extends** for class inheritance. It provides a **package** construct with an **import** statement, which allows the grouping of related classes that have convenient access to each other. **Public, protected,** and **private** declarations provide visibility and access control between classes and packages. Java also provides an **interface**

construct, which allows classes, and their descendants, to define and **implement** several interfaces as a set of methods. An interface can then be used by other classes as a form of contract. While Java only allows single inheritance for classes, a single class can implement multiple interfaces, and an interface can be defined as an extension of multiple other interfaces.

Visual Basic   Visual Basic 4.0 is a component-based language that does support object-based encapsulation, classes, methods, and attributes, as well as object messaging. However, it does not currently support inheritance. This means that inheritance in the analysis model will need to be mapped to a combination of communicates or aggregation associations, to use message delegation. Visual Basic makes it easy to write and use OLE automation servers, which behave as subsystems, service packages, or objects with public interfaces. Visual Basic provides encapsulation and visibility control mechanisms, expressed by keywords such as **public**, **private**, and **global**. These can be used to support the implementation of interfaces and facades. VB 5.0 provides support for defining ActiveX components, user defined events and more object-oriented features.

Chapter 7 provides some more detail on Visual Basic and reusable ActiveX components based on Microsoft's OLE/COM component model and interface definition mechanism.

6.7.2 Using inheritance

Inheritance is often used to define abstract classes that define a public interface. Subclasses can then specialize the class and supply the correct implementations of the operations defined in the public interface. In C++ virtual functions are used to declare functions that should be specialized in the subclasses. When a function is declared virtual, it need not have an implementation associated with it. In general, we prefer that functions be used as pure virtual, and we do not recommend overriding of default behavior.

Example

Consider a standard **Portfolio** and one of its specializations, **Account**. Further specializations of **Account** might include **Joint Account**, **Child Account**, or **Savings Account**. Each type of account has different rules as to who may sign, or when interest is calculated, or how many checks might be written. Further specializations of **Portfolio** might include **Stock Portfolio**, **Mortgage Portfolio**, or **Loan Portfolio**.

```
class Portfolio
{public:
      Portfolio() {}                          // Constructor
      Portfolio(IdNumber portfolio_id, Instrument balance, BankCustomer person);
                                    // Creates an initialized Portfolio
      virtual void deposit(Instrument amount);
      virtual void withdraw(Instrument amount);
```

```
      /* other public members */
   protected:
      IdNumber portfolio_no;
      /* other protected members */
   private:
      Instrument current_balance;
}

// Money is a simple form of instrument
// Account is a simple form of portfolio
class Account: public Portfolio
{public:
      Account() {}
      Account(IdNumber account_id,
         Money balance,
         BankCustomer person,
         String title);                        // Initializes account title
      void deposit (Money amount, String reason);
      void withdraw(Money amount, String reason);
   protected:
      String account_title;
   ...}
void deposit (Money amount)                   // Overrides the Portfolio definition
   {current_balance = current_balance + amount;
}
```

In Smalltalk virtual operation specialization can be achieved by defining a method in the abstract class with the implementation body **self subclassResponsibility**.

6.7.3 Using extensions

Recall that extensions are small use cases, types or classes that extend or modify the behavior of use cases, types or classes to which they are attached. Languages such as C++ do not provide direct support for explicit extension points and attached extensions. This means that extensions used to define variants in the use case model and analysis types need to be converted to some other mechanism in the design and implementation classes. There are several approaches, depending on exactly how the extension behavior interacts with the existing behavior.

If only a single extension is used at any one time, equivalent to selecting a single variant for an explicit extension point, **Extension1**, this is best implemented as calls on some number of virtual C++ functions, **Extension1a()**, ... **Extension1z()**, in an abstract base class. The abstract base class represents the unextended class. Each virtual C++ function represents a piece of the extension. Each function can then be specialized in an extending class to perform the right extending behavior. This abstract class can then be inherited by a concrete class, the "extending class," which can define the corresponding set of concrete functions for the extension. When a system is configured and installed, the proper extended class specialization and associated extension class need to be included in the installation. This is particularly simple when only one virtual function, **Extension1a()**, is needed.

These techniques are similar to the Strategy pattern (Gamma *et al.*, 1994). Strategy defines an abstract class that provides a standard interface to a set of alternative implementations, one for each extension. Each implements the same set of standard operations. The unextended class then has code that makes calls on these operations using a reference or a list of references to instances of these extension classes and makes calls on the extension operations.

If multiple extensions are to be associated with the extension point, the same idea is applied, but now the extended class must simultaneously be augmented with several extensions, each implementing one extension as a set of extension functions. There are several techniques that can be used to achieve this, such as in-lining of macros or template instantiations, or letting the extended class keep track of a dynamic list of extensions to invoke when the extension point is reached.

At the appropriate points in the extended class body, each of the currently attached extensions has its corresponding extension function executed. When a system is configured and installed, the various extension classes need to be included in the installation, and the extensions list must be dynamically created by "attaching" the extension classes to the instance of the extended class.

Another way of implementing an extension is to let the extension point raise an exception that is caught by the proper object, which then calls the objects that implement the extensions. This is more appropriate for implicit extension points.

Example

This example shows the IDL definition of an interface to an **Account** class. The **Withdraw** operation may raise the exception **Overdraft**, which would be trapped to handle some attached **Overdraft** extension.

```
interface Account: Portfolio
{
    exception Overdraft{Money amount}
    Account Create_Account(
        in IdNumber account_id,
        in Money balance,
        in BankCustomer owner,
        in String title
        );
    void Deposit(in Money amount, in String reason);
    void Withdraw(in Money, in String reason)
        raises (Overdraft);
}
```

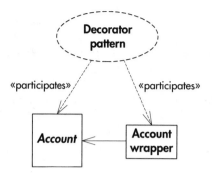

Figure 6.13 *The Decorator pattern used to implement strategies for **Account** overdrafts.*

Yet another way to implement extensions is to use the Decorator (or Wrapper) pattern (Gamma *et al.*, 1994). A decorator is used to attach additional responsibilities to an object. This can be done statically, or could be invoked dynamically to attach or detach responsibilities, even though this may be more than is needed with extensions. A Decorator class, shown in Figure 6.13, is used to wrap an original class, **Account**, with an extended class. The extended class has the same interface as the original and has a reference to the original class. A message sent to the extending class can execute new behavior before and/or after invoking the corresponding behavior in the referenced original class. A chain of extensions can be easily built up dynamically, using several wrappers. This works well, especially for implicit extensions, if the extending class can simply wrap existing operations in the original class. Since the decorator is wrapped around the extended object, extension code must be able to execute outside of the extended object, letting the unextended operation run completely.

Example

The Decorator pattern may be used in conjunction with the raising of an exception as illustrated in the previous example. In our simple implementation shown in Figure 6.13, the Decorator pattern defines **Account Wrapper** with the same interface as **Account**. An instance of the wrapper wraps each instance of the **Account** object, catches the **Overdraft** exception, and performs the operations provided by one or more attached extensions such as **Deduct Fee**.

6.7.4 Using parameterization, templates, and generation

To allow for variability, some components need to be parameterized, perhaps in the form of a template, rather than relying on mechanisms such as inheritance or extensions. The parameterized components are then preprocessed by a generator to construct the desired component.

Some programming languages have built-in mechanisms for parameterization that can be used to implement simple parameterized classes, for example generics in Ada and macros and templates in C++.

Example

As a simple example, the Account identity has different formats in different countries. In the USA WFB-6391-513401 may be a legitimate account number, while 2340-667987-4 may be viable in Sweden. This is represented as an attribute type with a parameterized definition:

Account

+ Identity: {Identity Type};   //Account identity implemented as parameter //

More powerful generation is often appropriate when several different parameters need to be bound to consistent values. This is the case when parameters are constrained to match with each other in some non-obvious way, or when several elemental components are combined together into complete components. An example here is a complex template, or a problem-oriented configuration language or 4GL. Generation becomes particularly important when the reusers are not sophisticated developers, and when many different variations are to be created.

Generation can sometimes be accomplished by a mechanism built into the language, by a simple external preprocessor, or usually by a more powerful generator language tool. A typical way is to write a script using the generation (modeling) language. The script can then be processed by the generator to produce the desired specialized components. Generators and preprocessors can be used both for implementation models and for design and analysis models.

Example

Microsoft Wizards are widely used in Visual Basic and Visual C++, and other Microsoft tools. They are simple generators that produce VB or C++ code skeletons and build files from simple dialogs. The dialogs present a series of panels that help the reuser to input values for a set of parameters. The dialog offers advice in setting the parameters and usually offers default choices. These parameters are then input to a simple preprocessor that selects an appropriate code or document template, and replaces embedded parameters with the chosen values to produce a specialized code or document file. Wizards are also used to create specialized forms and reports in Microsoft Access, and formatted documents in Microsoft Word.

The semantic generator used in Netron (Bassett, 1991, 1995, 1996), discussed in Chapter 4, uses a powerful generator to convert templates (called frames) with embedded parameters and editing commands that reference and modify other frames into specific implementations for COBOL and associated documents. The reuser typically edits a "top frame," setting parameters and making selections. The generator then assembles, selects and customizes other frames, then generates the output code, usually COBOL, configuration scripts, and documents.

Batory's P++ and Predator system generators (Batory, 1993, 1994), implement specific code components by selecting and combining a set of generic database and data structure code components, each implementing some orthogonal feature. For example, many data structure functions can be composed from an algorithm (such as sort, reverse, or search), a container (such as list, array, tree) and some datatype (such as integer, float, string). The preprocessor can, for example, generate an efficient component to sort trees of elements consisting of lists of complex numbers.

C++ provides a preprocessor that implements several mechanisms that can be used to support variability. These include simple parameter substitution, more complex conditional compilation and macros, and type templates. The C++ preprocessor provides the **#define** statement to define symbolic constants and macros that can be used to produce customizable components. The **#if** statement can be used to conditionally compile alternative sections of code, perhaps selected by the value of a symbolic constant, or to match alternative target systems.

Example

For example, we may parameterize the **Cash Dispenser** class containing the size of money bills it can process. We want these to be parameters, since this will compile into tight firmware for the ATM.

```
#define Money_height 66            //Defines a constant in millimeters
#define Money_length 155           //Defines a constant in millimeters
#define Money_type "US DOLLAR"     //Defines the currency name
#define Money_denomination 20      //Defines a constant in US dollars
#define How_many_bills(x) (x/Money_denomination))   //Defines an in-line macro
#if Money_type="US DOLLAR" ...
   #else ...
   #endif                          //supports conditional compilation
```

C++ also provides a type template mechanism that can be used to define families of related components, similar to the Batory datatype-composition mechanism described above. These C++ type templates have been used to build the C++ Standard Template Library components as a set of composable sub-components.

Example

The following C++ template defines a generic routine to manipulate lists of transactions of various types. It uses the generic List template from the C++ Standard Template library.

```
#include <list.h>      // Standard List Template, List<>
template <class T>
{
private:    T *vector;
            int current_number_of_elements;
public:     void Add (T item);
            T GetFirst();
            .
            .
};
                // This can now be specialized into a list of Transactions as follows:

List<Transaction_Type> Transaction_List;
```

Languages with strong type-checking, like C++ and Ada, may have to use preprocessor parameterization or type templates to handle type-parameterization. Smalltalk does not enforce any "compile-time" type-checking. Since it deals with typing at run time, much of the parameterization required or available in other languages is not necessary in Smalltalk. On the other hand, additional Smalltalk code may be required in order to do the type-checking at run time. Visual Basic supports a mixture; depending on compiler options, some simple types are checked at compile time, while some object types are only checked at run time.

6.8 Packaging and documenting object components and variants

The types, classes, interfaces, attribute types, objects, and subsystem components and variants need to be packaged and documented to support component-based development.

One aspect of this is that independent components and variants need to be organized in independent configuration items. The reusers can look for a desired piece of functionality, and find the corresponding components and variants that offer the functionality bundled in a configuration item.

Example

The following set of «configuration item»s (CI) are suggested for the **_Withdraw Money_** use case in the **Money Management** component system and the variants **Withdraw Cash** and **Withdraw Digicash** for the **ATM Cashier** and **Digicash Cashier** application systems:

Withdraw Money Types CI:

A single configuration item containing the object components for **Withdraw Money**:

- *Cashier Interface*
- *Account*
- *Withdrawal*
- *Dispenser*

Withdraw Cash Types Variant CI₁:

A single «configuration item» for the ATM interface variant of the {**Dispenses The Money**} variation point, corresponding to the use case variant **Withdraw Cash**. This configuration item consists of the type:

- *Cash Dispenser*

Withdraw Digicash Types Variant CI₂:

A single «configuration item» for the home-banking interface of the {**Dispenses The Money**} variation point, corresponding to the use case variant **Withdraw Digicash**. This configuration item consists of the type:

- *Digicash Dispenser*

We illustrate this with a portion of the component and application systems involved (Figure 6.14). Note that **Money Management** is used to develop either **ATM Cashier** or **Digicash Cashier**.

The **Digicash Cashier** application system, for example, defines a new configuration item, imports one from the component system **Money Management** and combines them in the following configuration:

Withdraw Digicash Types Configuration_A:

A «configuration» containing all the configuration items that make up a complete configured **Withdraw Digicash**:

- **Withdraw Money Types CI**
- **Withdraw Digicash Types Variant CI₂** ...

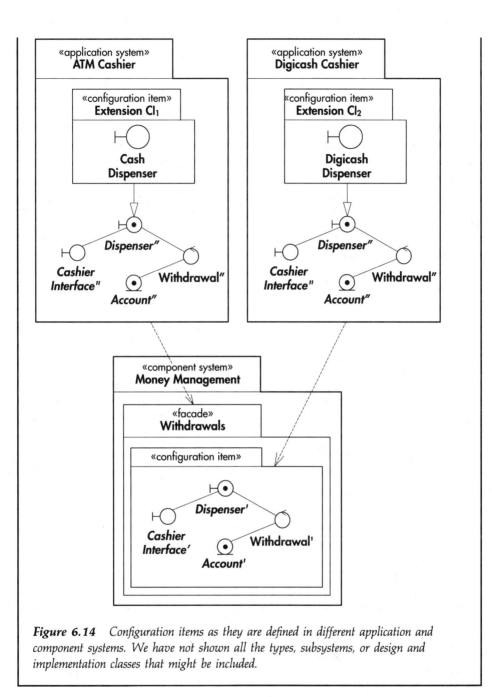

Figure 6.14 *Configuration items as they are defined in different application and component systems. We have not shown all the types, subsystems, or design and implementation classes that might be included.*

In simple C++ systems, we will use the file system to manage connections between several files that separate class headers (.h) files and class implementations (.cpp) files. A combination of configuration items and file-based configuration management systems are used to manage alternative variants. The UNIX *Make* tool is used to manage dependencies between these files. The C++ concept of *file scope* for variable and function names is used to encapsulate the name space across several files.

An important guideline is that the interfaces to the C++ part of each facade should be in its own .h file(s). This allows each set of operation interfaces to be managed and evolve separately. If the C++ interfaces corresponding to one facade changes, C++ files that only #include .h files from other facades do not need to be changed or recompiled. Each .h file can have subsidiary files to support some simple forms of variability, such as pluggable alternatives, perhaps using C++ parameterization or templates to handle renaming.

Component and facade documentation guidelines are aimed at making it easier for reusers to understand and choose between alternative components, reduce the cost of maintenance, and reduce unnecessary dependence between components. It may also be necessary to express how different variants depend on each other, that is, which require each other and which prohibit each other. Several books (Jacobson *et al.*, 1992; Booch, 1995; Goldberg and Rubin, 1995; Meyer, 1994; Lorenz, 1993) include documentation guidelines.

6.9 Summary

An object model shows the design of a system at some level of abstraction, and consists of types or classes organized into subsystems. The analysis model is used to build an object architecture that is reusable and robust when faced with new and changed requirements. The design model is derived from the analysis model and serves as a blueprint of the implementation.

Component systems often provide concrete components, abstract components, and associated optional variants. A system that reuses the component system can then import the components and some of the variants that fit with the abstract components.

Each use case variation point is traceable to one or several variation points in an object model. Each use case variant needs to be traceable to one or several variants in an object model. When possible, a good design heuristic is to let one type realize each individual variation point. This avoids the complexity of managing changes in a single variation point across several correlated types.

Interfaces at the design model level consist of a set of type definitions, containing just the public operation prototypes and type definitions that define the interfaces. State diagrams are used to model the ordering and interaction between the interface operations. Interfaces are used to better manage dependencies between classes, types and subsystems.

A subsystem that contains abstract types or classes is an abstract subsystem. A framework is in fact an abstract (implementation model) subsystem. The design model subsystem corresponding to the framework will use collaborations and patterns to describe the collaborations between instances of the classes or types.

Most sound design patterns can be identified from corresponding abstract use cases, which are then realized by a collaboration in which several types or classes participate to perform the use case.

The variability mechanisms most appropriate to types and class specialization are inheritance, extension, templates, parameterization, and generation.

6.10 Additional reading

The OOSE book (Jacobson *et al.*, 1992) provides extensive discussion of analysis and design models, and the use and mapping of various relationships, as well as some programming language issues and guidelines.

The Patterns book by Erich Gamma, Richard Helm, Ralph Johnson, and John Vlissides, *Design Patterns — Elements of Reusable Object-Oriented Software*, Addison-Wesley, 1994, describes some standard design patterns, and how these should be implemented. They also discuss a documentation style for patterns that is very similar to a use case description.

Paul Bassett, in *Framing Software Reuse: Lessons from the Real World*, Prentice-Hall, 1996, describes the Netron frame model in detail, and illustrates how frames combine a form of inheritance and generation. The book also discusses many other useful aspects of reuse technology and management.

7

LAYERED ARCHITECTURE

7.1 Architecture defines system structure, interfaces, and interaction patterns

Modern large-scale information systems are very complex, are impacted by constantly changing standards, and combine distributed computing, many technologies, and many systems and platforms. This complexity is intrinsic and cannot totally be avoided, but can be managed with a good software architecture. This chapter integrates the techniques discussed in the previous chapters into a comprehensive approach to software architecture for large-scale systems.

Software architecture is one of those illusive terms that we software engineers believe we understand but find difficult to define well. The concept behind the term is important. It affects how software is designed and structured and therefore also substantially influences the characteristics of the software systems. Up to now we have managed to use a simplified definition and approach to architecture. In this chapter, we provide more details and add new modeling techniques to help deal more systematically with the complexity *of large systems*. The following is a more careful definition of software architecture used as a starting point as we journey in this chapter towards a deeper understanding and more precise representation of layered architectures:

In an object-oriented system where implementation classes are organized in subsystems, the **software architecture** defines the static organization of software into subsystems interconnected through interfaces and defines at a significant level how nodes executing those software subsystems interact with each other.

There are several other definitions of software architecture, such as that of Garlan and Shaw (Garlan and Shaw, 1993; Shaw and Garlan, 1996), which is closest to ours in its focus on the concept of architectural style. They state that "the architecture of a software system defines that system in terms of computational components and connections among those components." While related, this and other definitions of architecture would require further explanation to be useful in terms of the modeling approach discussed so far.

7.2 A good architecture is crucial to maintain system integrity

Choosing the right architecture is one of the most important decisions a software engineering business can make. Software architecture is important in order to maintain the integrity of systems so that development and maintenance do not result in a patchwork of uncoordinated fixes. A well-articulated software architecture is also key to managing the complexity of software systems, allowing large organizations to work on parts in parallel.

With the right architecture in place, software engineers can design and implement the system more effectively and more predictably. Software engineers can build on well-defined interfaces with exactly the functionality and performance that they need. A good architecture acts as a guide to which components should be reused during the development of application systems. Without a clear definition of architecture and interfaces, components will seldom work well together and the software engineers will find it difficult and expensive to reuse components.

A good software architecture allows the component and application systems to evolve gracefully over time. The architecture must be defined and described in such a way that it can be easily modified and improved as new and changed requirements are implemented. In order to build an architecture that is change tolerant it is important to decide which parts of the software are likely to change, and which not. Structures that are most stable should have the most influence on the organization of the software into subsystems and interfaces. But at the same time, the architecture must enable anticipated change. The subsystem structure and interfaces must be designed for change. This is similar to building a house. Some parts (foundation and outer walls) change infrequently. Other parts (inner walls and partitions) change more often, while yet other parts (furniture in each room) change fairly often. It would be pointless to build houses where the outer walls can be replaced easily, and madness to glue or weld the furniture of each room to the floor.

The larger the organization, the greater the communication overhead will be as the software engineers try to coordinate their efforts, particularly if the organization is geographically distributed. A well-defined architecture, with explicit interfaces, can reduce this communication overhead since the architecture will provide the developers most of what they need in order to understand what others are doing.

Defining a software architecture is more difficult than developing an application system or component system. It is also one of the most important things to be done if the application domain or the technology used is new to the organization. But it then becomes even more difficult, since the architects have no prior experience, and even more important, since the developers who will build application and component systems also have less experience, and will need more guidance.

What type of architectures can be used to meet all these needs? There is no simple answer to that question. In our experience, using a layered architecture and applying it correctly is the right starting point.

7.3 A layered architecture organizes software according to generality

Application systems can be built from component systems. Component systems may in turn be built from other component systems in lower layers. We can see all of this as a kind of *layered system* composed of application systems at the top and component systems underneath, shown in Figure 7.1. A layered system is defined by a layered architecture.

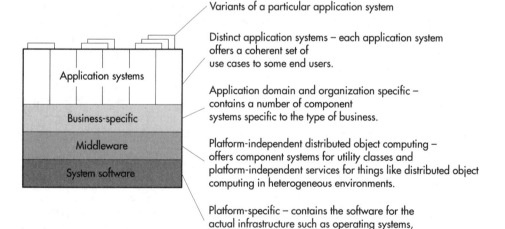

Figure 7.1 *A typical layered system consisting of both application and component systems.*

We define a **layered architecture** to be a software architecture that organizes software in layers, where each layer is built on top of another more general layer. A **layer** can loosely be defined as a set of (sub)systems with the same degree of generality. Upper layers are more application specific, lower are more general.

By software organization, we mean that the layering addresses how static constructs such as modules depend on each other at compile and link time. We do not mean the run-time "organization," or dynamic structure of the software. The dynamic characteristics of a system are defined by use cases, collaborations, process and node models. These dynamic models are used together with the layered static organization of the software.

Each distinct system is developed by a separate software team, following a specific software development process. Remember that component systems are created as common components to be reused only by developers, and are generally not used by end users.

The number of layers, their names and their contents are not fixed, but vary from situation to situation. The following is a typical layered architecture with four layers:

1   The topmost layer – *application system layer* – should contain one application system for each software system that offers a coherent set of use cases to some end users. Some application systems come in different versions, or variants, as described in Chapter 4. Application systems may interoperate directly with each other through their interfaces, and may also interoperate indirectly through some service or object provided by a system in one of the lower layers, such as an Object Request Broker (ORB), operating system, or business-specific service.

2   The next layer – *business-specific layer* – contains a number of component systems specific to the type of business. Such component systems offer use case and object components to the application engineers to build application systems and are often reusable by the application systems developed by a particular reuse business. The business-specific components are built on the middleware layer.

3   The *middleware layer* offers component systems providing utility classes and platform-independent services such as distributed object computing in heterogeneous environments. This layer often contains component systems for GUI builders, interfaces to database management systems, platform-independent operating system services, ORBs, and OLE-components such as spreadsheets and diagram editors. These components are used by application engineers and other component engineers so that they can focus on building business-specific component and application systems. Many of the CommonPoint frameworks by Taligent (Potel and Cotter, 1995; Taligent, 1994), are examples of component systems that probably would belong to this layer. One can also argue that OLE and CORBA Common Services might be generic middleware while ORB and COM are transport services that are at or just above the system software layer.

4   The bottom layer — *system software layer* — contains the software for the computing and networking infrastructure, such as operating systems, interfaces to specific hardware, and so on. However, it is increasingly the case that specific operating systems provide mechanisms for platform-independent access to services offered by system software. The distinction between the middleware and the system software layers is therefore somewhat arbitrary.

Example

In Figure 7.2, we show the XYB layered architecture. Different application systems such as **ATM Cashier** and **Payment** can be built from the business-specific component systems **Money Management**, **Account Management**, **Bank Customer Management**, and **Invoice Management**. Several of the application systems developed by XYBsoft, such as **Payment** and **Invoicing**, may need to execute on different machines and hence need to interoperate using middleware component systems such as **Java** and **HP ORB Plus**. At the lowest level, XYBsoft will build on commercial system software such as **NT Workstation** (on the desktop of managers and clerks) and **TCP/IP**.

Application systems such as **Payment** and **Invoicing** help a **Bank Customer** perform the XYB business processes such as **Sales From Order To Delivery**.

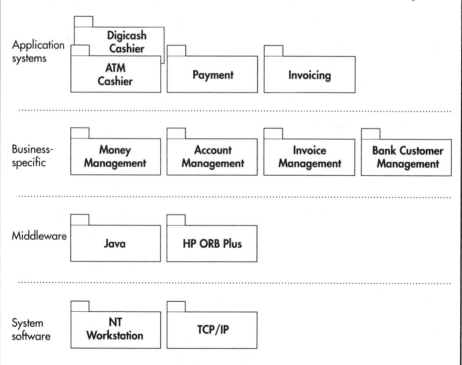

Figure 7.2   *An illustration of the XYB layered system.* **ATM Cashier** *and* **Digicash Cashier** *are two cashier application system variants.*

In this process, a **Buyer** first orders some goods or services, then the **Seller** invoices the **Buyer**, then the **Buyer** pays, and the **Seller** delivers the goods or services, either before payment or after. This example will be used several times in this chapter.

In general, it is hard to decide exactly which layer some things go into. For example, Java can be viewed in two ways. The first is as just another language, located in the system software layer. More interestingly, Java can be viewed as a key part of the organization's distributed object strategy. Software developers are using Java Object Request Brokers, exchanging Java objects, changing the ways they partition client–server applications by moving Java objects to different machines, and so on. In this view, a significant part of Java belongs to the middleware layer, or at least many parts of the middleware layer are written in Java. We have arbitrarily allocated Java to the middleware layer for our example.

A layered system has both a horizontal "dimension" for systems interacting within the same layer and a vertical "dimension" for static dependencies across layers, as shown in Figure 7.3. To keep systems manageable, we have decided that a system may not reuse components from higher layers. This would lead to static dependencies from some component systems to more specific systems in higher layers. This would increase the volatility of the component systems as they would depend on more application-specific application or component systems that are typically not as resilient to change.

However, it is still feasible to implement notification, call-backs and database triggers from lower layers even if the static dependencies are only permitted to lower layers. Any object or component that wants to subscribe to a notification, call-back, or trigger first

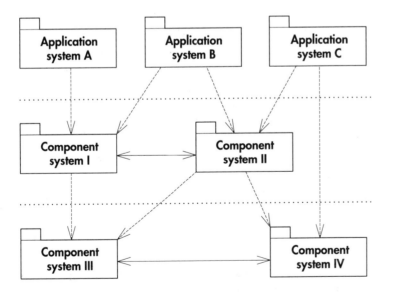

Figure 7.3 *System dependencies (dashed arrows) and interaction (full arrows) in a layered system. Systems in one layer may not depend on systems in higher layers.*

registers its interest with the (lower-level) object that may generate the notification by providing a pointer to itself or to some function to be called. The object then calls back by issuing a message to the registered object instance or function.

7.4 A layered architecture reduces software dependencies

A layered architecture allows software to be organized in layers according to application specificity. The further down the layers, the more general the components. The software engineering processes can then be customized to develop and evolve components with different levels of specificity. Different people with individual skills and interests can follow a tailor-made software engineering process and focus on appropriate layers. The direct correspondence between the type of system developed and the type of software engineering process used makes it easier to manage the organization − architecture, processes and team organization go hand in hand.

A layered architecture is *intuitive* enough to be understandable to someone without deep software engineering knowledge. This is very important since it allows for discussions of the architecture, operation, and performance of the reuse business in high-level terms. This is particularly important with people who have only a limited or high-level understanding of the technical side of the reuse business. These include partners, chief executive officers, customers, third-party vendors, and so on. In fact, many crucial issues may be discussed and addressed using only a simple illustration such as Figure 7.1 and some basic metrics such as:

- degree of reuse of/from component systems in different layers;

- initial and maintenance cost for the development or purchase of a specific component system;

- initial and maintenance cost for the development of application systems − compared to the cost before installation of the reuse business;

- time required for initial and further development of a specific component system;

- time required for initial and further development of an application system, compared to time required before installation of reuse business;

- quality of component systems;

- quality of application systems, compared to quality level experienced before installation of reuse business.

A layered system can also be defined with *enough detail* in terms of interfaces and facades to be useful to the developers. This allows distinct interfaces to be defined for different reusers of components, common services, object-request brokers, and other infrastructure. This simplifies the work of the reusers. Furthermore, the dependencies on lower layers are reduced by allowing dependencies only on components explicitly exported from the facades of lower layers. This reduces dependencies on internal, volatile parts.

Getting the layered architecture right is not easy, however. It is difficult both to develop it initially and to maintain it as technology and requirements change. By using the right modeling techniques and by proceeding in increments it is possible to improve the chances of success and to reduce risks. Such a systematic technique is suggested starting in Section 7.7. Briefly, the idea is to think of the whole layered system as one system and to develop a set of use case and object models for it. Then those models can be used to identify individual application and component systems, which can be further developed using individual software engineering processes.

There are several typical issues to address in the middleware layer and the business-specific layer. We will see how common off-the-shelf products and legacy software can be used in our layered architecture approach.

7.5 The middleware layer supports distributed object computing

Large organizations grow more and more dependent on enterprise-wide information systems. They need information to support them in a globalized, highly competitive market. To compete effectively, companies require *agility* – the ability to change processes and supporting information systems quickly. Many organizations want to empower their employees by providing them with easy access to corporate information. There is a growing trend to virtual organizations, distributed teams, cross-organization process support, and telecommuting. All of these trends require more support from distributed enterprise information systems that are easy to change. Such changes are simplified if they can be performed as a multitude of local changes (with a consistent global impact) to information systems and resources accessible to the whole enterprise. A distributed enterprise-wide information system is only practical to evolve and manage if it is independent of the physical location of the employee and the hardware and operating system platforms they use. The emergence of standardized platforms for *interoperable distributed object computing* is an important step towards globalized enterprise information systems.

While objects and components defined in a classical programming language, such as C++, provide important capabilities, these are limited to executing in one fixed address space, bound to one language. Contrast this with the vision of *interoperating distributed objects* written in a variety of languages, which can be distributed across networks and are supported by a variety of services for persistence, security, and naming. These objects will be packaged as individual components or suites of related software components, supporting high degrees of plug-and-play computing and allowing piece-wise evolution of shared components.

This requires a platform with a mechanism for marshaling messages to objects that are localized in a different address space, possibly on the other side of the world on a different type of workstation, running a different operating system. *Marshaling* here means encoding and decoding messages and parameters to and from a flattened form that can be transmitted across a network. There are several different emerging standards, such as Microsoft's COM/OLE, and OMG's CORBA augmented with CI Labs OpenDoc. The excellent *Distributed Objects Survival Guide* by Orfali *et al.* (1996) provides a comprehensive discussion and comparison of these and other systems and of document component standards. It is not our intent to provide a comprehensive description of these systems, but to highlight features that have affected our approach and to illustrate how our approach connects to these systems.

Given the pace of change in the industry, some of what we say in this section will most likely be outdated as you read this. It is our goal to give the flavor of how these systems can be used within the RSEB — *the essential message is that the CORBA/OpenDoc and COM/OLE techniques both map well to the RSEB approach.* We will show how to use layering to manage the complexity of several commercial off-the-shelf software products (COTS) and supporting technologies. It is important to note that despite many similarities, CORBA/OpenDoc and COM/OLE have many differences. For example, they have quite different models of interface navigation, interface composition, object identity, and object life cycle. They also have quite different approaches to multiple-language development and multi-platform deployment. These distributed computing technologies are influencing each other and are also being influenced by rapidly changing Internet technologies such as Java. However, it is still expected that CORBA and COM/OLE will coexist in many system implementations supported by an increasing number of bridges between them, such as the HP ORB Plus and the Iona ORBIX products. In 1996, OMG approved a proposal for a standard COM/OLE interoperation facility for CORBA.

7.5.1 CORBA

The Common Object Request Broker Architecture (CORBA) is a vendor interoperability standard designed to allow interoperability between components regardless of the platform, language, author, or vendor infrastructure.

> An **Object Request Broker (ORB)** is an implementation of the CORBA standard and is responsible for transparently marshaling and forwarding messages to objects distributed in heterogeneous environments (OMG, 1996e).

A key part of the CORBA specification is a language-neutral Interface Definition Language (IDL). IDL gives a precise description of types and exceptions and is similar to C++ interface and type declarations but permits multiple language bindings. CORBA objects can have multiple interfaces, perhaps composed or inherited from other interfaces.

There are many related CORBA products, together with a number of common services and facilities. Figure 7.4, adapted from OMG (1996e), is a standard way of showing the relationship of various CORBA services. There are four major kinds of

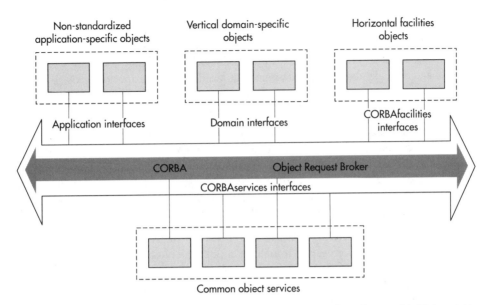

Figure 7.4 *OMG architecture and services reference model. (Adapted from OMG (1996e).)*

software services and objects, all defined by IDL interfaces. The dotted boxes represent categories of objects with object interfaces, while the rectangles represent one or more objects "managed" by the services. The following descriptions are adapted from OMG's online CORBA 2.0 executive overview (http://www.omg.org).

- The CORBA Object Request Broker (ORB) enables objects to transparently make requests and receive responses in a distributed environment. The ORB is the communications heart of the standard. It provides an infrastructure allowing objects to converse, independent of the specific platforms and techniques used to implement the objects. Compliance with the Object Request Broker standard guarantees portability and interoperability of objects over a network of heterogeneous systems. The ORB provides conventions for naming, locating, binding, and interacting with objects. There are numerous vendors of ORBs, such as IONA with its Orbix product and HP with its ORB Plus product. These products are fairly similar but provide some variation in services, language bindings, platform support, customizability, Internet interfacing, OLE gateways, and so on.

- CORBAservices is a collection of services (interfaces and objects) that support functions common in distributed systems. These components standardize the life-cycle management of objects. Interfaces are provided to create objects, to control access to objects, to keep track of relocated objects, and to control the relationship between styles of objects (class management). Also provided are the generic environments in which single objects can perform their tasks. Common Object Services provide for application consistency and help to increase programmer productivity.

- CORBAfacilities is a collection of common facilities and objects that provide a set of generic application functions that can be configured to the specific requirements of a particular installation. These are facilities such as printing, document management, database, and electronic mail facilities. Standardization leads to uniformity in generic operations and to better options for end users to customize their working environments.

- Domain Interfaces represent vertical areas that provide functionality of direct interest to end users in particular application domains. Domain interfaces and domain-specific objects may combine some common facilities and object services, but are designed to perform particular tasks for users within a certain vertical market or industry. For example, these could include business objects for banking and finance, spreadsheet objects, and GUI components.

- Application Objects are objects specific to particular industries or end-user applications. These correspond to objects in both the business-specific and application layers discussed earlier. The Application Interfaces provide IDL access to objects and component-based applications performing particular tasks for a user. An application is typically built from a large number of basic objects – some specific to the application at hand, some domain specific, some from object services and some built from a set of common facilities. These applications benefit greatly from the strengths of robust object systems development and the application interfaces are critical when considering a comprehensive system architecture.

More details on CORBA and the facilities can be found in a series of books published by the OMG (1996, 1996b, 1996c, 1996d, 1996e). See also the web (http://www.omg.org).

In the RSEB an ORB can be managed as a component system providing a facade that contains IDL interfaces to the ORB functionality. That component system should also include components, models, and documentation developed for the RSEB itself, such as wrappers that limit the interface to an ORB. This documentation and wrappers become even more important for complex applications that use multiple ORBs implemented in different languages, yet having (almost) the same interfaces. To help reusers set up the rather complex sequence of calls needed to use these ORBs, the component systems might include descriptions of abstract use case collaborations, and state transition diagrams that define call sequences for distributed objects such as control or boundary objects. Each set of additional object services and business-specific objects can be managed as separate component systems organized in suitable subsystems or service packages.

Example

Several of the application systems offered by XYBsoft such as **Payment** and **Invoicing** may execute on different machines and need to interoperate via distributed objects. One way to achieve such object distribution is to use an ORB, as shown in Figure 7.5. For the **Payment** and **Invoicing** application systems, this means that, for example, the *Account* and **Invoice** objects need to be distributed objects.

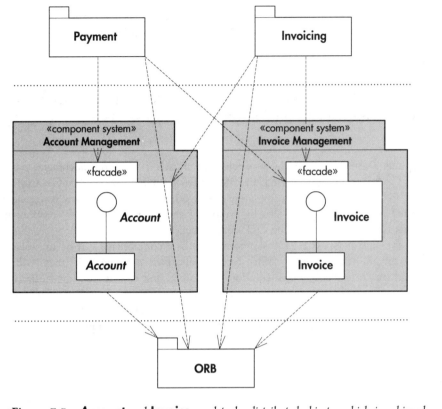

Figure 7.5 **Account** *and* **Invoice** *need to be distributed objects, which is achieved using an ORB that publishes the* **Account** *and* **Invoice** *interfaces. Several «imports» dependencies are shown.*

Note that the ORB is itself a component system in the middleware layer, while the **Account Management** and the **Invoice Management** component systems belong to the business-specific layer.

7.5.2 OpenDoc

According to Orfali *et al.* (1996), most of the component revolution on the open market has been driven from the desktop, from activities such as Component Integration Laboratories' OpenDoc and Microsoft's OLE/ActiveX. The problem with many desktop applications has been that they have become increasingly large, inflexible, and complex monolithic desktop applications. The goal is to replace these monoliths by suites of business components and applets that can be flexibly combined, within a standard container or compound document.

Component Integration Laboratories (CI Labs) is a consortium of system companies including Apple, Digital, Hewlett-Packard, IBM, and Lotus (now part of IBM but still responsible for the Notes product), as well as several large consumers, such as American Airlines and Citibank, concerned about an open systems definition of components.

> **OpenDoc** is a compound document architecture, implemented as a set of compound document components and services, aimed at development of rich user interfaces and document-oriented applications.

The component classes, called parts, implement a rich compound document framework. The OpenDoc model is based on IBM's SOM, itself based on OMG's CORBA standard. The OpenDoc model is completely object-oriented and allows new components to be created by subclassing and also by wrapping and aggregating other components. Furthermore, OpenDoc claims to be OLE compatible.

From an RSEB perspective, the standard OpenDoc components can be represented as one or several component systems. Since they form a framework, they will be implemented by an abstract implementation subsystem, and can be described using the use case and other object models to help in their use. Additional OpenDoc components can be developed by reusing and specializing standard OpenDoc components. These additional OpenDoc components can be organized in separate component systems with facades that export what other developers need.

7.5.3 OLE/COM and ActiveX

OLE (Object Linking and Embedding) started out as a rather complex mechanism for allowing Microsoft Office products to share parts of documents, such as embedded spreadsheets in documents. OLE has evolved substantially and has been recast as ActiveX – a fairly complete framework for reusable components that are easy to use in Internet applets, support distributed object computing, and adhere to more open standards. Numerous vendors offer products that can operate with OLE objects or offer tools and components that are OLE compliant. For example, it is relatively easy to define an OLE server in Visual Basic or Visual C++.

OLE is based on an underlying Component Object Model (COM). OLE/COM defines an architectural style for components (the component definition model), and provides several services such as compound document objects, structured storage, uniform data transfer, and OLE automation and scripting. The Compound Document classes of OLE offer approximately the same functionality as OpenDoc. The marshaling, notification, and navigation interfaces of COM are comparable to CORBA. With the development of NT 4.0, ActiveX now supports two kinds of distributed computing, one based on DCOM and the other on the Internet model. DCOM used to be called Network OLE (Orfali *et al.*, 1996; Brockschmidt, 1995) and is delivered as part of Windows NT 4.0 to let users deploy distributed applications made up of a series of OLE components.

OLE components are accessed through OLE Control Component (OCX) interfaces, now more correctly called ActiveX.

> An **ActiveX** interface is a collection of functions (sometimes called methods or member functions) that reusers can connect their software to.

Each interface is uniquely identified by a Globally Unique Identifier. COM/OLE is not as object-oriented as CORBA/OpenDoc. For example, COM/OLE does not support multiple inheritance of component interfaces and even single inheritance is not encouraged. This means that complex interfaces are created by composing interfaces either via containment and delegation, where a received message is forwarded via some pointer to some other component, or via aggregation. Each COM/OLE component can have multiple interfaces. COM/OLE components are thus not specialized via inheritance, but by parameterization, generation, and aggregation, as explained in Udell (1994).

From an RSEB point of view, all this means that interfaces to OLE components can be defined using facades and UML interfaces, but they are somewhat less elegant than the corresponding CORBA interfaces would have been, and they do not support multiple language bindings. One approach to OLE/COM ActiveX components (OCXs) in a layered system is to have one component system with the core OLE framework and components such as Microsoft Foundation Classes (MFC). Then separate component systems contain additional sets of components, for example spreadsheets, multimedia, and inference engines, represented as object types and classes or perhaps service packages.

Example

The Microsoft Office Suite of Applications consists of several applications that are continuously being reengineered to work increasingly well together and to expose more of their core functionality as OLE services. These applications are Word for documents, Excel for spreadsheets, PowerPoint for presentations, Access for database, and Mail. Using OLE and Visual Basic, these applications can be integrated into a variety of task-oriented solutions. The applications are thus suppliers of two interfaces: one user interface to the human user, and one interface to applications within the suite and other OLE objects.

MS Office is changing from monolithic applications built from hidden component systems to systems constructed from visible, shared, replaceable OLE components and ActiveX components such as spreadsheet tables, database tables, spell-checkers, paragraphs, diagrams, and so on (Figure 7.6), glued and customized by Visual Basic for Applications (VBA). These components are constructed internally using, for example, Visual C++ and the common Microsoft Foundation Classes (MFC). New office applications can be built by directly accessing these OLE components. End users can load and use these components directly without having to run the entire application.

Microsoft distributes an Office Developers Kit which shows how Visual Basic 3.0 and 4.0 can be used as a scripting language to the OLE components of Word, Excel, PowerPoint, Mail, and Access. Many other tools, such as ViSio by Visio

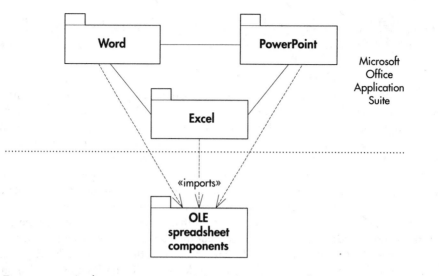

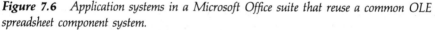

Figure 7.6 *Application systems in a Microsoft Office suite that reuse a common OLE spreadsheet component system.*

Corporation and Rose by Rational, can either invoke OLE servers through their OLE automation interface, or themselves be controlled or extended through their OLE server interfaces.

Some XYB home-banking services will be built as a combination of Java and OLE/ActiveX components discussed here for use in an Internet browser, or as combinations of components and customizable applications such as Microsoft Money, Intuit's Quicken, and Microsoft's Access database. Microsoft Money'97 has been re-architected to be compatible with Microsoft's new Open Financial Connection (OFC), a financial architecture and framework to facilitate such custom client application suites for banking and finance.

7.5.4 Comparing ActiveX/OLE/COM to CORBA/OpenDoc

Table 7.1 summarizes how different standards and products relate to the concepts of the RSEB.

The evolution of OLE and ActiveX has been driven from its use in the Office applications, the Visual Basic community, and now the Internet community. CORBA has evolved in steps as a standard for large-scale object distribution that allows vendors to implement their own products. Other middleware products have taken a variety of other approaches to provide a comprehensive distribution service. The Taligent CommonPoint frameworks and the Teknekron Rendezvouz software bus are two such examples.

Table 7.1 *Comparison of ActiveX/OLE/COM and CORBA/OpenDoc.*

	ActiveX/OLE/COM	CORBA/OpenDoc
Component system	Separate component systems for each set of components, for example spreadsheets. Components represented as object types or classes or perhaps service packages.	The ORB is one component system and each additional set of services is a separate component system. Component systems are organized in subsystems or service packages.
Application systems built by	Using OLE and DCOM to access components through their interfaces as OLE servers, embedding ActiveX components in Web browsers and other containers, adding extra functionality with a scripting language	Accessing components through an ORB without bothering about object location. Using OpenDoc components for rich UI and document-oriented applications.
Facade	Facades contain interface specifications and ActiveX/OCXs components that can be customized.	Facades contain IDL specifications.
Interface	OLE IDL, which defines interfaces as collections of functions.	OMG IDL – similar to C++ .h files.
Variability mechanisms	Parameterization, generation, and aggregation.	Inheritance and aggregation.
Distribution mechanism	DCOM, Internet.	An ORB.
Middleware layer	As defined by DCOM, ActiveX, OLE services.	The ORB, Object Services, Common Facilities. Common components for compound documents.
System software layer	Windows NT, Windows 95, some interoperability services provided on UNIX.	Each ORB should be capable of existing on multiple platforms, or interoperating with ORBs from other vendors.

7.5.5 Taligent's CommonPoint and Microsoft's MFC

Taligent Inc. was founded by IBM and Apple in 1992 as a consortium, with HP joining later. Taligent's goal was to exploit objects and frameworks as fully as possible, extending the frontiers of object technology to produce a truly object-oriented operating system and application development environment. Over time, the plans adjusted to produce the

CommonPoint Application System (essentially a set of component systems in the RSEB sense). In December 1995, Taligent became a wholly owned subsidiary of IBM.

> **CommonPoint** (Potel and Cotter, 1995; Orfali *et al.*, 1996) consists of an integrated set of over 200 closely collaborating C++ frameworks, such as Workspace, Document, User Interface, Graphics, Data Access, Remote Objects, System Management, Storage, and Communications.

The compound document model provides effective mappings to OpenDoc components and an interface to OLE objects. There is also a set of CommonPoint component and application construction tools. However, IBM is now unbundling portions of the comprehensive CommonPoint product as independent frameworks and class libraries to be used together with VisualAge.

The set of frameworks is complex to understand and use due to the sheer size and number of classes and methods (Laubsch, 1996). There are hundreds of classes and thousands of methods, and it takes a developer a considerable time to learn to use them effectively. It is therefore wise to restructure the CommonPoint frameworks into a set of more independent, consumable chunks, as IBM seems to be doing.

In the RSEB approach, we would define several component systems for these frameworks, rather than just one. Each component system would contain one or more closely related frameworks. The component systems would not only contain the implementation of the frameworks, but also CommonPoint documentation, interface specifications, and additional models such as use case models, developed by the RSEB itself to enhance reuse. There might be a single facade for each framework or, if appropriate, one combined facade for several frameworks. The facades of each component system would contain interfaces for the services provided by the framework and components to be customized. Reusers extending a framework would then import the components from the relevant facade and reuse them as-is or specialized via inheritance.

Another widely used framework is the Microsoft Foundation Classes (MFC). These provide many utility classes and mechanisms to the C++ programmer using Windows 95 or Windows NT 4.0 that provide many basic services, such as GUI classes, OLE and DCOM interfaces, and basic collection data structures. These are useful and essential to develop applications that take full advantage of the power of Windows. The MFC framework is used directly in almost all applications included in the Microsoft Office application suite, and indirectly through Visual Basic and ActiveX.

7.6 The business-specific layer supports rapid application development

This layer contains all the component systems that are specific to the business, but reusable in several applications. It is primarily these component systems that should be used by the application engineers.

The component systems in the business-specific layer capture and implement business-specific domain knowledge. These component systems are highly valued assets for the reuse business because they can support the organization as they use its knowledge to compete with other companies.

Example

The **Account Management** component system contains a **Risk** component. **Risk** is used to allow bank customers to estimate the risk they are exposed to on their accounts, for instance when an *Account* holds a foreign currency. The **Risk** component implements business rules that reflect XYB's understanding of how to estimate these kinds of risks. XYBsoft knows that XYB has good understanding of how to assess risks of this kind and therefore hopes to attract further customers by offering new banking services associated with risk management.

Several authors have discussed the vision of widely available, standard, domain-specific business object implementations, as a set of reusable objects or components that can be used to develop business applications more rapidly and effectively in some domain (Jacobson *et al.*, 1994; Taylor, 1995a; Shelton, 1995; Sims, 1994). Some of the authors have concentrated on the modeling aspects, while others have concentrated on specific implementations of business components and business frameworks that capture many business semantics. Typical business objects are **Account**, **Customer**, and **Invoice**. The representation of the business object may be in a natural language, a modeling language, or a programming language. Some business objects might be common to several business areas, such as Finance, Sales, or Customer, while others might be more specific to one area, such as Banking, Insurance, Manufacturing, and so on.

In a recent Request For Proposals (OMG, 1996a), OMG Business Object Management Special Interest Group (BOMSIG) define a business object as follows: "A business object is a representation of a thing active in the business domain, including at least its business name and definition, attributes, behavior, relationship, rules, policies and constraints. A business object may represent, for example, a person, place, event, business process or concept." Some authors use the term *business component* rather than business object. Some think that Java will be a good vehicle to distribute components from the business-specific layer, since these components will be easy to access from Internet repositories, and flexible to use and customize using scripting languages (JavaScript or VBScript) in browsers, allowing these components to run on almost any machine. One of the real challenges to developing business-specific components is making them able to interact with each other. This will require standardization work, such as the OMG BOMSIG is trying to encourage, in order to settle on the interfaces and division of responsibilities between different components (Harmon, 1995).

We define a **business object** as representing something concrete and significant in the business — a representation of members of the business or "some thing" handled or used by people in the business (Jacobson *et al.*, 1994).

In the RSEB, business objects are supported by software in one or more component systems within the business-specific layer.

The components that implement a business object might be delivered as separate service packages or subsystems, but more often because of size and complexity of interfaces will be delivered as complete component systems. In addition to well-defined facades and usage documents, these business object component systems may include use case and analysis models to clarify the semantics and usage. By making these into separate component systems, we will make these components' natural connections to the business models and their importance in the organization highly visible.

Example

The **Account** business object was identified while XYBsoft's business engineering experts analyzed their business. As the XYBsoft Application Family Engineering team defined the layered system, they suggested a component system **Account Management** to support account related functionality.

Example

Hewlett-Packard is beginning to invest in application-specific frameworks for classes of Financial, Manufacturing, Telecom, and Medical Information systems. These frameworks define additional services and mechanisms on top of the CORBA and COM models, aimed at providing common, customizable support of interest to the appropriate domain. Such services include management of working sessions and application workflow, and local private workspaces integrated with enterprise information. A prototype framework for the medical domain includes components that provide access to medical coded terminology, medical record management with audit trail for initialed changes, and synchronization. Some of the prototype components wrap legacy information systems, and others provide interfaces to some medical measurement instruments. The component model for this framework uses OMG IDL as the specification language to define interfaces, but adds interfaces to a basic component by aggregation, rather than by multiple inheritance. This allows the components to be implemented with either CORBA or COM as the distributed communication infrastructure.

7.6.1 Contents of the business-specific layer depend on similarity among application systems

The business-specific layer should contain components that allow application engineers to work effectively. What kind of components best support the application engineers depends on the nature of the application systems. Table 7.2 provides some guidelines as to which type of components should be most useful to develop application systems with

Table 7.2 *The contents of the business-specific layer depend on the nature of the application systems.*

Characteristics of application systems	What they will reuse from the business-specific layer
Independent applications with some common components and features	Some common entity types and related classes
Interoperating, but fairly different	Many entity types
An interoperating, integrated application suite	Some concrete and some abstract use cases. Most entity types, major boundary types, and some control types and classes
Separate applications that are built as customizations of a base of generic application functionality	Some concrete and many abstract use cases. Most types and classes are reused and specialized from common component systems
Interoperable applications that are built as customizations of a base of generic application functionality	Some concrete and many abstract use cases. Most types and classes are reused and specialized from component systems. Many types and classes are also reused as-is

certain characteristics. This table illustrates how the contents of the business-specific layer depends on the application characteristics. This dependence is less obvious than the fact that the contents of the middleware layer depend on whether support is provided for distributed objects.

Example

The application systems **Payment** and **Invoicing** communicate with each other during the business process **Sales From Order To Delivery**, as shown in Figure 7.7.

The business process of **Sales From Order To Delivery** is supported by the **Pay And Schedule Invoice** use case in the **Payment** application system and the

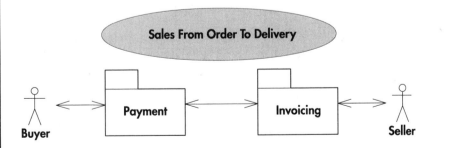

Figure 7.7 *The application systems* **Payment** *and* **Invoicing** *support* **Sales From Order To Delivery**.

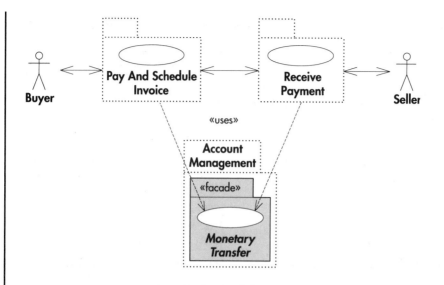

Figure 7.8 *The use cases* **Pay And Schedule Invoice** *and* **Receive Payment** *reuse the* **Monetary Transfer** *use case.*

Receive Payment use case in the **Invoicing** application system. These use cases are shown in Figure 7.8. The use case **Pay And Schedule Invoice** allows the **Buyer** to study invoices and decide whether, when, and how to pay them by issuing a request to the use case to schedule invoice payment. The **Receive Payment** use case informs the **Seller** when invoices have been paid and keeps track of outstanding invoices, helping the **Seller** take action on them. The abstract use case *Monetary Transfer* is reused from the **Account Management** component system.

Both the **Invoicing** and **Payment** application systems also reuse object components from the component systems **Account Management** and **Invoice Management** (Figure 7.9). These components include entity types for **Invoices**

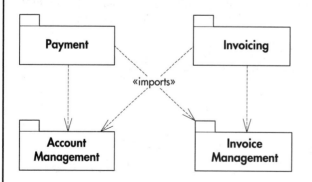

Figure 7.9 *The* **Payment** *and* **Invoicing** *application systems reuse use cases, entity and control objects from* **Account Management** *and* **Invoice Management**.

and **Accounts**, but also control types that take care of money transfer and processing an invoice payment. This means that the component systems **Account Management** and **Invoice Management** offer abstract use case components and some concrete entity and control objects. This is a common pattern. These concrete objects act as shared communication objects when integrating interoperable application systems.

7.7 Using multiple models when working with layered system architecture

It is easy to believe that the software architecture of a system can be captured in one diagram. In fact, most of what has been discussed in this chapter has dealt only with the static organization of the software, which can in principle be shown with only one diagram. But software architecture needs to take into account both the static organization of software and *how that software manifests itself in executing systems*. An object-oriented software architecture thus also defines the allocation of object instances to processes, process interaction, and the allocation of processes to nodes. The allocation of use cases to types, classes and processes and the performance of those use cases are also important to consider, even if the use cases themselves are not part of the architecture. It is not very practical to show all this information in one diagram. Instead several views are beneficial. Each view addresses one specific set of concerns. This is particularly true for complex layered systems, which involve many people, organizations, projects, concurrency, and technologies. These different views of the architecture must be coordinated so that they are consistent with each other while the architecture is iterated towards a steady state. This is difficult and requires careful attention to change management.

Kruchten (1995) proposes five main views of a system which are useful and often necessary to develop architectures. Kruchten's views correspond very well with the models discussed in Chapter 3. These models will be used in a slightly different way to develop architectures as we will see in the coming sections. They are used as follows:

- The concurrency model captures concurrency, processes, and synchronization aspects.

- The deployment model describes the mapping(s) of the software onto the hardware and reflects its distributed aspect.

- The design model and implementation model describe the static organization of the software in its development environment.

- The analysis model is used to represent and outline the most essential objects in the business; this is not part of the architecture per se, but is used to better understand what the architecture represents.

- The use case model defines the most important use cases that span across several application systems. While not part of the architecture per se, it is used to better understand what the architecture represents. The use cases are used to define how the elements of the architecture need to interact.

Note that only the concurrency, deployment, design, and implementation models are used to *represent* the layered system. The analysis and use case models are auxiliary models used to better understand the layered system. All these models contain only architecturally significant elements, which means that they are *abstractions* of the models of the individual application and component systems that comprise the layered system. These models are used by the architects in much the same way as application engineers use the models of an individual application system. The key difference is that architects think of the whole layered system as one system. We call this a *system of interoperating application and component systems (SIS)*, shown in Figure 7.3. These systems are interconnected through either communicates or imports. The architects use the models listed above to represent the layered system.

7.8 Representing a layered system as a superordinate system

The layered system is treated as a system in its own right, a system that defines the interoperating set of application and component systems as a whole. This system is called a *superordinate* system since it provides the big picture of the whole layered architecture, and corresponds to *subordinate* application and component systems. The models of the superordinate system are called superordinate models, consisting of superordinate use cases, subordinate subsystems, and so on. The idea is thus to develop a complete OOSE model for a layered system in two steps of abstraction. The first step treats the family of applications as if it were in fact a single superordinate system, ensuring end-to-end consistency. The second step develops models with much more detail for each of the individual interacting application and component systems.

What is really important is to use the superordinate and the subordinate models so that there is a precise relationship between them. This will be detailed below, but the idea is that each design subsystem in the superordinate system is traceable to one application or component system. The most important issue at the superordinate level is to identify the subsystems and the interfaces between them. The individual application and component systems must then conform to the interfaces defined at the superordinate level.

> The **superordinate system** is described with several models that together represent both the static and dynamic aspects of the layered system as a whole.

By representing the layered system as a single superordinate system separate from the individual application and component systems, it is possible to:

- represent only the part of the architecture that is most significant to the Application Family Engineering team as a group;

- manage the architecturally most important aspects of the layered system as a product, since it is represented as a system, as discussed in Chapter 4;

- coordinate the different views of the layered system as a whole – by treating the different.views as models of a system, we can use OOSE guidelines on managing the connections between the views;

- use similar software engineering processes and tools to work with the overall layered system and applications;

- more easily train skilled application engineers to work with architectures.

A system of interoperating systems (Jacobson *et al.*, 1995b) is a system that is implemented by a set of interoperating systems as shown in Figure 7.10. The systems **A** and **C** are application systems and **B** is a component system, described by their own set of use case and object models. The fact that **A**, **B**, and **C** are interoperating systems maintained by individual teams stresses the importance of keeping the models of those systems compatible with each other. This requires additional modeling techniques and extended development processes.

Such a set of interoperating systems can be also be represented as a single system **S**, as shown in Figure 7.11. Each one of **A**, **B**, and **C** is now represented by a corresponding subsystem, **a**, **b**, and **c**, in (the design model of) **S**.

The overall system **S** shown in Figure 7.11 is called the *superordinate system* and the interoperating systems **A**, **B**, and **C** are application and component systems. The superordinate system is used to model not only how the application systems interact

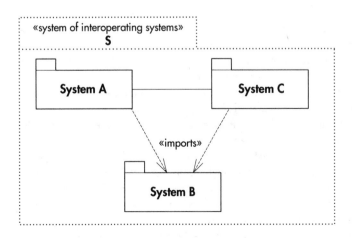

Figure 7.10 *A system of interoperating systems.*

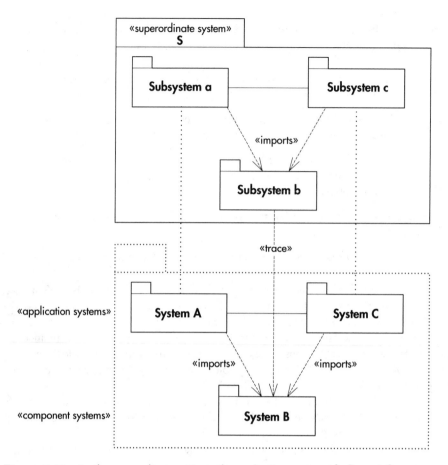

Figure 7.11   *In the superordinate system, the application systems* **A**, **B**, *and* **C** *are represented by design subsystems* **a**, **b**, *and* **c**.

but indeed the whole layered system. In particular, this includes how the various application systems import from component systems.

One of the main reasons for breaking down the layered system into separate application and component systems is to allow independent, yet manageable, development of these systems. This separation is particularly crucial when several application systems can be individually sold, delivered, and installed. Each application and component system may have its own development team which is fully responsible for the details inside the system. Each application, component system, and architecture development team requires its own set of models to manage their system. Each application and component system therefore has its own set of use case and object models, while the architects have their own superordinate models which provide the overall view used to define the dependencies among application and component systems. The architects, the *Application Family Engineering team*, are therefore responsible for defining interactions and interfaces between application and component systems and the facades provided by the component systems. These responsibilities and the associated process are elaborated in Chapters 9 and 10.

Remember that each system, be it the layered system, an application system, or a component system, is defined by individual sets of models. The only things that need to be consistent between the models of the different systems are the facades and the interfaces they supply.

The Application Family Engineering team needs to be careful not to make the superordinate models more detailed than needed for this overall view. The superordinate models should only contain what is significant for the Application Family Engineering team to deal with as a group. While this varies from situation to situation, the following guidelines, adapted from a Rational training course (Rational, 1995), suggest what to include:

- Superordinate system use cases that capture most of the collaborations involving more than one application system, and some interactions that involve both an application system and component systems.

- Some important abstract use cases or key mechanisms.

- Major object types and classes, but not most subtypes or subclasses.

- Types and classes that have high visibility, or that are core to the domain, typically corresponding to analysis types.

- All subsystems and exported interfaces, but not all individual classes or modules.

- All facades and their contents.

- All processes.

- All node types.

Example

As the Application Family Engineering team works on the **Account Management** component system, they envision several types and classes for transaction fees that implement different ways for the bank to charge the customers as they perform transactions. However, these classes are not visible to application engineers working on applications such as **Digicash Cashier**, **Payment** and **Invoicing**. Instead, these classes will only be used by other types and classes defined within **Account Management**. These transaction fee classes are therefore not deemed significant enough to be represented in the superordinate models.

The early architecture work entails many iterations where the interfaces and the facades go through several versions before the system collaboration patterns gradually stabilize. The Application Family Engineering team acts to control the evolution of the interfaces between the systems and to mediate between the different application and component system engineers. As they work to control the interfaces, facades, and dependencies they use primarily the superordinate design model to define the layering.

7.8.1 Using a superordinate design model to represent layering

> The **superordinate design model** contains a subsystem for each application and component system.

Each such subsystem is an abstraction of the corresponding application and component system, and leaves out details not relevant to the Application Family Engineering team. The subsystems are connected with «trace» links to the corresponding application and component systems. These traces support impact analysis of change and ensure that the models of the superordinate system and the individual application or component systems are synchronized. The design model of the superordinate system is used to:

- define the application systems on a high level and define how they interoperate;

- define the reusable design classes, types, and subsystems and organize them in component systems;

- define the component system facades and also to detail which systems import from which facades;

- allocate use cases defined in the models of the superordinate system to the application and component systems.

Note that the components and the facades cannot be defined thoroughly in the first iterations of the architecture work. Instead they evolve as the architecture stabilizes.

The design model of the superordinate system is organized in non-overlapping layers to reflect the layering of the application and component systems. Each subsystem belongs to one layer and may depend only on subsystems in that layer or in lower layers. The term "layer" is only important as an architectural pattern that conveys a simple image of the superordinate system — the precise picture of the intersystem dependencies can only be understood by looking at the subsystem dependencies.

Example

The business process of **Sales From Order To Delivery** is supported by the interoperating **Payment** and **Invoicing** application systems. Both **Payment** and **Invoicing** reuse the *Account* component defined in the component system **Account Management**.

The design model of the superordinate system contains a subsystem for each of the application and component systems. For example, the application systems **Payment** and **Invoicing** are represented as subsystems in the **Application Layer**, and the component system **Account Management** is represented as a corresponding subsystem in the **Business-specific Layer** (Figure 7.12).

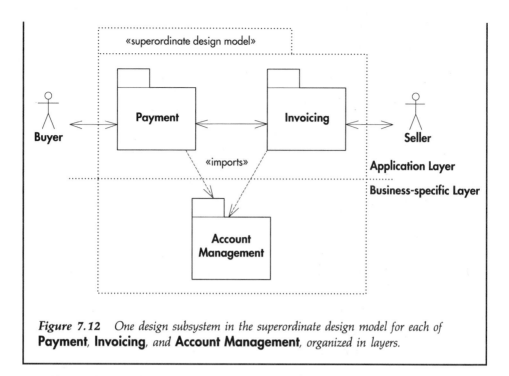

Figure 7.12 *One design subsystem in the superordinate design model for each of* **Payment**, **Invoicing**, *and* **Account Management**, *organized in layers.*

The use cases defined for the superordinate system are used to identify the superordinate subsystems, but legacy systems and Commercial Off The Shelf (COTS) products also substantially shape the architecture.

7.9 Use cases in relation to a layered system

It is important to understand how the interoperating application and component systems interact with each other. This can be defined in terms of use cases that span across several interoperating systems in the layered system. We represent such use cases as *superordinate use cases* in the superordinate system. Each superordinate use case can be allocated to the application and component systems, by splitting them across these systems. This involves two steps. First, allocate the use cases to design subsystems in the superordinate system, as shown in Figure 7.13. A part of a use case allocated to an individual subsystem is called a use case *segment*.

Then the superordinate subsystems are used to define the responsibilities of the corresponding application or component system. Each application or component system will in turn offer a number of use cases that correspond to the use case segments allocated to the subsystem in the superordinate design model. Together, the set of application or component system use cases offer behavior that is equivalent to the superordinate use cases (Figure 7.14).

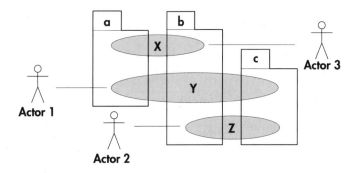

Figure 7.13 *The superordinate use cases* **X**, **Y**, *and* **Z** *are allocated to the subsystems* **a**, **b**, *and* **c**. *Different segments of each use case are assigned to each subsystem.*

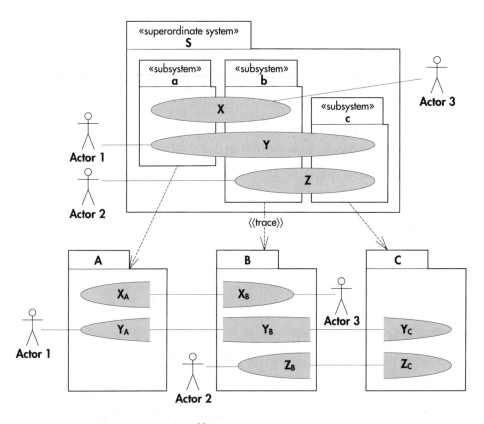

Figure 7.14 *Each use case (such as* **X$_A$**) *in an application or a component system corresponds to a segment of a superordinate use case (such as* **X**). *Note that the system's application and component systems,* **A**, **B**, *and* **C**, *and the superordinate system,* **S**, *are each treated as separate systems with their own unique models.*

Example

The business process of **Sales From Order To Delivery** is supported by the interoperating **Payment** and **Invoicing** application systems. Together, these application systems perform the superordinate use case **Pay Invoice**, which handles payment of issued invoices. The **Pay Invoice** use case is responsible for assisting the **Seller** to issue invoices, supporting the **Buyer** in deciding which and when to pay, and then making sure that money is transferred from the *Account* of the **Buyer** to that of the **Seller**.

The superordinate **Pay Invoice** use case is divided between subsystems that correspond to the application systems **Payment** and **Invoicing**, and the component system **Account Management**. Together the use cases **Pay And Schedule Invoice** and **Receive Payment** (Figure 7.15) perform a behavior that is

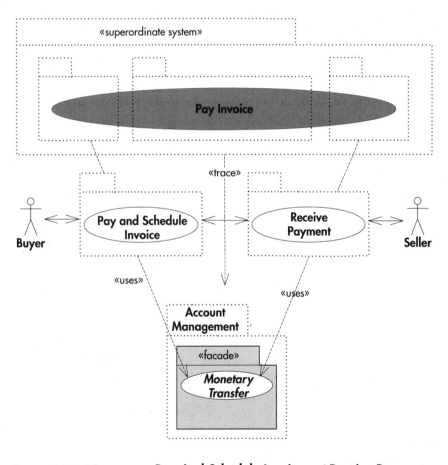

Figure 7.15 *The use cases* **Pay And Schedule Invoice** *and* **Receive Payment** *together perform the* **Pay Invoice** *use case defined for the superordinate system.*

equivalent to that defined by the superordinate use case **Pay Invoice**. Note that the superordinate use case **Pay Invoice** need only be described at a level where the subsystem interfaces can be defined.

7.9.1 Describing use cases for the superordinate system

When end users use a system of interoperating systems, they do not have to know which of the interoperating systems are involved. Instead each end user can think of the whole system of interoperating systems as performing use cases on his or her behalf. Each use case in the superordinate system is comprised of *superordinate transactions* that may involve more than one application and component system.

In principle, the use case model for the superordinate system could define all superordinate transactions. However, that is not practical. Instead the use case model for the superordinate system should define only transactions that are relevant to the Application Family Engineering team.

Furthermore, the descriptions of the superordinate transactions should be confined to what is architecturally significant, excluding parts of individual transactions that are contained wholly within one application or component system.

Example

The use case **Pay Invoice** could have an (oversimplified) description something like the following:

1   The **Buyer** activates the use case. The system presents the invoices that have not yet been paid.
2   The **Buyer** chooses which invoices to pay and decides when to pay them.
3   The system registers the payment orders and at the proper time executes payment of the invoices, by deducting the amount from the account of the **Buyer** and transferring it to that of the **Seller**.
4   As an invoice is being paid, a message is sent to the **Seller** and a receipt is sent back to the **Buyer**.

Sequence diagrams can be used to define how each use case for the superordinate system is divided among the design subsystems that correspond to the application and component systems.

Example

Pay Invoice involves the interactions between application and component systems as shown in Figure 7.16.

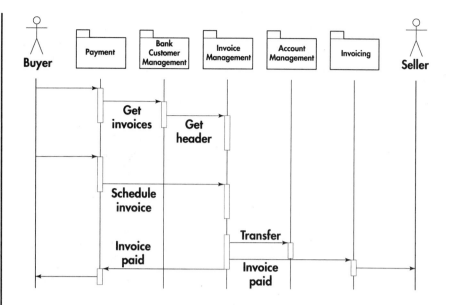

Figure 7.16 *A sequence diagram describing the flow of* **Pay Invoice**.

A selection of the available **Invoice**s is fetched. One or more **Invoice**s are chosen and scheduled for payment.

Later, when a scheduled **Invoice** is due for payment, **Invoice Management** is invoked by a timer and the **Invoice** is paid by transferring money from the account of the **Buyer** to that of the **Seller**.

The **Invoice** state is set to paid and **Invoicing** and **Payment** are informed via the notification **Invoice paid**.

7.9.2 Using interfaces for more explicit separation of system responsibilities

It is important to define explicit interfaces between interoperating application and component systems in order to separate the responsibilities of the teams that develop them. As described in Chapter 6, interfaces define a set of public operations, exceptions, state-machines, pre- and post-conditions, and attributes. The static structure of the interface may be defined using, for example, IDL or C++ .h files and the dynamic structure may be further defined using, for example, UML state diagrams (Booch *et al.*, 1997a).

Example

The **Invoice** component offered by **Invoice Management** allows peers to register for notification on the state changes of an **Invoice**, using the **Invoice Tracking** interface to the **Invoice** component. This is used, for example, by

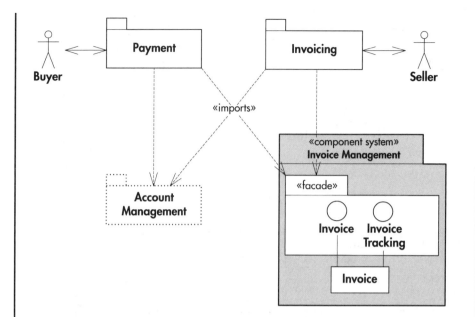

Figure 7.17 The **Payment** *and* **Invoicing** *application systems reuse the* **Invoice Tracking** *interface of the* **Invoice Management** *component system.*

Invoicing after it has created a new **Invoice** to the **Buyer**, to allow the **Seller** to register for notification on paid and overdue invoices. The creation of the **Invoice** object results in a notification to the actor **Buyer**. The **Buyer** then uses the **Payment** application to pay the **Invoice** which notifies the **Seller**.

Note that only the **Invoice** and **Invoice Tracking** interfaces are exported in the facade for reuse, not the **Invoice** type itself; see Figure 7.17.

The **Invoice Tracking** interface to the **Invoice Management** component system would be defined in IDL roughly as follows:

```
#include <financialtypes.idl>
module InvoiceManagement {
...
interface Invoice_Tracking {
    exception Invoice_Issued{Date when}
    exception Invoice_Paid{Customer who}
    exception Invoice_Overdue{Date when, string why}
    Account Create_Invoice(
        in Customer buyer, in string title, in Money amount);
        raises (Invoice_Issued);
    void Register_For_Notification(
        in any peer, in NotificationType what);
```

```
    void Schedule_Invoice (in Account wherefrom, in Time when)
      raises (Invoice_Paid);
    . . .
  };
};
```

Application systems can interact either through a shared object such as in the example above or directly with each other. In the latter case the application systems would interact through interfaces that either of the application systems supply instead of through a shared object interface. As an example, **Payment** could instead supply an interface which **Invoicing** could use to register a new **Invoice** to be paid.

Only the Application Family Engineering team is allowed to change the facades and the interfaces between systems. The developers of the application and component systems may suggest changes to facades and interfaces but they may not change them. This is managed by letting the Application Family Engineering team own the superordinate set of models. Note that the same interfaces and facades are used in the superordinate models to define the same imports and interactions between the corresponding subsystems as between the "real" application and component systems. In fact, the interfaces between the application and component systems must be *identical* to the interfaces between the subsystems in the superordinate design model to maintain consistency.

7.10 Actors of the application and component systems

Each application and component system may *interact with* both end users and other application or component systems. However, when looking at the world from inside

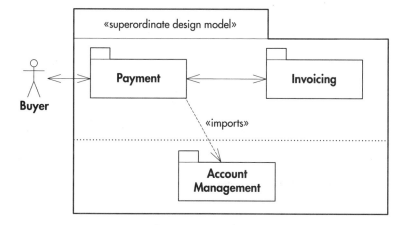

Figure 7.18 *The* **Buyer** *actor plus the* **Invoicing** *and* **Account Management** *subsystems constitute the environment of the subsystem* **Payment**.

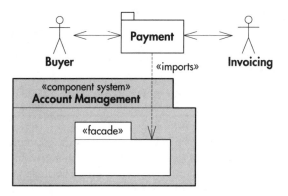

Figure 7.19 *The application system* **Payment** *interacts with the* **Buyer** *and* **Invoicing** *actors and imports from a facade of the component system* **Account Management**.

an application or component system, it is desirable to remove dependencies on specific application or component systems. This is done by representing the application and component systems that a system interacts with as actors, as shown in Figures 7.18 and 7.19.

Since each application and component system details a subsystem defined in the superordinate system, it has to be capable of interacting with the same environment. This means that each application and component system must be able to interact with all actors and all subsystems that the corresponding subsystem interacts with. Therefore each application and component system must have actors that correspond to:

- all actors that the corresponding subsystem in the superordinate model interacts with, and

- all subsystems *in the same layer* that the corresponding subsystem interacts with.

No actors are defined for interaction with and imports from lower layers since the services and objects offered from lower layers are imported into the system that uses them. The imported objects then become part of the system itself and thus are no longer outside the system like an actor. One reason why this is often desirable is that imports from lower layers often involve type or class specialization — which is difficult to show adequately with actors.

Example

The **Payment** subsystem in the superordinate design model interacts with the **Buyer** actor and the **Invoicing** subsystem. It also imports from the **Account Management** subsystem in the lower layer.

Both the superordinate **Buyer** actor and the superordinate **Invoicing** subsystem will be represented as subordinate actors of the application system **Payment**. Reuse from the component system **Account Management** is expressed as an import from a facade.

7.11 Use cases for the application and component systems

Each application and component system may have its own use case model. These are ordinary use case models, as discussed in Chapters 3 and 5. We have already shown how use cases defined for the superordinate system can be "composed of" use cases defined in application and component systems. It is simplest when one superordinate use case corresponds to one use case in each application and component system involved, but it is sufficient for the application and component systems to offer use cases that somehow work together to behave equivalently to the superordinate use cases.

Example

The superordinate use case **Pay Invoice** is decomposed into use cases for the component (or application) systems as follows. This superordinate use case

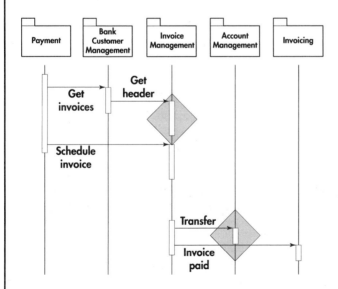

Figure 7.20 *The grayed rhomboids highlight activities that provide input from the superordinate design model when defining subordinate use cases in the* **Invoice Management** *and* **Account Management** *systems.*

involves the subsystems **Invoice Management** and **Account Management**. These correspond to component systems with the same names. Figure 7.20 is a sequence diagram that highlights the behavior of those subsystems as they interact with other subsystems.

The behavior depicted results in the definition of two abstract use cases in the **Invoice Management** and **Account Management** component systems, **Get Header** and *Monetary Transfer* (corresponding to the Transfer message in Figure 7.20). *Monetary Transfer* is reused in the **Payment** and **Invoicing** application systems. Note that both of the use cases defined for the component systems may also be "involved" in other superordinate use cases.

At this point, we have finished identifying the application and component systems and defined their facades and interfaces. Once we have decomposed the use cases and defined the subordinate actors and use cases for each subordinate application and component system we can model each system as discussed in Chapters 5 and 6.

7.12 Wrapping legacy systems to fit the architecture

Before we have completely finished with the architecture, we have to consider how to integrate our new application and component systems with existing systems. In most situations when a reuse business is installed, there already exist significant legacy systems that do part of what the new applications should do. There are many compelling reasons for starting afresh and not reusing any part of the legacy systems, but equally there are many pragmatic and economic reasons to build the new set of systems based on the existing legacy systems.

A **legacy system** is a pre-existing system that was created using other design methods and technologies, yet still manages significant business data and continues to support important business processes.

There are a number of possible approaches to take when dealing with legacy systems, but we will only consider reuse of legacy systems by wrapping them in new technology. This allows an incremental approach to replacing or upgrading the legacy systems. We start by encapsulating the appropriate services from each legacy system with an object wrapper.

A **wrapper** is here a piece of object-oriented software that encapsulates the legacy system and manages some interactions with it.

Software engineers can then treat these legacy systems as if they were truly object-oriented, or at least well-defined, components. Later, the services offered by these legacy systems can be taken over by new systems and the wrapper revised or made obsolete.

It is also important to plan for legacy integration as part of new systems development. This has an impact on how the architecture will be partitioned into component systems, how to define how the new systems interact with the legacy information systems and the ever changing user interfaces. The right choice of component definition and integration technologies will greatly help in flexibly wrapping existing systems.

In the RSEB this is done by creating one or several separate component systems for each legacy system to be wrapped. These component systems will provide an appropriate set of objects and operations to create, fetch, store, and manipulate objects corresponding to data and procedures in the legacy system. Tools such as the ParcPlace-Digitalk PARTS Wrapper can do some of this work, but an efficient design and implementation of the encapsulation can become a significant effort in itself.

The component system facade of a legacy system wrapper will export an appropriate set of components of various types to allow requirements capture, robustness analysis, design, and implementation of new services. This means that other systems that reuse the component system will treat the legacy systems as if they were remote object systems. The wrapper component system provides object definitions of the "objects" that can be fetched and stored in the legacy system. Note that more than one component system and more than one facade may be defined for a single legacy system. This is useful when a legacy system does not map well to the layered architecture. By providing several wrappers for one legacy system it is possible to define several interfaces to the legacy systems.

This wrapping approach is similar to the approach taken by David Taylor (1995a) who suggests that legacy systems can be wrapped by relatively autonomous business objects, or the use of OLE to provide an object-based interface. Other techniques for creating appropriate wrappers are the Facade pattern (Gamma *et al.*, 1994) and the client–server patterns developed by Wolf and Liu to encapsulate legacy systems (Coplien and Schmidt, 1995).

Developing the wrapper may sometimes require a lot of new code or some modifications to the legacy system, but this is not always the case. For example, if the legacy system has a well-defined interface and communication protocol, it may be

---

Example

As XYBsoft begin to develop their suite of application systems, they decide to base it on their existing **Customer-Account Transaction Manager**, developed in COBOL 20 years ago. The system contains critical business data regarding accounts and customers that can be accessed through the low-level interfaces **Account Data** and **Customer Information**. Since the Application Family Engineering team wants to be able to evolve account and customer management independently, they choose an architecture with two component systems, **Account Management** and **Bank Customer Management**. They therefore define these component systems together with suitable interfaces to **Account** and **Bank Customer** and let each wrap different aspects of the legacy system, as shown in Figure 7.21. In the future they expect to move from the existing **Customer-Account Transaction Manager** to new technology.

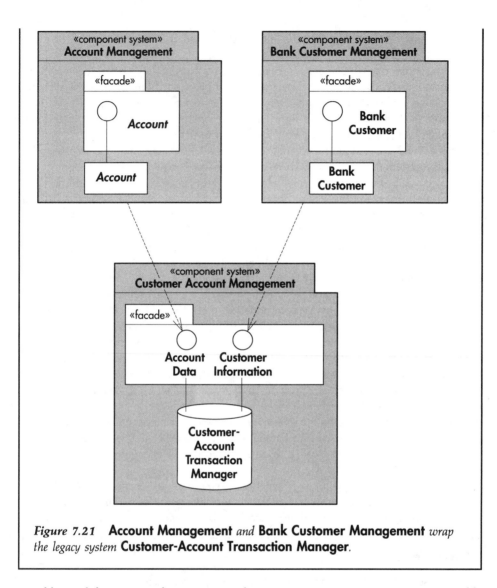

Figure 7.21 **Account Management** *and* **Bank Customer Management** *wrap the legacy system* **Customer-Account Transaction Manager**.

possible to define its interface in IDL and treat it as an existing CORBA-compatible component, and let various ORB services access it as needed.

7.13 Distributed processes and nodes for a layered system

The distribution of a system across several computation units and multiple processes complicates the architecture a lot. It is therefore important to treat the distribution explicitly and model the process structures and the system's physical division onto different hardware units. These models are essential to capture requirements on performance, integrity, fault-tolerance, concurrency, scalability, and system availability. It is important also to model how the processes and the nodes relate to the other models of the system of interoperating systems. Each use case defined for the superordinate system, for example, has to be distributed among the processes, maybe by means of interaction diagrams. This is important in order to verify system performance, liveness, and so on.

A distributed system is one with several simultaneously advancing computations, possibly synchronizing and communicating. A distributed system is said to be parallel if the "simultaneously advancing computations" overlap in time.

A **process** is used to represent a single "advancing computation" in most computing environments; that is, a **thread of control** in a computing environment that can be carried out concurrently with the threads of control represented by other processes.

An example of a thread of control is the main function in C++. We define the *behavior* of a process as the behavior defined for its thread of control. A heavyweight process can "contain" (or create) other smaller lightweight processes or threads, whose programs cooperate to perform some behavior. Threads are created in the context of a heavyweight process. A thread is a single path of execution through a program, a dynamic model, or some other representation of control flow. Both process and thread are stereotypes of the UML active class construct.

The problems inherent in the engineering (requirements capture, design, implementation, test, and maintenance) of distributed systems is similar to a juggling problem: The more balls a juggler needs to handle, the more complex the juggling task. It might even be that the complexity of the juggling task grows exponentially for each new ball added! Now, each ball can be likened to a process. For each new process added to a system it becomes even harder to understand and engineer. Thus, distributed systems are in most cases harder to develop compared to sequential systems consisting of only one process.

A **node** represents an abstraction of a hardware device in the system's implementation. A node is used to describe one node type, for example a computer or a device, in a physical network that executes the system's functionality.

Processes are allocated to nodes; processes that are allocated to the same node are (physically) distributed together in the system's implementation.

When objects are allocated to processes, their (instances) reside in the same address space as the process. Objects of a single type or class can be allocated to different processes. Objects of different types or classes can be allocated to the same process. Another aspect of distribution is that multiple application systems may share objects at run time.

Example

It is often convenient to have separate processes for dealing with different actors. The **Payment** and **Invoicing** applications involve different actors which can

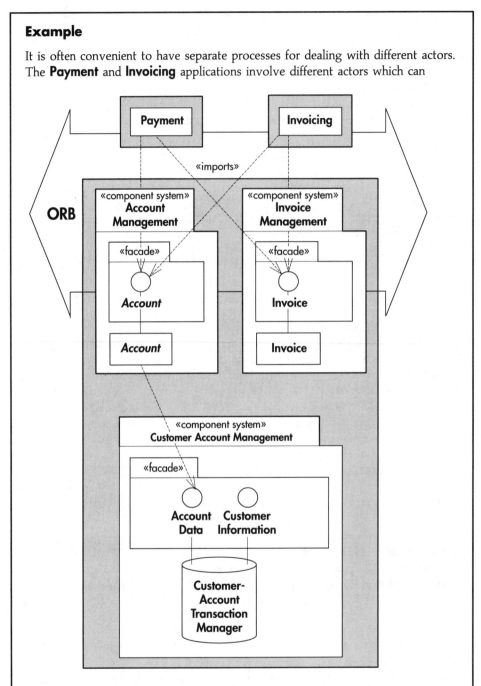

Figure 7.22 **Payment** *and* **Invoicing** *are both allocated to independent processes (gray rectangles).* **Account Management** *and* **Invoice Management** *are both allocated to a common legacy system process. An ORB marshals and forwards requests between these processes.*

operate fairly independently since they only interact through **Invoices** that change state. The application systems are furthermore often implemented on different hardware. They should therefore be allocated to different processes.

In an earlier example, Figure 7.5, we saw how the **Account** and **Invoice** objects could be shared in a distributed environment by using an Object Request Broker. The **Payment** and **Invoicing** applications then import the interfaces to those component systems and use the objects as if they were available in the same process as the application itself.

The architects believe that later they want to allow the **Account** and **Invoice** objects to be located anywhere in their distributed system, as long as they are reachable through the ORB. But for the first few releases they decide that these objects belong entirely to the same process as the legacy system **Customer-Account Transaction Manager**. From an architectural point of view they can think of the legacy system as executing within one single process, as shown in Figure 7.22.

However, the actual decision of how to distribute objects to processes should be delayed as long as possible. This will allow the distribution to be changed easily as the system's performance can be monitored. By using well-defined interfaces between different application systems, and also between component systems, it is easier to delay this deployment of objects to processes. Interfaces can thus, if necessary, be implemented as proxies that forward messages from one process to the process that houses the real object. With tools to support object distribution to processes, such as Forté or DCOM, it is even possible to delay the distribution until run time.

While lightweight processes and mutexing over shared data are very important in system design on many platforms, we do not discuss it in this book. Instead we assume that either the middleware layer or the system-software layer provide appropriate primitives, and that the use of these primitives can be modeled using UML. The UML documents and books will provide more information regarding processes, nodes, threads, and so on (Booch *et al.*, 1998; Jacobson *et al.*, 1998; Rumbaugh *et al.*, 1998).

7.14 Summary

Software architecture defines the organization of software at a high level and deals with how systems are decomposed into elements and how these interact with each other. Good architectures are tolerant to change, understandable, and enable the design of the desired system functionality with suitable performance.

A *layered system* organizes software into layers, where each layer is built on top of another more general layer. A layer can loosely be defined as a set of systems with the same degree of generality. The further down the layers, the more general the components. The number of layers, their names and their contents are not fixed, but vary from situation to situation. We call the topmost layer the *application system layer*, since it consists of application systems. The next layer contains those component systems used to build application systems and is called the *business-specific layer*. The business-specific components are built on the *middleware layer* and provide platform-independent components for things like distributed object computing. The *system-software layer* consists of specific operating systems, GUI systems, and so on.

A layered system can be thought of as a system of interoperating systems. The architecturally relevant pieces can be defined as a system using several superordinate models. These models include an analysis model, a concurrency model, a deployment model, a design model, an implementation model, and a use case model.

Each application and component system is represented as a subsystem in the superordinate design model. The environment of such a subsystem will be represented as actors of the application or component system in question. Each use case defined for the superordinate system is distributed over the application and component systems involved.

Application and component systems in one layer communicate via interfaces with other systems in the same layer. They may also reuse components provided via facades exported from component systems in lower layers.

7.15 Additional reading

Philippe Kruchten provides an excellent discussion of the needs of multiple views on software architecture in "The 4 + 1 View Model of Architecture", *IEEE Software*, November 1995.

Systems of interoperating systems and superordinate systems are discussed in detail in the "Systems of Interconnected Systems" article by Ivar Jacobson, Karin Palmkvist, and Susanne Dyrhage, *ROAD*, May–June 1995.

The excellent book *The Essential Distributed Objects Survival Guide*, by Robert Orfali, Dan Harkey, and Jeri Edwards, Wiley, 1996, provides a comprehensive discussion and comparison of several distributed computing systems, such as CORBA and OLE/COM.

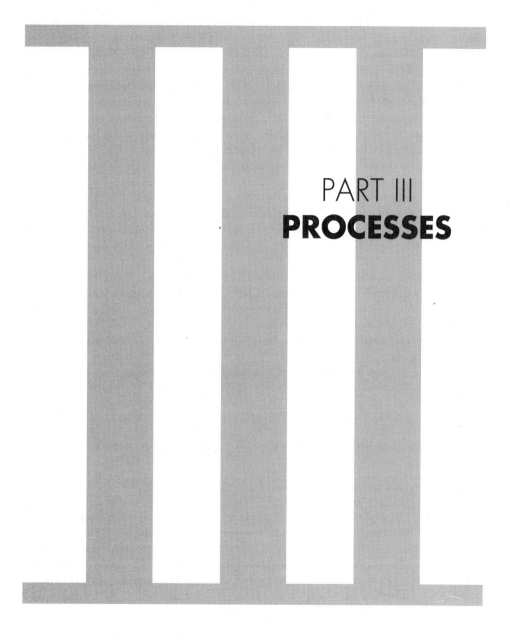

PART III
PROCESSES

Many business organizations find that competition is forcing them to improve their performance not just by the few percent a year that has been sufficient in the past but by 10 times as much. A change of that magnitude means they have to change the way they work radically. Not only do they need a large change, but they need it quickly.

A little historical insight will help. In feudal times a local artisan bought a few local materials, fabricated them in his local shop, and sold them to a few local customers. Chances are he couldn't read and write. He kept his simple affairs in his head.

Business affairs are different today. Materials come from all over the world. They pass through a stocking, manufacturing, inspection, warehousing, and distribution sequence. Supervising this series of activities requires a substantial administrative operation. People, materials, process and machinery, and product have to be in the right place at the right time. Keeping this complex manufacturing or service operation going are staff departments like purchasing, engineering, accounting, and marketing.

Within the past few years a couple of new ideas have been gaining ground. One of them is that business processes exist to deliver value to customers. Companies have discovered that the denizens of these scores of coordinating departments find it easy to get involved in turf battles. Such is the joy of administrative conflict that they take their eye off the customer and, perchance, competitors as well.

The second new idea is that much of the coordination of business processes can be taken over by information systems. Among other effects, everyone can work off the same database. Armed with pertinent information, both workers and managers can better focus on the needs of the users of their product. Reworking the operations of a business to implement these two ideas is called business process reengineering (BPR) — or sometimes, just business engineering.

What do we have to change? These two ideas seem simple enough, but observers note that more than half the attempts at BPR fail. On the other hand, Deloitte & Touche Consulting Group's Seventh Annual Survey of North American Telecommunications (1996) reported that 70 percent of the responding companies had initiated reengineering projects during the previous 12 months. The concept of BPR, difficult as it may be, seems to be gathering steam.

We apply business engineering in two ways. The first is reengineering the business processes of the organization that will benefit from the application systems developed by the reuse business. The second is reengineering the software development process itself.

Reengineering the business processes, as will be discussed in Chapter 8, involves:

- analyzing current practices and assets, making use of object-oriented business engineering and use-case methods;

- developing and carrying out an incremental change plan.

The rest of Part III explains the types of processes and organization that will exist in a working reuse business — after it has been reengineered. To get there and to sustain the operations of the reuse business takes management vision, organization, and financing. Getting there and managing a reuse business is covered as supporting processes in Part IV, but in Chapters 9–12 we concentrate on the software engineering processes themselves.

Chapter 9 describes the overall set of business use cases (processes) for the Reuse Business and what people with different competencies need to do to perform them.

We will see how an organization can be structured into competence units to support the processes. This high-level business model provides a framework for the more detailed treatment of the key software engineering processes which are described in the following chapters.

Chapters 10–12 detail the three key business use cases:

- in Chapter 10, the process for engineering the layered architecture – Application Family Engineering (AFE),

- in Chapter 11, the process for building a component system – Component System Engineering (CSE),

- in Chapter 12, the process for developing one application system using components – Application System Engineering (ASE).

Chapters 10, 11, and 12 have the same overall structure and follow a similar line of thought, namely OOSE. We describe an incremental engineering approach to building architectures, finding and engineering the reusable component systems, and developing applications.

OBJECT-ORIENTED BUSINESS ENGINEERING

8.1 Business process reengineering achieves dramatic improvement

Business Process Reengineering (BPR) is "the fundamental rethinking and radical redesign of business processes to achieve dramatic improvements in critical, contemporary measures of performance, such as cost, quality, service and speed" (Hammer and Champy, 1993; Hammer and Stanton, 1995). It implies a comprehensive view of the entire operation. It is the thinking through of what you do, the way you do it, and why. In short, BPR makes you focus on a redesign to serve your customers better.

The risks involved in a BPR project are significant. They fall roughly into two categories: those associated with the change process itself, and those arising from the technology employed. Most of the books about BPR tackle only the first set of risks — the soft factors. We do not underestimate the need to address these risks; that need remains. (In fact, we address it in Part IV.) But we are convinced that BPR's success rate can be dramatically improved by employing methods that offer more concrete guidance to the reengineers. A well-defined reengineering process not only increases the chance of a successful project, but reduces the "soft factor" risks. This is one thing that sets our reengineering approach, *Object-Oriented Business Engineering*, apart from other approaches to business process reengineering – its strong focus on risk-reduction by building object models of a business following a well-defined process. The models should be based on objects because then you get a very close mapping between real objects like "people," places, and things and objects in the information systems.

Example

The XYB banking consortium wants to develop a suite of new applications to support the rapidly growing electronic home-banking (or home finance) market. The market is changing rapidly, and banks have to compete on the rapid provision of new and innovative services to an increasingly computer literate and diverse bank customer base.

To do this, the XYB has to radically change its operating procedures, its organization, and its mission-critical information systems – in short, to reengineer itself. Because this new style of distributed, virtual, electronic financial institution will depend so critically on rapidly developed and deployed software systems, the XYBsoft software development organization also needs to reengineer itself. It needs to identify the new application problem domains that support the new business processes, build a transition organization, define an architecture, start producing component systems for the new banking world, and quickly develop the new applications.

Business engineering can be applied in two ways when installing a reuse business.

- The processes and the organization of the *reuse business itself* can be developed and modeled using business engineering – as discussed in Chapters 9–14. The reuse business itself would be something like a software development department; we use XYBsoft as an example of such a reuse business.

- Business engineering can also be used as a technique to better understand the *target organization* and its needs for information system support. The target organization is the organization that will have its processes improved in terms of time to market, quality, predictability, and so on, as a result of the application systems developed by the reuse business. The models developed in a business engineering program are an excellent starting point to define architectures, find reusable components, and develop application systems that add value for the customers (see Chapters 10–12).

In this chapter we will only illustrate how business engineering can be applied to a target organization – the XYB.

8.2 A well-defined process for business process reengineering

Business engineering according to Jacobson *et al.* (1994) is a process where the current organization is analyzed and a new organization is envisioned and designed. Figure 8.1 shows the key activities in business engineering. Also, the information systems required to support the business are identified and developed in parallel with the business engineering.

There is no standard recipe for engineering a business. The exact path depends on the kind of people in the organization, the kind of customers, and the kind of problems. The business engineering process must therefore be customized and discussed with managers and employees to make sure that they will be able to understand the results and models. The big picture must be in place before the project starts; details and adjustments can be handled along the way.

In Table 8.1, we describe the Business Engineering process, showing it as five sequential steps, BE1..BE5. In reality, many of these steps will be carried out concurrently, as Figure 8.1 shows.

Table 8.1   *The essential steps of the Business Engineering process.*

BE1:   **Creating a business reengineering directive** – define the goals of the engineering effort at a level that can be discussed with managers and employees. Explain the situation of the business and why it must be engineered. The reengineering directive is a management responsibility.

BE2:   **Envisioning the new business** – based on knowledge of the existing business, try new ideas and new technologies in order to envision the new business. Also gather information and compare with "best in class" companies. This vision is formulated in terms of goals, objectives, and high-level descriptions of future business processes. The vision is the input to the first iteration of forward engineering and implementation.

BE3:   **Reverse engineering the existing organization** – to get an accepted common picture of the existing business. Describe in detail only those parts of the business that are important and that must be engineered. What you choose to reverse engineer will depend on the results of envisioning.

BE4:   **Forward engineering the new business** – incrementally develop and describe the new business and develop the information systems that will support it. The results define what the business will do in terms of business processes, how the business will be organized internally in order to perform the processes, and instructions for the people in the new business.

BE5:   **Implementing the new business** – incrementally and while the existing processes are operating. Start with a part of the business where success is certain and learn more about the process for business engineering to reduce risks in further reengineering. This creates a success story before going on with the rest of the business.

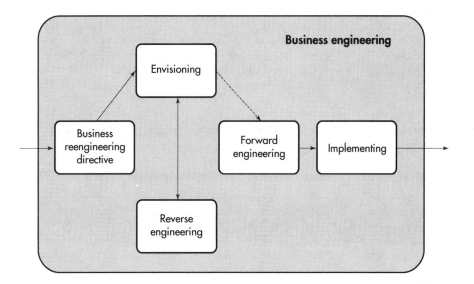

Figure 8.1 *An informal illustration of the work steps in business engineering [adapted from Jacobson* et al., *1994]. Arrows indicate the main direction of information flow.*

8.3 Business engineering delivers models as a chart for the future

Object-oriented business engineering (Jacobson *et al.*, 1994) is a well-defined process that results in a number of models of the business. Many find engineering approaches less attractive, because engineering means some kind of modeling, and modeling means viewing the organization as a set of building blocks in a machine-like way. However, modeling languages supply a common language that simplifies communication between people when discussing the business, and the models provide a shared understanding of the subject matter which reduces the risk of misunderstandings. Models give a good starting point when proceeding to improve the business, and are invaluable for continuous process improvement. It is important that the models are intuitive enough so that all the people working in the business are able to understand the most important pieces.

Others think that formal modeling approaches limit their creativity, because of the particular syntax and semantic rules. But a structured approach to reengineering does not really limit creativity. Instead, it helps focus creativity on the right problems.

The object-oriented business engineering models are similar in spirit to those of Object-Oriented Software Engineering (OOSE). The biggest difference is that the "system" being modeled is now a business organization instead of a software system. Hence we will find who the customers are, represented as actors, and the different ways they will use the business, represented as business use cases. The business use cases are described in terms of interacting objects (that is, people with specific competencies in different roles and the things they manipulate) that perform the business use cases.

An object-oriented business engineering project will result in the implementation of a new organization defined by business actors, business use cases, worker types (an abstraction of people with a specific required competence), business entity object types (workproducts) and competence units (organizational clusters of workers).

8.4 Using business actors and use cases to represent value-adding processes

A **business system** is used to represent an organization unit that we want to understand better in order to make it more competitive.

For example, the XYB bank. To create an adequate model of the business it is important to understand its environment.

A **business actor** represents a role that someone or something in the environment can play in relation to the business.

For example, in the environment surrounding the XYB bank business system there are several business actors. These include the **Bank Customer**s that the business is supposed to serve and **Buyer**s and **Seller**s, who use the new bank services to process invoices. A real person can take on several roles in relation to a business system. For example, John Bigbux might be both a **Bank Customer** and a **Buyer**. Other organizations such as the United States Internal Revenue Service (IRS) or the Federal Inter-bank Clearing Organization may also take on a role as an actor.

The notations we use are an extension of the OOSE notation described in Chapter 3. We use a stick figure to represent a business actor, as shown in Figure 8.2. Business processes are modeled as business use cases, using ellipses, also shown in Figure 8.2. The term "business process" and the more precise term "business use case" are used interchangeably in the remainder of the book.

Each business use case represents a specific workflow in the business. A business use case description defines what should happen in the business when the use case is performed. More precisely:

A **business use case** is a sequence of work steps performed in a business system that produces a result of perceived and measurable value to an individual actor of the business.

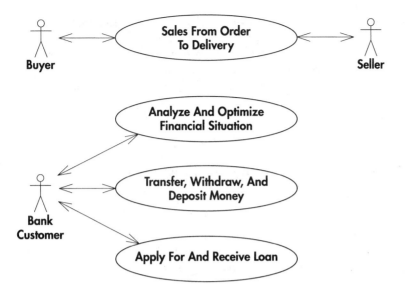

Figure 8.2 *The business use cases offered by the XYB to its actors. Arrows are* «*communicates*» *associations.*

Business actors and business use cases communicate by issuing requests. We indicate this with «*communicates*» associations between business actors and use cases.

Example

The business engineers envision several business use cases for the XYB, as shown in Figure 8.2. In reality, there would be many more.

- In the business use case **Sales From Order To Delivery** a **Buyer** is assumed to know what to buy and from where. The **Buyer** orders the goods or services, then the **Seller** invoices the **Buyer**, the **Buyer** pays and finally the **Seller** delivers the goods or services. The XYB acts as a broker in this business use case, connecting the **Buyer** and the **Seller** to each other.
- The business use case **Analyze And Optimize Financial Situation** enables a **Bank Customer** to analyze and optimize finances.
- The business use case **Apply For And Receive Loan** allows a **Bank Customer** to borrow from the XYB.
- The business use case **Transfer, Withdraw, And Deposit Money** allows a **Bank Customer** to make transfers between accounts, withdraw and deposit money, and also to define future automatic transfers.

The use case and actor model provides a *usability view* of the business, that is, *how the business adds value to customers and partners*. Furthermore, it will be easy to see how each person involved in the organization participates to perform the business use cases that serve the business actors. For each business use case there are diagrams and documents that show how people with certain competencies act to carry out the use case.

8.5 Using workers and entity types to represent people and results

In order to organize a business it is necessary to identify the competencies required by the employees, the roles they need to play, and the "things" that one or several of the employees use or handle as they perform the business use cases:

- The **case worker** represents people with a certain competence who have contacts with the actors as an essential part of the job.

- The **internal worker** represents people with a certain competence, such as specialists, that work within the business.

- A business **entity object** represents a "thing" that is handled or used in the business, such as a *Sales Order*.

- A **work step** describes a piece of work a worker may be asked to perform.

We want to define different worker types for the different competencies required in a business. The workers can act in one or more roles as they participate in the business use cases. But it is the worker types that can be used to define the organization – based on required competencies.

Workers communicate with each other and with entity objects to perform the workflow of the business use cases.

Workers that communicate with each other or with a business actor or with work objects are connected by a **«communicates»** association.

The workers may also access entity objects, which is also depicted by «communicates» associations.

Example

The following is a very brief description of how the workers participate in the business use case **Sales From Order To Delivery**, as shown in Figure 8.3.

1   A business actor **Buyer** orders some goods or services by direct contact with the business actor **Seller**.
2   The **Seller** invoices the business actor **Buyer** through the (case) worker **Payment Requester**.
3   The **Buyer** pays via the **Payment Requester** who transfers money between the entity object **Account** of the **Seller** and the **Account** of the **Buyer**.
4   Finally the **Seller** delivers the goods or services directly to the **Buyer**.

The worker **Payment Requester** adds value to the **Seller** by issuing the entity object **Invoice** and maybe also by keeping track of outstanding payments. The **Payment Requester** worker also adds value to the **Buyer** by simplifying transactions like this and by providing better control and availability of invoice payment.

Note that **Account** and **Invoice** are types of entity objects in the business model, not to be confused with the related *Account* and *Invoice* entity types in the OOSE models.

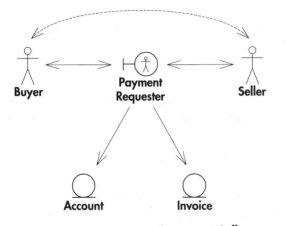

Figure 8.3   *Business actors (**Buyer** and **Seller**), a worker (**Payment Requester**), and business entity objects (**Account** and **Invoice**) that participate in the business use case **Sales From Order To Delivery**.*

The clear connection just illustrated between workers and business use cases is important in order to optimize the workers for the business use cases in terms of time to market, quality, and cost, and to ensure that their work steps are coordinated.

Traditionally, processes or projects have been defined by work steps assigned to individual people, one work step to one person. By grouping the work steps as responsibilities of the workers, it is much simpler to find suitable people to perform the processes since each worker clusters work steps that should be performed by one individual with a certain competence. Staffing in terms of individual work steps, on the other hand, would mean that for each work step you have to decide who should do it. It is harder to identify a person with a suitable competence level if you just consider individual steps – not clusters of steps. Other BPR approaches also define workers or roles, but after the identification of work steps. We prefer to find the workers first (that is, the required competencies) and then assign the detailed work steps. Furthermore, each worker is responsible for performing a handful of work steps, which means that a business use case can be understood in terms of a handful of workers instead of dozens of work steps.

To illustrate these concepts, let us see what really happens when a real person approaches the business. Described in terms of object-oriented business engineering, the following happens in a typical business use case such as **Apply For And Receive Loan**:

- First, an instance of a business actor is created. This corresponds to a real person such as Mr Eager contacting the bank. Normally it is too early to know the type of actor, but let us here assume the actor **Bank Customer**.

- At the same moment a business use case instance is also created. Again, it is too early to know which type of use case.

- Similarly an instance of a case worker is created. This corresponds to an employee within the bank, such as Mr Swift, being contacted by Mr Eager. Once again, it is too early to know which type of case worker.

- The **Bank Customer** and the worker instance together determine the **Bank Customer**'s business at hand. This corresponds to Mr Eager and Mr Swift deciding what to do.

- It is now possible to discern the type of actor, use case, and case worker. We can thus tell which use case commences (in this case **Apply For And Receive Loan**), which business actor (in this case **Bank Customer**) Mr Eager represents and which worker Mr Swift represents.

- From now on the workers, staffed by employees, can act to fulfill the **Bank Customer**'s needs as defined by the use case.

- It may become necessary to engage a new worker in the use case. This corresponds to Mr Eager or Mr Swift contacting some other employee, for example Ms Agile, who has the necessary competence.

8.6 Grouping workers into competence units according to skills

It is the people and information systems that make the business processes happen. In this respect we can think of people and information systems as *resources* that enact the workers as they participate in the business processes.

Resources such as individual persons and information systems are organized into **resource units**.

A resource unit may be a traditional department, section, or a group with a functional responsibility. A resource unit may also have a *resource owner*, similar to a manager, that people report to, as discussed in Jacobson *et al.* (1994).

In a traditional organization resource units define responsibilities and reporting paths. Resource units are often used to keep people who work with functionally related tasks together even when they have quite different skills or competencies. This is not necessary in a process-driven organization where the operations are carried out by people and information systems performing business use cases (business processes). The people and information systems that enact the workers of a business process may come together from several resource units. We prefer to talk of competence units rather than resource units since we focus on the competencies that need to come together to enact a process. A process such as launching a new product then draws workers (enacted by resources) with complementary skills from several competence units such as marketing, developing, and packaging a product.

Example

The case worker **Payment Requester** and the **Invoice** class of entity objects both belong to the competence unit **Invoice Processing**. Mr Ready is the resource owner for people that get involved in the competence unit **Invoice Processing**, such as Ms Agile and Mr Swift.

A **competence unit** contains workers with similar competencies and entity object types that these workers are responsible for.

The purpose of a competence unit is to maintain and develop a certain type of competence within the business and also to improve the types of material (that is, the entity objects) and documentation used. Competence units help better understand what competencies exist, to simplify hiring and training the right people, and simplify the staffing of business processes. Most often there is a one-to-one relationship between a competence unit and a resource unit, which simplifies management and training. A resource may have the different competencies required for many different worker types, but most often for worker types within one competence unit. In other words, for most situations you may think of people as being organized in competence units. For the rest of the book we will ignore the distinction between resource units and competence units; we will talk only of competence units and say that each competence unit has a resource owner, and so on.

A business process type, that is, a business use case, is typically owned by a manager, or executive worker, known as a *process owner*. The process owner is responsible for defining the business use case and appointing process leaders. A particular instance of a business process may be led or supervised by a *process leader* worker, like a project leader running a project. The people enacting the workers report to the process leader on a daily basis, not to their resource owners who, instead, are responsible for their long-term training and career path. The manager of a resource unit should not be in charge of daily operations since this works against the whole idea of cross-organization business processes. A resource unit manager who is responsible for the daily operation of an organization is highly likely to put the interests of the resource unit above the interests of the organization as a whole.

8.7 Information systems must support the business use cases and workers

The workers are staffed by people who use information systems to communicate:

- with each other,

- with the business actors, and

- to access or manipulate entity object resources.

Using object-oriented business engineering as input, it is a straightforward process to identify the information system models. The following is a very simplified approach (see Figure 8.4):

- Identify an information system actor for each worker that will interact with the information system.

- Some of the business actors interact directly with the information systems of a business, which means that they also will show up as information system actors.

- Each worker and business actor needs streamlined information system support for his or her work steps in a business use case. Therefore, define a *specific information system use case for each business use case that each worker or business actor is involved in*. This means that each business use case will be supported by several information system use cases – one for each worker or business actor. Sometimes it may make sense to combine the information system use cases targeted at different workers or business actors into one information system use case.

- The business entity objects represent the important things the employees work with. Such important things often need to be managed persistently and therefore are represented also as information system *entity types*.

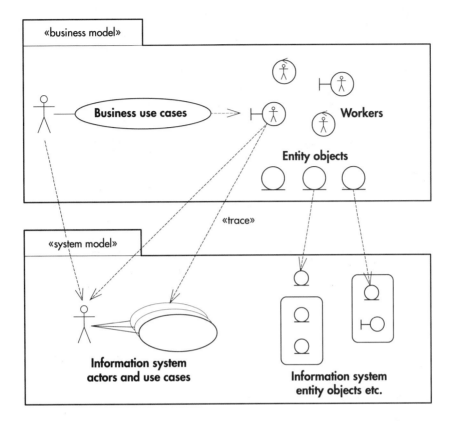

Figure 8.4 *The workers participating in business use cases and also some business actors map to information system actors that use information system use cases. Business entity objects often correspond to information system entity objects.*

Example

The XYB wants to support the invoice payment in the business use case **Sales From Order To Delivery**. They create the information system use case **Pay Invoice** which allows a **Seller** to send **Invoices** to a **Buyer**, and the **Buyer** to pay **Invoices** from the **Seller**. Both the **Seller** and the **Buyer** interact directly with the information system use case **Pay Invoice**, which means that *individuals that act as the business actors* **Seller** *and* **Buyer** *will also be acting as the corresponding information system actors* **Seller** and **Buyer** (Figure 8.5).

Furthermore, the **Account** and **Invoice** types of business entity objects will be represented as the corresponding information system entity types, **Account** and **Invoice**.

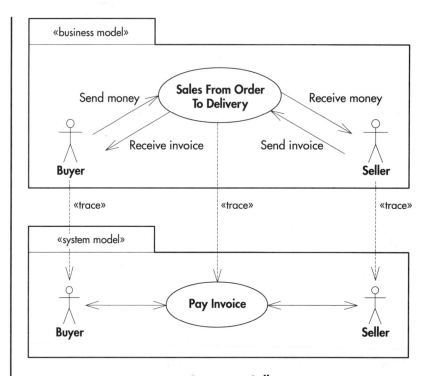

Figure 8.5 *The business actors **Buyer** and **Seller** interact via a business use case supported by an information system use case **Pay Invoice**, used by corresponding information system actors.*

8.8 Summary

Object-oriented business engineering is a reengineering technique that involves:

- creating a vision of the desired processes, organization, information system architecture, and application systems,

- analyzing current practices and assets, and

- developing and carrying out an incremental risk-sensitive change plan.

Think of an organization as a *business system* that interacts with *business actors* such as customers, suppliers, and so on. A business actor that interacts with the business provides something to it and gains something of value in return. A business process is what a business does as it provides something of measurable value to an actor. We use the more precise term *business use case* instead of the more common term "business process." As a business performs a business use case, people with various competencies collaborate in order to enact the use case. A worker is a set of roles conducted by someone with a certain competency in the organization.

Competence units group workers with similar competencies and entity types that these workers will be responsible for. The purpose of a competence unit is to maintain and develop a certain type of competence within the business, including types of entity objects to be used.

The workers use information systems to communicate with each other and with the business actors, and to access or manipulate entity objects. Each business actor and worker that uses the information system gives rise to an information system actor. Information system use cases and entity types can be identified from workers and business entity types.

8.9 Additional reading

For more details on the object-oriented business engineering approach used as a basis here, consult the book, *The Object Advantage: Business Process Reengineering with Object Technology*, by Ivar Jacobson, Maria Ericsson, and Agneta Jacobson, Addison-Wesley, 1994. Note that some terminology has been changed.

Many pragmatic guidelines on how to succeed with BPR can be found in the book *The Reengineering Revolution – A Handbook*, by Michael Hammer and Steven A. Stanton, HarperBusiness, 1995.

Another perspective on using objects to model business processes can be found in David Taylor's book, *Business Engineering with Object Technology*, Wiley, New York, 1995.

9

APPLYING BUSINESS ENGINEERING TO DEFINE PROCESSES AND ORGANIZATION

9.1 Processes and organization of the Reuse Business match architecture

One of the most critical challenges that a reuse business faces is how to structure and organize its software engineering processes and organization. Effective reuse requires significant software engineering organization and process change, typically spanning several projects or even multiple organizations within a company. Furthermore, the system and the development organization must harmonize; that is, the organization must match the system's architecture. Such a sweeping change can only be accomplished with management support and a suitable transition process. The changes can only be sustained and systematically improved with well-defined process and organizational support. Often the changes occur in parallel with or as a consequence of changes to other processes within the company, but this is not elaborated in this chapter; instead we focus on the software engineering processes.

Fortunately, all this is fairly simple in principle, given that you have a clear vision of an architecture. The layered architectural style naturally leads to a structure of processes and an organizational model which separates developer concerns.

Unfortunately this is not as simple in practice. There are several factors that complicate matters, such as the difficulties in understanding and managing complex architectures and organizations. Another factor is not knowing everything from the outset, such as all the requirements, business needs, organizational problems, and market forces. We address these types of difficulties in four ways:

- The architecture, reuse business processes and organization are all developed *incrementally* in order to reduce the risks associated with the changes.

- The architecture and the component and application systems are developed based on *input from business models* of the *target organization,* which improves the usability of the systems developed.

- The layered architecture is represented using *explicit techniques* such as superordinate system models. The use of modeling techniques with well-defined meaning makes it easier to understand the architecture and also to engineer and manage it.

- The reuse business organization itself is represented using *explicit techniques* such as the business engineering process and modeling language for object-oriented business engineering. A well-specified object-oriented business engineering process and modeling language make it easier to get reengineering going, which reduces the risks of getting stuck. The object-oriented business models also improve the understanding of the organization and thus the ability to manage it.

Over the years, the software engineering community has discovered the importance of following a well-defined software engineering process. A well-defined process details the competencies, roles, work steps, methods, responsibilities, and deliverables of the people developing the software. While most software process work is directed at coordinating the work of teams, even individual programmers can benefit. As an outgrowth of work on large team process definition, and work at the Software Engineering Institute on process maturity, Watts Humphrey (1995) has developed a lightweight personal software process that individuals can use to optimize their own performance, as well as that of small teams.

A software process describes milestones and metrics, making it possible for the development activities to be coordinated and managed effectively. Whereas no single Reuse Business process will suit every situation, a general model of reuse processes and organization can be used as a good starting point for customization. This is the way we intend to use the Reuse Business model we describe. The Reuse Business defines three software engineering processes each with a specific responsibility, as shown in Figure 9.1:

- One **Component System Engineering** process staffed by a team for each component system.

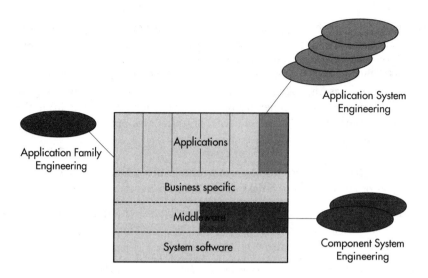

Figure 9.1 *The various Reuse Business software engineering processes and their relations to the layered system.*

- One **Application System Engineering** process staffed by a team for each application system.

- One **Application Family Engineering** process staffed by a team for the entire layered system (System of Interoperating Systems), particularly focused on the definition of the division into systems and the interfaces between them.

The process and organizational models that will be presented here are significantly simplified for presentation. For example, we do not define the detailed work steps and properties of the individual workers, although this would be essential for these processes to be directly usable.

9.2 Software engineering processes in the Reuse Business

The Reuse Business performs business use cases (business processes) that add value to its customers, who are represented as actors. Business use cases are performed by cooperating *workers* within the Reuse Business. Let us now introduce a few of the most important actors:

- **Customer**s request application systems, place requirements on them, and usually pay for the systems.

Customers are also involved when deciding on the features, priorities and roll-out plans when developing new versions of component systems and the layered architecture as a whole. **Customer**s can be both internal, such as a business process owner, or external, such as another company.

- An **End User** is someone who will use an application system when it is installed in the target organization.

End Users need to participate in engineering the application systems by suggesting new features and usability requirements. Some **End User**s are also involved as a source of information when developing new versions of component systems and the layered architecture as a whole.

- A **Manufacturer** receives a new version of an application system when developed, then customizes, configures, produces, and delivers complete applications to **Customer**s.

These business actors are shown in Figure 9.2, represented by the stickman symbol. This figure is a more accurate rendition of the informal figure previously used in Chapter 2.

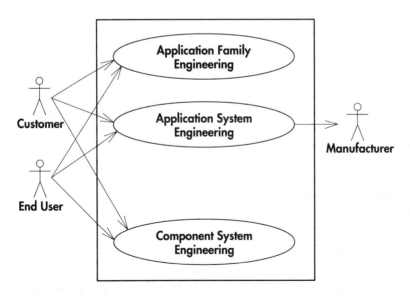

Figure 9.2 *A simple business model of the Reuse Business, showing the business use cases and the business actors. Arrows indicate the main interactions between business actors and business use cases.*

Notice that component systems, facades, application systems, and the layered system do not appear on this diagram. They will appear as business entity objects in other diagrams.

- The business use case **Application System Engineering** develops new versions of application systems as requested by a **Customer**.

- The business use case **Component System Engineering** develops component systems to be used by **Application Engineer**s.

- The business use case **Application Family Engineering** develops the product plan and engineers the layered system.

Figure 9.2 illustrates these business use cases as ellipses, with arrows indicating that the **Customer**s and **End User**s provide input to them.

Example

As XYBsoft begins to install a reuse business, they appoint a **Software Engineering Business Manager**, who is given the responsibility to lead their software development department into a full-fledged reuse business.

The **SEB Manager** and a team consisting of his superior manager, his fellow managers, and the key developers begin the transition to the reuse business. One of the first things they need to do is to decide on the business actors.

The team agrees that the business actor **End User** best corresponds to the real bank customers. Furthermore, XYB already has a well-functioning central software distribution and installation group, which the **SEB Manager** and colleagues match with the business actor **Manufacturer**.

Since they are developing internal support systems for the XYB they decide that the XYB business process owners should be the **Customer**s. As it turns out, the XYB business engineering team has already defined four major XYB business processes, and assigned process owners.

These processes are: **Sales From Order To Delivery, Analyze And Optimize Financial Situation, Apply For And Receive Loan**, and finally **Transfer, Withdraw, And Deposit Money**. These business processes will be used to define the suite of application systems and overall architecture to be managed by XYBsoft.

Each of the business use cases (processes) **Application System Engineering, Component System Engineering**, and **Application Family Engineering** is a *software engineering process* (SEP) derived from the general OOSE software engineering process as discussed in Chapter 3 (Jacobson *et al.*, 1992). **ASE** is an elaboration of the OOSE software engineering process, customized to assemble application systems quickly from component systems. **AFE** is an elaboration of the OOSE software engineering process, customized to develop a layered architecture in terms of a superordinate system, superordinate use cases, interfaces, subsystems, and facades. **CSE** is an elaboration of the OOSE software engineering process, customized to design for variability.

Each of the business use cases (processes) should be supported by a number of tools integrated into a complete *software engineering process support environment* (SEPSE).

There are also several other non-software engineering processes, which we will not model here. These include **Transition To A Reuse Business** and **Managing The Reuse Business**, both of which are key to establishing and operating a successful reuse business. They will be described in detail in Chapters 13 and 14.

As explained in Chapter 8, the business use case model is transformed into an object model, showing objects representing interacting workers and entity objects. Figure 9.3 shows a simplified model of the RSEB workers and the entity objects they manipulate.

The **Application Family Engineering** process controls the facades between the layers, thus fixing the points of interaction between the processes for **Application System Engineering** and **Component System Engineering**. The facade exports component use cases, classes, subsystems, and so on. In CSE the **Component Use Case Engineer** and the **Component Subsystem Engineer** create reusable components by capturing component use cases from the requirements of the **Customer**s and the **End User**s and then designing and implementing them. In ASE the **Application Use Case Engineer** and the **Application Subsystem Engineer** reuse components to build application systems to meet **Customer** and **End User** needs. Then the **Tester** tests the application systems and delivers them to the **Manufacturer**.

Let us now look at each of the software engineering processes in somewhat more detail.

Application Family Engineering This software engineering process captures the requirements from a range of **Customer**s and transforms these requirements into a suite of application systems. The process produces an architecture that defines the layers and facades of the component systems. The workers involved need to understand what current and potential **Customer**s will need and want in the future, in order to envision appropriate use cases. The use cases are then transformed into a suitable architecture through an architecture robustness analysis and design. Candidate application and component systems can be defined during the architecture robustness analysis and aligned with existing products, such as legacy systems, GUI builders, object request brokers, and so on during design.

It is then possible to decide when to engineer (or buy) the various application and component systems, which can be done by a set of concurrent processes for **Component System Engineering** and **Application System Engineering**.

Application System Engineering This process builds application systems by selecting, customizing, and assembling components from component systems. The **Application System Engineering** process begins when a **Customer** requests an application and the process starts with requirements capture. The purpose of requirements capture is to collect

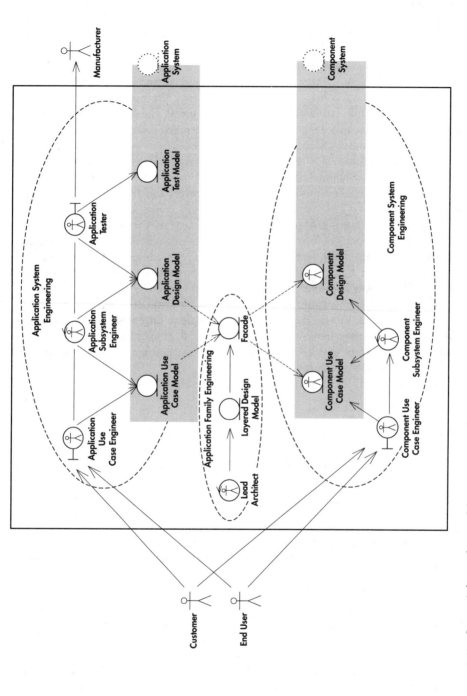

Figure 9.3 *Some of the workers and business entity objects that participate in the software engineering processes of an RSEB. Application and Component Systems are aggregations of other entity objects, such as Application Use Case Model, highlighted by the grayed field behind them.*

and organize requirements from the **Customer** and the **End User**s. The application system is then incrementally analyzed, designed, implemented, and tested – by reusing and specializing components. Even if the Application Engineers try to reuse as much as possible, they often have to analyze, design, and implement system features that have little or no support from the component systems.

ASE involves workers such as requirements analysts, architects, designers, and testers. The Application Engineers use the tools, modeling languages, and process instructions provided with the component systems that they reuse.

Component System Engineering This process designs, constructs, and packages components into a component system. **CSE** begins with requirements capture, which is based on information from a wide range of sources such as business models, domain experts, and application **End User**s. After having analyzed the requirements for consistency, commonality, and variability, the results of the requirements capture are used to incrementally architect, design, implement, and test the component system.

CSE concludes with certifying and packaging the component system for reuse and easy retrieval. The reusers need to follow a process and use tools that assist and guide them to effective use of the provided components. The component engineers develop or acquire process (SEP) and tool (SEPSE) components that are useful or essential when reusing elements from their component system. Then, the reusers combine these process and tool components into software engineering processes and tools optimized for their work.

Most of the work for a component system is performed by similar types of workers to those in **ASE**, but also involve component engineers that are specialists in making the component system accessible to reusers. Certification and packaging is performed by these workers or by dedicated component supporters.

Example

The **Application System Engineering** teams will mostly use Java as they integrate components into applications, because they want the inherent portability and flexibility in moving distributed objects to the right nodes. The **Component System Engineering** teams will be using C++, but will specify all component interfaces in OMG IDL.

The Component Engineers who develop the **Account Management** component system soon learn that some functionality in the legacy system that they must wrap is not as flexible as they hoped. **Overdraft Management** in particular will be difficult to implement in the component system as flexibly as required.

The Component Engineers therefore decide to implement the first generation of the component system so that it does not accept overdrafts at all. They also describe a working procedure (that is, a process component) that can be followed by the Application Engineers who wish to implement their own custom procedures, such as allowing an overdraft but taking a fee for it.

> Custom overdraft management is difficult to implement using the first generation of the **Account Management** component system, since it will require the Application Engineers to create their own wrappers for the legacy system. The Component Engineers therefore suggest that the Application Engineers should assign one person to the task of implementing custom overdraft management. That person needs to be acquainted with both the legacy system and the wrapper tools used. The Component Engineers also provide a set of test scripts that can be run to verify the overdraft transactions.

Remember that workers involved in **Application System Engineering** have different goals, skills, rewards, and time-scale than Component Engineers. The Component Engineers, for example, focus on building robust, specializable systems that are well documented for reusers, not end users:

Application Engineers	**Component Engineers**
Assemble and customize into applications	Generalize for reuse and work on architecture, systems, and domain issues
Capture individual **Customer** demands	Capture and analyze requirements from several sources including several **Customer**s. Coordinate well with other analysts, domain experts
Like to quickly satisfy **Customer** and **End User** needs	Prefer working on high-quality, reusable components

Let us now further see why we chose these three business use cases for the Reuse Business.

9.2.1 Separate business use cases to allow software engineers to focus on key value added

The business use cases (that is, the business processes) just presented have been chosen to separate concerns so that individual teams can focus on "one thing" when they perform them, to give maximal value to their specific customer.

Each software engineering team must contain people that together have both sufficient domain and software engineering expertise. This is particularly true for the **Application Family Engineering** team. Each team must also have a sufficient overlap of competencies for them to be able to communicate effectively and credibly with each other, and with **Customer**s and **End User**s.

It is essential to have one business use case, **Application System Engineering**, for all the work associated with building an application system for an *individual* **Customer** so that the engineers can concentrate on adding value to that one **Customer**. The ASE use case ends at the hand-off to a **Manufacturer** since there are so many ways of doing manufacturing and distribution of applications which are outside the scope of this book. For example, it is sometimes desirable to have several **Manufacturer**s of one application system, particularly in a worldwide distributed organization. The **Manufacturer**s can make some customizations to match local needs.

There is a separate business use case for engineering a component system to enable component systems to be built concurrently. This is simplified if each component system is built by a distinct instance of **CSE** and a separate team.

So far we are consistent with the discussion in Chapter 1, describing how most systematic approaches to reuse make a clear separation between creators (**CSE**) and reusers (**ASE**).

There is one business use case that is responsible for building and improving the layered system: **Application Family Engineering**. We have decided to separate the **AFE** business use case from the **CSE** business use case. In the domain-engineering approach to reuse as discussed in Chapter 1, the overall system architecting, domain analysis, and component engineering are combined into one process. Our rational for separation is:

- **Application Family Engineering** deals with high-order architecture while **Component System Engineering** deals with the detailed architecture and design of one component system. This involves different people, even if there is some overlap.

- It is in **Application Family Engineering** that product line decisions are made, deciding which applications to develop and when. By having this in a business use case separate from **Component System Engineering** it is easier to enable managers and marketing personnel to focus on the right issues and provide valuable input to that process.

- By separating **Application Family Engineering** and **Component System Engineering** into distinct processes, it is easier to manage concurrency between them. **Application Family Engineering** can evolve the layered system and the facades incrementally while processes for **Component System Engineering** can work incrementally on individual component systems, as long as the Component Engineers comply with the facades. The facades define what people other than the Component Engineers know about each component system in an application family.

- Separate processes for **Component System Engineering** can be instantiated while the process for **AFE** is still active. The need for a new component system is often identified in the **AFE** process, which then "spawns" a distinct focused sub-project for **CSE** which can be funded and allocated to one team.

However, when the reuse business is first introduced into the organization, or if the architecture is simple, it may very well make sense to combine an instance of **Application Family Engineering** and **Component System Engineering** into one project. This is particularly true if the organization is not used to operating concurrent processes nor to working in an incremental, iterative way.

9.2.2 Incremental, iterative engineering

It is well known that incremental, iterative approaches to system design and implementation reduce risk by producing operating designs early and focusing resources on the key features and structure of the evolving system. Many authors have discussed the benefits of an incremental, iterative process for developing systems in general and OO systems in particular (Boehm, 1988; Gilb, 1988; Booch, 1994; Jacobson *et al.*, 1992; Kruchten, 1995). In fact we believe that OO methods provide a more seamless notation that makes it easier to use the more dynamic and iterative models.

> The concept of **incremental, iterative development** is simple: instead of producing the complete system as a single, monolithic release, the approach is to build up the complete functionality of the system by deliberately developing the system as a series of smaller increments, or releases.

For each increment in a project, discoveries and refinements made in later models are used to update earlier models. Each increment will include additional functionality. Some of the reasons for incremental, iterative development are:

- Each iteration results in a system increment, which can be carried out in a shorter time period than if all functionality is delivered at the same time. This allows a useful subset of functionality to be deployed sooner. This is particularly true when powerful tools can be deployed that allow application systems to be generated from use case or object models, such as domain-oriented modeling languages, application generators, scripting tools, or domain-specific kits (Griss, 1995a; Griss and Kessler, 1996).

- Several shorter increments allow more effective planning for both anticipated and unanticipated changes in requirements and technology since the changes can be accommodated in a subsequent iteration usually without disrupting the current one.

- Changing the number and length of iterations controls risk and manages time-to-market issues more effectively than one large increment. If some requirements take longer than expected to implement, or if the market window changes, a subset system can still be released on time by using the output of an earlier increment.

- Iteration provides earlier feedback from Customers and End Users, and allows changes to the product in subsequent iterations without having to re-implement everything.

- Iteration improves rapid learning by the workers of the reuse business. The developers' problem and technology experience grows with each iteration. This experience can be used to refine tools, processes, organization, and designs.

In both OOSE and Object-Oriented Business Engineering (see Chapter 2 in Jacobson *et al.* (1992), and Section 6.4.3 and Chapter 11 in Jacobson *et al.* (1994)), systems are developed incrementally in a series of stages, leading to the release of a series of versions. This is done to accommodate requirements and technology change during the system life cycle, as well as to deal with different system configurations.

Not all system requirements can be fully known at the outset of a project. New requirements are discovered or created as experience is gained. Each iteration therefore starts with a *delta requirements specification*. This leads to changes to each of the models.

To keep these changes manageable and understandable, the system should be structured and released so that changes can be associated with distinct subsystems or modules, each having distinct versions. A complete system is then configured from appropriate versions of the subsystems.

The way this incremental work is organized is to first develop an information system use case model to some level of detail. Then the use cases are prioritized to deliver the most important functionality first. Another useful prioritization is to explore and develop the most risky parts first, so as to control risk as early as possible. In fact, the results of these two different approaches to priorities often coincide – the most important use cases are generally used the most and therefore stress the system the most. On completion of an increment, the next set of use cases can be refined and implemented.

As each set of use cases is implemented, each of the object types that participates in them will receive additional operations and attributes and perhaps some modifications. Each increment is thus developed as one iteration through the software engineering process, but there are also numerous short iterations within each "increment iteration," such as improving the use case model as new analysis objects are discovered or correcting the design model as a system is tested.

Figure 9.4, adapted from Kruchten (1996), illustrates an iterative approach to architecture and system engineering, including rquirements capture, design, testing,

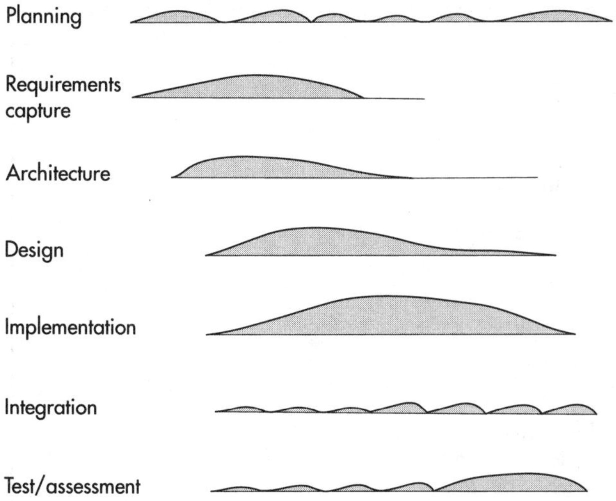

Planning

Requirements capture

Architecture

Design

Implementation

Integration

Test/assessment

Figure 9.4 *Each iteration involves at least one cycle through all the steps from requirements capture to testing. (Adapted from Kruchten (1996).)*

measurement, analysis, and then further iterations. Note how the architecture stabilizes after a few iterations and then changes only slightly as the focus is shifted towards design and implementation. Note also how integration and test is carried out in all iterations. Kruchten suggests that such an approach not only mitigates risks, but also helps build teams and improves training, architecture familiarity, tool acquisition, and the initial run-in period for procedures and tools. An iterative approach also helps refine and better understand the requirements.

The incremental, iterative approach used in this book is based on an integration of the techniques in OOSE, Object-Oriented Business Engineering, and Kruchten (Jacobson *et al.*, 1992; Jacobson *et al.*, 1994; Kruchten, 1995).

Example

The XYBsoft team decides to start by developing application systems to support electronic **Invoice** payment. An **Application Family Engineering** team is created and they define the two application systems **Payment** and **Invoicing**. As shown in Figure 9.5, **Payment** and **Invoicing** can be built from the component systems **Account Management** and **Invoice Management**. The **Account Management** component system might initially offer entity objects for things like **Bank Customer** and *Account*.

The **AFE** team defines the layered system with facades between the layers. Then they initiate concurrent development of the two application systems and the two component systems. They themselves iteratively design, implement, and perform unit tests on the systems, and they also perform integration testing to confirm that they interoperate effectively. Then they release the two application systems for beta-testing. The plan is to transfer these two application systems to product status within four months, as soon as they have gained enough feedback from their **Customer**s and **End User**s.

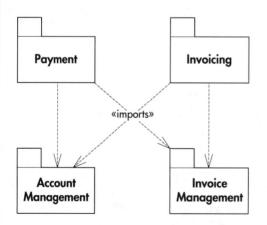

Figure 9.5 The **Payment** *and* **Invoicing** *application systems import from the* **Invoice Management** *and* **Account Management** *component systems.*

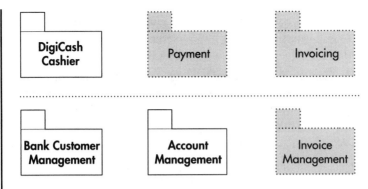

Figure 9.6 The **Account Management** *component system is split into* **Account Management** *and* **Bank Customer Management** *as the* **Digicash Cashier** *application system is added.*

Concurrently with collecting feedback on these two application systems, the **Customer**s also begin to involve XYBsoft in developing the new **Digicash Cashier** application system. As they start to collect the requirements they discover that the **Digicash Cashier** application system offers some use cases that deal with the **Bank Customer** but with no connection to *Account*. These use cases update customer addresses and marital status.

The **AFE** team observes that some software developers are skilled at *Account* issues and others at **Bank Customer** issues such as addresses. They use this information to restructure the organization as they take the next iteration over the architecture. They now decide to split the **Account Management** component system into two interdependent component systems: **Account Management** and **Bank Customer Management**, as shown in Figure 9.6. Each component system

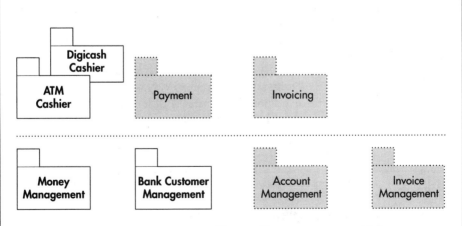

Figure 9.7 A new component system, **Money Management**, is added to capture the commonality reused by the application systems **ATM Cashier** and **Digicash Cashier**.

is quite complex and involves issues such as security, globalization, performance, and legal issues. They estimate that each of the component systems will need to be further developed and maintained by a 5–10 person team.

Later XYBsoft will develop the **ATM Cashier** application system. When they work on **ATM Cashier** they choose to extract what is common to **ATM Cashier** and **Digicash Cashier** into a separate component system, **Money Management**, as shown in Figure 9.7.

9.3 Organizing workers into competence units

Each competence unit consists of worker types which are effectively definitions of competencies required by people to fulfill the necessary roles. Each competence unit has a resource owner and is staffed by people acting as different types of worker.

A **resource owner** is responsible for staffing and funding, for training individuals as reuse workers and for solving problems in resource allocation.

One example is the **Software Engineering Business Manager**, who is responsible for the reuse business as a whole.

The workers perform the business use cases (that is, the business processes) by interacting with each other and with business actors and by using entity objects as discussed in Chapter 8. There is a **Process Owner** appointed for each type of business use case, such as **Application System Engineering**. A **Process Owner** is responsible for the design, improvement, and appropriate configurations of the business process description.

There is a **Process Leader** appointed for each individual (instance of a) business use case (staffed by a team). The **Process Leader** reports to the **Process Owner** and is responsible for supervising the execution of an instance of a process and may in many ways be compared with a project leader or project manager.

Example

The business use case for **Application System Engineering** is performed by workers such as an **Architect**, **Use Case Engineer**, and **Subsystem Engineer** (Figure 9.8). They cooperate with each other and use business entity objects such as the **Use Case Model** and the **Design Model**.

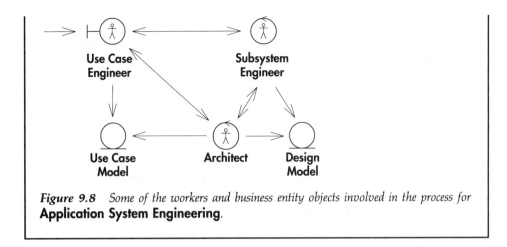

Figure 9.8 *Some of the workers and business entity objects involved in the process for* **Application System Engineering**.

The competence units that we have chosen each represent a type of skill required in a reuse business. These include traditional competencies such as requirements capturers, architects, designers, and testers. But, there are also competencies that are unique to a reuse business, such as component engineering and component support, required to package and facilitate the components for reuse. We now turn to an examination of the workers in each of the competence units.

9.3.1 Requirements Capture Unit

The **Requirements Capture Unit** contains the workers required when capturing the requirements for the layered system, an application, or a component system. The **Use Case Engineer** is the most important worker in the **Requirements Capture Unit**:

- A **Use Case Engineer** is responsible for specifying a use case and the associated user interfaces. Often it is wise to let one person be responsible for one actor type and all information system use cases that have that actor as its most important one. At other times it is better to assign one person to be responsible for all information system use cases that are involved in one business use case. A **Use Case Engineer** for the superordinate layered system is titled **Superordinate Use Case Engineer**.

- A **GUI Coordinator** evaluates and suggests the GUI component libraries to use. The **GUI Coordinator** coordinates the definition of the graphical interfaces and is, for example, responsible for resolving user interface conflicts between other engineers, particularly the **Use Case Engineers**.

9.3.2 Design Unit

The **Design Unit** contains the workers required when doing robustness analysis, design, and also implementing the layered system, an application, or a component system:

- A **Subsystem Engineer** is responsible for defining the types or classes within an analysis or design subsystem (including variability requirements) and for coordinating with other workers responsible for other subsystems. We have further assumed that a **Design Subsystem Engineer** implements and unit tests interfaces to the design subsystem and also the software inside it. This assumption is only feasible when it makes sense for the same individual to do design, implementation, and unit testing. A **Subsystem Engineer** for the superordinate layered system is titled **Superordinate Subsystem Engineer**.

- A **Use Case Designer** is responsible for defining a collaboration for a use case, that is, allocating a use case to analysis and design objects, and to subsystems. A **Use Case Designer** for the superordinate layered system is titled **Superordinate Use Case Designer**.

Other relevant workers may include domain experts and system integrators.

9.3.3 Testing Unit

The **Testing Unit** contains the workers required when testing the layered system, an application, or a component system. The **Tester** is the most important worker in the **Testing Unit**:

- A **Tester** performs system tests above the level of unit testing. This includes the testing of use cases, subsystems, the whole system, and selected configurations.

Example

As XYBsoft begins to collect requirements for the new **Digicash Cashier** application system they need another **Application System Engineering** team for this. They figure that the **Payment** application system will be easy to move from beta status to product status and therefore can be handled by fewer people than were involved in developing the beta release. They therefore decide to take out of the **Payment** team one **Use Case Engineer**, one **Subsystem Engineer**, and one **Tester** to form the nucleus of a new **Digicash Cashier** team for **Application System Engineering**. These three people, however, lack the competence required to develop support for use cases that involve secure withdrawal and deposit of electronic cash, such as Digicash and Cybercash. They therefore start to look for someone that has experience in this area and also in Microsoft Money'97 and Open Financial Connectivity (OFC), which XYBsoft plans to use later.

When the **Digicash Cashier** Application Engineers decide to use the OFC framework for inter-organization financial transactions, they also decide to use some new related toolsets, involving several wizards and a financial interface language to express financial business rules. They realize that in order to use

---

these additional toolsets they also need to update the process for **Application System Engineering** to add steps to define, inspect, and test the language scripts. The **Process Owner** for **Application System Engineering** is consulted to develop an appropriate extension.

9.3.4 Component Engineering Unit

The **Component Engineering Unit** defines additional workers required when developing a component system. A **Component System Engineering** team is thus comprised of the same type of workers as an **Application System Engineering** team, with some important additions:

- A **Reuse Process Engineer** develops and acquires process (SEP) components that the reusers can combine into optimized software engineering processes. This includes developing work steps for process handbooks, checklists, training material, examples, and guidelines for reuse mentors to use.

- A **Reuse Support Environment Engineer** is responsible for the development and acquisition of tool (SEPSE) components that the reusers can combine into toolsets that support component reuse. The **Reuse Support Environment Engineer** must make sure that the component system is engineered so that powerful reuse tools can be engineered or bought for the reusers.

- A **Facade Engineer** is responsible for making the facade useful to the reusers. The **Facade Engineer** suggests the tools and techniques to use for implementing variability points and variants.

9.3.5 Architecture Unit

The **Architecture Unit** contains the workers required when defining the architecture of the layered system, an application, or a component system:

- An **Architect** is responsible for a system as a whole, that is, the essential parts of the use case, analysis, design, and test models and decides on most architectural patterns to use in the system. The **Architect** for the superordinate layered system is titled **Lead Architect**.

- A **Distribution Engineer** is responsible for defining the processes and nodes in the system, how they are interconnected and how they interact with each other. The **Distribution Engineer** suggests how the design objects can be allocated to processes.

Remember that architecting is a complex and difficult job that can be done well only by excellent and experienced architects.

The **Architecture Unit** has the following responsibilities (Philippe Kruchten, Rational Software Corporation, provided a lot of useful insight):

- Design and maintain the layered system (the superordinate system) and maintain its integrity.

- Assess technical risks related to software architecture.

- Propose the order and contents of the iterations to the next release and assist in planning them. The team must help avoid working on less important problems and concentrate on the most important ones.

- Assist **Application System Engineering** teams and **Component System Engineering** teams in their work by communicating the architecture and suggesting solutions to problems.

- Assist marketing with future product definition.

9.3.6 Component Support Unit

Workers in the **Component Support Unit** are skilled at packaging and facilitating the reuse of component systems, and are mostly concerned with maintaining the facades and distributing the component systems so that the reusers can access the desired components. There is no separate business use case for supporting components; instead component support is integrated with the business use cases **Application System Engineering** and **Component System Engineering** as illustrated in Figure 9.9.

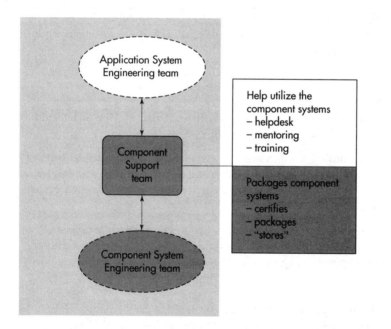

Figure 9.9 *A team from the* **Component Support Unit** *fills the gap between the* **Component System Engineering** *and* **Application System Engineering** *teams.*

The **Component Support Unit** consists of the following workers:

- The **Component System Trainer** helps the engineers to reuse the component systems by training them, mentoring them, developing examples, and so on.

- The **Component System Supporter** is responsible for answering questions and responding to complaints about a component system – a kind of help desk. The **Component System Supporter** is responsible for keeping track of reusers, their support requests, and also for correcting minor defects in the component systems.

- The **Component System Librarian** is responsible for organizing and managing the repository of baselined component systems, component SEPs, SEPSEs, training material, and so on. It is important that the repository is organized according to the architecture and managed to be a cost-effective asset that is easy to search and reuse from, and not become a "black hole" of lots of nice things that no one ever reuses.

Example

When XYBsoft develops the **Payment** and **Invoicing** application systems, they decide to have one team for each application system. They also establish one combined team responsible for the layered system as a whole and also for the individual component systems. This combined team then also serves as some kind of **Component Support Unit**.

When XYBsoft decides to develop the **Digicash Cashier** application system, they decide that there is a need for one point of contact to which the different **Application Engineer**s can turn when they want to use any component system. XYBsoft considers creating a separate team for the **Component Support Unit**, but do not want to introduce too much organizational change at this time. Instead they opt for an interim solution where they appoint one person in the **Application Family Engineering** team to be responsible for supporting the component systems. This person and his manager agree that as soon as the architecture stabilizes, he will be the resource owner for people who will staff a team for the **Component Support Unit**.

9.3.7 Expressing Application System Engineering in terms of workers

We will show how to express a business use case in terms of workers. We have chosen to illustrate **Application System Engineering**, as shown in Figure 9.10, since it is the simplest. Each of the three software engineering business use cases (that is, Software Engineering Processes, or SEP) will be presented in greater detail in terms of how the workers participate in Chapters 10, 11, and 12.

The **Use Case Engineer**s, together with the **Customer** and the **End User**s, specify the use cases which are then used by the **Use Case Designer**s as input to various **Subsystem Engineer**s who define the types within the analysis subsystems based on the

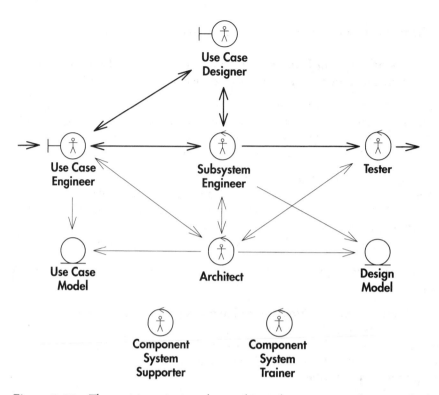

Figure 9.10 *The most important workers and some business entity objects involved in* **Application System Engineering**; *thick arrows indicate the main flow of communication. We have not shown how the* **Component System Supporter** *and the* **Component System Trainer** *help all the other workers use the component systems, since that would complicate the diagram.*

use cases. The analysis model is then used by the **Subsystem Engineer**s as they organize the system into software classes which the **Subsystem Engineer**s implement and unit test. The **Use Case Engineer**s, **Use Case Designer**s and **Subsystem Engineer**s plan and schedule subsystem, use case, and system tests that **Tester**s then perform.

The **Architect** is responsible for the models as a whole and coordinates the different models within the application system and also coordinates the application system models with those of the superordinate layered system. The **Component System Supporter** and the **Component System Trainer** help the **Application Engineer**s to use the component systems.

9.3.8 This organization model allows different competencies to thrive

The competence units that we suggest in this chapter are generalizations of several software engineering, reuse process, and organization models. They are adapted primarily from OOSE (Jacobson *et al.*, 1992; Jacobson *et al.*, 1995b; Griss, 1995c) and Object-Oriented Business Engineering (Jacobson *et al.*, 1994), work conducted at HP (Griss,

1995b; Fafchamps, 1994; Cornwell, 1996), the STARS Conceptual Framework for Reuse Processes (CFRP) (STARS, 1993) and work on software architectures by Rational in collaboration with customers (Booch, 1996; Kruchten and Thompson, 1994). This evolutionary approach is important since it ensures that the suggested organization into competence units is built for real-life software engineering, based on experiences from dozens of reuse- and architecture-oriented software engineering projects in which Rational (Kruchten, 1996) and HP (Jandorek, 1996) have participated independently.

The competence units **Requirements Capture**, **Design**, **Testing**, and **Architecture Unit** are all common in many organizations, but may go under different names. All these competence units have different skills and require different training. The requirements capturers, for example, need only be specialists in capturing, organizing, and making cost estimates on requirements, and do not need to understand in detail how to design the software.

A reuse business must support more processes than the core software engineering processes we discuss in this book, for example **Tendering**, which is estimating and proposing how much a certain application system will cost to develop. A reuse business must also provide a process for **Fixing Defects In Application Systems**. These additional processes further motivate a breakdown into these competence units since they involve only some of the workers and competence units. **Tendering**, for instance, will mostly involve the requirements capturers and analysts, while **Fixing Defects In Application Systems** will mostly involve designers, implementers, and testers.

The **Component Support Unit** has been separated out to stress that supporting existing component systems and training others to use them requires separate skills than developing them (Griss, 1995b; Cornwell, 1996). There is usually only one team for **Component Support** in a reuse business.

In practice, factors such as size of teams, size of component systems, and geographic distribution will also have a significant effect on how best to staff the workers into teams, projects, departments, and divisions.

Several of the workers we present here are not unique to *reuse-driven* software engineering businesses, and are found in any well-organized software engineering business. Nevertheless, the reuse principles affect all workers and individuals in a reuse-driven software engineering business. Our goal is to present a reasonably complete model of a software engineering business that can be made reuse-driven. How to make an organization reuse-driven can only be understood by looking at the whole situation.

Some organizations may not be able to develop their own components or aim for a full-scale reuse business organization, for example if they cannot afford the investment in people and money. In this case we suggest creating a combined *component infrastructure team* containing some of the workers of the **Design Unit**, **Testing Unit**, **Architecture Unit**, **Component Engineering Unit**, and **Component Support Unit**. This component infrastructure team is then responsible for:

- acquiring and adapting Commercial Off The Shelf (COTS) products and components,

- integrating a complete architecture,

- maintaining the component repository, and

- training and supporting the **Application Engineer**s as they build application systems.

9.3.9 Reuse business workers use business entity objects to build systems

A **business entity object** here represents some important architectural construct, such as a use case or a node type.

Each class of an entity object belongs to a competence unit, like the workers:

- The use case model belongs to the **Requirements Analysis Unit**.

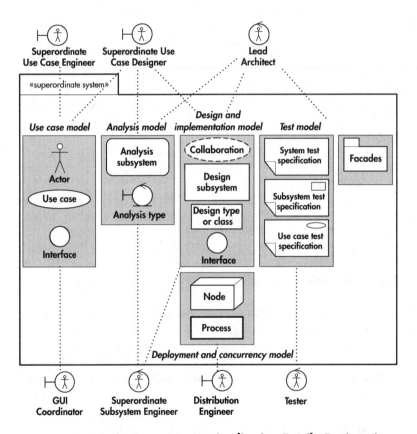

Figure 9.11 The workers involved in **Application Family Engineering** own the business entity objects of the superordinate system. The individual interests of the workers have been indicated with dotted lines.

- The analysis, design, and implementation models belong to the **Design Unit**.

- The test model belongs to the **Testing Unit**.

- The deployment and concurrency models and the system as a whole belong to the **Architecture Unit**.

The workers involved in **Application Family Engineering** work in terms of the superordinate system which consists of superordinate use case, analysis, design, concurrency, deployment, and test models (Figure 9.11).

Example

The **Lead Architect** of XYBsoft is responsible for entity objects such as the **Facades**. The **Lead Architect** is also responsible for the layered system as a whole, which means that he or she will decide on major patterns in the different models of the superordinate system. The **Lead Architect** is made responsible for the architecture document to reflect this overall responsibility and ownership. This document presents the business entity objects of the superordinate system, that is, the architecturally relevant use cases, interfaces, processes, and so on. The intention is that the document should be updated once every month and serve as the common ground that all Application Engineers and Component Engineers need to understand in order to build systems.

The workers involved in **Component System Engineering** work in terms of a component system which consists of component use case, analysis, design, implementation concurrency, deployment, and test models. Note that the facades offered by a component system are owned by the workers involved in **Application Family Engineering** (in fact the **Lead Architect**).

The workers involved in **Application System Engineering** similarly work in terms of an application system which consists of application use case, analysis, design, implementation concurrency, deployment, and test models.

9.4 Interplay between Reuse Business processes

Once the process for **Application Family Engineering** has developed the superordinate design model, the development of the application and component systems may begin. The superordinate design model defines the layers, the facades, and the interfaces between the application and component systems. The following is a simplistic procedure for developing an application or component system. More details will follow in Chapters 11 and 12.

1   Create an application or component system for each superordinate subsystem.

2   Perform requirements capture for that application or component system. Use cases are found from the superordinate use cases that are allocated to the design subsystem, as shown in Figure 9.12. If it is a component system, it is important to perform a systematic commonality and variability analysis. If the system is an application system, it is essential to reuse from the use case models of component systems.

3   Perform robustness analysis and design, implement, and test the system, by reusing components.

The above procedure gives the impression of a waterfall approach by first fixing the interfaces between the application and component systems and then developing each one

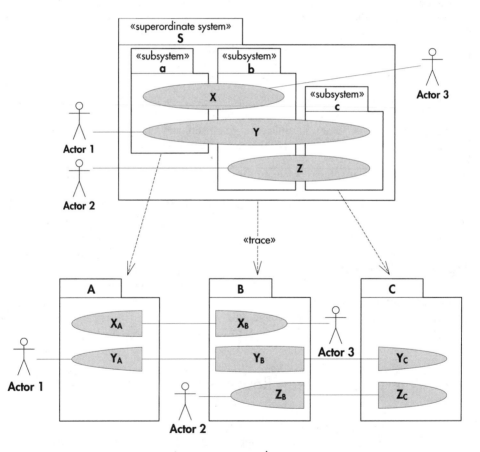

«application systems» and   component systems»

Figure 9.12   *Each use case (such as* **X_A***) in an application or component system corresponds to a segment of a superordinate use case (such as* **X***).*

independently. But this is not practical. There is a necessary mix of work on the layered system as a whole and on the individual application and component systems. It is not possible to devise the complete layered system without looking deeper into the individual application and component systems. Neither is it feasible to develop the application and component systems without any stable high-level architectural vision. These different processes therefore have to be interleaved and executed incrementally.

Example

Now XYBsoft is concurrently developing the **Digicash Cashier** application system and moving the **Payment** and **Invoicing** application systems from beta to product status. They know that this is difficult to manage, yet they cannot delay the **Digicash Cashier** application system since that imposes even greater risks. They believe that their highly experienced staff, including a cutting-edge **Software Engineering Business Manager** and an experienced **Lead Architect**, will be able to handle this. However, they decide to reduce the risk further by choosing to hire someone with substantial experience in version control and configuration management and by acquiring CM tools that simplify version control.

As some Application Engineers progress with the **Digicash Cashier** application system, they note that the other system needs to be able to present the bank transactions that a bank customer has done. They ask the Component Engineers responsible for the **Account Management** component system how best to do this. The Component Engineers suggest implementing a retrieval of the last 5–7 transactions. They also add a **Transaction** interface to the **Account Management** component system, and update the **Account** interface so that an account can be requested to deliver the past transactions. The Component Engineers realize that this is a matter of changing the facades to the component system and therefore discuss this with the **Application Family Engineering** team who decide to update the facade that exports the **Account** interface, as shown in Figure 9.13.

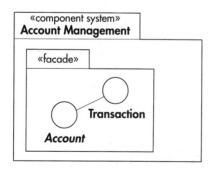

Figure 9.13 *The facade of* **Account Management** *is updated to refer to the new version of the* **Account** *interface and the new* **Transaction** *interface.*

Later the Component Engineers improve **Account Management** to also export **Transaction**. The changed facade is certified and packaged for reuse and transferred to the team responsible for component support. The **Component Trainer** distributes the new facade to the **Digicash Cashier** Application Engineers who learn how to use the components and import the interfaces from the facade.

9.5 Summary

In principle, a layered architectural style leads to a process and an organizational model which separates developer concerns. But there are several factors that complicate matters, such as difficulties in understanding complex architectures and organizations, and the problem of not knowing from the outset all the requirements, business needs, organizational problems, and so on. We address these types of difficulties in four ways:

- We use *explicit techniques* such as superordinate system models to represent layered systems. By doing this we improve understanding of the architecture and thus improve also the ability to engineer and manage it.

- We use *explicit techniques* such as object-oriented business engineering models to represent reuse business processes and organizations. By doing this we improve understanding of the organization and thus improve also the ability to manage it.

- The architecture, business processes, and the organization are all developed *incrementally* in order to reduce the risks associated with the changes.

- The component and application systems and the architecture are developed based on *input from business models* of the target organization, which improves the usability of the systems developed.

The following are the competence units that we suggest you organize a reuse business into:

- one competence unit for capturing requirements on systems – **Requirements Capture Unit**

- one competence unit for designing and implementing systems – **Design Unit**

- one competence unit for testing systems – **Testing Unit**

- one competence unit for the additional skills required to engineer each component system to become as reusable as possible – **Component Engineering Unit**

- one competence unit for architecting the superordinate layered and the individual application and component systems – **Architecture Unit**

- one or more competence units that package and facilitate the use of component systems – **Component Support Unit.**

The Reuse Business interacts with the business actors: A **Customer** orders an application system and places requirements on it. An **End User** is someone who will use an application system when it is installed in the target organization. A **Manufacturer** receives a new version of an application system when developed, then customizes, configures, produces, and delivers complete applications to **Customer**s.

The key business use cases are all software engineering processes (SEP) – **Component System Engineering** and **Application System Engineering**. The use case **Application Family Engineering** develops the product plan and the layered system.

9.6 Additional reading

For more details on the object-oriented business engineering approach and how that can be applied to software engineering processes, consult *The Object Advantage: Business Process Reengineering with Object Technology* by Ivar Jacobson, Maria Ericsson, and Agneta Jacobson, Addison-Wesley, 1994.

"Beyond methods and CASE: The software engineering process with its integral support environment" by Ivar Jacobson and Sten Jacobson, *Object Magazine*, January, 1995, presents the idea of comprehensive tools support for a software engineering process.

The article by Martin L. Griss, "Software reuse: A process of getting organized", *Object Magazine*, May 1995, discusses both the reuse process and reuse organization needed to ensure significant software reuse, based on HP experience. See also the August 1996, Hewlett-Packard Journal article by Patricia Cornwell, on HP's Domain Engineering process and organization.

A series of papers by Victor Basili and colleagues on the Experience Factory and the Component Factory provided additional insight into the reuse process and organizing for reuse: Victor R. Basili, Gianluigi Caldiera, and Goivanni Cantone, "A Reference Architecture for the Component Factory", *ACM Transactions on Software Engineering and Methodology*, **1**(1), 53–80, January 1992, and Victor R. Basili, "The experience factory and its relationship to other improvement paradigms". In *Fourth European Software Engineering Conference Proceedings* (I. Sommerville and M. Paul, eds), pages 68–83, Berlin, Germany, September 1993. Springer-Verlag.

10

APPLICATION FAMILY ENGINEERING

10.1 Developing an architecture for an application family

Architecture is critical to effective software engineering. The architecture should be a common vision of the systems, shared by customers, management, application and component engineers, and the Application Family Engineering team. The right architecture will guide the developers to reuse the components they need and provide well-defined interfaces to simplify the development of application and component systems. The architecture also shapes the organization of the software developers in the reuse business, matching processes to the layered system.

> The **Application Family Engineering** process develops and maintains the overall layered system architecture.

The layered architecture defines the structure of a family of systems, called the layered system. As described in Chapter 7, this layered system is represented as a superordinate system defined by use case, analysis, design, and test models. Figure 10.1 shows the superordinate design system for part of the architecture developed by XYBsoft. These models are used to define which application and component systems to develop, what functionality they should offer, and how they relate to each other. Remember that each application and component system is itself a system and corresponds to a subsystem in the superordinate design model.

The following example is also used in Chapter 7.

Example

XYBsoft's superordinate design model of the layered system contains subsystems for each of the application and component systems. For example, **Payment** and **Invoicing** and **Account Management** are represented as subsystems in the appropriate layers, shown in Figure 10.1.

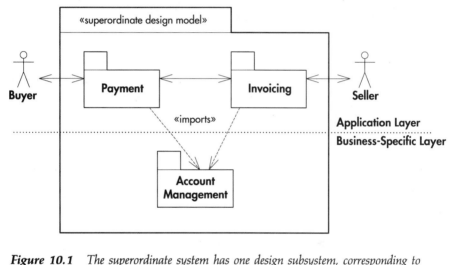

Figure 10.1 *The superordinate system has one design subsystem, corresponding to each of the application systems* **Payment** *and* **Invoicing**, *and to the* **Account Management** *component system, organized into two layers.*

The **Application Family Engineering** process starts by treating the layered system as one complete system. The process carries out requirements capture, robustness analysis, design, implementation, and testing of that single superordinate system as a whole, with a focus on finding subsystems. Each subsystem is treated as a component or application system which is developed by a separate process, **Application System Engineering** or **Component System Engineering**. The **Application Family Engineering** process involves so many iterations that it is not right to think of it as a sequence of steps. The approach to iterative **AFE** is inspired by Kruchten (1995). Table 10.1 shows the steps and the iterations and the process is illustrated in Figure 10.2.

Table 10.1   *The essential steps of the Application Family Engineering process.*

AFE1:   **Capturing requirements that have an impact on the architecture** – Find out who the customers and the end users are and the needs and expectations they have. Make a first approximation of a product plan and use it to decide which parts to focus on. Perform the first iteration of requirements capture and analysis to find actors and use cases. Select the most important 5–20% of the use cases and describe them. Do some analysis of use case variability.

AFE2:   **Performing robustness analysis** – Use the selected use cases to identify candidate application and component systems using a high-level analysis model.

AFE3:   **Designing the layered system** – Use the first version of the analysis model to prepare a prototype design model that defines the layered system in terms of application and component systems. Take advantage of legacy systems, third-party products, GUI toolkits, utility class libraries, object request brokers, and so on. Use interaction diagrams to divide the use cases among the application and component systems in order to precisely define facades and interfaces. Develop a first version of the concurrency model and the deployment model.

AFE4:   **Implementing the architecture as a layered system** – Use the product plan to schedule the work on each application and component system. Review the architecture and the plan. Implement the first version of the most important and risk-sensitive application and component systems, facades, interfaces, and processes. Integrate legacy systems and Commercial Off The Shelf (COTS) systems such as object request brokers.

AFE5:   **Testing the layered system** – Test each application and component system both by itself and also as part of the layered system as a whole. Testing the layered system is particularly important for application systems that interoperate. Test against the most notable risks and measure its performance. Capture lessons learned.

Repeat step 1 (requirements capture) for an additional set of use cases. Reassess risks. Perform a more thorough step 2 (robustness analysis) for the combined use cases, identifying how to integrate the new or changed use cases into the robustness analysis. Prepare a design model from the use cases and the analysis model, defining the next version of concurrency model, deployment model, application and component systems, facades, interfaces, and integration of COTS and legacy systems. Revise the product plan. Identify the highest-payoff application and component systems and decide which ones to start developing (possibly none if the architecture still seems too brittle); use this information to focus the next iteration.

In Chapter 13 we describe how a reengineering directive for the software development organization is used to optimize the reuse business to a specific set of objectives, for example time to market or quality. That reengineering directive can be used to decide priorities for the iterative approach. When there is ongoing business engineering of the target organization, the reengineering directive for that organization can also be used to optimize the reuse business.

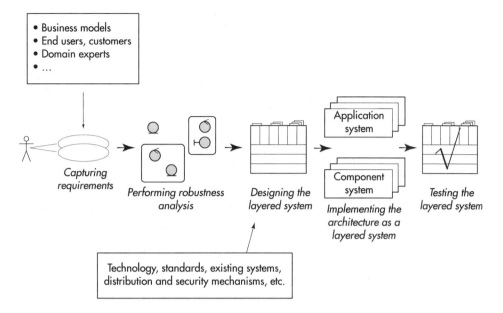

Figure 10.2 *A summary of the sources of information and the work steps in the*
Application Family Engineering *process.*

By doing the market analysis, business modeling, and customer installation in an
iterative fashion as well, it is possible to reduce risks and time to market not only for the
development cycle, but for the whole life cycle from idea to delivery.

Example

While XYBsoft has been defining its services and layered systems, rapid changes
in technology and Internet banking standards have been taking place. (Actually,
while we were writing this book, the XYB technology example changed
radically.) Microsoft and others have been particularly active, and consequently
XYBsoft has several new standards and technology components to consider.

Microsoft's Open Financial Connection (OFC) provides an API and set of
standard services that enables Microsoft Money to be used as part of the
interface ("home teller") to services introduced by banks. Microsoft is
participating in the definition of electronic commerce standards. OLE components
have become ActiveX components, with greater support for WWW-based
browsers. A simplified form of Visual Basic, VBScript, with a freely available
portable interpreter makes it possible to use these technologies and Java
technologies as part of several customizable end-user interfaces and
programmable business rules in business objects. Microsoft has also accelerated
the production of distributed OLE (now called DCOM), interoperation with
CORBA, and secure NT, forcing XYB to reconsider the architecture of several
layers.

These changes also affect the bank's decisions regarding the services they themselves should provide, the services they out-source and those they should not offer. The pace of new service introduction is increasing, suggesting that the various layers and component systems should be as loosely coupled and as little dependent on each other as possible. Aiming at such a modular architecture has a significant impact during the design step, AFE3, and also during implementation in AFE4.

The Microsoft initiative leads the Application Family Engineering team to decide that one version of the **Digicash Cashier** application system should be based on OFC. Furthermore, they see that they can support a customizable **Overdraft** management system much earlier than expected by choosing to use VBScript as the customization language, and several ActiveX components as a starting point.

Microsoft's increased emphasis on Internet technology makes the Application Family Engineering team question their initial choice of Java as the application programming language. They do not yet feel ready to move away from Java, since Microsoft wants to support Java as well, but they note "sticking to Java" as one of the biggest risks to be closely monitored, and resolve to do some early tests.

Often there may be an existing system architecture, or the beginnings of one. Sometimes the architecture is predefined by business or infrastructure standards. If so, these AFE steps can be applied as a technique to improve the structure and increase the potential for reuse. A suitable approach is first to develop an initial superordinate system design model that maps onto the existing architecture, taking into account appropriate implementation constraints. Reverse engineering a superordinate system design model can essentially be done as described in AFE3. Then continue iterations of process steps AFE1–AFE5 to suggest changes to the architecture.

10.2 Planning the product schedule according to use case priority

To identify the most important 5–20% of use cases, start by estimating the value the customer places on each use case. By the value of a use case, we mean the value placed on the services provided if that use case were implemented. For a use case designed to support a worker, it is possible to estimate how much the use case can help to improve some important aspects, such as time to market, quality, or the reduced cost of the business use cases that the worker participates in. Use that information to plan the incremental development. Sometimes it is not possible to assign a value to each use case independently, but a number of use cases can be assessed together. Also estimate the marketing window for each use case. Then schedule the next increment to analyze, design, implement, and test the most valuable use cases.

As use cases are designed and evolved to support additional requirements, it will become necessary to change existing application systems or to introduce new ones. We incorporate the new systems in the product plan and use it to plan and staff marketing, training, and engineering. A product plan may include other types of product considerations, such as product definition, positioning and packaging, product structuring, and so on.

It is important to align the plan with the business objectives of the organization. Is time to market the key issue, or is it quality, or portability, or compatibility with other applications? In Chapter 13 we will examine a more thorough treatment of how to optimize towards different goals. In Chapter 14, we will explore several reuse process and product metrics that can be used to estimate development costs and schedules.

The order in which application systems are developed and delivered helps define the order in which component systems are needed. The order of development is also influenced by the costs of developing the different systems and the benefits they provide when they become available.

It is important to plan for the extra learning and training time required to use the component systems and for developing training materials and examples for the Application Engineers. With complex frameworks such as Taligent's Commonpoint, ET++, Interviews, MFC, MVC, or MacApp, containing many hundreds or thousands of methods, the learning curve is steep (Laubsch, 1996). Cookbooks, pre-configured systems and examples should be prepared, and training is needed to ensure that the benefits are realized cost-effectively.

10.2.1 Using iteration to deal with complexity, uncertainty, and risk

There are many risks associated with developing systems, including technical feasibility, changing market conditions, changing technology and standards, and changing organizational situations. Many questions must be addressed as the project proceeds. Some can be anticipated at the outset, for example: Will the applications be easy to port to other platforms? Can the database handle the load at peak time? Will the processes be able to deal with node failures in distributed environments? Will the most critical applications really add value to the end users? And many more.

A well-defined process helps the engineers organize their work so that they avoid many traps, such as unclear responsibilities and hand-offs. Techniques such as using superordinate systems to represent layered architecture improve understanding and manageability. Business engineering driving requirements capture improves the usability of the systems and helps identify the most important requirements that will impact on the architecture. But still, many risks remain.

The only way to really address any technical issues beyond doubt is to implement and test enough of the layered system to verify that the most important and risk-exposed use cases work.

We cannot wait until all the requirements, application systems, and component systems have been analyzed and designed. Instead the use cases that have most impact on the architecture are selected, analyzed, partially designed, implemented, and tested in a first iteration according to the AFE steps above. Then another iteration is carried out, this time with use cases that have the second most significant impact on the architecture, and so on. By keeping the iterations short the software architects can reduce the most prominent risks early.

Example

XYBsoft believes that CORBA combined with Java is a suitable technology base for their applications. But they are also concerned that these technologies are new and fairly unproven in the industry. They therefore decide to build the first version of their layered system by implementing some use cases that will test the feasibility of using an ORB and Java.

During market analysis XYB finds that what customers desire most is the ability to pay invoices over the Internet. XYB therefore decides to start by developing a business model for electronic payment and then to develop application systems to support invoicing.

To ensure that they take the right perspective on the business processes, they begin by considering why there is a need to pay invoices in the first place. By thinking broadly they hope to capture the essential characteristics of these processes and to develop information systems that support the processes optimally.

The analysis leads them to the business use case **Sales From Order To Delivery**, which the **Buyer** invokes. In the **Sales From Order To Delivery** process a **Buyer** first orders some goods or services, the **Seller** invoices the **Buyer**, the **Buyer** pays in some way, and finally the **Seller** delivers the goods or services.

During requirements capture they identify the use case **Pay Invoice** which supports payment as defined in the business process **Sales From Order To Delivery**.

During robustness analysis and design, the **Pay Invoice** use case is divided between the application systems **Payment** and **Invoicing**, both of which reuse the component system **Account Management**, as shown in Figure 10.3.

First Iteration goal: By implementing a small part of the **Pay Invoice** use case, the architects hope to partially verify that the chosen ORB meets the performance requirements.

They plan to concurrently develop and test **Payment**, **Invoicing**, and **Account Management** through several iterations. By measuring the performance of the applications, they estimate that the current ORB implementation will suffice for their most likely market scenarios during the next two years. Following that period, however, they predict a higher load on the applications than the ORB can currently cope with. They believe that future ORB implementations will resolve this performance problem, but they note the problem as a major risk to address.

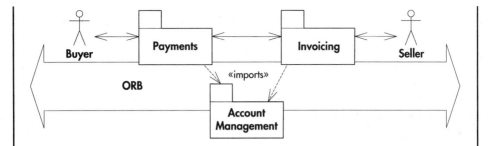

Figure 10.3 *The application systems* **Payment** *and* **Invoicing** *interact with each other via an object request broker accessed through the* **Account** *interface imported from the* **Account Management** *subsystem.*

XYB decides that the next most important use case to support is **Transfer Between Accounts**. This use case will help to further validate the chosen technology.

Another difficulty is that it is *not possible to know exactly what applications will be developed and changed* in the future. The problem is that a good picture of the application systems is needed in order to build the right components. It is desirable to prepare for both anticipated and unanticipated future evolution in technologies, standards, and business needs, which unfortunately involves a lot of guesswork and introduces a substantial risk that the resulting components will turn out not be useful to the Application Engineers. A moderate approach is therefore recommended to reduce the risks of all these uncertainties: Decide on a development strategy and use that strategy to plan the development of the individual application and component systems; see also Section 13.2. Make an assessment of the value added, costs incurred and risks introduced by the suggested components.

The most important technique to reduce these and many other risks is to adopt an iterative approach, using already ordered application systems as the main input when defining the architecture and components. An iterative approach is also useful when *requirements and technology keep changing*, since the relatively short duration of each iteration allows projects to be redirected faster.

In order to reduce risk, the team should analyze the risky areas quickly. They should verify the most important use cases, even if their implementation is highly volatile. A system that cannot support its most important use cases is useless, even if it is built on proven technology.

For the **Application Family Engineering** team to be effective in dealing with risk and uncertainty, they need to develop and evolve a good picture of all the technical risks. They also need a clear idea of likely business use case priorities and changes, so that they can relate each technical risk to the use cases most likely to encounter it and then prioritize, design, and implement the use cases to manage these risks in the best possible way. See also the discussion on risk assessment and management using prioritization and the spiral process model (Boehm, 1988, 1991).

During the first few iterations it is often practical to let the **Application Family Engineering** team develop the initial component systems and perhaps also the application systems, which allows them to understand the issues thoroughly and avoids the overhead of formal communication between teams. It is best not to create individual component and application systems in the first iterations, but to let only the **AFE** team work with the corresponding subsystems. By postponing the introduction of additional teams and systems, the **AFE** team can reduce the problem of managing the many changing versions of interfaces at a time when the architecture is still unstable.

As the architecture begins to stabilize, separate component systems may be created and assigned to other teams who will evolve them concurrently with the system architecture. This requires a carefully structured source control process for version control and configuration management to avoid having **Application Family Engineering**, **Application System Engineering**, and **Component System Engineering** processes "going round in circles." But the source control process needs to be smooth enough to let necessary interface changes propagate quickly to the developers that need them. Concurrent evolution of the architecture and the application and component systems is difficult to manage due to the inherent dependencies. Begin cautiously. Avoid concurrent engineering of several application and component systems and iterations that overlap in time, until experience is gained.

One additional procedure that helps address technical risks is the use of separate "tiger teams" to rapidly prototype thin slices of a complete system to explore new technology or feature-set risk. Participation in industry and technology standardization groups is also important in reducing risk by gaining early access to and influence over emerging standards.

10.3 AFE1: Capturing requirements that have an impact on the architecture

We are all too familiar with system development efforts that failed to consider the real needs of customers and end users. Large amounts of money were invested, systems were implemented and organizational changes were made, yet the resulting system did not produce the desired improvements in business performance.

It is therefore *essential* to understand how the family of applications is meant to operate together to support not only individual end users but the entire target organization. Only by understanding the needs of the organization will customers get the most value out of the applications. Without this understanding, it is not possible to determine the layered system and a set of component systems that will be useful when developing the family of applications.

Thus it is important to tie the architecture and reuse plans to a good understanding of the *business, market, and customer needs and trends*. If we do not know why and how the applications will be used (or won't be used) then we are in trouble! Without knowing how the applications will be used it is not possible to predict accurately how the business processes will be affected, nor to suggest radical and accurate changes to the applications. And it is far too risky to engineer an architecture or even think about reuse.

When capturing and analyzing the requirements, a high-level use case model is used to represent architecturally relevant requirements. We should focus on requirements that are important across the board, such as requirements on application interoperability and compatibility. Architecturally relevant requirements need to be implemented early to simplify the development of individual application systems.

10.3.1 Understanding the market and the customers

The following questions may help to understand who the key customers are, and what they need:

- Who are the current customers and end users and how can they be categorized or segmented? How is the market changing? Is it growing? What are the key segments?

- How are the current customers and end users changing? What kind of customers and end users do you want to attract in the future?

- What is the relationship between the customers and the end users? Are they the same individuals, do they ever meet, how well do they understand each other, and so on?

- What kind of products are the current and potential customers buying? What do they and the end users think of your products and others' products?

- How successful are the customers in their business, what challenges are they facing, how well do the envisioned products fit their needs and help them seize business opportunities?

- What are the desires and expectations of current and desired future customers and end users and what do you believe they really need? The best way to know the needs of the customers and end users is to model the processes that they participate in. By doing so it is possible to indicate where applications can add value.

- What kind of activities would the customers like to out-source, what is their core business, where do they primarily add value?

- What official and de facto standards determine the process, data, and systems with which the customers must operate or interoperate?

Example

The XYB performs a market analysis which indicates that their traditional private customers will choose a bank according to the following prioritized desires:

- Security, to protect their assets
- Simplicity of day-to-day activities, such as payment, withdrawals, and transfers
- Availability, for example of Internet and ATM teller machines
- Competitive fees and rates of interest
- Wide range of services, including tax advisors and stock brokerage
- Rapid introduction of new types of services
- Support for financial analysis
- Openness of applications to allow for integration with other toolsets, such as financial advisors.

Karlsson (1995) discusses how the Porter and GE market models can be used to shape a reuse strategy. The model shows how existing and new customers must be considered, as well as market trends and the potential impact of competitors, suppliers, customers, and new entrants to the market. The key idea is to determine the features needed by customers, the customer criteria for choosing between competing products (applications), how applications might evolve, and what combinations of features seem important. Other reuse and domain engineering methods such as Synthesis, FODA, and ODM also stress the importance of customer and market analysis input to determine the current and future needs and features desired (Arango, 1994; Kang, 1990; Simos, 1995a).

Knowing the needs of the customers and end users, your own strengths and weaknesses, and the competition, it is possible to determine the *opportunities* and decide where to add value.

Example

The XYB management decides that they probably cannot compete on interest rate. Neither will they be able to compete on range of services. Instead they choose to offer services that will simplify the day-to-day activities, such as payment, withdrawals, and transfers between accounts.

A key success factor will be to offer these services so that they require no training and can be accessed at virtually any place, and offer easy access to customers' accounts not only at their bank, but also (for a fee, of course) linked accounts at other financial institutions.

10.3.2 Finding superordinate actors and use cases

Finding actors and use cases that shape the architecture is best done by a group of people gathered around, for example, a whiteboard. Start by defining potential actors. Many of these will be found from the business actors and workers of the business model of the target organization. Then concentrate on finding the use cases based on the requirements. Make a first draft of the use case descriptions and iterate. At this point some kind of

CASE tool may become important, as the details and connections start to become more complex.

Review the actors and use cases informally and present the model to the customers and end users to get their feedback. Then describe the use cases and change the structure of the use case model as appropriate. When the model is ready, review it formally.

There is no strict ordering of these work steps and they do not need to start and finish in sequential order. In fact, new actors and use cases may be found and similarities between use case descriptions factored out into new abstract use cases throughout requirements capture.

Searching for architecturally relevant superordinate actors and use cases can be done as in ordinary OOSE but the results can be documented with less detail. The descriptions of the use cases for the superordinate system will not be as exhaustive as in an OOSE use case model. For example, they should not include descriptions of behavior that will be contained within the individual application and component systems. This distinction will of course be difficult to discern in the first iterations. When in doubt, one piece of advice is to allow for details in the descriptions during the first iterations. Later, as the architecture stabilizes, move the detailed specifications to the use case models of the application and component systems. Also, there will probably be only a few «extends» and «uses» generalization relationships in the superordinate use case model. These are difficult to identify at this stage because of the lack of detail in the use case descriptions. However, they are useful for identifying component use cases, and such relationships will be more common in the use case models of the individual application and component systems.

The following example is repeated from Chapter 7.

Example

The use case **Pay Invoice** could have an (oversimplified) description something like the following:

1   The **Buyer** activates the use case. The system presents the invoices that have not yet been paid.
2   The **Buyer** chooses which invoices to pay and decides when to pay them.
3   The system registers the payment orders and pays the invoices at the proper time, by deducting the amount from the **Buyer**'s account and transferring it to the **Seller**'s account.
4   As each invoice is paid, a receipt is sent back to the **Buyer**.

When there is a business model of the target organization, the above procedure for finding actors and use cases should be extended as described in the next subsection.

10.3.3 Finding information system actors and use cases from business models

We strongly believe in a business engineering approach to identifying information system actors, requirements, and use cases. We will focus on this approach, although in some cases, when business engineering is inappropriate or unavailable, some aspects of more traditional domain engineering can be used to identify the family of applications in conjunction with the process described in this chapter.

Business engineering is probably the most comprehensive technique for capturing and understanding the needs of customers and end users (Jacobson *et al.*, 1994). It is particularly well suited to developing application systems for an *internal customer*, such as the sales or human resources department. With an internal customer it is generally easier to know the current and future business processes, and what application systems they need.

Business engineering also works quite well when the reuse business develops applications for one customer out of many with similar processes, such as when developing *customized systems for one or more companies in a particular type of industry*. The reuse business can then develop a generic business model that captures the common characteristics of those customer organizations. Such a model can also be useful when developing *a family of applications for the open market*, if the model can be used to capture the essential characteristics of the customer organizations.

Although the business engineering approach works well for many business information systems, it may be less obvious for other types of systems, such as embedded systems. Here, we recommend a similar set of techniques (or more traditional domain engineering, as described in Chapter 1), but we have to apply the Reuse Business in a slightly different way to succeed. By thinking of the total system, consisting of both hardware and software, as a single system and by developing high-level use case and object models for it, it is possible to analyze the requirements on the embedded system in a systematic way. The responsibilities of the total system use cases can be allocated to types defined in the object models of the total system, similar to how business use cases are allocated to business entity types and workers. Then think of the hardware as actors of the information system and define one information system actor for each object type in the high-level total system model. Define a specific information system use case for each total system use case that each object is involved in. Only then can the architects work with the software and hardware in parallel to define the precise separation of the software (information system use cases) and hardware (information system actors in this case). This separation of hardware and software is similar to the separation of responsibilities between people and information systems for a business information system. The decision about what is best supported by an information system and what by a worker (or by hardware) needs to be made for each object type in the business or total system model of the embedded system. Define the precise responsibilities of each information system use case by deciding what to support with people, hardware and software respectively by assessing characteristics such as quality of performance, speed, flexibility, error detection and correction, investment cost, and maintenance cost. A more detailed discussion of this approach to identifying hardware requirements is beyond the scope of this book. Here, we will focus primarily on developing a family of applications for the business information systems needed by an organization.

The models developed during object-oriented business engineering can be used as a starting point to define the layered system, similar to how information systems can be defined as discussed in Chapter 8.

Example

The business engineering team is instructed to proceed in quick iterations to deliver results as soon as possible to the application family engineers. The business engineers develop the following business use case model in their first iteration (Figure 10.4).

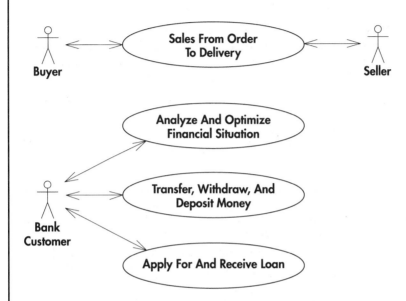

Figure 10.4 *The business use cases offered by the XYB to its bank customers.*

In the business use case **Sales From Order To Delivery**:

1   A **Buyer** orders some goods or services.
2   The **Seller** invoices the **Buyer**.
3   The **Buyer** pays.
4   The **Seller** delivers the goods or services.

The business use case **Analyze And Optimize Financial Situation** enables a **Bank Customer** to analyze and optimize finances.

Apply For And Receive Loan allows a **Bank Customer** to borrow money from the XYB.

Transfer, Withdraw, And Deposit Money allows a **Bank Customer** to make transfers between accounts, withdraw and deposit money, and also to define future automatic transfers.

There are several other sources of requirements that have an impact on the architecture, such as:

- Application system end users who were not modeled in the business model. For example, a system administrator is an end user who is usually not represented in a business model since most business models focus on the customer-oriented processes, while a system administrator adds value to the organization by enabling the other workers.

- Corporate software development strategies that the whole organization has decided on. These include strategies for a standard IT architecture, a component reuse program, openness, interoperability, distribution, platform independence, heterogeneous environments, compatibility, and quality.

- Legacy systems, corporate databases, and other information systems that the new systems must work with.

- Business trends and trends within the IT industry, competitors, literature, domain experts, and so on.

A business model connects with the needs of the organization and therefore provides the most *relevant* input when identifying the use cases. A business model also provides a *straightforward* way of finding use cases. For each worker and business actor, decide if it will use the application systems. If so, identify an information system actor and give this actor the same name as the worker or the business actor. Look for similarities between workers and business actors in order to spot use cases that several information system actors will use. Identify a use case for each business use case that the worker or the business actor is involved in. Give the use case a name that reflects the work steps it supports. Sometimes it makes sense to use a single use case to support several workers, business actors or several business use cases.

Sometimes the reuse business develops software for several target organizations where each organization has been defined using distinct business models. Then, define use case and analysis models of the whole layered system based on one business model, then take the next business model and improve the use case and analysis models based on the new input, and so on. Eventually, after using several business models as input, the use case and analysis models will stabilize as each new business model adds fewer new requirements. Another approach could be to synthesize a generic business model from the end-user models and then use the synthesized model to drive the requirements capture. A synthesized model is also more appropriate for a reuse business that plans to develop custom systems and component systems to support several unconnected organizations within a target industry area.

Example

As the architects look at the business use case for **Sales From Order To Delivery**, their initial suggestion is to create one actor for each of the workers involved. But then they realize that they want to replace all of the workers with software systems, so they suggest that the information system will have actors exactly corresponding to the actors of the XYB business.

The XYB marketing personnel decide to advocate implementing only the **Payment** application system involved in the business use case **Sales From Order To Delivery**. The architects then suggest a use case model consisting of the **Pay Invoice** use case and the **Buyer** and **Seller** actors. Since **Buyer** and **Seller** are allowed to use the information system of the XYB they will give rise to the **Buyer** and **Seller** information system actors.

10.3.4 Improving the business model

Not only does the business model have a strong influence on the resulting information system, but the process of developing the information system may in turn suggest changes to the business model. On the one hand, the information system design may identify technology restrictions that hinder or prevent the organization from performing as the business models describe. On the other hand, new technology can also be discovered that allows more dramatic improvements than were originally envisioned. In either case, the business models must be updated, which also is an iterative process. Some way of tracing requirements and concepts from the business model to the information system models and back is required for effective connection between these models. This is what *traces* are used for.

Example

As the architects consider how best to support overdraft management in use cases such as **Pay Invoice**, they see an opportunity for a new type of customer service. The service they envision is an electronic assistant that could inform a **Bank Customer** about important contingencies.

They foresee a mechanism whereby a **Bank Customer** could be allowed to define certain events that he or she would like to be informed about, such as when a scheduled invoice payment might or does result in an overdraft. Furthermore, they propose that such alerts could be communicated by a variety of media such as mail, fax, phone, and email.

As they discuss alerts with the business engineers, a completely new business use case **Alert** is introduced (Figure 10.5). As the **Alert** business use case is validated with some key **Bank Customer**s, it turns out that most **Bank Customer**s would primarily want this kind of alert for overdrafts and changes in interest rates.

The **Alert** business use case will be supported by two use cases: **Alert Setup** for defining alert conditions and **Alert Notification** for issuing an alert to a **Bank Customer**.

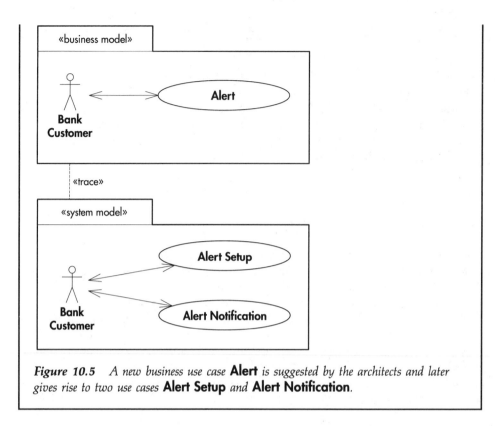

Figure 10.5 *A new business use case* **Alert** *is suggested by the architects and later gives rise to two use cases* **Alert Setup** *and* **Alert Notification**.

Having captured the requirements on the family of application and component systems it is now possible to identify the individual application and component systems. Most likely there is already some idea of what they are, but the following process steps provide further guidance and allow the systems to be identified with greater precision.

10.4 AFE2: Performing robustness analysis

Candidate application and component systems can be found through superordinate system robustness analysis, by identifying analysis types and then clustering them into subsystems which represent candidate application and component systems. Start by looking at the superordinate use cases and the business model of the target organization and identify analysis types for the superordinate system. Then describe how the use cases and the business model are related to the analysis types. Finally, cluster types with high coupling into subsystems.

10.4.1 Finding superordinate analysis types from use cases

Superordinate analysis types can be found from use cases much as in ordinary OOSE, as described in Chapter 3. For each use case, identify analysis types that represent roles played when the use case is performed. Remember not to make this superordinate analysis model too detailed. Choose fewer types when in doubt and iterate later if more granularity is required. Do not spend too much time describing the types or the detailed relationships between them.

In the next step we use the "boundary-control-entity object" (B-C-E) pattern from Chapter 6. The B-C-E pattern is used to find suitable objects to support use cases, which is most useful at this subordinate level when identifying candidates for and delimiting the different application and component systems.

We start by identifying a boundary type for each combination of an actor and a use case. The boundary types at this superordinate level are used to identify and delimit the different application and component systems. These types are generally too coarse-grained to help identify the detailed user interface, which is dealt with as the application and component systems are developed.

Similarly, identify a control type for each use case, and an entity type for each type of entity objects that will be supported by the information system. The control and entity types should implement the business rules that pertain to either the processes or the entity objects involved. Use acquaintance associations to connect entity types with each other. Document how these entity types are related and traceable to types of entity objects in the business model.

Connect the control and boundary types to other types with «communicates» and «subscribes to» associations for triggers and notification, and «extends» and «inheritance» generalizations to structure the types.

Example

The XYB is building a new system, XYBhomeBanking. The business model used as input to developing the XYBhomeBanking system contains the entity objects **Account** and **Invoice**, both of which are involved in the business use case **Sales From Order To Delivery**.

The use case **Pay Invoice** supports the business process **Sales From Order To Delivery** and interacts with the two actors **Buyer** and **Seller**. The **Application**

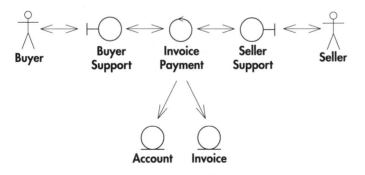

Figure 10.6   *The analysis objects that participate in the use case* **Pay Invoice**. *All relationships are communication associations.*

Family Engineering team can therefore define two boundary types combining these actors and use cases, **Buyer Support** and **Seller Support** (Figure 10.6). Since the information system use case **Pay Invoice** involves account and invoice management, there should be corresponding entity types.

Furthermore, one control type **Invoice Payment** is identified for the use case itself. All interaction with the **Account** and **Invoice** entity objects in the **Pay Invoice** use case goes through the control object **Invoice Payment**.

Note that these analysis types are high-level abstractions of the actual implementation. Each of the analysis types would correspond to several classes, perhaps even to separate application or component systems!

The superordinate analysis model is used to capture essential characteristics of the application domain at a high level, which makes the model particularly useful when discussing important object patterns and interactions. Look explicitly for patterns of object composition and interaction that help remove or encapsulate interdependencies, or better understand what the family of application systems will do. One such pattern is the Observer pattern suggested by Gamma *et al.* (1994) which is used to let objects subscribe to notification of state changes in objects. The Observer pattern can be represented as a «subscribes to» association in the analysis model.

Example

As a new **Invoice** is registered by **Seller Support**, the **Invoice Payment** object informs **Buyer Support**. Similarly, as **Buyer Support** pays the **Invoice**, the **Invoice Payment** object informs **Seller Support**. In both these situations the **Invoice Payment** object has a «communicates» association to the other objects, which implies a static dependency on them. A different solution can be used to make **Invoice Payment** almost totally independent of the types **Seller Support** and **Buyer Support** (Figure 10.7).

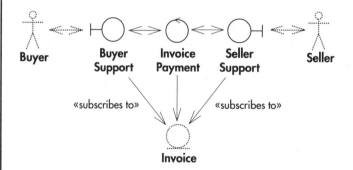

Figure 10.7 The analysis objects **Seller Support** and **Buyer Support** use «subscribes to» to monitor state changes in the **Invoice** object. All other associations are «communicates».

Let the **Invoice** object issue notifications as soon as the state of an **Invoice** is changed. Then both **Buyer Support** and **Seller Support** can subscribe to the relevant state changes, which is modeled as a «subscribes to» association directed from **Seller Support** and **Buyer Support** to **Invoice**.

Example

A **Bank Customer** who uses the **Payment** application may sometimes need information about an *Account* used for **Payment** and therefore may need to invoke the **Digicash Cashier** application system. **Digicash Cashier** allows a **Bank Customer** not only to deposit, withdraw, and transfer money between *Accounts*, but also to look at the *Account* history and so on.

A **Bank Customer** would perhaps like to double-click on the user interface representation of an *Account* and then the **Digicash Cashier** application system would present the transaction history for that *Account*. This navigation path to presenting the transaction history for an *Account* can be represented with an «extends» generalization from the *Cashier Interface* boundary type to the **Buyer Support** boundary type. Together with the «extends» there would be criteria for invoking the **Digicash Cashier** application system, such as when a **Bank Customer** requests more information on an *Account*.

Distribute each use case across the analysis types by sketching the flow of the use case in terms of the objects, using collaboration diagrams and use case descriptions. It may even be useful to use sequence diagrams for some of the use cases, particularly those that are most important and complex.

Example

Figures 10.6 and 10.7 are examples of collaboration diagrams for the use case **Pay Invoice**. The use case description re-expressed in terms of these analysis classes would be something like:

1   The **Buyer** activates the use case through the boundary object **Buyer Support** which presents the invoices that have not yet been paid.
2   The **Buyer** uses the boundary object **Buyer Support** to decide which invoices to pay and when to pay them.
3   The control object **Invoice Payment** registers the payment orders and at the proper time executes paying the invoices, by deducting the amount from the *Account* of the **Buyer** and transferring it to the *Account* of the **Seller**. The **Seller** is informed through the boundary object **Seller Support**.
4   As an **Invoice** is paid, a receipt is sent back to the **Buyer** through the boundary object **Buyer Support**.

10.4.2 Identifying subsystems as the first prototype iteration of the layered system

Subsystems in the superordinate analysis model are used to identify potential application and component systems. As described in Chapter 3, in ordinary OOSE the aim is to find subsystems that are relatively independent, but have good cohesion between their respective types or classes. Independent subsystems with high cohesion have increased maintainability and reusability since other subsystems will have limited dependencies on the facades and interfaces they offer. To some degree this limitation of dependencies comes automatically from the "B-C-E" pattern as the three different analysis object stereotypes are used.

The most important criterion for defining individual application systems is that it should be possible to deliver them and to upgrade them as separate products. Choosing the right application systems is therefore a marketing decision. One helpful heuristic is to make application systems fairly small and independent, like the trend towards Internet applets and application suite applets. Small application systems are easier to change in response to changes in other systems. Furthermore, small application systems generally have simpler dependencies on other systems, which makes it easier to sort out which application systems need to be updated when other systems change. Furthermore, each applet can be developed and released (almost) independently. Too many small applications, on the other hand, may be difficult to manage.

As a first approximation, make an application system for each supported business use case. Put entity types used solely by a set of types in a single subsystem into that same subsystem. Group other entity types into coherent clusters in their own subsystems. Each subsystem cluster is a candidate for its own component system. Many component entity types can be found by looking directly at common business entity types.

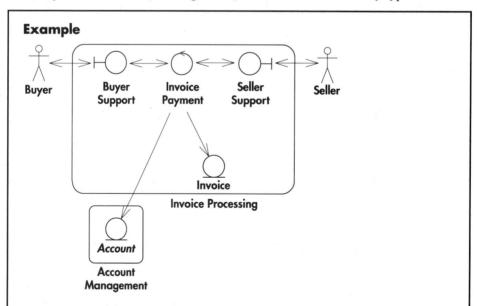

Example

Buyer Buyer Support Invoice Payment Seller Support Seller

Invoice

Invoice Processing

Account

Account Management

Figure 10.8 Initial packaging of superordinate analysis types into different subsystems.

As a first step, we group all analysis types specific to the business use case **Pay Invoice** in one subsystem **Invoice Processing**, which leaves the entity type **Account** in a separate subsystem which we call **Account Management**, as shown in Figure 10.8.

It is sometimes desirable to define separate subsystems for individual boundary types. This may be useful when there will be alternative subsystem implementations for the boundary types or when such separation would simplify the operation and maintenance of the applications. Keep each control type in the same subsystem as the boundary type that primarily uses the control type, or make one separate subsystem for the control type.

Example

As a next step, a separate subsystem is created for each of the boundary types in order to simplify later development of several variant application systems for both types of user. These subsystems are called **Payment** and **Invoicing**.

A separate subsystem is also created for each of the entity types **Account** and **Invoice**, called **Account Management** and **Invoice Management**.

The control type **Invoice Payment** is allocated to the same subsystem as the **Invoice** type.

These changes lead to the superordinate model shown in Figure 10.9.

We use this last subsystem partitioning in the rest of the book.

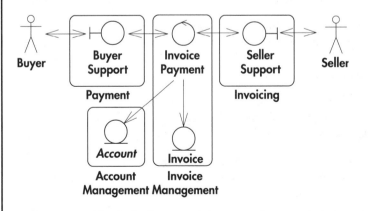

Figure 10.9   *The final allocation of the superordinate analysis types to several subsystems.*

10.5 AFE3: Designing the layered system

We transform the analysis model and its subsystems into a superordinate design model, which is used to define the layered system in terms of subsystems organized into layers with facades between them. Each of these superordinate design subsystems ultimately can be implemented as a separate application or component system.

The subsystems initially can be suggested by the analysis subsystems, but will have to be adjusted and expanded to match the implementation environment as described in Chapter 3. We adjust the subsystems by considering aspects such as performance, scalability, robustness to errors and malfunctions, testability, maintainability, and security. We also consider existing standards, target technology, and legacy systems.

These adaptations must strike a careful balance between a simple, elegant architecture and a pragmatic integration of existing software and adherence to standards, which requires great skill and experience on the part of the **Application Family Engineering** team. Using a preexisting piece of software in the layered system or obeying some standard always imposes additional constraints on the architecture. These constraints are not necessarily bad, but may improve productivity and understanding by imposing a good architecture.

A good idea at this point is to sketch a number of possible architectures which are then evaluated and compared. We need to develop and prioritize a set of criteria against which we compare the alternative architectures.

10.5.1 Making the layered system manageable

The following guidelines help define subsystems that lead to a manageable layered system, particularly from a version control and configuration management perspective:

- Small systems allow for faster and more independent changes to each system.

- Smaller systems typically have fewer dependencies on other systems, but reduced dependencies like this have to be consciously designed into the architecture. If the system is too small, however, it will depend on relatively many utility classes compared to its own number of classes.

- Small systems can be developed in smaller teams which simplifies communication as the system is developed. But teams cannot be too small, else important competencies may be missing (see Chapter 9).

- Having many small systems makes it more difficult to ensure consistency and interoperability between them, particularly if they are developed in many different places. A few larger systems are easier to handle in these respects.

- A system should belong to only one layer, that is, a layer contains only whole systems, since that clarifies the relationship between that system and other systems.

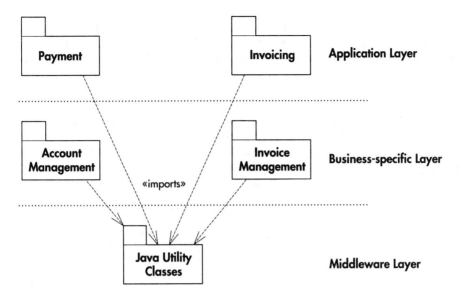

Figure 10.10 *Utility classes are useful to systems in several layers.*

- A system in one layer may import from and have dependencies on component systems in the same layer or in layers further down. Restricting the reuse of component systems to those only one layer down is often too much of a constraint. An example is utility classes such as Stacks, Queues, Lists, and Numbers that belong to the middleware or the system software layer but are useful in both the business-specific layer and the application layer, as shown in Figure 10.10.

- An application system may have dependencies on other application systems.

It is important to avoid too many dependencies between systems that need to interoperate, because too many dependencies make it more difficult to change the systems. Instead, try to resolve such dependencies using a few powerful design patterns or architectural patterns such as middleware frameworks and systems. For example, provide only a narrow interface to a system, to localize the point of connection (like the Facade pattern by Gamma *et al.* (1994)).

10.5.2 Using middleware for application interoperation

At this point, it is time to decide which middleware services are required, such as distribution of the system's functionality across several nodes and processes. Try first to buy, else reluctantly build, component systems that provide those services. In some cases it will be necessary to add a component system wrapper for a purchased software system to ensure that it fits the architecture. Create (at least) one component system for each preexisting piece of software, Commercial Off The Shelf (COTS) software, or software of a specific type of technology, for example an ORB or a DBMS.

Packaging each into its own component system, with facade and conforming documentation, will simplify management of each as a "member of the architecture." One component system per independent commercial system helps simplify division of responsibilities among the developers, and allows independent evolution of these systems by their vendors.

Many applications need to interoperate via shared instances of entity objects, such as in distributed enterprise-wide information systems where people work with (business) objects in a shared repository. A suitable architectural pattern (Buschmann, 1996) for sharing objects is an object request broker, implemented in some commercial ORB, since an ORB makes object distribution transparent which greatly simplifies the work of the application and component engineers. Using the ORB pattern, objects can call other remote objects through a "broker" that forwards the call to the node and process that hold the desired object. This forwarding of the call is made transparently so that the caller does not have to know whether the called object is remote or not.

Example

In the XYB layered system both **Invoice**s and **Account**s are obvious candidates for object sharing. XYBsoft decides to use an ORB to manage this sharing and distribution. Since **Account** and **Invoice** objects need to be accessed efficiently from any node in the distributed environment, the ORB may even allow these objects to "roam" the network, or to be transparently replicated in some way, using proxies that are accessed at dynamic lookup time.

Shared entity objects provide an important asset in the enterprise and many people and applications depend on them. Changes to their implementation and their interfaces must be tightly managed to avoid dramatic impacts. The use of an ORB that can find the objects or access their interfaces dynamically, using proxies or run-time interface resolution, can greatly decouple this part of the system.

Many applications need to be informed when some entity object, located in some other application or data server, changes state. In the analysis model such "triggers" are well represented using «subscribes to» associations. Also, many applications often need to interact in close coordination. The use of «communicates» and «subscribes to» associations, and the «extends» generalization between boundary and control types in the analysis model, indicates that the corresponding application systems need to be able to invoke one another or communicate in some other way. This means that an action in one application system should invoke an appropriate action in another application system. One example is a CASE tool, where an editor may need to invoke a CM system or a C++ environment.

In situations where there is close interaction between applications, it is desirable that application systems are developed and can be maintained sufficiently independently that:

- applications can be changed without automatically affecting others;

- additional applications can be added without dramatic impacts on existing applications;

- additional applications are able to interact immediately with existing applications;

- additional entity types can be added, and moved around the distributed environment.

To help here we use notifications, events, or triggers. Some distributed databases and other middleware provide direct support for notifications. For example, the OMG defines an event service as a common CORBAfacilities service that can be used for notifications. Similarly, a software bus architecture can be used. A software bus allows applications to interact via a standardized set of messages that can be used to invoke one another (Garlan *et al.*, 1995; Purtilo, 1994; Coplien and Schmidt, 1995; Teknekron, 1994; Cooley, 1993). There may also be more specialized message sets that only a subset of the applications understand and use to communicate with each other. The message sets that all applications can respond to is defined in an interface and specialized message sets can be expressed as subtypes of that interface.

Event services and software buses can then be implemented using software bus messages or the event services for an ORB.

Example

The XYB actor **Bank Customer** wants to be able to invoke other applications from within an application system simply by double-clicking on the user interface representation of, for example, an **Account** or a **Transaction**. The «extends» generalization from the **Cashier Interface** boundary type to the **Buyer Support** boundary type represents one such relationship that can be implemented by a software bus message from the **Payment** application system to the **Digicash Cashier** application system.

The architects suggest a general design guideline where double-clicking on a user interface object should result in an **Invoke (OnObject: any)** message to the software bus, unless the current application itself can manage it. The different applications connected to the software bus then listen for the messages and get activated when relevant.

XYBsoft architects now combine the object request broker (ORB) with a software bus. They implement a software bus style of interaction by defining a **BusManager** as an object service using the ORB's naming and event services, as shown in Figure 10.11. Each object that plans to broadcast any messages will send them via a message to the **BusManager**. The **BusManager** will maintain a list of all objects desiring to listen to this (or any) message, and resend the message to them. Objects that plan to listen to bus messages need to register themselves with the **BusManager** service. Thus applications that interact with the bus by broadcasting a message effectively do so by sending to and receiving

---

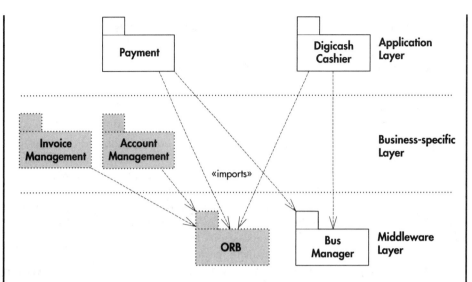

Figure 10.11 *Adding a software bus to the ORB.*

from the **BusManager** service. Applications can invoke and communicate with each other by sending messages through the bus and share objects through the distributed object mechanism of the ORB.

Systems such the TIBCO TIB (Teknekron, 1994) and HP Softbench use non-ORB based broadcast message servers and standard message protocol (Cooley, 1993).

By choosing to define the **BusManager** service as an object facility and by using the ORB as discussed above, XYBsoft hopes to achieve even more flexible interoperation as well as consistency in application behavior.

10.5.3 Achieving consistency and adherence to architecture standards

The consistent appearance and behavior across multiple applications is one of the most appreciated characteristics of the Macintosh, and more recently Windows 95. A consistent appearance and behavior helps end users learn new applications and become productive almost at once. Of course, consistent appearance and behavior has been achieved through a number of factors but most important to the Macintosh is the MacApp framework, referred to as an "expandable application" (Schmucker, 1986):

- the MacApp framework, which is a framework (an abstract component system in our terminology) for developing a Macintosh application;

- the MacApp Developers Guide, which is a style guide for developing applications with a Macintosh look and feel.

The consistency includes the user interface and the model of behavior; for example, all Macintosh applications have the same **Save** and **Print** commands. One way to achieve such consistency is to create a number of component systems or frameworks that support the building of consistent user interfaces, models of behavior, and so on. Make sure that the look and feel of the application systems is consistent with applicable standards, which will help users learn and use the applications much more easily. The latest Microsoft environments, such as Windows 95 and Windows NT 4.0, offer essentially the same degree of inter-application consistency, through the Microsoft Foundation Classes (MFC), Windows subsystem, common development tools such as Microsoft Visual C++ and Visual Basic, and common ActiveX libraries.

This consistent appearance and behavior is not just limited to GUI. Having a consistent mental model and compatible implementation of many entity types greatly simplifies the end users' (and application developers') task.

Example

Accounts, stock portfolios, Smartcards, and so on can all be treated as a form of **Portfolio** containing various types of **Instrument** such as money and stocks. This provides a simple mental model which enables the construction of a consistent way of using the systems. A user may then, for example, ask any **Portfolio** for its value and a graph of how the value has changed over time.

Bear in mind that consistency is an issue primarily for the set of applications used by each individual actor (actually person, since one person can be several actors); it is not necessary to enforce consistency across all users.

It is important to ensure that the architecture adheres to other (de facto or official) standards that apply, for example CORBA, compound document standards, Windows API, compliance with Windows 95 look and feel, and so on. Consider also if the layered system needs to connect to the Internet and, if so, which mechanisms or tools to use, and what sort of browser metaphor to encourage. The principles, strategies, and style guides for the design and implementation of the system should be documented in a *Design Guidelines* document. A typical *Design Guidelines* document gives guidance on the following:

- General design and implementation guidelines regarding issues such as: detecting, handling, and reporting faults, memory management, and fault tolerance.

- Coding standards regarding code layouts, commenting, naming, and so on.

10.5.4 Acquiring component systems

Buying component systems is difficult. It is so difficult that some organizations have developed separate processes and built teams with well-developed human networks for buying software. Not only is it important to assess the quality of component systems as such, but equally important is the "quality" of the vendor.

Many large companies such as Ericsson and HP have well-defined processes for external technology provisioning. Ericsson, the telecommunications company, uses the following prioritized criteria (Asker, 1994):

1   Right technology – the technology must fit the application systems. One way to verify the appropriateness of the technology is to prepare in advance a list of desired characteristics and then assess the component system according to these characteristics.

2   Right vendor – is it a leading vendor capable of further developing the component system?

3   Right customer relationships – is there capability to support and assist customers in achieving their goals and objectives?

4   Right commercial deals – what are the initial acquisition cost, maintenance and support cost, cost during the first year, cost for extra licenses, estimated cost of changing vendor, required number of licenses?

Korson and McGregor (1991) and McGregor and Sykes (1992) suggest a number of criteria to use when evaluating an object-oriented class library. Many of these apply equally well when evaluating a component system or framework for purchase. The many vendors of OCX and ActiveX components provide an enormous potential for reuse on the open market and substantial leverage to any application builder. However, some of these are very small companies, which adds some risks regarding their capability to support a buyer. Great care should be taken to be sure that multiple OCX/ActiveX components acquired from different vendors are well supported, and will evolve as the OLE/DCOM models and tools evolve. Look carefully at interactions between the components, and also at confusing naming conflicts. Some may even have to be repackaged into your own component systems, with wrappers and so on. Certainly, most will need new document-ation, and perhaps guidelines on effective use within the architecture.

Similar criteria can also be applied to assess a subcontractor who will develop a new component or application system or when acquiring components from someone within the organization.

10.5.5 Integrating legacy systems

As discussed in Chapter 7, legacy systems should be incorporated in the layered system without letting them dictate the overall architecture. The suggested approach is to first design the architecture to meet business needs. Then each legacy system can be encapsulated using one or more object-oriented wrappers. Each wrapper presents one coherent set of interfaces to the legacy services. Over time the legacy systems can be replaced by one or more new systems.

The specifics to accomplish legacy wrapping are (Jacobson and Lindström, 1991):

1   Prepare a use case model of the legacy system by reverse engineering its functionality.

2   Prepare an analysis model based on the use cases.

3   Define the required interfaces to the legacy system.

4   Implement the wrappers which supply the interfaces and transform messages sent to the wrapper interface into requests to the legacy system and vice versa.

Sometimes it may be feasible to make one use case model, one analysis model and one design model for a set of related legacy systems, such as when several legacy systems are tightly interwoven. Based on these combined models, one or several component systems can be developed that together wrap the legacy systems. Also, thinking of the set of legacy systems as a system of interoperating systems may be a good way to see the "whole picture."

Example

As described in Chapter 7, work on an enterprise information framework at Hewlett-Packard included the need to plan and support the interfaces to several legacy systems. As an example, a medical application system's customization of the framework used loosely coupled CORBA-compatible data management components to handle legacy medical systems. Starting from an information model of the legacy data, each of these components acted as an independent wrapper, effectively consisting of entity and control types that provide appropriate data access to the legacy systems. Each of these components is responsible for accessing the legacy services, and for coordinating or mediating multiple accesses. The plan is to later adapt and reuse these wrapper components for other kinds of data access, which allows the developers to replace specific services from the legacy systems incrementally.

At other times, it makes sense to provide several separate component systems to encapsulate different parts of a single legacy system.

There are several problems associated with integrating existing systems together. Incompatible architectures, technologies, or mechanisms can make this a trying experience or sometimes even impossible.

Example

As shown in Chapter 7, the component systems **Account Management** and **Bank Customer Management** are used to wrap different aspects of the legacy system **Customer-Account Transaction Manager**. We have repeated this as Figure 10.12, for convenience. The **Account Management** and **Bank Customer Management** are suppliers of the necessary interfaces and implement the wrapper code.

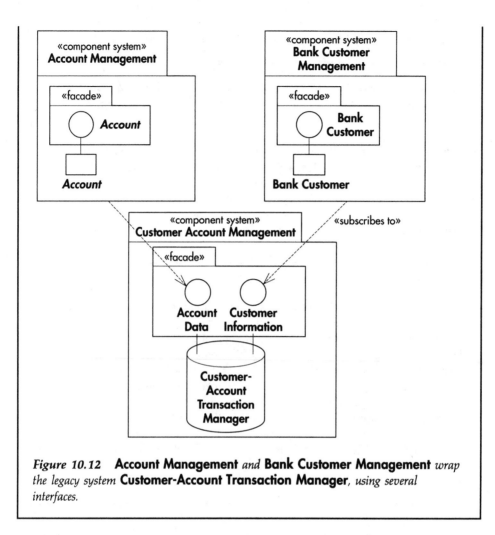

Figure 10.12 **Account Management** *and* **Bank Customer Management** *wrap the legacy system* **Customer-Account Transaction Manager**, *using several interfaces.*

10.5.6 Adapting architecturally incompatible component systems

Garlan *et al.* (1995) give a wonderful description of several problems in a project where they integrated systems from different vendors, claiming all to be caused by architectural mismatch. They divided these problems into six categories including excessive code, poor performance, a need to modify the systems and reinvent existing functions, and an error-prone construction process. The cause seemed to be that the different systems made incorrect assumptions about each other. Many systems, for example, are designed as if they are the center of the universe and assume that other systems will conform to their interaction models, interfaces, and communication primitives. Garlan *et al.* (1995) suggest several strategies for detecting and dealing with such architectural mismatch, including checking assumptions that component systems make about each other, modifying components, and adding wrappers to reduce mismatch. They suggest always limiting the interface to a COTS or a legacy system to what is necessary and letting no other system have further dependencies on it, to reduce the impact of changing technology.

Example

Using an ORB as the object distribution mechanism will impact the design of most other application and component systems – they have to make calls on various object services, such as naming. They also have to publicize their interfaces in appropriate ways. Still, the dependencies on a specific ORB implementation is contained by the use of IDL to define the interfaces of the distributed objects.

Wrappers can sometimes be created quickly by using a flexible scripting language, such as Visual Basic or VBScript. For example, using the features of Visual Basic 4.0, the wrapping program can be easily made into an OLE server, and expose component class methods which can then accessed remotely using DCOM. Also, Visual Basic can be used to combine several systems together, with small programs helping mediate the typical incompatibilities.

10.5.7 Defining and maintaining interfaces and facades

Different systems interact as they perform superordinate use cases. To manage system interaction, we need to define the interfaces carefully, and decide what to expose through the facades.

Use cases in the superordinate model define how the different application and component systems need to interact. By defining collaborations for the use cases and drawing sequence diagrams, as shown in Sections 7.9 and 7.11, we can quite carefully determine what sort of messages they exchange, and in what order.

After estimating the performance of the use cases in different situations, and comparing with the requirements, we can make the final decisions as to how the corresponding systems should interact, and what designs give the best performance/ flexibility trade-offs. We also need to decide on strategies for capturing errors or exceptions, and implement these in the interfaces.

Each interface can now be defined or updated by looking at the use cases in which they are involved, and defining their operation signatures. The interfaces supplied by a subsystem should be as generic as possible, and not specific to its "client" systems. Instead the interfaces should define how the subsystem may be used by *any* subsystem, maybe even by systems developed by other vendors or by the customer.

Example

(Repeated from Chapter 7 to illustrate some results of this work step.)

The **Invoice Tracking** interface to the **Invoice Management** component system would be defined in IDL roughly as follows:

```
#include <financialtypes.idl>
module InvoiceManagement {

    . . .
interface Invoice_Tracking {
    exception Invoice_Issued{Date when}
    exception Invoice_Paid{Customer who}
    exception Invoice_Overdue{Date when, string why}
    Account Create_Invoice(
        in Customer buyer, in string title, in Money amount);
        raises (Invoice_Issued);
    void Register_For_Notification(
        in any peer, in NotificationType what);
    void Schedule_Invoice (in Account wherefrom, in Time when)
        raises (Invoice_Paid);

    . . .
};
};
```

Here we have assumed that there is one IDL module for the component system
Invoice Management. The **Invoice Tracking** interface supports, among
others, the operation **Schedule_Invoice** which schedules an **Invoice** to be paid
at a certain time from the specified **Account**. The exception mechanism is used to
signal that an **Invoice** has been paid by raising an exception that others can
catch.

Finally, decide how to group the exported actors, use cases, analysis types, design classes
(and types), service packages, and interfaces. Define one or more facades for each
component system, as discussed in Section 4.5. Put the exported constructs into as many
separate facades as needed to keep them as independent as possible. When the
components are packaged into the facades, it is likely that changes to components will
be suggested to better accommodate the various reusers.

Watch out for name collisions and redundancy between different component
systems. Make sure that each Application Engineer can reuse from a compatible set of
component systems, without confusion of names.

The interfaces and the facades will undergo many changes during the initial
architecture work. They will also change as the application and component systems are
developed. The architects need to handle change requests to facades and interfaces as a
continuous activity. The architects will have to establish new versions of them and make
sure that the support organization (or tools) distributes the new versions to the
application and component engineers. As the architecture gradually becomes more stable
the changes will be less frequent. The facades and the interfaces between the application
and component systems are owned and changed by the workers of the **Application
Family Engineering** team.

10.6 AFE4: Implementing the architecture as a layered system

The architecturally significant parts of the layered system are implemented by coding the subsystems that will later be the individual application and component systems to a point where the *architecturally relevant use cases can be tested*. Do not implement each (sub)system completely in the first version. Instead plan for evolution and implement the systems iteratively to deliver them in a series of increments.

First, spend substantial time on engineering a robust architecture for each subsystem. Then perform a systematic commonality and variability analysis, but develop only the minimal subset of components really needed for requested and scheduled application systems. Do not develop "nice-to-have" or "perfect" components. It is too risky and difficult. Using these components, implement each subsystem sufficiently to support and allow the architecturally relevant use cases to be tested. Make sure that you consider concurrency and distribution early since they generally introduce new sources of errors and complicate decisions about interfaces, performance, error recovery, and so on.

The result is an architecture that should allow for graceful evolution to meet anticipated needs and is reasonably robust in the face of unanticipated changes. See further discussions on trade-offs between proactive and reactive development of components in Chapter 13.

As appropriate, involve internal and external experts, customers, and key end users in reviewing the models developed so far. It is important that they understand the requirements on functionality, reuse, flexibility, and so on.

10.7 AFE5: Testing the layered system

The best way to develop a high-quality architecture is to design and build it right the first time, invest in systematic reviews and inspections to detect defects early, and to test it to remove remaining deficiencies. However, since it is so difficult to develop architectures, several iterations are required to get it right. But by following a well-defined process it is possible to increase the "quality of each iteration," by avoiding many misunderstandings and common mistakes, by using the most important sources of input, and so on.

A well-defined process does not preclude the need for testing. Instead testing and planning for testing should be integrated in the process. Testing therefore begins during requirements capture with the planning of the tests. The different models such as the use case model and the design model are used to define the specific tests, such as use case and subsystem tests.

The primary focus of testing the layered system during **Application Family Engineering** is to see if the critical interfaces and designs work as intended. Layered system testing involves testing processes, object distribution, error recovery, persistence, and other common collaborations. It also includes tests of performance and of how well the architecture scales when additional application systems and end users start using the application family. It is essential that the architecture is tested early in the target environment, not necessarily for all tests, but for the important ones. Delaying target environment tests imposes too great a risk.

As discussed in Chapter 3, use cases are used to "drive" the testing work steps, similar to how they are used to "drive" the rest of the incremental, iterative development. At each iteration, an additional set of use cases is analyzed, designed, and tested to extend the architecture to support additional interfaces and interactions. The most important things to test should therefore be tied to the use cases that use or stress them most. Once an increment has been tested, the results need to be analyzed and the list of risks updated. Each increment probably eliminates some of the risks, while others remain or may even have been aggravated.

With the right-sized development increments, each increment will not require much rework of previously tested increments. For example, Gilb (1988) suggests rather small increments and short intervals for each cycle, sometimes only a few weeks. But in practice there will always be some changes that require previously tested interfaces and designs to be retested using a regression testing suite.

Testing is particularly important when there are *interoperating application systems*, because testing each application or component system in isolation is not enough in those conditions. As soon as a new system that interoperates with the other systems is added, it is important to test all use cases that involve the new system in interaction with other systems.

10.8 Managing architectural change

Many requests for new types of application systems or component systems can result in changes in the architecture. Changes in technology and standards, the unanticipated availability of new third-party component systems, problems with existing vendors, changes in market or competition, end-user complaints about features, usability or performance, or changes in business processes can also motivate changes in the architecture. These requests and changes have to be managed carefully, to ensure that the layered system architecture is responsive to real needs, but does not change in an uncontrolled way. For each change request, analyze potential impact on existing and planned systems, on scheduled products, costs, documentation, and education needs.

Some application systems are easy to develop with the existing component systems, in which case it is only necessary to briefly go through the AFE process to see if some component system or architecture needs to change when developing a new application system. Other application systems, however, may be more difficult to develop using the available components. In that case, either develop the application system even if the component systems do not provide suitable support, or schedule the development so that the component systems can be improved to support it. If application or component engineers complain about component systems, this too may be an indication of a necessary architecture redesign. The underlying problem may also be that the engineers require more or better training in how to use the component systems effectively. However, component systems that are complex to understand and use indicate that something may be wrong.

If competitors launch new competing products, it may become necessary to re-evaluate the competitive advantages, strategy, and so on, which in turn may lead to placing substantially changed requirements on the application family and thus impact the architecture. Likewise, a changed market analysis will affect the business model from which the architecture is derived. As soon as the business model has been changed and validated, it will be necessary to revise the architecture.

10.9 Expressing Application Family Engineering in terms of workers

Figure 10.13 and Table 10.2 indicate how different workers are involved in different parts of **Application Family Engineering**. The workers are described in more detail in Chapter 9.

The business entity objects **superordinate use case model, analysis model, design model, implementation model, test model, concurrency model,** and **deployment model** have been omitted from the Figure 10.13 to simplify it. See also Section 9.3.9 for a discussion of how the workers use business entity objects.

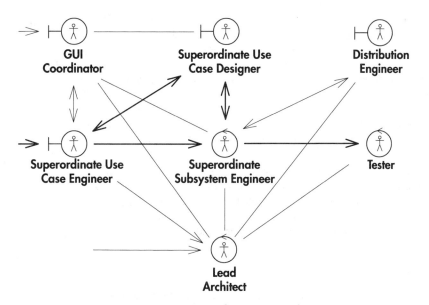

Figure 10.13 *Workers involved in* **Application Family Engineering**. *Arrows are* «communicates» *associations, and the darker arrows indicate most frequent interaction.*

Table 10.2   *Workers involved in the **Application Family Engineering** process.*

AFE0: If there already is a sound architecture as a base, it is represented using the superordinate design model, by the **Lead Architect**, **Distribution Engineer**, and **Superordinate Subsystem Engineer**. The **Distribution Engineer** is responsible for defining the processes and nodes in the system, how they are interconnected and how they interact with each other. A **Superordinate Subsystem Engineer** is responsible for defining the types within a subsystem in the superordinate design model.

AFE1: Requirements capture is performed primarily by business engineers and by the **Lead Architect**, **GUI Coordinator**, **Distribution Engineer**, and **Superordinate Use Case Engineer**s. The **GUI Coordinator** evaluates and suggests what GUI component libraries to use and coordinates the definition of the graphical interfaces. The **Software Engineering Business Manager** develops an application product plan. The **Superordinate Use Case Engineer**s develop a use case model of the superordinate system assisted by the **GUI Coordinator**. When possible, a business model of the target organization should be used as input. The **Tester**s start planning how to test the architecture.

AFE2: The **Superordinate Use Case Designer** suggests analysis types from the use cases and the **Superordinate Subsystem Engineer** groups the analysis types into subsystems, one subsystem for each candidate application and component system.

AFE3: The **Lead Architect** considers legacy systems, third-party products, and so on, and defines a layered system using the design model. The **Lead Architect** is responsible for looking at middleware, GUI toolkits, utility class libraries, and object request brokers, and factors these out into separate component subsystems. The **Distribution Engineer** considers distribution and works on the deployment and concurrency models. The **Superordinate Subsystem Engineer** defines the interfaces and the facades that each application or component system will provide. The **Superordinate Use Case Designer** distributes the use cases among the application and component subsystems.

AFE4: The **Software Engineering Business Manager** uses the product plan to decide when to implement each application and component (sub)system.

AFE5: The **Tester** is responsible for testing the architecture and helping prepare test specifications in parallel with the work steps above. First the application and component (sub)systems are implemented and locally tested. Then they are tested as part of the whole layered system, where the superordinate use cases are tested. As the architectural elements are tested, they are incrementally baselined.

During the work outlined above, the **Lead Architect**, **GUI Coordinator**, and **Distribution Engineer** are responsible for the quality of the different models of the layered system.

10.10 A leaner approach to Application Family Engineering

Some organizations can build their application systems by simply integrating existing components. They add value by combining the parts into a greater whole but do not develop any substantial software themselves. For such organizations we have sketched out the following "lean approach" to defining an architecture and the applications that make up that architecture. The approach is basically to take one quick iteration through all the steps of the AFE process to define the architecture by integrating the architectures of the existing component systems. However, this approach is not an option for most software development organizations today since the open market of available components has not reached a sufficient degree of maturity.

Do requirements capture and robustness analysis as normal, but during design and implementation integrate only components that can be acquired or adapted. These include ActiveXs, ORBs, and legacy systems. The testing step need only verify that these components work together. After the first quick iteration, the different processes for **Application System Engineering** can be launched for each application system. Note that these processes will have to work using only the existing components and architectures; they cannot expect many new components to be created within the reuse business itself, apart from a few components developed by the application engineers themselves over time as pluggable variants or alternatives within the integrated architecture.

10.11 Summary

The process for **Application Family Engineering** develops and maintains the layered system, represented as a superordinate system with use case, analysis, design, deployment, and concurrency test models, as shown in Figure 10.2. Business actors and workers are used to identify actors and use cases for the layered system. These use cases are studied to identify the architecturally most relevant analysis types, which are grouped into subsystems that are molded to suit the target implementation environment. During design, the layered system is adapted to Commercial Off The Shelf products and legacy systems, and defined using explicit interfaces and facades. Finally the architecture is implemented and tested using the key use cases as drivers.

Application Family Engineering proceeds in iterations, where at first only a small fraction of the use cases are selected, analyzed, designed, implemented, and tested according to the steps above. These use cases are selected so that they are the most relevant to defining the architecture. Then the second most relevant use cases are selected, and so on. Based on the resulting architecture, the application and component systems are then developed in separate processes: **Application System Engineering** and **Component System Engineering**.

10.12 Additional reading

Use *A System of Patterns* by F. Buschmann, R. Meurier, H. Rohnert, P. Sommerland, and M. Stal, as a catalog of architectural patterns that can be combined into a suitable architecture. The book, published by Wiley in 1996, provides advice on implementing the patterns and discussions of the pros and cons of the individual patterns.

The "Systems of Interconnected Systems" article by Ivar Jacobson, Karin Palmkvist, and Susanne Dyrhage, *ROAD*, May–June 1995 describes how to work with systems of interoperating systems in general.

The book by John McGregor and David Sykes, *Object-Oriented Software Development: Engineering Software for Reuse*, Van Nostrand-Reinhold, 1992, contains an excellent discussion of the technical criteria to be used in evaluating object-oriented libraries, and many other guidelines related to a fractal, incremental, iterative, component-based software development process.

COMPONENT
SYSTEM
ENGINEERING

11.1 Building flexible component systems

A good component system allows reusers to build their systems more quickly, more effectively, and less expensively. The reusers of a component system are most often **Application Engineer**s but may also be other **Component Engineer**s. These reusers require well-designed, flexible component systems that match their skills and needs.

> The **Component System Engineering** process develops use case, analysis, design, implementation and test models for a component system, similar to the ordinary OOSE software engineering process described in Chapter 3, but with a focus on building and packaging robust, extendible, and flexible components, see Figure 11.1.

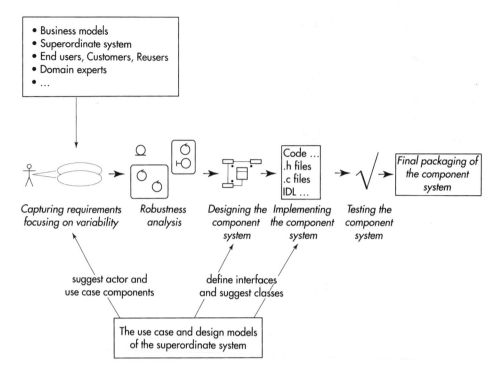

Figure 11.1 *A summary of the sources of information and the work steps in the* **Component System Engineering** *process.*

Component engineers use a variety of input, such as business models, models of the superordinate system, and input from end users, customers, and domain experts to determine the features and range of variability needed in a particular component system. The models of the superordinate system are used to suggest actors and use cases and to define the interfaces of the component system as discussed in Chapter 7.

There is one **Component System Engineering** process for each component system, which means that there will be several concurrent processes, each building a different component system. There will also be several concurrent processes for **Application System Engineering** and one concurrent process for **Application Family Engineering**. A component system must export the facades and interfaces defined in the superordinate system and comply with the facades offered by other component systems that it reuses from. An application system must comply with the interfaces defined in the superordinate system and the facades offered by component systems. Since these systems have inherent dependencies on each other, the concurrent processes (ASE, CSE, AFE) that develop them have to synchronize.

The work steps, described at a high level, are shown in Table 11.1.

In reality, just as for **AFE**, these steps will not proceed sequentially, but will be part of an iterative, incremental life cycle.

Table 11.1 *The essential steps of the **Component System Engineering** process.*

CSE1:	**Capturing requirements focusing on variability** – Collect input from reusers, business models, models of the superordinate system, domain experts, customers, and end users. Prepare a use case model of the component system and make sure that variability requirements are captured. Assess the value and cost of each use case and decide whether or not to include it in the next release. Also analyze how best to organize the facades and requirements on processes (SEP) and the tools (SEPSE) to be used with the component system.
CSE2:	**Performing robustness analysis** – Use the use cases to identify analysis objects and packages and express variability. Use facades to export the analysis components.
CSE3:	**Designing the component system** – Use the analysis model as an input to prepare a design model of the component system. Adapt the design model to the implementation environment. Use sequence diagrams to distribute the use cases among the subsystems in order to precisely define interfaces. Use facades to export the design components.
CSE4:	**Implementing the component system** – Implement the new version of the component system, review the implementation, and select technology for delivery. Use facades to export the implementation components.
CSE5:	**Testing the component system** – Test the component system for reuse.
CSE6:	**Final packaging of the component system** – Document and package the component system and its facades for easy use and retrieval by reusers.

11.2 CSE1: Capturing requirements focusing on variability

The purpose of requirements capture is to identify and organize the requirements as use cases. Requirements capture for a component system is similar to requirements capture for a traditional OOSE system, but with a greater focus on identifying commonalities and variability among several application systems.

Getting requirements right for a single application is difficult. There are several people involved, each with a slightly different viewpoint. The models are often ambiguous. The goals move as the development proceeds and the implementation environment may affect the early requirements specifications. It is even more difficult to establish requirements for a component system, since:

- a component system must meet the needs of several application systems;

- a component system is not developed to be installed and used immediately, but rather to serve as a reusable asset for many years to come;

- a more diverse set of people will provide the requirements for a component system, in order to understand current needs and predict future ones;

- engineering the right variability requires careful trade-off and considerable experience.

It is therefore important to have a systematic technique for collecting inputs, and for structuring and comparing potential requirements. The business model of the target organization and the superordinate layered system provide a useful starting point for requirements capture. Our technique draws from several domain engineering methods (Arango, 1995), especially FODA (Kang, 1990), CFRP (STARS, 1993), and ODM (Simos, 1995b; STARS 95).

11.2.1 Using business models, the superordinate system, and other component systems as input

Many component actors and use cases can be identified from the models of the superordinate system. See Chapter 7 for a discussion of how to divide the superordinate use cases over design subsystems. Each superordinate subsystem corresponds to an application or component system, as shown in Figure 11.2. Identify one candidate component use case for each use case segment that is allocated to the component

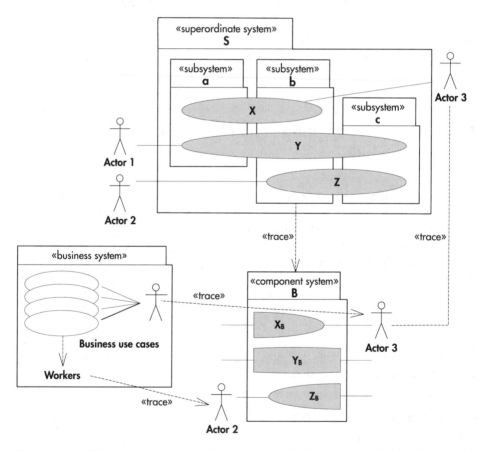

Figure 11.2 *The component actors and use cases can be found and specified based on models of the business and the superordinate system.*

subsystem. Identify component system actors from superordinate system actors and from other superordinate subsystems that the component subsystem interacts with.

Example

The models of the superordinate system contain an interface **Invoice** that the component system **Invoice Management** supplies, as described in Chapter 7.

Study the business actor or worker profiles to see what knowledge and preferences people that can enact them have and use that information to specify the actors of the information system. Study the workers and the business entity types to better understand how to build the right component use cases. Identify business rules, constraints, and pre- and post-conditions and map those to use cases or entity types. Relate new and changed information system use cases and actors to the business actors, workers, and business entity types to see how they support the business processes.

Define and maintain «traces» from business actors, workers, and business entity types to component actors and use cases as illustrated in Figure 11.2. This helps with changing the requirements as the business understanding grows, simplifies validation of system requirements, and helps explain the component system in a business context. Sometimes, technology restrictions make it impossible to implement business use cases as planned. Similarly, new technology may offer new opportunities to improve the business use cases. Also define and maintain «traces» from the superordinate models to component actors and use cases as illustrated in Figure 11.2. Among other things this helps component system engineers to give feedback on the layered system as a whole.

If the component system reuses other component systems such as middleware, then study the facades of those component systems. Try to understand how reused component systems might evolve in order to anticipate and isolate changes.

11.2.2 Using input from customers, end users, reusers, and component system supporters

Talk to customers and key users, and observe how they use the systems to better understand their situation and needs. Customers particularly can help determine the importance and value of many requirements. Use the analysis of customers and end users performed during **Application Family Engineering** to determine which customers and end users to talk to.

Relate component use cases to application system use case models to make sure that the components really add value and are not "ivory towers." If no such application systems exist, envision at least three situations where each use case component will be reused and assess its viability from that. Decide how to develop the component system in increments based on the product plan, customer demand, and the needs of reusers.

As reusers work with existing component systems, they will often identify problems and limitations, as well as opportunities for improvement. They report these to the

Component System Supporters who gather them together and discuss them with the component engineers. Reusers will also provide feedback on their development processes (SEP) and tools (SEPSE). Changes to the reusers' processes and tools may also influence the design of the component systems. An environment such as Visual Basic will affect how components are defined, implemented, packaged, and documented.

Example

The **Account Management** component system supports custom **Overdraft** management using VBScript as discussed in Section 10.1. The reusers and some potential customers like VBScript very much. In fact, the reusers like it so much that they suggest using VBScript in the component system **Invoice Management** for custom handling of overdue invoice payments. The **Software Engineering Business Manager** decides that the increased flexibility and ease of use justifies the extra work to revise the **Invoice Management** component system.

Remember that problem reports do not necessarily identify the real problem, but only a symptom of it. Discuss problem reports with the reusers and component system supporters and then suggest how to improve the component use cases.

Develop and maintain a glossary of terms that can be used when describing application use cases, types and classes, and so on. Prepare a glossary document for each exported facade and include the appropriate terms from the component system glossary. The terms can be imported by reusers and can help them to use the same vocabulary consistently as they discuss requirements and designs.

11.2.3 Using other sources of input

Use existing applications within the company or developed by other vendors as input. These systems ("exemplars" in the ODM domain engineering process (Simos, 1995a; STARS 95)) often help identify key requirements and features, and provide insight into architectures and designs.

Component engineers must keep up to date with the evolution and trends of the business domain and with the information technologies used, such as the rapid changes in the Internet, WWW, Java, and ActiveX technologies. Business domain experts and experts in information technology should be involved to help select and explain the novel features of exemplar systems.

Use related work in the literature and standards publications where components and frameworks, or identified patterns or designs, may already have been factored out. See, for example, the OMG task force on business objects, financial and insurance frameworks, banking and financial standards, or database kits (Batory, 1994). Identify areas where changes are likely and prepare the component system to facilitate these changes in upcoming versions.

Many standards and handbooks include glossaries that may be relevant to the component system. These also help improve the understanding of the domain and subsequently of the component systems (STARS, 1993).

Make sure that you address not only the functional requirements, but also all other requirements such as performance, quality, software size, and understandability.

11.2.4 Expressing commonality and variability in the use case model

Use the following rules of thumb when building the component use case model:

- Factor out common variations as separate use case variants, for example common parameter settings and extensions.

- Represent commonalities as use cases with variation points to represent variability.

- Define for each variation point the characteristics of a valid variant.

- Specify the criteria for reusing each actor and use case, perhaps by specifying the requirements it fulfills. Define and document which actors, use cases, and variants must coexist in a system, and which ones cannot coexist.

Example

The **Account Management** component system offers a use case component **Monetary Transfer**. Different reusers of that component system need different strategies for handling overdrafts. As shown in Figure 11.3, the **Component Engineer**s define a variation point {**Account Overdrawn**} to deal with overdrawn accounts. The component system also provides a number of variants for dealing with overdrafts. One deducts a fee for each overdraft, while the other does not permit overdrafts at all. These variants are associated with the variation point {**Account Overdrawn**}. The facade documents the restriction that these two variants may not both be reused by the same application system.

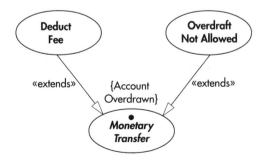

Figure 11.3 *The abstract use case component* **Monetary Transfer**, *together with two alternative variants for handling account overdrafts.*

11.2.5 Reviewing and packaging actor and use case components for reuse

Ensure that the future plans for a component system are consistent with the strategic and operational goals of the business. Validate with the managers the high-level requirements and impacts on time to market, quality, and cost for the application systems that can reuse the component system. Discuss how the changed component system allows the company to improve its strength in some market segments, address new market segments, or withdraw from some market segments.

Decide which component actors, use cases, and variants to export and group them into one or more facades to make them as reusable as possible. Make sure that reusers can use the components together with components from other component systems. Try to make the facades as independent as possible since that generally reduces maintenance costs. Group components that are reused together in the same facade. See also the discussions of facades in Chapters 4 and 5. Organize the components into separate configuration items to reflect the facade organization.

Validate the component system by verifying that the use case models of systems that reuse it can be updated easily to match the new use case components.

Gather a good mix of customers, end users, business domain experts, information technology experts, **Component System Supporter**s, and reusers and let them review the new version of the component use case model. Use the business model and the models of the superordinate system as a frame of reference. Let the reviewers examine several application systems that have been or could be developed using the component system. Let them identify weaknesses, trouble spots, or "corner cases" where some of the design assumptions might not apply. Develop suggestions for improving the component systems. Use these ideas to carefully revise and improve the use case model and then verify the changes with the reviewers.

Example

As the reviewers review the first draft of the use case model for the component system **Account Management** they discover that the component use case **Monetary Transfer** does not allow for time-outs due to communication problems over the telecommunications network. They furthermore point out that different installations of the component system must allow for different lengths of time before canceling the transfer.

Prepare a list of risks added when changing the component system and suggest a way to reduce each risk. Typical risks are: adding new components that have not yet been reused, low functionality coverage, and bad packaging of components.

11.3 CSE2: Performing robustness analysis to maximize flexibility

The purpose of robustness analysis is to find a robust and reusable object structure that can provide the specified component use cases. This structure is essentially an architecture for the component system. Robustness analysis for a component system is similar to traditional OOSE robustness analysis, but with a greater focus on identifying commonalities and variability. See also the discussion in Section 7.6 regarding the choice of appropriate business-specific components to support rapid application development.

The superordinate design model also provides significant input. Candidate entity types can be found by looking at design types in the superordinate model. The superordinate design type itself or some of its properties can be used to suggest a component entity type. Candidate entity types can also be found by looking at the business entity types and their properties.

As discussed in Chapter 6, several default patterns help map use cases into a set of interacting analysis components. Candidate boundary types can, for example, be identified for each interface that the component system uses or supplies. All interaction with actors of the component system should go through boundary objects.

Let us now turn to how analysis types can be found from use cases. Distribute each use case across the analysis objects by defining a collaboration, using collaboration diagrams and use case descriptions rewritten in terms of analysis objects. Describe the role of each analysis object and how it participates in the use cases.

Example

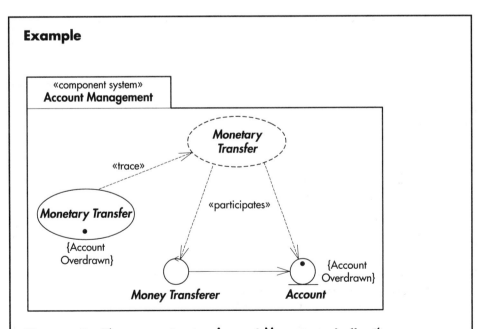

Figure 11.4   *The component system* **Account Management** *offers the use case* **Monetary Transfer** *and the related analysis objects that perform the use case.*

> The use case component **Monetary Transfer** defines a procedure for transferring money to, from, and between **Accounts**. The analysis objects **Account** and **Money Transferer** together implement the corresponding collaboration (Figure 11.4).

Define and maintain «traces» from workers and business entity objects to analysis types. Also define and maintain «traces» from the superordinate use case and design models to analysis types.

11.3.1 Structuring the variability

Identify variation points and variants that support the variability defined in the use case model. Allocate each variation point to one analysis type when possible since this makes it easier to attach a variant – the variant only has to "hook" into one type.

When an actor is optional, allocate one dedicated boundary type for that actor, and make it optional as well.

As discussed in Chapter 6, several patterns and modeling techniques can be used to make a flexible object model. OOSE provides two types of relations that may be used for this, the «subscribes to» association and the «extends» generalization. The «subscribes to» association resembles the Observer pattern (Gamma *et al.*, 1994) and the «extends» generalization can be used to represent the Decorator pattern. Another pattern that may be useful is the Strategy pattern, as shown in the next example.

Example

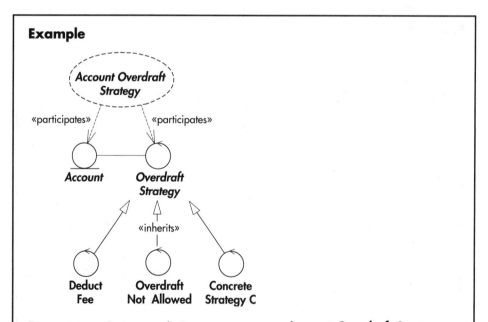

Figure 11.5 Custom overdraft management as an **Account Overdraft Strategy** pattern.

One way to implement the variation point **{Account Overdrawn}** is to use the Strategy pattern (Figure 11.5). Gamma *et al.* (1994) define the Strategy pattern to allow for families of interchangeable algorithms (see also Section 6.7.3). The Strategy pattern consists of three participating objects: *Context*, *Strategy*, and *ConcreteStrategy*.

In our example the **Account** will be the *Context* which has a need for an interchangeable algorithm for **Overdraft** management, and has a reference to an abstract *Strategy* object, **Overdraft Strategy** in our example. The abstract **Overdraft Strategy** is specialized into different *ConcreteStrategies* **Deduct Fee** and **Overdraft Not Allowed** which each implement a variant of the algorithm. The idea here is that the context (the **Account**) can use different strategies (**Overdraft Strategy**) for dealing with overdrafts. The **Account** object must provide an interface for the **Overdraft Strategies** so that they can ask the **Account** for any information that they need during their execution.

Look also for patterns that are specific to your organization or application domain, such as entity-object patterns, and suggest useful commonality and variants.

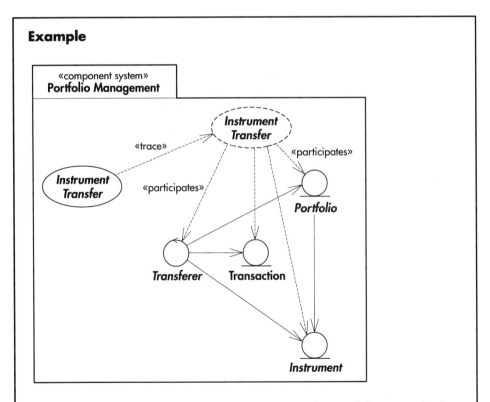

Example

Figure 11.6 *A banking-specific design pattern, expressed as a collaboration, related to an abstract use case, **Instrument Transfer**.*

The following example was used in Chapters 5 and 6 to discuss several levels of reuse. The same example is used here as an illustration of a domain-specific pattern that can be defined as a reusable component in a component system.

The **Portfolio Management** component system contains the abstract use case **Instrument Transfer**, which moves an arbitrary instrument type, for example money, from one **Portfolio** to another. As illustrated in Figure 11.6, this use case is realized by a collaboration involving several analysis objects, in which **Transferer** is responsible for the transaction and creates a **Transaction** entity object to document the transfer. We will not detail this collaboration, but suffice it to say that **Transferer** also transfers each **Instrument**, and updates the corresponding **Portfolio**. A **Portfolio** here includes accounts, loans, stock portfolios, and so on.

If the analysis model shows many objects with complex interdependencies, this is often a sign of a bad design. Try to remove complex dependencies by applying some design pattern or by introducing additional types, such as abstract types that contain the dependencies.

Example

The **Portfolio** and **Instrument** components above can be designed using the Composite pattern (Gamma, 1994). Both types should inherit from another abstract type, in this case **Asset**, which provides a virtual operation for computing the value of something, either an individual **Instrument** or a **Portfolio**

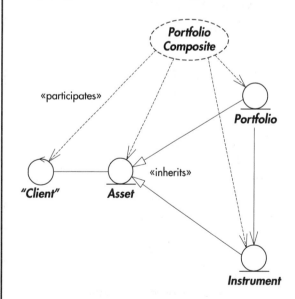

Figure 11.7 *The **Portfolio Composite** pattern used to create an abstract type **Asset**.*

of **Instruments** (Figure 11.7). Clients of the **Portfolio** and **Instrument** types that need to compute the value of both **Portfolios** and individual **Instruments** can then be designed as clients of the abstract type **Asset** only.

11.3.2 Packaging the analysis types for reuse

The analysis components can be grouped into subsystems and service packages in much the same way as described in the OOSE process:

- For each optional set of functionality make one service package that contains analysis types and variants that together offer that functionality.

- Divide the mandatory types and variants into service packages, each with limited dependencies on other service packages.

- Group the service packages into subsystems.

Decide which service packages to export and package them into a number of facades and configuration items that make them as reusable as possible, as discussed in Section 11.2.5.

11.3.3 Assessing the reusability and quality of the analysis model

Review the analysis model as described earlier for the use case model. Verify that:

- all component actors, use cases, variation points, variants, and legal combinations of use case variants are supported by the analysis types;

- the systems that reuse this component system can be modeled effectively using the analysis components, and that the component analysis model can be extended easily by reusers;

- dependencies from the component system itself to facades of other component systems that are likely to change in the future are limited. One way to limit dependencies is to narrow the imported facades as much as possible, so that only a limited subset of the available functionality gets imported, or to devise a "concealing" wrapper to put around the reused component system.

It is also useful to "stress" the reusability of the analysis model, for example in brainstorming sessions where component supporters and reusers suggest odd reuse situations and explore corner cases. Any suggestions that do not fit very well with the architecture are analyzed to see how likely they are, by checking with customers and reusers. They are then mapped to the use case and object models and worked into the component system like any other type of requirement.

Karlsson *et al.* (1995) have a thorough treatment of how to assess the reusability and quality of reusable software. They use the following criteria:

- Portability

- Adaptability, that is, modularity and generality

- Understandability

- Confidence, that is, maturity and fault tolerance of components.

11.4 CSE3: Designing the component system

The procedure for the design and implementation of a component system is similar to ordinary OOSE system design and implementation:

1   Identify one candidate design class for each analysis type. Identify one candidate design subsystem and service package for each analysis subsystem and service package. Decide which variability mechanism to use for each variation point, as discussed in Chapter 6. If the component system is abstract (a framework) then try to factor the component system into subsystems such that each is a sub-framework. Try to decouple these sub-frameworks as much as possible, perhaps even introducing specialized classes that isolate the dependencies. Define «trace» links between the analysis model and the design model.

2   Reorganize the design model based on the *Design Guidelines* document prepared by the **Application Family Engineering** team as discussed in Section 10.5.3. Try to reuse components, frameworks, and other products such as OLE or OpenDoc.

3   Make sure that the component system can supply the interfaces that clients expect. These interfaces are defined in the superordinate design model as interfaces between subsystems. Since these subsystems correspond to application and component systems, the interfaces should be the same as those in the design model of the superordinate system.

4   Divide the responsibilities of the use cases over design objects using interaction diagrams. Use the sequence diagrams to design for the right performance by breaking down use case performance requirements to performance requirements on individual object operations. Each operation that an object performs can potentially result in an exception. Use the sequence diagram to look for possible exceptions in objects that receive messages and suggest how to improve robustness in the face of errors and malfunctions.

5   Define methods on the classes based on the interaction diagrams.

6   Allocate design objects to processes.

7   Implement and unit test the classes.

The above steps are not performed in a strict sequence as the numbering may suggest, but may involve many iterations.

Most of the design patterns suggested in Gamma *et al.* (1994) can be used to develop the design model. Gamma *et al.* suggest procedures for selecting and implementing a pattern based on required variability; see, for example, Sections 1.7 and 1.8 in Gamma *et al.* (1994). List or document in the *Design Guidelines* the patterns used frequently, starting with patterns such as Observer, Strategy, Composite, and Decorator from the Design Patterns book (Gamma *et al.*, 1994). Allow the engineers to learn these patterns and then let the pattern catalog grow as more patterns are employed and discovered. This pattern catalog also serves as a common vocabulary for the developers.

McGregor and Sykes (1992a), describe criteria due to Korson and McGregor (1991) for evaluating class libraries. These criteria are also very useful when designing a component system. They include measures for completeness of the class library and how to use inheritance.

11.4.1 Reviewing and packaging design components for reuse

Review and package the design model similarly to reviewing and packaging the analysis model. Also make sure that all analysis types have been traced to design classes and that «trace» links are defined accurately from the design model to the analysis model.

Each **Application System Engineering** team follows a process for **Application System Engineering**. This process may be unique to each **Application System Engineering** team, adapted to suit the application system, the reused component systems, and the tools used. The component engineers offer kits (Griss, 1995c) containing not only the component system, but also suitable tools (SEPSE) and process (SEP) elements for reusing it. The application engineers define their process for **Application System Engineering** by integrating process and tool elements from several component system kits and streamlining them for their type of application system.

Example

The **Account Management** component system is developed as a C++ framework. The Component Engineers do requirements capture, robustness analysis, and design using the Rational Rose tool and suggest that the Application Engineers also use the same environment. They then choose to use the HP Softbench C++ environment as they implement the component system and suggest that the Application Engineers also use the same environment. They customize the Rational Objectory 4.0 process to the needs of the Application Engineers and to the specific needs when reusing **Account Management**. Objectory is a configurable software engineering process based on OOSE, but for industry-strength software development.

The Component Engineers furthermore use Rose and Visual Basic to build an ActiveX component that allows the Application Engineers to define custom procedures for dealing with **Account Overdrafts**.

Make sure that reusers can reuse the component system without encountering name collisions with components in other component systems they reuse.

11.5 CSE4: Implementing the component system

There are many languages that can be used to implement components. We have used C++, Smalltalk, Visual Basic, and Java as examples in this book. In addition to the discussion on C++, Java, and Visual Basic in Chapter 6, we will show some simple guidelines for C++ and Smalltalk here.

11.5.1 Implementing in C++

Implementing an OOSE design in C++ is a fairly straightforward task. Table 11.2 summarizes some aspects of doing this.

Make all public member functions virtual, because it is impossible to foresee which public member functions will need to be overridden in some future subclass.

An attribute type in the design model should correspond to types in C++, like **enum, int, float**, and **char***, or derived types, like **array**, or user-derived types like type-defined enumerations. An attribute type might also be implemented as a class.

Karlsson *et al.* (1995) suggest further guidelines to use when implementing reusable classes in C++. See also McGregor and Sykes (1992).

Table 11.2 *Implementing the design model in C++.*

Design	C++
«Design package»	Files, directories, and configuration items in the CM system
«Design class»	One or more classes
Abstract class	Class with protected constructor
Operation	Member function or, for class operations, static member function
Virtual operation	Virtual member function = 0
Operation group	–
Inheritance	Public inheritance
Attribute type	(a) An existing class (b) A type, such as **enum** or **int** (c) A new class
Attribute	Member variable or, for class attribute, static member variable
«Acquaintance»	Member variable (by reference)
«Consists of»	Member variable (by value)
«Communicates»	Sending messages
«Depends on»	If the CM system has a good mechanism for expressing dependencies between packages, use it

11.5.2 Implementing in Smalltalk

Table 11.3 shows one way of implementing an OOSE design in Smalltalk.

Table 11.3 *Implementing the design model in Smalltalk.*

Design	Smalltalk
«Design package»	Categories or configuration items in the CM system
«Design class»	One or more classes
Abstract class	Abstract class
Operation	Method (Instance or Class)
Virtual operation	Method implemented as "self subClassResonsibility"
Operation group	Protocol or method category
Inheritance	Inheritance
Attribute type	(a) An existing class (b) An aggregation of existing classes by means of Collections (c) A new class
Attribute	Instance/class variable
«Acquaintance»	Instance/class variable
«Consists of»	Instance variable
«Communicates»	Sending messages
«Depends on»	If the CM system has a good mechanism for expressing dependencies between packages, use it

11.5.3 Packaging the implementation for reuse

Review and package the code modules of the implementation model similarly to the review and packaging of the design model. Define «trace» links between the design model and the implementation model. Some tools can use these traces for round trip engineering so that changes in the implementation can be used to update the design model.

Example

The Component Engineers decide that the component system **Account Management** needs four configuration items: one for the **Account** and **Transaction** types, one for the **Risk** type, and one for each of the two pre-built strategies for dealing with **Overdraft** (that is, do not allow an overdraft at all or take a fee for each overdraft).

The configuration item for **Risk** contains C++ files.

The configuration item for **Account** and **Transaction** contains C++ files and the **Overdraft** ActiveX component that allows custom procedures for dealing with account overdrafts.

The configuration items for the two different overdraft strategies contain VBScript programs that specialize the **Overdraft** ActiveX component.

11.6 CSE5: Testing the component system

Testing reusable systems is complex; it is impossible to test a class, framework, or system in all situations where it will be reused. Inheritance is particular tricky, since inheritance gets around the object's normal encapsulation barrier — which introduces a significant opportunity for uncontrolled changes. The use of inheritance is often coupled with a need for extensive white-box testing and scenario-driven testing, that is, testing the internal design of the class and testing it against likely reuse scenarios.

McGregor and Korson (1992), Lorenz (1993), Goldberg and Rubin (1995), and Karlsson (1995) provide extensive discussions of testing classes and frameworks, how to change traditional testing, and the importance of providing reusers with reusable test specifications. They also discuss testing reusable components and frameworks based on different ways of expressing variability. They introduce several concepts.

Widened   Test only component functionality that is actually reused in any application system.

Narrowed   Completely test abstract use cases or units that offer only functionality required by all reusers.

Configurable   For modules that can be combined into different configurations, test each unit and also each configuration of units.

Example

The component system **Account Management** is first developed to support the application systems **Payment** and **Invoicing**. The first iteration of test specifications for the component system therefore focuses on moving money between accounts. But the Component Engineers know that with the development of the **ATM Cashier** application system scheduled next year, the component system must support withdrawals from and deposits to accounts. They decide to include some tests for withdrawals and deposits as well. But they focus their testing on moving money between accounts since that is what the Application Engineers need most right now.

Testing has its own life cycle which starts with test planning and ends with a test report. Start planning the tests early in the development process, preferably during requirements capture.

Testing is performed on three different levels in OOSE (see also Chapter 3).

Unit testing   Ensure that a unit matches its specification. By *unit* we mean either an individual class, a group of classes, or other sub-programs, such as member functions in C++.

Use case testing   Test the collaboration between instances of the classes in use cases. Use the interaction diagrams as test specifications.

System testing   Test the entire system when the use cases have been tested.

Since it is not possible to test all configurations of a system, focus on important cases:

- Test each unit and use case as for any OOSE system; that is, test them without considering a specific reuser.

- Then test the complete component system with a complete system test, with several concurrent use case instances executing; that is, test it with all provided functionality "in use" but still in isolation − without considering a specific reuser.

- Test *likely* configurations with a complete system test; that is, test with some chosen variants available either in the component system or in specific application systems.

- Test a few carefully selected *unlikely* or *corner-case* or *boundary-case* configurations to see how robust the component system is in different respects, to gain an appreciation of the limitations of the component system.

- Test the configurations *actually* ordered with a complete system test; that is, test with the variants that will be used in an application system that has already been ordered.

If this is a new version of an existing component system, perform regression tests on the systems that reuse it.

11.7   CSE6: Final packaging of the component system for reuse

The use case and object models help reusers learn how to reuse from the component system, but are seldom enough in themselves. The learning curve for complex component systems is in fact a major obstacle to substantial reuse. Microsoft Foundation Classes (MFC), Taligent CommonPoint and even MacApp would be too hard to use without extensive examples, "cookbooks," and specialized tools. One approach is to package components, component systems, software engineering processes, tools, and examples together as a coherent entity — a *kit* (Griss, 1995c). Such a kit may include:

- A road map or tutorial for learning how to reuse the component system.

- Terminology and required prerequisites such as that the reusers must be skilled C++ programmers.

- The *Design Guidelines* document, defining key collaborations and patterns.

- An explanation of why the different facades were chosen and what they contain.

- A software engineering process (SEP), with step-by-step guidelines on how to reuse the component system — clearly showing what reusers have to add, configure, and parameterize, and which special tools to use.

- A set of tools (SEPSEs), for assembling, engineering, and testing application systems from the component system; for example, CM tools, repositories, builder tools, generators, scripting tools, problem-oriented languages, and help tools.

- Guidelines on how to choose between optional variants, including non-functional aspects of the components such as efficiency, portability, and reliability. Also other guidelines on how best to use the components.

- Examples of how components have been reused, including sample models and code that can be used as a starting point.

- Prefabricated test-beds and specifications that can be reused to verify application systems.

- Fragments of end-user documentation that can be combined into complete documentation to describe application systems.

- Training material and information for the Component System Supporters when training and supporting reusers. Remember that the Component System Supporters will themselves require appropriate training. Give reusers who are already using an earlier version of the component system adequate training to ensure a smooth transition.

- Other material such as references to related component systems, platform requirements, and revision history.

Example

Visual Basic (VB) exemplifies many of the kit features described above, and is an interesting component-based application construction environment. VB has become very popular since 1990, because of its features, a growing set of third-party components and tools, and significant support by Microsoft (Udell, 1994). Microsoft uses Visual Basic for Applications as an embedded glue/customization/macro language for its extensible applications, and as an integration and automation language for OLE-based applications.

VB's power comes from the careful balance between:

- simple object and component model;
- easy-to-use, interpretive glue and customization language;
- range of built-in and third-party components and add-on tools;
- openness, granularity, and packaging of components (called controls); and
- integration of visual, property-sheet, and language-based customization.

VB is extensible enough to be the basis for a family of compatible, domain-specific kits, and has inspired the design of several similar systems. VB illustrates many important kit features:

- *VB components* comprise several compatible parts, including an icon for the toolbox, code, help element, visual resource for Windows, a property sheet, and event procedure stubs.
- The VB *framework* is built on the Windows API. Many Windows messages are converted into VB events, which are dispatched to named VB methods. The framework is generic, but enforces a Windows GUI and event-driven communication.
- VB's interpretive generic Basic *language* glues components together and specifies behavior as method bodies and global procedures. The language includes extensions for objects, methods, properties, event-driven programming, OLE access, and external routines. Property sheets associated with each component are a form of "template language."
- A developer can load a *sample application* and modify it incrementally, or copy pieces from another sample VB application to create a new application.
- VB's development and execution *environment* and *tools* include a visual "builder." An iconic form of a component is copied from the toolbox and instantiated, creating a default property sheet and event routine stubs. Using browsers and editors, the developer customizes the component's appearance and behavior, changing graphical attributes, properties, event actions, and method bodies. Syntax checking and interpretation support rapid and incremental development. Simple generators ("wizards") help construct customized components, subsystems, and complete applications.

Procedures written in C and C++ can easily be linked in. Third-party components and tools cover many domains (for example, database, finance, instruments), and include a cross-reference facility, component development kit, source code management, help builder, and basic compiler.

Develop and maintain all the documentation, examples, tools, and so on that accompany the component system, *in coordination* with the component system itself.

Let a separate team perform acceptance tests before the component system is included in the reuse repository and made available for reuse by the application engineers. Check that all required documentation, components, and tools are provided. Inspect all documentation to ensure that it has the right format, and uses the appropriate terminology and concepts. Inspect each facade to ensure that it is well described. Use the examples provided; install them and execute them. Make sure that the indicated SEP and SEPSE processes and tools can be used to reuse the component system effectively.

Once certified, the component system should be cataloged, entered into the repository, tested for access and retrieval, and then announced.

11.8 Expressing Component System Engineering in terms of workers

Table 11.4 and Figure 11.8 indicate how different workers are involved in component system engineering. The workers are described in more detail in Chapter 9. Note that in the following steps, as the **Component Engineer**s develop the models of the component system, the **Facade Engineer** incrementally updates the facade and validates it with the reusers.

The **Architect** and **GUI Coordinator** coordinate the models of the component system and also coordinate them with the models of the superordinate system.

The **Reuse Process Engineer** and **Reuse Support Environment Engineer** ensure that the component system allows effective ASE processes (or CSE when reused by higher-order component systems) and tools to be engineered and deployed.

Table 11.4 *Workers involved in the Component System Engineering process.*

CSE1:	The **Use Case Engineer**s develop a use case model based on input from reusers, from the models of the superordinate system, from related business models, and so on. The **Reuse Process Engineer** analyzes the needs and the preferred development style of the reusers and prepares requirements on process (SEP) and tool support (SEPSE) for them.
CSE2:	The **Use Case Designer** identifies analysis types from the use cases and the **Subsystem Engineer** groups the analysis types into subsystems.
CSE3:	The **Subsystem Engineer** develops the design model based on the analysis model, but adapts it to the implementation environment. The **Use Case Designer** distributes the responsibilities of the use cases among the subsystems. The **Reuse Process Engineer** defines SEP components for the reusers. The **Reuse Support Environment Engineer** selects tools (essentially SEPSE components) and technology for delivery to and for use by the reusers of the component system as they localize, import, and specialize components.
CSE4:	The **Subsystem Engineer** implements the design model.
CSE5:	The **Tester**s are responsible for testing the component system and help prepare test specifications in parallel with the activities above. As the components are tested, they are incrementally baselined.
CSE6:	The **Component System Librarian** packages the component system as a kit, includes the component system and related material in the reuse repository, and announces its availability.

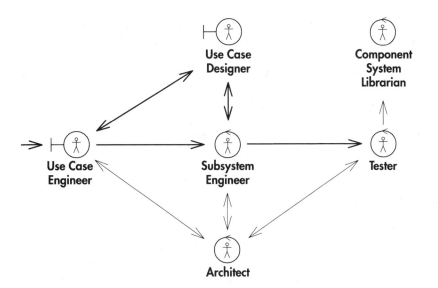

Figure 11.8 *Workers involved in Component System Engineering. Arrows are* «communicates» *associations, and the darker arrows indicate the most frequent interaction. The* **Facade Engineer***, the* **GUI Coordinator***, the* **Reuse Process Engineer***, and the* **Reuse Support Environment Engineer** *have been omitted to simplify the figure.*

Example

The **Application Engineer**s tell the **Component System Supporter** that they would like to use VBScript for custom overdraft processing. The **Component System Supporter** suggests this to the **Reuse Process Engineer** and the **Reuse Support Environment Engineer**. They talk with the reusers and with the **Lead Architect** for the whole layered system. They then decide to make a first prototype. The reusers and a few selected end users approve the prototype, and the **Lead Architect** concludes that the technology fits the architecture. XYBsoft then schedules the development of the custom overdraft kit based on Visual Basic.

11.9 Summary

The **Component System Engineering** process develops use case, analysis, design, implementation and test models similar to the ordinary OOSE software engineering process described in Chapter 3. Figure 11.1 summarizes the steps which focus on building robust, extendible, and flexible components. The component engineers use a variety of sources as input, such as business models, models of the superordinate system, and input from end users, customers, and domain experts.

Business actors and workers are used to identify actors and use cases, which in turn give rise to analysis types grouped into subsystems that are adapted to the implementation environment. The use case and design models of the superordinate system are used to define the interfaces of the component system, and also to suggest actor and use case components.

Components are grouped into a number of facades to make them as reusable as possible. The component system is developed and maintained as a component system kit – that is, together with all the documentation, examples, tools, and so on that accompany the component system.

11.10 Additional reading

The Patterns book by Erich Gamma, Richard Helm, Ralph Johnson, and John Vlissides, *Design Patterns – Elements of Reusable Object-Oriented Software*, Addison-Wesley, 1994, describes some standard design patterns, and how these should be implemented. They also discuss how OO features can best be exploited to produce reusable components.

Software Reuse: A Holistic Approach, edited by Karlsson, Wiley, 1995, contains many detailed design and implementation guidelines for the use of C++ to create reusable components and frameworks. The contributors discuss many aspects of modifying the normal software life cycle to support "design for reuse".

The book by John McGregor and David Sykes, *Object-Oriented Software Development: Engineering Software for Reuse*, Van Nostrand-Reinhold, 1992, contains many useful component development and testing guidelines.

Mark Lorenz, in his *Object Oriented Software Development: A Practical Guide*, Prentice-Hall, 1993, provides numerous C++ and Smalltalk coding and documentation guidelines for reuse.

APPLICATION SYSTEM ENGINEERING

12.1 Building application systems from reusable components

Of the three processes in a reuse business, **Application System Engineering** (ASE) is important because it is closest to the business by serving customers and end users directly. In providing this service, it not only generates external revenue, but serves as a conduit for feedback to **Component System Engineering** and **Application Family Engineering**. The ASE process develops use case, analysis, design, implementation, and test models, as in other software development (see Figure 12.1). The possibility of reusing components throughout the series of models provides a way for application engineers to find components that fit and can be reused very early in their process, well before the coding stage. ASE conducts this model building within the scope of the architecture established by **Application Family Engineering** and fine-tuned by **Component System Engineering**.

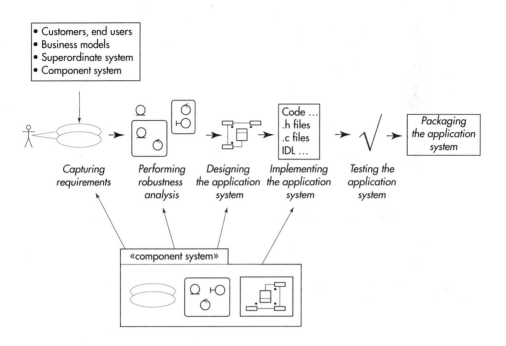

Figure 12.1 *An informal illustration of the activities involved in* **Application System Engineering**.

The presence of an architecture and reusable component systems goes a long way toward cost-effective development of quality products meeting functionality requirements within time-to-market windows. In this chapter, therefore, we focus on three aspects of application system development: the architecture of the family or domain, the five-stage modeling process, and the reuse of component systems. In most other respects, **Application System Engineering** is merely our old friend, OOSE, under a new name.

There is one **Application System Engineering** process for each application system, which means that there may be several concurrent processes, each building a different application system. There will also be processes for **Component System Engineering** and **Application Family Engineering** with which the **Application System Engineering** process must synchronize.

The work steps, described at a high level, are shown in Table 12.1.

Once again, we have described the process steps as if they occur sequentially. In reality, there will be many iterations between steps. Note that some requirements probably cannot be met by simply reusing from existing component systems, even after negotiating changes. These will have to be captured, architected, designed, implemented, and tested by performing more conventional incremental OOSE development.

Develop the application system *in increments* all the way from requirements capture to testing, to reduce time to market and cost; see also Chapter 9.

Table 12.1 *The essential steps of the **Application System Engineering** process.*

ASE1:	**Capturing requirements** – This is initiated by a customer in order to prepare a use case model of an application system, by reusing use case components. Collect input primarily from the customer and end users but also from business models and the models of the superordinate system. Assess the value and cost of each use case, negotiate and decide whether or not to implement it in the next release.
ASE2:	**Performing robustness analysis** – Use the use case model as an input to assemble and specialize analysis model components. Only extend the architecture provided by the component systems when necessary.
ASE3:	**Designing the application system** – Use the analysis model as an input to assemble and specialize design components.
ASE4:	**Implementing the application system** – Use the design model as an input to assemble and specialize implementation components.
ASE5:	**Testing the application system** – Assemble and specialize test specification components and then test the application system.
ASE6:	**Packaging the application system** – Package the application system for use by the application manufacturers, installers, or end users.

Example

As the Application Engineers develop the **Digicash Cashier** application system, they first want to support the use case **Transfer Between Accounts** since that is wanted most by the home-bank customers. They reuse the **Money Management** component system and specialize the use case **Transfer Between Accounts** and the corresponding object types and classes. They encounter no real difficulties since all they have to do is to specialize the user interface for the use case so that it can be used over the Internet.

Later they will take on the more difficult use cases **Withdraw Digicash** and **Deposit Digicash**. These use cases are more difficult since they involve creation and consumption of Digicash.

Be careful that customers and end users do not focus too much on quickly producing just what seems immediately feasible, rather than what is really required. Develop a reasonable roll-out plan, and prioritize and schedule the design and implementation of use cases based on a combination of need and feasibility. Keep asking the question "Are we spending our resources correctly if we build this functionality now, or should we renegotiate the requirement with the customer to maximize reuse of the component systems?". Such adjustments of the requirements can have a significant effect on the amount of reuse and consequent economic benefits.

If your organization has not itself developed any components, the only items available for reuse will be acquired components and component systems, such as Commercial Off The Shelf software, or legacy systems that have been adapted for reuse. Probably only design and implementation components will be available, but no use case and analysis components. In this situation, develop the use case model as in traditional OOSE as suggested in Chapter 3. Use this use case model when performing robustness analysis, design, implementation, and testing, but remember to design and implement the use cases in terms of existing components such as OLE components and legacy systems. Use tools such as Visual Basic for Applications or VBScript for assembling components into applications.

Even if Application Engineers mostly focus on quickly adding value to a specific customer, they often need to extend and adapt the architecture provided by the component systems to the needs of the customer. The Application Engineers should try not to change the component systems, but instead to extend their architectures as they develop the analysis and design models of the application system.

12.2 ASE1: Capturing requirements

In this section, we discuss how to develop the use case model to match the requirements, much as described in Section 3.5 and in Jacobson *et al.* (1992). Make sure that you address not only the functional requirements, but also all other requirements such as performance, quality, software size, understandability, and product management requirements.

Use the glossaries supplied with the component systems to achieve a consistent terminology. Import the glossaries from the component systems, and add new glossary entries specific to the application system. Watch out for name collisions when reusing from several component systems.

12.2.1 Using business models and the superordinate system as input

Some actors and use cases can be identified from the models of the superordinate system as discussed in Sections 7.10 and 7.11. This can be done as described in Section 11.2.1 but instead targeted towards an application system. Make sure that the application system offers use cases for all interfaces that it supplies.

A business model of the target organization can be used to identify further requirements on actors and use cases (see Section 11.2.1). Define and maintain «traces» from business actors, workers, to information system actors and use cases. Also define and maintain «traces» from the superordinate models to actors and use cases. This is illustrated in Figure 12.2.

Use the design model of the superordinate system to determine which component systems to reuse. Decide which other application systems this one should interoperate with and find out additional requirements and constraints from them.

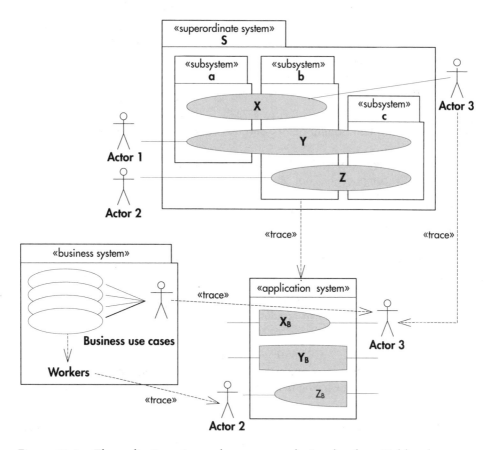

Figure 12.2 *The application actors and use cases can be found and specified based on models of the business and the superordinate system.*

12.2.2 Using customer and end-user input to focus on value added

Get customers and end users involved in the requirements capture, selecting the right mix of customers and end users according to the analysis given in Section 10.3.1. If the customers already know the available component systems, they can discuss the requirements in terms of use cases offered by the component systems which can serve as "catalogs" from which to pick and specialize.

If the customers and end users do not know about the available components, it is often easier to elicit information from them by talking about concrete usage situations or scenarios (that is, use case descriptions of instances). Scenarios help in understanding what the customers and end users think they need, which is most important when identifying and describing the use cases. These scenarios can also be used later to help develop test cases. Let the customers and end users first envision the application system by sketching scenarios as they perceive them, without necessarily knowing what reusable components are available. Later, add knowledge of the component systems to synthesize the envisioned scenarios into a use case model based on available component use cases.

If the application system must be configurable, it can be developed in much the same way as component systems, described in Chapter 11. Analyze the variability, express it using the mechanisms described in Chapters 4, 5, and 6, and then package the use cases, types, classes, and service packages into configuration items and facades suitable for the **Manufacturer**s. We will not discuss these issues much further in this chapter.

12.2.3 Locating component actors and use cases that meet the needs

If the facades are well documented, they are the best guide to what requirements can be met easily by the components. Look at example systems that use the component systems for ideas on how to reuse them.

The layered system and the business models provide a straightforward way of finding components to reuse:

- Use the layered system as a reference model to understand how the application system "rests" on the component systems.

- Make sure that you understand the purpose, architecture, and key features of the component systems and their facades. The glossaries help you to understand the terminology and purpose of related components.

- Try to understand the 7 ± 2 most important use case and object components in each facade, and then try to understand the other use cases, types and classes — which are often related to the most important ones with generalization and dependency relations.

- Try to map requirements to the use case components during requirements capture and then map the use cases to object components. When several components almost match the requirements, choose according to functionality and other characteristics such as cost of adaptation, maturity, maintenance cost, quality, additional functionality, and size.

- The business model will provide additional information about the actors and entity objects.

Example

The **Money Management** component system has a use case model with three main use cases and a number of pre-built variants. The use cases are **Transfer Between Accounts**, **Withdraw Money**, and **Deposit Money**. A reuser who understands these use cases should easily be able to understand the use case variants, such as the different pre-built strategies for **Overdraft Management**. A reuser who understands the principal object components, such as **Cashier Interface**, **Withdrawal**, **Deposit**, **Transfer**, **Dispenser**, **Money Receptor**, and **Account**, should similarly be able to understand their variants.

All of these components will be found grouped into a number of facades, each targeted at a certain usage:

- The **Withdrawals** facade exports the ***Withdraw Money*** use case and the
  Withdrawal, Dispenser, Account, and ***Cashier Interface*** types.
- The **Deposits** facade exports the ***Deposit Money*** use case and the ***Deposit,
  Money Receptor, Account***, and ***Cashier Interface*** types.
- The **Transferals** facade exports the **Transfer Between Accounts** use case
  and the **Transfer, *Account***, and ***Cashier Interface*** types.

Note that the ***Account*** and ***Cashier Interface*** types and related classes appear in
several facades. This way all the facades offer a complete set of components for a
specific purpose. The ***Account*** and ***Cashier Interface*** types and related classes
are each defined in one configuration item. All the facades include these
configuration items and export them to reusers as required.

12.2.4 Reusing and specializing component actors and use cases

Define application system actors and use cases by reusing and specializing actor and use
case components. In some cases, the match will be obvious, because the requirements
match exactly. In others, it is more difficult to interpret the requirements in terms of
available use case components. Negotiate with the customer to change the requirements
to improve the match with available components. Try to avoid implementing use cases
that cannot be built from use case components, since they are generally far more costly
and complex to design, require more lead time, and are more error-prone. Read more
about reusing actor and use case components in Chapter 5.

Adapting a component beyond the intended specialization incurs additional costs
both up-front and in subsequent maintenance. Try hard to avoid such adaptation or keep
the extent of the change to less than 10%. Experience in other reuse situations indicates
that the cost of reusing a component jumps to 50% or more of the cost of developing
from scratch when changing more than 10% of the component (Selby, 1989). The costs
can be even higher, because extra testing and maintenance may be incurred later.

Verify if the scenarios suggested by customers and end users can be performed by the
use cases. Also indicate additional use cases that the customers and end users might not
have considered at first, but can be supported at a low cost by the component systems.

12.2.5 Packaging, ranking, and assessing actors and use cases

If appropriate, suggest to the customer that some of the complicated use cases should be
developed into component use cases. It will typically cost more and take longer to
develop a use case as a reusable component than simply as part of a single application
system, but the new use case component and the improved quality that comes with
making it into a component can benefit other application engineers. By waiting for a
component an application system gets delayed, but subsequent application systems can
be developed quicker.

One way to evaluate the value of each use case is to go through the business use
cases one by one and estimate the benefit of each information system use case. This

estimate can then be compared to the estimated cost to design, implement, and test the use case. When it is difficult to estimate the cost of use cases, it may be appropriate to develop a prototype in order to learn more about the issues involved in implementing them. Rank the use cases according to the cost–benefit analysis and the amount of influence they have on the architecture – use cases that have a major influence on the architecture should be developed early. Use this ranking to develop an incremental roll-out plan for the application system.

Example

As the Application Engineers look at the use case **Transfer Between Accounts**, they realize that it is much easier to develop than the use cases **Withdraw Digicash** and **Deposit Digicash**. They therefore suggest breaking the application system **Digicash Cashier** into two smaller application systems. One, called **Transferring**, deals with use cases such as **Transfer Between Accounts**, and the other, called **Withdraw And Deposit**, handles the rest of the use cases, including **Withdraw Digicash** and **Deposit Digicash**.

The **Lead Architect** and the **Manufacturer** approve of the suggested change. The marketing department thinks this is a great idea so they schedule the first of the two application systems, **Transferring**, to be shipped to customers four months earlier than expected and the second application system to be shipped two months later than expected. This delivery plan assumes that the application system **Withdraw And Deposit** will not break the architecture and design developed for the application system **Transferring**. The **Application Family Engineering** team notes this assumption as a risk.

Present the use case model to customers, end users, architects, and so on for review. Include some **Component System Supporter**s in the review team to verify that component systems have been used correctly and optimally. Try to understand how reused component systems might evolve in order to anticipate and reduce the consequences of changes in them. Make sure all requirements are agreed on, including requirements on time to market, quality, and cost.

Example

Two of the end users suggest that many end users will want to run Microsoft Explorer and therefore it may be more important that the application is optimized for Microsoft Explorer rather than for Netscape, with support for embedded ActiveX components and VBScript.

The marketing department indicates that many users may want to integrate the application system with other applets they develop themselves using Microsoft

---

Money'97. They therefore suggest implementing a suitable API that other OCXs and ActiveX components may use.

The marketing department points out that it is important to allow for transfers of any type of currency and also of any denominations, possibly including small coins and micropayments.

It is now fairly easy to perform robustness analysis, design, implementation, and testing of the application system, given the use cases and other requirements and the components of the analysis, design, implementation, and test models.

12.3 ASE2: Performing robustness analysis for flexible application systems

The robustness analysis aims at building a system structure that is flexible when faced with future system requirements. Sometimes most of this work has already been done as the component systems have been developed. Build the application system so that it is consistent with the style of the reused component systems but add further architecture that is specific to the application system. This is fairly easy for use cases that are reused as-is, but sometimes requires more work, such as when completely new use cases are introduced.

When an actor or a use case is reused as-is, the corresponding collaboration and participating analysis types can also be reused as-is. Follow the trace links to the collaboration and the analysis types and import the corresponding configuration items, as described in Section 6.4. When an actor or a use case is reused and specialized with a provided variant, the corresponding analysis types and variants can be reused similarly. For example, a use case may be specialized by setting a parameter or by adding an extension at an extension point – which might correspond to subtyping an analysis type. Either reuse existing variants or develop new ones by reusing as much as possible of component analysis types. Aim at reusing existing types when possible and only consider creating completely new analysis types that do not specialize any existing analysis types when reuse is impossible, since this will further increase work in later phases.

Example

As discussed in Chapters 5 and 6, the **Withdraw Money** use case has three variation points that are directly traceable to the types in the analysis model, as shown in Figure 12.3. The **{Account}** variation point, for example, maps directly to an abstract type, **Account**.

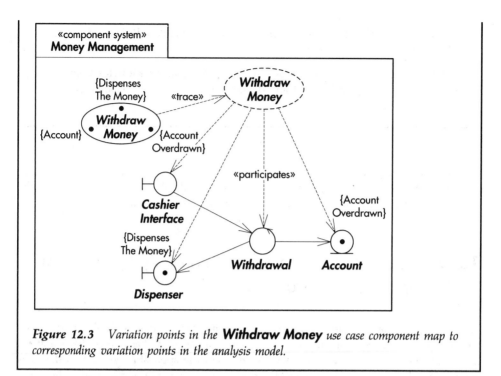

Figure 12.3 *Variation points in the* **Withdraw Money** *use case component map to corresponding variation points in the analysis model.*

Use the normal OOSE approach to improve the architecture of the application system and to identify additional analysis types and variants. Distribute each use case across the different analysis types, by defining collaborations using collaboration diagrams and use case descriptions.

Business entity types and properties in the models of the target organization will correspond to entity types in the application systems. Note that many of the business entity types have already been mapped to component entity types, others may require some component-entity types to be specialized, while others still may require completely new entity types in the application system. Define and maintain «traces» from business entity types to analysis types.

Assign each analysis type and attribute type to a service package and a configuration item according to the guidelines in Section 6.8.

Review the analysis model similarly to the review of the use case model. Try to reduce the number of new analysis types. Verify that all actors and use cases are supported by the analysis types.

12.4 ASE3, ASE4, and ASE5: Designing, implementing, and testing the application system

Try to reuse design and implementation components as much as possible; see also Sections 6.4, 6.5, and 6.7. The procedure for design and implementation is similar to that of **Component System Engineering**, but with more focus on iteratively meeting or negotiating adjusted customer requirements and with less focus on variability.

Reuse and specialize collaborations that define how component use cases map onto design classes. Divide the responsibilities of the new and specialized use cases among design classes by reusing, specializing, and adding further interaction diagrams. Try to reuse and specialize components as much as possible; only extend the architecture and add new classes and types or change existing components when reuse is impossible. When reusing components that need to interact, but cannot be directly connected because of incompatible interfaces and architectures, consider approaches such as the following (Garlan *et al.*, 1995):

- Wrap one of the components using a wrapper (or a Decorator (Gamma *et al.*, 1994)) that can transform requests from other components into the appropriate messages for the component.

- Introduce a Mediator object (Gamma *et al.*, 1994) between the components that helps them interact. According to Gamma *et al.*, a Mediator " ... encapsulates how a set of objects interact. Mediator promotes loose coupling by keeping objects from referring to each other explicitly, and it lets you vary their interaction independently."

Example

The Application Engineers initially develop the application system for **Transfer Between Accounts** without considering the Microsoft Money'97 customization framework or the Open Financial Connection (OFC) services. However, for the use cases **Withdraw Digicash** and **Deposit Digicash**, some users want a connection to Microsoft Money and its OLE components.

Unfortunately, the current implementation of the **Money Management** component system does not allow that to be done easily since it was developed for an object request broker and its interfaces were defined in IDL. The Application Engineers choose to tie the component systems Microsoft Money'97 and **Money Management** together using the HP ORB Plus bridge between CORBA and OLE/COM. That bridge can transform requests between their proprietary ORB-based **Money Management** and Microsoft Money'97. The bridge behaves somewhat like a Mediator pattern (Gamma *et al.*, 1994).

Package and review the design and implementation model similarly to the review of the analysis model.

The testing and quality assurance for an application system is quite similar to the testing of any ordinary OOSE system. The tests include usability tests by **End User**s, administrators, and **Manufacturer**s. Make sure that you reuse test drivers and test specifications from the reused component systems.

Configurable application systems should include a comprehensive set of test specifications that can also be configured and extended to develop test suites for a configured system. Also provide a set of sample configurations that can be used as a known, tested starting point for some installations. See further guidelines on how to test configurable systems in Section 11.6.

12.5 ASE6: Packaging the application system for easy installation

Fully document and package the application system according to corporate standards before releasing it. Many of these standards are common to the release of almost any product and seem obvious – though are often forgotten! Application systems may be packaged by the Application Engineers or by the **Manufacturer**s.

The application system must provide a **Manufacturer** with the following:

- A description of the purpose of the application system as a whole.

- A brief introduction to how the application system works and what it does. This introduction can probably be described in terms of use cases.

- An installation guide, that is, a process description for customization and installation of the application system, together with examples.

- Descriptions of platform and environment requirements, dependencies on other application systems, and so on.

- References to a help desk that supports the application system.

- Documentation of the application history; which changes have been made to which versions and when.

- Descriptions of frequently asked questions, and known defects, limitations, and difficulties.

- Configuration items containing test specifications, test drivers, test-beds, and so on.

People have to be trained to provide not only mentoring and training to end users but also installation and support of the application system. It is important to describe how the application systems are configured, customized, and tested by the **Manufacturer**s or perhaps even by the **Customer**s. Use descriptions (including training material and test specifications) similar to those for component system kits; see Section 11.6.

Follow a certification process similar to that of Section 11.7 to ensure that all relevant work products are provided with the application system, to check that they are consistent with appropriate documentation standards (such as style of language and contents of the document headers), and consistent with each other and with other systems they interoperate with. Provide appropriate versions of each work product and tools, and check that they are correctly marked with version information.

Archive the packaged application system in a repository so that all installers can access the models and documents. The application system may need to be classified and cataloged; include or reference all materials and tools to be used when installing it.

Example

The **Manufacturer** suggests that updates to the application systems should be distributed over the Internet to simplify distribution. The **Manufacturer** is assigned to find out how to package the application systems so that they can be shipped this way.

12.6 Expressing Application System Engineering in terms of workers

Table 12.2 and Figure 12.4 indicate how different workers are involved in different parts of **Application System Engineering**. The workers are described in more detail in Chapter 9.

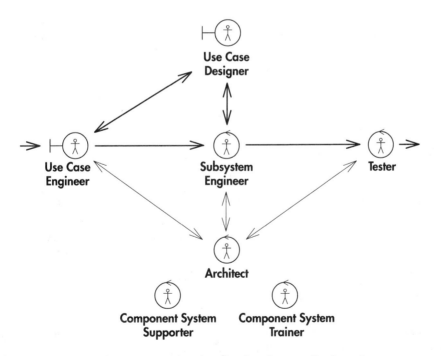

Figure 12.4 *Workers involved in* **Application System Engineering**. *Arrows are* «*communicates*» *associations, and the darker arrows indicate the most frequent interaction.*

Table 12.2 *Workers involved in the* **Application System Engineering** *process.*

ASE1:	Requirements capture is initiated by a **Customer**, that is, someone that requests an application system. The **Use Case Engineer**s use input from the superordinate system, business models, **Customer**s, and **End User**s to develop a use case model by reusing from component systems. They assess the architectural impact, value, and the time and cost required to implement each use case. They then negotiate and decide whether or not to support it in this release. The **Component System Trainer** and the **Component System Supporter** help the **Use Case Engineer**s to use the component systems.
ASE2–5:	The **Architect**, **Subsystem Engineer**s, **Use Case Designer**s, and **Tester**s incrementally perform robustness analysis, design, implementation, and testing of the application system, preferably by reusing and specializing components from the component systems. As the components are tested, they are incrementally baselined. The **Component System Trainer** and the **Component System Supporter** help the **Application Engineer**s to use the component system.
ASE6:	The **Tester**s are responsible for packaging the application system for reuse and retrieval by the **Manufacturer**, who is responsible for ensuring that the application installation process and tools are suitable for this application system.

During the work outlined above, the **Architect** is responsible for the quality of the models of the application system and also coordinates them with the models of the superordinate system.

12.7 Summary

The **Application System Engineering** process develops use case, analysis, design, implementation and test models similar to the ordinary OOSE software engineering process (Jacobson *et al.*, 1992), see Figure 12.1. The most important difference from OOSE is that instead of developing each model from scratch, we improve quality and reduce time to market and costs by reusing components from component systems. The Application Engineers primarily use customers and end users for input on requirements.

The business models and the models of the superordinate system define the interfaces that the application system must supply and define the component systems that the application system can reuse from. The architecture of the reused component systems guides the application engineers as they architect and design the application system.

Application System Engineering is performed as a sequence of controlled iterations. Each iteration implements a set of use cases that add value to the customer and end users, but is also targeted at reducing one or more of the remaining risks associated with developing the application system.

12.8 Additional reading

For a different perspective on "design with reuse" see *Software Reuse: A Holistic Approach*, edited by Karlsson, Wiley, 1995. The book provides many detailed design and implementation guidelines for the use of components, frameworks, and C++. The contributors also provide a detailed discussion of how to change the development life cycle to accommodate development with reuse.

PART IV

ORGANIZING A REUSE BUSINESS

Systematic reuse will not happen by itself. It takes a conscious effort on the part of management to organize for reuse. Each specific reuse business must be reengineered and optimized to meet its specific business objectives and situation. Each situation will require an organization and management structure best suited to its needs. While one should start from the standard Reuse Business model described in Chapter 9, each situation will require a specialized set of software processes, organizational structures, and management guidance.

This part of the book discusses the strategic organizational and management activities needed to transform a particular software engineering organization into a reuse business, a specialized instance of the Reuse Business. Becoming a reuse business is not a one-shot effort. There are a number of ongoing management and organization issues, involving trade-offs, economic decisions, and continuing improvement and change.

Chapter 13 describes the systematic transition to a reuse business, combining the systematic object-oriented business engineering process-driven approach with the techniques of systematic change management and reuse-specific guidelines. This leads to an incremental adoption process. We describe process and organization changes, guidelines, and when to use reuse pilots to bootstrap the process. We describe how to customize and adapt the basic Reuse Business model to a variety of scenarios. We explain how to model the organization structures needed to support the Reuse Business, and how object-oriented business engineering can be used to partition the reuse roles and departments. We also discuss tools and technologies that help manage the process, help package the component systems, repositories, generator applications, and components, and so on.

Chapter 14 describes how the various processes are managed, the techniques and metrics used to manage trade-offs, resolve conflicts, and ensure progress, and the organization needed to support a reuse business. We also describe reuse-oriented economic, process, and workproduct measures and estimates, and how these might be used to manage the reuse business and achieve business goals.

Chapter 15 concludes with a final discussion of how the key architecture, process and organization principles of the Reuse Business work together to address the critical business and software issues facing your organization. Management must lead the reengineering of the software engineering part of your business to overcome the obstacles and achieve success.

13

TRANSITION TO A REUSE BUSINESS

13.1 A systematic, incremental transition controls risk

A systematic transition of an organization is needed to install a fully functional reuse business. Introducing large-scale reuse requires simultaneous changes in several aspects of business, people, process, organization, architecture, tools, and technology. There are so many changes that, without a systematic, incremental approach, it is easy for the transition to stall in a welter of detail. We use a systematic object-oriented business engineering approach as a framework for organizing the change, combined with techniques and guidelines for organizational change management and pragmatic reuse adoption.

Key elements of this transition include:

- assessments of business, process, domain, and organizational reuse readiness,

- the design of a multi-step, pilot-driven transition plan to install the new processes into an existing software engineering organization,

- the customization of the generic RSEB and organization design, and

- training, tool development and deployment.

There are a variety of different approaches to deal with large-scale organization and process change that can be used by a software engineering organization to introduce or improve its reuse practice. Some approaches develop process and organizational models, others deal with people issues during change, and some focus on explicit reuse success factors. We have combined three of these techniques into our systematic **Transition to a Reuse Business**.

13.1.1 Business engineering provides a systematic transition framework

Business engineering (BE) provides a process-centered perspective on organization and systems design, with explicit envisioning, modeling, reverse engineering, and forward engineering steps. The key idea is to identify a set of cross-functional processes that the organization wants to execute effectively, and then to optimize the organizational structure, policies, and information systems across the entire organization to remove cross-organizational barriers. For the transition we will use the Object-Oriented Business Engineering approach described in Chapter 8 (Jacobson *et al.*, 1994) and extended at Rational.

Important business process reengineering (BPR) guidelines, including the use of pilots and the importance of management leadership, are provided in a handbook by Hammer and Stanton (1995).

13.1.2 Organization change management addresses people issues

Organization change management is a systematic approach to managing change that is directed at handling the many people issues. Such issues include fear, politics, organizational stress, lack of knowledge, and so on. People have real difficulty changing without well-articulated, convincing reasons, lots of encouragement, support, and leadership, and participative ownership of the process.

Figure 13.1 illustrates several key organizational change elements, which include:

- identifying and assessing stakeholder issues,

- unfreezing to overcome fear,

- the use of change agents and champions,

- dealing with objections but focusing on successes,

- the importance of providing specific support to "cross the chasm" (Moore, 1991), and

- effective management leadership and vision to stay on course.

A significant step is to assess the stakeholder issues, and to develop and execute a detailed change management plan, with explicit communication and awareness building. New job definitions, performance evaluation, rewards, and recognition must be aligned.

Figure 13.1 *Change management essentials.*

The organization change guidelines we use have been adapted from the Price Waterhouse Change Integration Team model (Price Waterhouse Change Integration Team, 1995) and an HP internal change management model (HP PSO Americas, 1995).

13.1.3 Pragmatic reuse adoption proceeds in increments

Incremental reuse adoption is a collection of pragmatic guidelines, maturation models, and milestones that detail how a reuse organization can plan its incremental reuse evolution. The reuse research and practice community has learned that most successful reuse programs seem to naturally grow and mature through a series of distinct stages. Figure 13.2 illustrates how this maturation proceeded at HP. At each stage, a set of

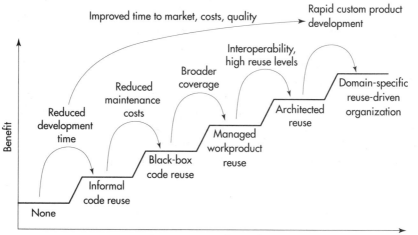

Figure 13.2 *Stages in Hewlett-Packard's systematic reuse adoption, each driven by business needs (from Chapter 1).*

new skills and activities are mastered by individuals and adopted by the organization. These include:

- black-box code reuse,

- library and workproduct management,

- architected components and systems,

- application and component engineering skills,

- reuse-oriented process and organization management,

- new tools and technology.

As experience grows, it is also common to expand the scope and level of the reuse program across the organization. Once mastered, it takes time to consolidate the new skills into a sustainable, institutionalized organizational practice with more process rigor before proceeding to the next stage.

Most reuse adoption approaches suggest starting small, with a subset of the organization, and once this proves successful, incrementally scaling to more of the organization and greater levels of reuse. Generally, the incremental, pilot-driven approach can show results sooner, confront problems sooner, contain risks more effectively, and begin with less investment.

Most of the pragmatic reuse experience has already been discussed in Chapter 1. At Hewlett-Packard, we have observed that the transitions occur in response to a clear business need. As the organization at all levels recognizes the need, and is able to commit and invest in the changes needed for the next stage, increased levels of reuse can be introduced. These further levels require organizational structures to support reuse, and increased amounts of architecture and process rigor. These steps are illustrated in Figure 13.2, which is an example of a simple reuse maturity model used at Hewlett-Packard. Such maturation and adoption issues are discussed in greater detail by Davis (1994b), Griss *et al.* (1993), Frakes and Isoda (1994), Hooper and Chester (1991), Karlsson (1995) and Jandorek (1996).

It is critical to engineer architecture, process, and organization for effective reuse. In a survey of the impediments that block effective reuse, Frakes and Fox (1996) indicate that most people do not even try to reuse, largely because organization support in the form of training and motivation is missing. The next most important impediment is difficulty encountered in integrating independently developed software components, largely due to poor software engineering processes that have failed to capture and express architecture and variability requirements. The architectures, processes, and organization need to be evolved in steps to gain experience in the small before building in the large.

13.2 The incremental transition process

If we now combine the key elements drawn from the three techniques into the Object-Oriented Business Engineering framework, we can provide a high-level view of the transition process (Figure 13.3). In particular we advocate a more aggressive approach and

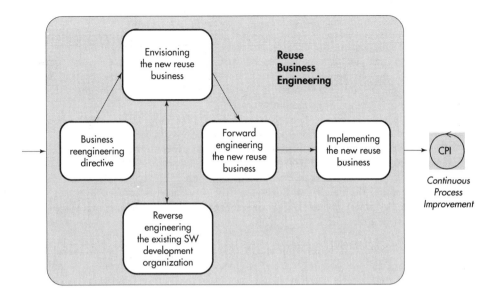

Figure 13.3 *Transition to a reuse business as Object-Oriented Business Engineering.*

earlier architecture focus than illustrated by Figure 13.2. In practice, the steps are carried out partially in parallel, with significant iteration and incremental roll-out. We label the steps as TRA*n* (Table 13.1) and they are detailed in Sections 13.3–13.7.

An organization that changes its software engineering activities into a reuse-driven software engineering business goes through the steps shown in Table 13.1.

Steps TRA1–TRA5 will be discussed in more detail in this chapter, while TRA6, Continuous Process Improvement (CPI), is dealt with as part of the ongoing management of a reuse business in Chapter 14.

Table 13.1 *The essential steps of transition to a Reuse Business.*

TRA1:	**Creating a directive to reengineer the software business** – The management of the company creates and publicizes a reengineering directive, as a clear statement of the high-level reuse business goals and their rationale. The directive defines and communicates the initial business, process, architecture, organization, and reuse goals. It defines the scope of the changes and establishes accountability. Management empowers an initial group of people (the transition team) to envision the reuse business.
TRA2:	**Envisioning the new reuse business** – Based on business needs and the initial **Application Family Engineering** efforts, the RSEB transition team develops a high-level vision of the new architecture, software business processes, and organization. They identify stakeholders, champions, and early adopters. The specific goals are documented in an objective statement. Some transition plans are developed, in which several versions of a reuse business might be defined as intermediate points for incremental adoption. Significant communication begins and key stakeholders are engaged in the transition.

Table 13.1 *The essential steps of transition to a Reuse Business (cont.).*

TRA3:	**Reverse engineering the existing software development organization** – The transition team identifies and studies the existing architecture, software assets, software processes, organization, tools, and baseline measures. The goal is to understand and baseline current software engineering practice, identify assets, determine the status of reuse, and understand organization issues.
TRA4:	**Forward engineering the new reuse business** – Develop the desired software engineering processes (SEP), organization, and appropriate software engineering environment and tools (SEPSE).
TRA5:	**Implementing the new reuse business** – The new model is installed into the business. People are trained, and processes, organization, architectures, and systems are (incrementally) replaced.
TRA6:	**Continuous Process Improvement** – As the new business becomes operational, collect and analyze reuse process and product metrics to measure progress, identify key areas for further improvement, and then make small process changes.

13.2.1 Workers involved in the transition

The transition to a reuse business is carried out mostly by the **Process Owner**s, **Resource Owner**s and the following workers:

- The **Owners Of The Reuse Business** (executives) are not workers of the Reuse Business per se, but more like actors of it. They are responsible for giving enough direction and funding during the setup and execution of the reuse business. They are responsible for the reengineering directive in step TRA1 (Table 13.1). They also need to participate in other steps in order to follow up progress and in particular during step TRA2 to understand the envisioned reuse business.

- The **Software Engineering Business Manager** (**SEB Manager**) is responsible for the (Reuse-Driven) SEB organization, reporting to the **Owners Of The Reuse Business**. The **Software Engineering Business Manager** ensures that the architecture and the organization are well aligned, and is responsible for the evolution of the application and component system roll-out plan.

- The **Transition Driver** leads the incremental work of establishing the reuse business, constructing plans, enacting them, and following them up.

13.2.2 Transition in focused iterations

There are primarily two reasons to transition in iterations. First, the architecture needs to stabilize, which takes 2–3 iterations. Secondly, an organization cannot change in one big leap, but instead has to learn and institutionalize the new processes gradually.

Fortunately, getting the architecture stable and the organization able to perform the processes go hand in hand. As the architecture stabilizes it makes sense to get more people involved since their interaction can be controlled through the interfaces of the architecture.

Each iteration through steps TRA1–TRA5 ranges from roughly 3 to 12 months. Each should have a small number of clear goals. The first iterations are generally geared to getting the big picture of the layered architecture and starting reuse awareness programs, while also focusing on the most critical software engineering processes. In general it is better to start small with a core team and then scale up, but the exact scope depends on the experience of the team and available consultants. Then, as experience is gained, other processes are studied in more detail and more people are engaged to spread the successes. The following suggestions for the first four iterations serve as an example:

- The purpose of the *first iteration* is to get an initial understanding of the application family, focus on the architecture, and begin reuse awareness in the organization. The following things are also done:
    - high-level envisioning of the reuse business,
    - initial market analysis,
    - a business model of the target organization with the focus on understanding which application and component systems should be developed for the first product release,
    - engaging key customers, and
    - establishing a transition team.

The transition team initiates the process for **Application Family Engineering** and finds suitable people to enact the workers.

Example

In the face of the pressing requirements to deliver a suite of applications in a short time, XYB decides in October 1995 to initiate their transition to a reuse business in four iterations as suggested above. At the same time they appoint a **Software Engineering Business Manager** and a **Transition Driver** whom they charge with establishing a functioning reuse business within two years. The chief executive officer, Vee P. van der Bank, assumes the role of **Owners Of The Reuse Business** and wants the **SEB Manager** and the **Transition Driver** to report directly to him.

The planning begins immediately. The iteration plans suggested by the **Transition Driver** are accepted in November when they are reviewed for the second time by the **Owners Of The Reuse Business**. The first iteration will begin in November and will focus on getting the architecture in place and beginning reuse awareness. The subsequent iterations will begin in May 1996, in October 1996, and in May 1997, the last iteration finishing in January 1998.

In November an **AFE** team is created. Together with some experienced consultants, the **Transition Driver** prepares a draft version of a process description for **Application Family Engineering**. XYB hires an experienced reuse and change management consultant to help the **AFE** team follow the process in the first two architecture iterations, to reduce risks.

Together with the **Lead Architect**, the **Transition Driver** and the **Software Engineering Business Manager** prepare a first version of the product plan. They decide to start with the application systems to support electronic invoice payment and then focus on different variants of ATMs – for Digicash and regular ATMs. The **Application Family Engineering** team start working on this and come up with the two application systems **Payment** and **Invoicing** and the component systems **Account Management** and **Invoice Management**.

In parallel to the architecture work, the **Transition Driver** forms the nucleus of a transition team. They begin to study XYBsoft to better understand how it performs, who the stakeholders are, and what their attitudes are. They envision a first version of the reuse business, and sketch out process and worker definitions.

The transition team also begins training a team of five people who will be the first **Component System Engineering** team in iteration two. These people not only will learn how to become component engineers, but also help the transition team to validate their six-week training program. After the two-week boot camp and the four weeks of training and workshops, the participants report that the program only partially lived up to the goals. They certainly learnt what OO, frameworks, Rational Rose, object request brokers, and Visual Basic are all about, but they failed to see how to use these together to build component systems. After numerous lively discussions, the transition team decides to acquire part of the training from external resources, and also decides to add a two-week workshop where the participants actually capture requirements, analyze, design, implement, and test a fragment of a component system.

In March the **Application Family Engineering** team has completed a first implementation of the layered system and begin testing. The testers detect three critical problems with the architecture, one of performance and two regarding inconsistent data in the **Account Management** component system. The **AFE** team assigns two people responsible for solving these problems. In April the **AFE** team has resolved one of the problems with inconsistencies and the performance issue, but the other problem with inconsistencies remains. The **AFE** team decides to move that problem to the top of the risk list but do not want to delay the second iteration, so they forward the risk to be addressed in the second iteration.

The **Lead Architect**, **Transition Driver**, and **SEB Manager** report progress to the board of managers in April. The board approves the results and decides to begin the second iteration in May.

It is important that all the people in the future reuse business come to accept the direction of the transition process, even if they will not be directly involved in the work until later iterations. Getting such acceptance from all stakeholders is the purpose of the reuse awareness program.

- The purpose of the *second iteration* is to stabilize the architecture (particularly the interfaces and the facades) and get more teams under way to incrementally build the new organization. This involves further envisioning of the reuse business, market analysis, key customer contacts, and **Application Family Engineering**. The transition team initiate a process for **Component System Engineering** and establish a suitable team.

Example

During the second iteration the **Application Family Engineering** team begin to look also at the **Digicash Cashier** application system. The transition team start looking at the process for **Component System Engineering** and the types of workers that should be involved.

The component engineers can most often develop a component system in parallel with the **Application System Engineering** processes that need it, given that the **ASE** processes are few and the parallelism can be handled informally. This is often practical during the first few iterations when the architecture has not yet stabilized and the number of people involved is fairly small. But as the organization grows, and more application systems come to depend on the individual component systems, the component systems should be developed first. The **ASE** processes should then use the component systems as they are, but suggest changes for later versions.

- The purpose of the *third iteration* is to bring even more teams into the change and involves further and broader **Component System Engineering**. Processes for **Application System Engineering** are initiated on customer demand and suitable teams are established.

Example

During the third iteration the **Application Family Engineering** team begin to look also at the **ATM Cashier** application system and they identify the need for a new component system **Money Management**. The transition team focus on the process for **Application System Engineering** and the types of workers that should be involved.

- The purpose of the *fourth iteration* is to achieve steady state in the reuse organization, and involves several application customer contacts resulting in further **Application System Engineering** processes and corresponding teams. There is also further **Component System Engineering**, of both new component systems and new versions of component systems developed in earlier iterations. A separate **Component Support** team is established as defined by the **Component Support Unit** to leverage reuse and improvement of component systems.

The next iterations focus on capitalizing on the reusable assets by expanding scale and scope in several directions, such as:

- Expanding or enhancing the architecture to cover more of the planned application family

- Expanding the number or variety of the component systems

- Supporting an increased number of component engineering or application engineering projects

- Supporting multiple versions of component systems and application systems

- More pervasive organization and process changes

- More geographic distribution of teams.

13.2.3 The written transition plan

Prepare a *transition plan* with intermediate milestones to meet the long-term goals over several years. The plan should define:

- how to evolve the architecture,

- which application and component systems to develop,

- which processes to define,

- which teams to create and train, and

- how to schedule reuse awareness programs

as indicated in Figure 13.4. The plan should detail the kinds of metrics to collect and when to start collecting them (see Chapter 14 for more details). Even if all the details are not clear initially, it is useful to have an explicit transition plan to avoid growing pains when scaling.

Changing an organization is costly, involves many risks, and takes a lot of time. By starting from a generic model for a Reuse Business, it is easier to understand the environment and find the right processes and workers in the organization with less cost and risk.

A specific reuse business can then be envisioned, starting from the ideas of Chapter 9. The various processes and workers can be detailed, along the lines of Chapters 10–12,

	1st iteration	2nd iteration	3rd iteration	4th iteration
Business need and opportunities	Reengineering directive	Product plan	Customer orders	End-user feedback
Application family and architecture	Architecture outline	Architecture baseline	Component systems	Application systems
Teams established	Architects	Component engineers	Application engineers	Component supporters
Processes defined	AFE	CSE	ASE	Custom ASE & CSE processes

Figure 13.4 *Examples of the key focus in different iterations along the business, architecture, organizational, and process dimensions.*

during the forward engineering activities. The risks and the time it takes can be minimized by acquiring a complete RSEB framework, toolsets, knowledge transfer, and expertise.

The iterative approach discussed so far follows a very aggressive schedule. This is necessary to some organizations which have no alternative but to adopt a fully functional reuse business as a strategic necessity. Either they change quickly or they will die. Perhaps they see opportunities with very limited time-windows. But *most organizations should take a more careful approach* with lower risks and more time for the organization to adapt to the changes. These organizations should start with a pilot to learn the basic skills and evaluate different approaches before committing themselves to a whole-hearted transition to a reuse business. Risk and cost often can be reduced by starting with a small pilot project, and then incrementally expanding the scope. Action and results help develop credibility.

13.2.4 Starting with a pilot to begin awareness and reduce risks

We have found from our experience at HP (Griss and Collins, 1995) and Rational (Brändermar, 1996) and from the experience of others in managing large-scale change (Moore, 1991; Hammer and Stanton, 1995) that the use of *carefully chosen pilots* is essential.

The importance of *early success to gain and retain management and engineer interest* cannot be overstated. Stakeholders, especially management, can lose interest, unless there is some early and visible evidence that change is beginning to happen and yield benefits. Pilots lead to early success and rapid understanding of the organizational and infrastructure issues that typically impede reuse programs (Frakes and Fox, 1995, 1996). Furthermore, pilots are usually smaller, and so can be started with less investment and run with less risk. Generally, we recommend selecting a small, fast-paced set of projects to create and reuse components in an important, but not critical, area.

Example

In early 1995, before XYB created the reuse business, they carried out two pilot projects. One project was assigned to see if there were any stable products for integrating object request broker products, OLE, and Web browsers.

The second pilot was targeted at getting a better understanding of how reuse could work in an XYB setting. XYB used the CASE tool Rational ROSE together with C++ and OLE to develop some throw-away component and application prototypes to see how reuse would work in their domain and whether these tools and environments could be used effectively together. They also wanted to get a rough estimate of the improvement in reduced time to market that they could expect from reuse.

Remember, however, that running a pilot requires much less rigor than running a full-scale reuse business. Do not make the mistake of trying to use the same informal process, organization, and communication mechanisms for the full-scale approach.

13.3 TRA1: Creating a directive to reengineer the existing software business

The first step in developing a business reengineering directive is to obtain and articulate upper management's and other key stakeholder's buy-in. The absence of solid management commitment can be a major inhibitor to a successful reuse program. Commitment is demonstrated by vocal support, provision of resources for the program, and managerial decisions to enable its progress.

13.3.1 Gaining management commitment to reengineer

The introduction of a reuse business involves a number of changes that can only be effected and led by senior management. It is crucial to make a compelling case to management. Senior management commitment is essential to success, but the case also has to be made to all levels of management. Depending on their level and inclination, different managers will need different kinds of convincing. It is important to understand the business issues that they confront, and their prior beliefs with respect to software engineering and reuse as a solution. Different organizations must take different approaches to reuse, and the balance of the case will depend on individual personalities and the culture of the organization. Upper management might be willing to take the long view, but is often inexperienced about software engineering (and software reuse in particular). Middle management is most likely to be concerned about the immediate impact on project cycle-time, and the extra cost of initial learning or extra development work. If middle managers do not feel secure within the company it is likely that they will be protecting their own turf and will avoid hazards that they think might harm their careers. One of the biggest challenges to upper managers will be to support middle managers as they participate in incremental adoption of the reuse business while continuing to deliver products to customers.

The following help convince management:

- "Selling" the RSEB as an effective concept. This involves showing that the basic technical concepts and most architectural, organizational, and managerial risks and solutions are well understood.

- Mentioning that other companies "like our own" have significant reuse programs; that they have recognized the competitive benefits, and are working successfully to overcome the obstacles.

- Showing the critical business needs that an RSEB can address, and clarifying the benefits and outlining costs.

- Explaining what architecture is, why it is crucial, why it is costly, and why it takes time to develop it.

- Analyzing the risks and providing a credible plan with estimates for return on investment (ROI) based on a market analysis. To avoid bias, it is better if someone other than the reuse proponents does the market and risk analysis.

Example

The CEO of XYB arranges a series of breakfast seminars for the executives as part of the RSEB evaluation. They invite several speakers and companies such as the Component Based Reuse Business (CBRB) who provide processes, tools, and mentoring for starting up a reuse business.

Once there is a management consensus to proceed, the next step is to prepare a reengineering directive.

13.3.2 The reengineering directive articulates a case for action

The reengineering directive clearly and effectively tells the entire organization that top management has looked ahead and determined that reuse is the direction in which the company must go. Getting there will take substantial investment. It will necessitate changes in architecture, organization, and business processes. Everyone in the company, from top to bottom, will have to persist for several years to achieve the goal of widespread reuse.

The directive should provide a clear and compelling picture of several key issues:

1 **The business environment**
   What is the business situation? What is changing? Who are the customers? Who are the competitors?

2   **The customer's expectations**
Describe what the customers expect in the future.
Explain why reengineering into a reuse business is necessary. Is it to meet time-to-market requirements or quality requirements, or to reduce cost? Sketch a time-plan.

3   **The competitive situation**
Describe how competitors have improved to meet the customer's needs, and how this changes the competitive situation.

4   **The organization's business challenges**
What are the business goals?
Explain why the business is unable to meet new requirements in the face of the changes in the business's environment and why some simple, incremental improvements won't do.

5   **A diagnosis of the company**
Explain why is it likely that systematic reuse can solve the problems of the business.
Define the scope of the transformation and communicate the level of management support.

6   **The risks of not changing**
To eliminate any doubt about the need for reengineering, this section should warn about the risks of not reengineering, such as the high cost of maintenance when not reusing systematically.

7   **The initial strategy**
What we should do to start the change.

Example

A simplified XYB reengineering directive

1   **The business environment**
We have been a bank that values our personal relationship with our private customers. We have maintained those relationships through local offices and want to continue them, but we recognize that information technology is providing the means for banks to institute other types of relationships.

2   **The customer's expectations**
It is clear, based on reports from our local officers, that most customers want to maintain a personal relationship with a bank officer. At the same time more of them now have access to a personal computer and they want to be able to perform simple operations such as paying invoices and obtaining information about their financial standing through their screens. Moreover, they would appreciate the ability to make simple financial analyses online, while still having a fallback, when needed, to a bank officer in person. Other requirements, discovered by market analysis, include:

- Simplicity of interaction with the bank's system
- Competitive fees and interest rates
- Better availability of a wider range of services
- Faster provisioning of the services
- Interaction across national borders.

All of the above must be accomplished at a high level of security.

3   The competitive situation

The combination of a deregulated financial market and merging of our competitors into larger organizations has increased the pressure on us to operate at lower cost and to offer a wider range of services. Other traditional banks like ours have used information technology to expand their offerings. International banks have entered our market by employing low-cost information systems rather than local offices. New organizations like *The VirtualBank PLC* in England have begun to address our market with no local offices at all, relying entirely on a network connected to a central database. As a result of their economical operations, these organizations are profitable with competitive interest rates and fees.

4   The organization's business challenges

We want to capitalize on the new opportunities that the global and networked financial markets are opening up. We also need to stop the loss of customers to more technologically advanced competitors. So far the loss is slow, but the pace is growing.

5   A diagnosis of the company

The predominant reason for our loss of customers is that competitors offer superior services at lower prices. They can do this because, taking advantage of new technology, they are operating more efficiently than we are. We believe that some of them are developing new services up to 10 times faster than we do and at development costs five times lower than us. A five-percent improvement each year is not enough if we are to match them. How are they achieving these almost unbelievable numbers? They were happy to tell us. They installed reuse businesses! Our response is clear. We must adopt reuse. And we must adopt it at a pace that enables us to beat them in our market on at least three of the customers' requirements within three years.

6   The risks of not changing

Some of our former competitors failed to adapt to the rapid delivery of services that information technology now makes possible and that customers have come to expect. They did not have the financial strength to endure until they could change. They are no longer in business. We can endure, but we must change.

7   The initial strategy

To accommodate the challenges of this rapidly changing environment, we believe our application suite must be composed of components rather than being built as a single monolithic application. The set of components must be interoperable, customizable, and configurable. A high proportion of them must be reusable. The prototype Digicash ATM and Invoice Payment applications are examples of this approach.

We can carry out this strategy because we have excellent knowledge in the banking domain. We have talented software developers. To assist them, we have already signed an agreement with Component Based Reuse Business (CBRB). They are among the best at providing the training, tools, processes, and mentoring that we need. They have helped many other companies to make this transition.

Three years from now, we must:

- Deliver new applications five times faster than we currently do
- Deliver application upgrades 15 times faster than we currently do
- Make our services available over the Internet.

Accomplishing the last goal means that we have to make our customer interfaces easier to use. They will not receive the training that you receive internally.

To meet these difficult goals, we have formed two teams. One is the Change Spearhead team under Harry N. Hurry. It will plan changes in the organization and communicate progress within XYB. The other is the Application Family Engineering team headed by Stable N. Sturdy. In the first year, the Application Family Engineering team will focus on getting the most important software right. That will enable us to scale up the effort in the succeeding years. In years two and three, more of you will receive a total of two months' training in object-oriented technology, business engineering, software engineering processes, domain architecture, tools, and reuse.

With this vision of the next three years, with the changes in organization we need to carry out this reuse plan, with the training in new processes that you need, we are confident that we can surpass our competitors, just as we have done for the past hundred years. We depend on your skill, enthusiasm, and professionalism, as always.

Vee P. van der Bank

13.4 TRA2: Envisioning the new Reuse Business

With management committed to change, we start by developing a vision of the new architecture, business processes and organization, and improving the initial transition plan. We establish objectives and scope, and explain how the business, people, process, and technology issues will be addressed. To do this well it is necessary to understand the existing business, clarify the business goals, do a customer and user analysis, and have a good understanding of the generic RSEB model from Chapter 9.

In parallel to the envisioning, the transition team will also do a pass through Reversing the existing business (TRA3) to get a more detailed understanding of the existing software business to further shape the reuse business goals. Which are the processes most important to reengineer? How much reuse is already under way? Can ongoing reuse activities be used as a success story and starting point to springboard the process, or is it based on a conflicting model? What sort of organizational issues need to be addressed? Are people ready for change? Wasmund (1993) discusses critical success factors for reuse. Boehm (1991) discusses an approach to systematic software risk analysis.

13.4.1 Begin addressing key organization and stakeholder issues

Identify the stakeholders that will be affected by the change, such as:

- customers,
- employees,
- owners,
- suppliers and partners,
- managers, and
- teams.

Map the workers defined for the generic RSEB to individual people within the organization. Then decide how best to involve these people in the transition program and get them enthusiastic to the point where they start suggesting improvements in the processes and job definitions (worker types).

Example

The developers within XYBsoft can roughly be grouped in three categories:

- 25% young recruits
- 25% banking domain experts
- 50% COBOL programmers.

Most of the young recruits and domain experts seem to be eager to try (or at least are curious about) this new approach. These people will likely fill most of the workers in the **Application** and **Component System Engineering** teams. Among the programmers there are two that qualify immediately for the **Application Family Engineering** team and for project managers. Many of the programmers will also become excellent testers since they know the types of problem that tend to exist within the domain. All the programmers are offered the two-month training program, to get them going under the new paradigm and help them improve their value on the job market.

But there are several dozen programmers who feel really uncomfortable about the new situation. The **Software Engineering Business Manager** knows that some of them would like to retire and some can continue to support the current software base for at least 5–10 years. But there are still some who do not like this new situation at all. The **Software Engineering Business Manager** does what he can to help them find alternative jobs, which works out well for most of them. But a handful of programmers do not want this and begin complaining about the whole situation to other employees. This leads to a meeting where, after having discussed different alternatives, they are asked frankly either to change attitude or to find another job. They all decide to quit.

Make an initial assessment of the needs and concerns of the stakeholders, and gather more detail later as the change proceeds. Deal with their concerns systematically as part of the ongoing communication and transition. Speak to each group; ask what they need, what they fear, what they think of the program and the other people they will need to coordinate with. Explicitly seek their support and involvement. Ensure that they are motivated and that they feel the plan will provide some value to them. Develop specific plans targeted at key stakeholders to involve them in "owning the reuse business transition." Identify potential champions and early adopters to lead the way.

To get full benefits from reengineering to a reuse business, it is important to operate across traditional functional borders. The new model must align programs and remove inconsistencies. However, it is necessary to *balance the political needs of organizations with cross-organization needs*. Project managers must work horizontally, build teams, peddle influence. Having to cross barriers slows things down, so managers must be prepared to push.

13.4.2 Creating an application family vision

Initiate the first iteration of **Application Family Engineering**, as discussed in Chapter 10. Establish the **Application Family Engineering** team and provide substantial mentoring if the time pressure is high. Acquire tools and training. If possible use or develop a business model of the target organizations that will use the application systems. Identify application and component systems to support business processes, workers, and business entity objects. Use the analysis of customers and end users to better understand their needs. Determine how stable the application domain and key subdomains are.

Example

In parallel to the changes to XYBsoft, the whole bank is being restructured to take advantage of global customer service, new networking infrastructure, deregulation and merger of banking, insurance, brokerage, and cable television (CATV) companies. The bank's BPR experts must therefore be involved in **Application Family Engineering** so that the **Application Family Engineering** team can better understand how to support the business processes of the emerging bank.

Use the early results from **Application Family Engineering** to sketch an application family and a product plan.

Example

As discussed in Chapter 10, XYB find that customers most desire the ability to pay invoices over the Internet. XYB therefore decide to start by developing a business model for electronic payment and then to quickly develop application systems to support this. They first define the application systems **Invoicing** and **Payment** and the component systems **Invoice Management** and **Account Management**. Looking a bit further down the line, they see that customers desire to be able to handle electronic cash, which suggests a **Digicash Cashier** application system and a new version of the existing ATM, which will be recast as the application system **ATM Cashier**. These systems also need the component systems **Money Management** and **Bank Customer Management**.

13.4.3 Describing the reuse business vision based on the generic RSEB

Examine the specific *business needs* and determine the sort of reuse business that best supports them. The RSEB model needs to be customized to the organization's business strategy, which may need to be clarified and articulated. For reuse it is particularly important to relate the business strategy to the development of a future family of related application systems, see Section 13.4.2.

We then *customize the RSEB* model to focus on the needed benefits. As described in Chapters 1 and 2, possible benefits include one or more of the following, each of which requires a slightly different reuse business strategy:

Timeliness of delivery (time to market)   High levels of reuse can dramatically reduce the time it takes to develop an application system. Focus on producing enough component systems and technology to support rapid evolutionary development.

Productivity improvements   Reduction in development and maintenance costs is the other benefit most often associated with reuse. Because of reuse, less has to be developed, and less will be maintained redundantly. Focus on developing those components that will be used many times, to reduce development and maintenance cost.

Quality   Software quality improves as defects are found and fixed as the application systems are used. Also, the cost of investing more in inspections and testing for reused software will be amortized over the application systems where it is reused. Focus on those component systems that relate to the most error-prone, most used and most complex parts of applications.

Standardization   Several reuse programs are using reusable software to impose internal technical standards. Focus on reusable (or portable) components that contain the standards or encapsulate standard infrastructure. In many cases, it is easier to enforce use of standard components than it is to enforce a written standard by manually checking exact compliance.

Interoperability, Compatibility Using stable architectures and standard COTS and proprietary component systems will ensure common behavior and interoperability within the whole application family.

New business opportunities A well-architected, high-quality set of reusable components can enable several direct and indirect business opportunities. Direct opportunities include the ability to sell reusable workproducts. Indirect opportunities include quick customization of solutions for niche markets, and the creation of customization or system integration businesses.

Example

XYBsoft decides to take the RSEB presented in Chapter 9 as a first approximation of their own new processes, but they make a few changes:

- They think of implementors as a separate competence unit. They therefore define an **Implementors** competence unit which contains the new worker **Implementor**, who in Chapter 9 was "part of" the **Subsystem Engineer** worker.
- Some of the people in the **Application Family Engineering** team have already been using the domain engineering method FODA (Kang, 1990) and like its strong emphasis on explicit features (in Chapter 4 we roughly defined a feature as *"a use case, part of a use case or a responsibility of a use case"*). The transition team decide to augment and adapt the processes and the workers of the reuse business to take this into account.
- Given the type of applications and Microsoft's involvement in home banking, XYBsoft decides that Visual Basic Script is probably the best technology for integrating components into application systems.

Given the emphasis on time to market, XYBsoft decides that they need to develop first a stable architecture and then as soon as possible a substantial set of component systems. They therefore plan two iterations through **Application Family Engineering** with a focus on architecture to allow for a broadened emphasis on several component systems.

Use the business objectives and goals as input to customize the generic RSEB by envisioning several alternative reuse business use case models. Define who the business actors are and what they provide and require. Look at the most important business use cases and develop high-level worker and business entity object models for those, such as sketched in Chapters 9–12. Propose technology and tools that can leverage processes and worker productivity. Develop market, environmental, and organizational scenarios and play them out against the envisioned reuse business alternatives, and see how the reuse business copes with these "what-if scenarios." Simulate or otherwise estimate performance and evaluate it against current performance and competitor benchmarking. Iterate quickly and avoid getting into details that can be dealt with during TRA4 (Forward engineering).

Example

XYBsoft takes the description of how workers participate in **Application Family Engineering** presented in Chapter 10 as a first approximation but want to adapt it to their use of FODA (Kang, 1990). They therefore suggest an additional worker **Feature Engineer** who is responsible for maintaining a feature map (which defines features and how they relate to each other) of each application or component system and for making sure that the feature map is consistent primarily with the use case model, but also with the object models.

The **Application Family Engineering** team plans to start working according to the suggested process but know that they will need to come back and revise the process description.

Document the vision and goals in an *Objective Specification*.

Reuse business objective specification

Include high-level descriptions of the future reuse business actors and processes, emphasizing how they differ from current processes. For each process, name the customer, supplier, and other types of partners. Describe the input, activities, products of each process, and the workers involved.

Define measurable high-level (but precise) properties and goals for each process, such as cost, quality, life cycle, lead time, and level of customer satisfaction. Each goal should be traceable to the business and reuse strategy.

Indicate the tools and technologies that may support the processes, with special emphasis on CM systems and component-based software engineering tools.

Describe how the processes may need to change in future business scenarios, due to new technologies, market changes, new interfaces to the environment, and different categories of workers.

Provide a list of critical success factors and risks to monitor.

13.5 TRA3: Reversing the existing software business

Assess the feasibility of investing in reuse and the organization's readiness for change to operate as some form of RSEB. To do this it is necessary to have a clear understanding of the existing software engineering processes, and the business processes they connect with. Some of these processes will have to remain or coexist with new processes. Others will have to be significantly changed or replaced. Study the current organization to determine the existing processes, tools, and issues. This can be done by developing a lightweight business model, but avoid doing too much work.

It is important to understand how the existing business *operates in practice*, rather than just what is "in the books." Focus on the *primary processes* that will shape the RSEB – the entire organization does not have to be understood in detail. A useful way to structure the assessment is to use a reuse maturity matrix (see the discussion below).

13.5.1 Assessing reuse feasibility

By asking several questions regarding business need and application family opportunities it is possible to see if reuse is a feasible choice. Then examine organizational readiness and process and technology needs to see how big a change might be needed. The following are sample questions to ask.

Business opportunities and needs   What are the drivers motivating change? Can these be addressed by some form of reuse? Does the organization perceive the need for change? How big are the needed changes? How aware are people of the competition?

Application families and domains   What kind and variety of application systems are produced? Do they obviously form an application system family? From what variety and kind of workproducts are they produced? Is there a visible subsystem or subset of workproducts that appear to be potentially reusable? Is there some level of formal or informal reuse already under way? Is there a common architecture defined or used? What sort of domain experience is there? What sort of future application systems are anticipated, what sort of technology and domain changes are anticipated? What legacy systems exist?

Organizational readiness   How experienced are the people in software development, in software processes, in the domain, in technologies such as object orientation and Visual Basic, and in reuse? How stable is the organization? How distributed is the organization? What sort of management structure exists? What level of management support and sponsorship exists? What cultural and historical issues exist that might support or impede reuse? What values drive people? Who are the stakeholders? How amenable or resistant to change is the organization? Are there other changes or initiatives under way that might compete for attention? Are people willing to try new technologies and processes? How risk averse are people? Do people understand basic economic and investment models such as return on investment (ROI)? What are the key cultural, communication, and political issues?

Process and technology needs   What sort of software process is followed? How mature is the process? What sort of tools and technologies are used, and what restrictions are there? What tools must be used because of target hardware or customer requirements? What sort of new tools and processes would developers accept? What performance do the processes have, that is, what is their time to market, quality, cost and so on?

Karlsson (1995) and Davis (1994b) provide several questionnaires that may be used to further assess reuse status and readiness. Prieto-Diaz (1991a) also suggests several key issues to investigate. These may be helpful in developing the objective specification and detailed reuse transition plan.

Several reuse researchers and practitioners, inspired by the SEI Process Capability Assessment (Humphrey, 1989), have proposed a variety of different reuse maturity models (Davis (ed.), 1992, 1994b; Prieto-Diaz, 1991). These models are more complex and have more dimensions than the simple stair step shown in Figure 13.2. They identify several observable attributes such as business and economics, technology, process, organization, reuse level, and several levels of maturity along these attribute dimensions. The maturation along each attribute dimension corresponds to an increased degree of systematic process and greater levels of investment, yielding higher reuse levels, more stable architecture, and increased benefits such as reduced time to market. Such matrices can be used to quickly assess where to focus in a reuse readiness assessment. See also the discussion in Karlsson (1995).

13.6 TRA4: Forward engineering the new Reuse Business

The key activities in this step are to develop the detailed process and organizational models, and plan tool acquisition and integration and knowledge transfer.

13.6.1 Designing the processes and workers starting from the generic RSEB

Start by customizing the generic RSEB process and organizational models described in Chapter 9, acquire SEPSE (tool) components and then prepare communication and training:

1   Develop more detailed models of the business actors and use cases most relevant in this iteration. Use the envisioned processes as a starting point, detail the goals for the business actors and use cases, and add

-   modeling guidelines,
-   criteria and heuristics,
-   document templates,
-   review criteria, and
-   examples.

The quickest and probably most cost-effective way to do this is to start from some existing process framework such as Rational's Objectory and specialize it to the organization's unique practices and culture. Note that the process chapters 10 to 12 are a good starting point, but are incomplete. For example, they contain no document templates, few heuristics, and no detailed review criteria. A process framework is a generic model of the processes and workers of a Software Engineering Business that can be specialized to the unique needs of an organization, but still contains most of the necessary details (not included in this book). The first iteration through this step is most often focused at detailing the **Application Family Engineering** process; the next iteration will probably define the process for **Component System Engineering** in more detail.

2   Develop a specialized worker and business entity object model that can offer the new and changed business use cases. Use the envisioned workers and business entity objects as a starting point:

-   Add responsibilities and step-by-step work descriptions for the workers.
-   Detail the attributes and relationships between the business entity objects, such as how the different software artifacts relate to each other. Introducing an additional term to represent features, for example, would require that it is well understood in relation to other terms.
-   Define document templates for the business entity objects.
-   Define how the workers interact in the business use cases and with the actors.
-   Define what skills and experiences the different workers need to have.

Example

During the first transition iteration the focus for XYB is to get the process for **Application Family Engineering** implemented. The pressure to get started with **Application Family Engineering** is high and XYBsoft have already started to prepare a business model of the target organization. The transition team now decide to implement the process in two steps. First the requirements capture and robustness analysis steps and corresponding workers are detailed and implemented together with some guidelines on acquiring Commercial Off The Shelf software such as object request brokers. Then two months later the design, implementation, and testing steps and corresponding workers get detailed and installed.

3　Connect goals for business actors, use cases, workers, and business entity objects to business goals.

4　Look at each business actor, use case, worker, and type of business entity objects and suggest how to support them with suitable tools, that is, Software Engineering Process Support Environments (SEPSE) and other information systems. Recall that each component system might include a specialized process (SEP) and specialized tools (SEPSE) for **Application System Engineering** that should be installed together with the component system itself to make most effective use of the components. A systematic way of doing this is sketched in Chapter 8. Generally it is not cost-effective to develop proprietary tools, especially not in the first iterations of the **Transition to a Reuse Business** since the number of tool users is small in the first iterations. Instead try to buy suitable tools, and then to integrate and adapt them to the needs of the reuse business. Remember that the tools should support or at least allow for the flow of work among the workers in the software engineering processes – not just provide modeling capabilities.

5　Decide on technology for distributing the process documentation and the tools to the organization, for example as documents, WWW pages, or CD-ROMs. Prepare plans for training and mentoring the workers and business actors. Remember that component systems should be distributed as "kits" together with suitable tools, examples, and process fragments as discussed in Chapter 11.

6　Decide on metrics collection; this is discussed in Chapter 14.

7　Develop a communication plan that defines how to communicate with the different stakeholders during the business implementation.

8　Specify and assess risks.

Example

During the first iteration the transition team and the **Application Family Engineering** team prepare a list of risks. They note the following as the highest risks:

1　The competition will beat XYB in providing equal or better services.
2　The organization cannot or will not change to an effective reuse business, due to anxiety and lack of ability.
3　Commercially available products for integration of OLE, the object request broker, and Web technology are not yet stable.

To deal with these risks, XYBsoft decides to strengthen the team that surveys the competitition. They consult with several companies that help organizations change, and they hire an experienced software architect to reduce the risk of integrating different technologies.

9　Start training change agents and develop training for reuse workers to follow the new processes and use the new tools (Tirso, 1991).

13.6.2 Choosing tools to support the workers in the business processes

Different workers have different needs for tool support. Some tools support the process itself, while others more directly support the construction and testing of software artifacts. Architects and component developers need facilities to develop OO models, as well as coding and testing tools. Managers and librarians need metrics tools, project management tools, and tools to manage multiple versions and configurations of components.

Today, there is no comprehensive set of reuse tools that can be immediately used to provide an optimal SEPSE for a customized RSEB. There are several existing reuse tools, but they typically only support part of the reuse process, seem inadequate to directly support the RSEB, and may in fact not be very effective to support even simpler approaches to reuse. These reuse tools, and other software development tools, can be used as tool components and integrated to a complete tool environment (SEPSE). Most have to be significantly adapted to the specific reuse processes and environments.

The following kinds of tools might be used to build the Software Engineering Process Support Environment (SEPSE):

- Software engineering processes such as Rational Objectory and HP Fusion.

- Software engineering environments such as HP Softbench and Microsoft VC++ and VJ++.

- OO CASE tools such as Rational ROSE and Paradigm Plus.

- Reuse process definition tools such as Extended Intelligence RPM.

- Workflow and process definition and enactment tools such as LBMS Process Engineer and HP OpenPM.

- Libraries and repositories such as Hitachi Object Reuser, STARS Asset, ObjectSpace ObjectCatalog, Visual Basic Component Manager, and Microsoft Repository.

- Catalogs, databases, general classification and search tools (Frakes and Pol, 1992), class library browsers, and WWW based library browsers (Poulin, 1995).

- Configuration management systems, such as Microsoft Visual Source Safe and PVCS, Rational Apex, and HP WebCM.

- Project management and progress management tools, such as Rational Summit and Microsoft Project.

- Generators, builders and visual development tools, such as Visual Basic, PowerBuilder, IBM VisualAge, Netron CAP, and Visual C++ Wizard tools.

- Metrics tools, such as Logiscope.

These tools need to be assembled and integrated into a variety of specialized environments to support the various workers. We are not suggesting that it is simple to integrate an arbitrary set of tools into a working software engineering process support environment (SEPSE). This can be a most frustrating task as many tools have not been designed to work well together to support the complete life cycle of software engineering. The following are examples of toolsets we believe support the workers well:

- Application engineers need tools that allow them to reuse, integrate, and adapt components to match a customer's requirements. The **Use Case Engineer** will use OO CASE tools that allow reuse of use case components and allow changed and new use cases and actors to be modeled, and GUI builders to sketch user interfaces. The **Subsystem Engineer**s will use CASE tools to reuse and develop new object models and application builder tools such as Visual Basic to integrate code components into complete applications. The **Tester** will use test environments such as VisualTest.

- Component engineers need tools that allow them to develop and package components for reusers. Here the **Use Case Engineer** will use similar tools to an **Application Use Case Engineer** but will also use tools to represent business models of the target organization. The **Subsystem Engineer**s will use CASE tools to develop component object models and implementation tools such as Visual C++, Borland Delphi, and Smalltalk. The **Facade Engineer** will use tools such as Rose and Visual Basic to package component systems for easy use and retrieval. The **Tester** will use test environments similar to the testers of application systems.

Example

ParcPlace-Digitalk PARTS Wrapper uses Visual Smalltalk as a scripting and integration language. In the PARTS Wrapper components are used to build applications. A component (or part) could be a traditional object, but can also be a COBOL program, database interface, or encapsulated communication protocol. The product is aimed at making it easy to encapsulate legacy applications in an OO-compatible manner. These legacy systems are then extended and augmented by pure OO techniques, perhaps in PARTS' visual programming environment. Application logic is created either by visually drawing links between parts, or by writing or modifying Smalltalk code. The available components are organized in catalogs in the form of palettes that contain all components available to the developer. PARTS comes with over 60 components, some as small as buttons or boxes, while others are larger templates, aimed at encapsulating other code.

- The **Application Family Engineering** team need tools that allow them to capture high-level requirements and express them as a superordinate system (that is, a representation of the layered system at a high level). Here the **Superordinate Use Case Engineer** will use similar tools to a **Component Use Case Engineer**. The **Subsystem Engineer**s will use CASE tools to develop high-level object models and implementation tools such as Visual C++, Delphi, and Smalltalk to implement some core mechanisms. They will substantially use tools such as IDL environments and Visual Basic to specify interfaces and facades and also configuration management tools to control the evolution of the facades.

- The **Librarian** needs tools for configuration management to help keep track of component and facade versions. The **Librarian** also needs to provide tools that allow reusers to browse and search for components and facades. The **Component System Trainer** needs tools and techniques for distributing the components to reusers. The **Component System Supporter** needs tools for capturing and tracking support requests, perhaps submitted using a simple email or WWW interface.

There are a large variety of object-oriented and object-based development tools that support rapid assembly of applications from objects or components. These environments, such as Microsoft Visual Basic, HP's Visual Plus, PowerBuilder, IBM's VisualAge, and ParcPlace-DigiTalk VisualWorks are application frameworks with builders. They provide a large variety of built-in services and tool functionality and components that make it easy to create an application that immediately enjoys many standard desktop and client–server features. They also provide a combination of object or component libraries and browsers, some form of GUI and data-access application framework, an interpretive or rapid compile language, and visual environments that aid in the rapid selection, customization, and assembly of components. Different environments provide varying support for client–server application development and integration with OLE or CORBA.

Finally, some CASE tools support customizable notation, scripting languages, and OLE control of the tools and enable other tools and environments to access the model database. These capabilities enable the construction of generators that can create complete application systems by putting together domain-specific components following a script. For example, Rational Rose, Visual Basic, and Visual C++ can be combined into an environment that simplifies specializing the components for custom needs.

Example

The transition team suggest a suite of tools and environments consisting of:

- HP Softbench
- Rational ROSE for C++, VB and Java
- Visual C++ from Microsoft
- Visual Basic for Applications from Microsoft
- Visual Test from Rational
- The ORB Plus environment from HP
- The Rational Objectory process product.

During their start-up phase they will use only the file system for configuration management but will switch to a commercial CM system during the third iteration.

13.7 TRA5: Implementing the Reuse Business

In this step, we initiate the roll-out of the new processes and tools, change the organization structure, train engineers, and set up metrics collection procedures. Most of this activity involves normal project management, but there are some key change management issues. Most important is to allow time for "unfreezing," to allow people to overcome fear of change, and let go of past issues. Provide assistance in "crossing the chasm" of the unknown (Moore, 1991), using a combination of "vision pull" and "pain push," with lots of communication, education, and support.

Example

There is of course a risk that XYB employees and managers will not believe that the reuse business can deliver what it promises. Such doubts are natural but can become harmful if they come to dominate the climate at XYB. There are several ways of addressing such a risk, including early successes at pilots, communication about risks and concerns, and successes in other organizations.

Support in the form of continuous communication, training, and prompt management attention to issues as they arise are key to sustaining the change process. Use both management and grassroots modes of communication. Use credible spokespeople and involve and empower diverse, cross-functional steering teams. Communicate using multiple channels, and opportunities presented by email, Web, newsletters, and talks. The **SEB Manager**, **Process Owners**, **Resource Owners**, and the transition team should deal with objections, but must focus on successes and firmly lead the way. Ensure that **Resource Owners** and **Process Leaders** support organizational change by words and action. Show commitment to the new way by removing barriers and terminating obsolete systems and measures.

Motivate the employees by providing specific training and establishing new career paths for the new worker positions. Redefine job evaluation and reward systems.

Collect and display metrics. Most unsuccessful reuse programs fail to deliver early, tangible results, causing people, especially management, to lose interest.

13.7.1 Management leadership is crucial to engineer commitment

There are many process and organizational changes that upper management (**Owners Of The Reuse Business**) need to initiate and sustain. Investment will be needed for architecture, development of component systems, organization changes, acquisition of products and tools, and training. Time and encouragement will be needed for incremental learning and improvement. The need for upper management leadership is particularly strong since reuse links multiple software development projects and requires long-term investment, support, and commitment to sustain. Reuse should become a way of life for the organization where managers and engineers know how and when to make reuse decisions. They need education, direction, and incentives to change.

In some organizations, it makes sense for the **Software Engineering Business Manager** or the **Owners Of The Reuse Business** to support initial iterations with extra money, extra time, or extra people. Also, extra training and consulting can be provided, to help these iterations face lower risk. Experience shows that direct financial incentives to individuals does not lead to effective changes in long-term team behavior. It is better, as indicated above, to support the teams, providing additional people or helping to reduce risks.

Management commitment helps create and sustain engineer commitment. Software developers need encouragement to try reuse and stay with it, despite fairly radical changes in culture and process. Most engineers will not have had any training in reuse, and so will tend to have an incomplete view of the impact of reuse and the real work and costs associated with non-reuse scenarios. Engineers will often be uncomfortable in depending on others to provide key components. They will conceal their discomfort, saying "reusable code is too slow, a reusable component will not meet our specific needs, it is too hard to understand reusable code, it's quicker to write our own, and using reusable code destroys our creativity."

Factors that influence how they react includes the local culture of "inventiveness." Does the culture and reward system support people taking time to develop general components and package and document them well? Management needs to make changes in expectations to allow this. Do people feel encouraged to work to standards, or is "individual creativity" the key factor? A different kind of creativity and innovation may be needed. Stress the excitement of new ideas, that the job will be better and more predictable, and that reuse will enable the engineer to more rapidly explore alternative solutions. Component engineers and supporters will become experts in their field and many will depend on them, which will make them a sought-after resource within the organization.

13.7.2 Implementing the processes and competence units in your organization

Design your reuse business organization by adapting the RSEB processes, worker models, and competence units to the specific needs. Determine the number and size of teams, based on the estimated size and number of the component and application systems.

In theory, the workers and the competence units can be mapped to arbitrary people and organization units, as long as the people have the skills required. In practice, however, it is essential to allocate people to workers in a way that aligns well with the organization. Ideally there should be one organization unit or resource unit (for example, a department or a group) for each competence unit. This is seldom possible to achieve in full, particularly during the transition to the reuse business. As the transition progresses, however, it should be a goal to align the organization with the competence units, where each competence unit is managed by a **Resource Owner** that reports to the **Software Engineering Business Manager**.

Make sure that the required workers can be assigned, without too much tension, to people within the organization at each milestone towards the "final" organization. This requires substantial flexibility from the people involved and should be supported by the **SEB Manager**, **Process Owner**s, **Process Leader**s, and the **Resource Owner**s. There are a few guidelines to keep in mind during the transition to the final organization:

- Do not have people involved in both **Application** and **Component System Engineering** at the same time – these workers run with agendas that differ too much for one person to assume both types of worker responsibilities. This is because the production of high-quality reusable assets can take significantly longer (sometimes twice as long or more) than a non-reusable asset. Individuals could periodically rotate between **Application** and **Component System Engineering**, but at any one time they should have a clear assignment. The same person may, however, participate in several different **Application System Engineering** processes or **Component System Engineering** processes.

- Keep component supporters as a separate team. These people should be trained as facilitators more than in engineering of components. They do, however, need to be in the close vicinity of or in close communication with the application engineers to facilitate their work. However, during the start-up of the reuse business it is often feasible to combine the **Component Support** and **Component System Engineering** teams, though different individuals will usually enact different workers such as **Architect**, **Subsystem Engineer**, **Component System Supporter**, and **Librarian**.

- Sometimes the **Tester**s can be integrated into the **Application Family Engineering**, **Application** and **Component System Engineering** teams. This may not always be feasible; some organizations prefer to keep some tension between the software engineers and the QA people "defending the quality."

- The **Application Family Engineering** team can generally be reduced (perhaps by a factor of 3) as the architecture stabilizes after iteration 2 or 3.

- The same person should not work as both **Architect** and **Process Leader** because he or she cannot then be committed enough to architecting. Furthermore, the **Process Leader** is responsible for resolving conflicts within the team, including conflicts that the **Architect** is involved in.

During the first iterations an organization typically builds its internal **Application Family Engineering** and transition team with the assistance of external consultants, who may play the role of team members or mentors.

During the first iterations, much of the communication and training can proceed more informally than in a full-scale reuse business. As the reuse business gains momentum and scales up in subsequent iterations, the **Application Family Engineering** and transition teams will switch from a learning mode to a teaching mode as they help bring reuse into other parts of the organization.

Having the right organization is crucial – having the right people to do the job is even more important. Make sure that you hire skilled people and train those you have to be able to participate in the very complex environment of a full-scale reuse business. The following workers are particularly important to staff with excellent and motivated people:

- **Lead Architect**
- **Transition Driver**
- **Software Engineering Business Manager**

Try to have all personnel that participate in a process such as **Application Family Engineering** seated in the same place — the communication barrier is otherwise difficult to overcome (Coplien and Schmidt, 1995).

As part of the work that led to the reuse organization discussed in Chapter 1, Danielle Fafchamps investigated 10 different HP reuse organizations, summarizing them in four different organizational models. She discusses in detail the risks and benefits of each structure (Fafchamps, 1994).

We have also examined other reuse organizations at HP, and at AT&T. They differ in the degree to which the component engineers and the people in the **Component Support** team have full-time responsibility for component systems. They differ in the extent to which they are embedded within **Application System Engineering** teams and hence, more directly involved with application development. They also differ in the degree to which a single manager is able to coordinate interactions between the teams. For example, if the teams are relatively independent, they tend to drift out of alignment.

13.7.3 Team management in a process organization

In a process organization **Process Leader**s report to **Process Owner**s. In the simplest case each **Process Leader** for **Component System Engineering** reports to the corresponding **Process Owner**, and the **Process Leader**s for **Application System Engineering** report to the corresponding **Process Owner**. The **Process Owner**s for **ASE** and for **CSE**, the **Process Owner**s for **AFE**, and the manager for the **Component Support** team all report to the **Software Engineering Business Manager** (Figure 13.5). When the **Process Owner**s and manager for the **Component Support** team cannot themselves resolve their controversies, the **SEB Manager** is responsible for doing so.

The **AFE** team, **ASE** teams, **CSE** team, **Component Support** team, and **SEB Manager** together constitute a Reuse-driven Software Engineering Business.

It is important to balance the relative status of component engineers and application engineers, which somewhat depends on the amount of funding provided for component development as compared to the funding for application development. It depends also on the way in which the company provides that funding. On the one hand, if it treats the cost of component development as overhead, it makes the component engineers feel "second class" in comparison to the direct-charging application engineers. On the other hand, if it sets up a scheme to transfer component systems to an **ASE** team as a priced asset, it makes component engineers feel that they are producing a product of value. Moreover, because they have to pay for the component system, application engineers also feel that they are getting a product of value. If they do not agree with the value placed on an asset, that leads to another issue to be resolved. Sometimes a simple incentive program can help jump-start the reuse process.

It greatly simplifies management to let the **Process Owner**s of **AFE**, **ASE**, and **CSE** report to a single manager, such as the **SEB Manager**. Some organizations, however, they have preferred some other mechanism, such as a Reuse Council, composed of representatives of the interests involved, and depend on this council to resolve issues of conflict, priority, and funding.

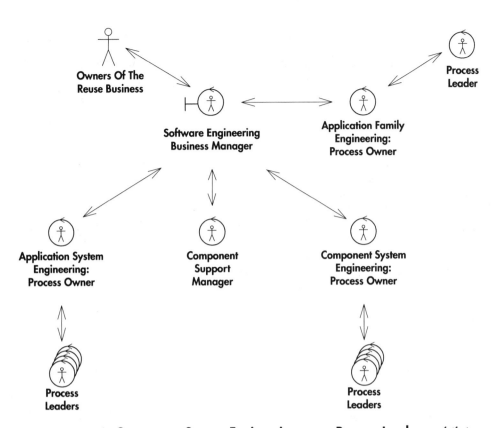

Figure 13.5 *The* **Component System Engineering** *teams,* **Process Leaders** *and their* **Process Owner** *are on the same organizational level as the* **Application System Engineering** *teams,* **Process Leaders** *and* **Process Owner**.

The guidelines on management and responsibilities presented in this section may seem obvious. Yet we have seen many reuse efforts fail — or sometimes be clumsily rescued at the last minute — because companies did not establish an appropriate organizational structure. Other efforts have failed because the **SEB Manager** or the Reuse Council lacked the inputs, such as those from metrics or reviews, that would reveal the true nature of the problem.

13.8 Summary

Transitioning to a fully functional reuse business can be one of the most difficult tasks that a software engineering business can undertake. It takes time, typically measured in years. It expends substantial sums of money, both the investment kind and the operational kind, before recovering that money in increased operational effectiveness. It changes the organizational structure and the way people work, which can be disruptive.

The transition affects more than the software people. The scope of change is akin to that typically addressed by a business process reengineering effort, which can affect people and the organization throughout the entire company.

Many businesses, in reality, have little choice. The advances in information technology have made it possible to operate the business processes in dramatically more effective ways. But a business can take advantage of these advances only through software reuse. Building software systems in the old ways to operate reengineered processes would just take too long and cost too much.

Nevertheless, a business should not plunge into reengineering and reuse until at least part of its executive structure sees that this path is indeed the one that it must follow. Then the initial order of business is to set up a planning group to gather the facts that convince most of the rest of the executive structure that reengineering and reuse are, indeed, essential to the continued health of the business. Of course, extensive change involves more than management. Consider other stakeholders, the company's readiness to change, and existing experience with reuse.

With this general understanding, the transition program has the backing to start. Many companies have begun with pilot efforts, running a small-scale implementation before scaling up to organization-wide reuse. Unfortunately, backing may weaken over the years, as other important issues demand attention. Reuse champions can maintain backing by such methods as:

- Metrics that demonstrate success on financial measures or achievement on non-financial measures.

- Broadband communications that keep the goals and methods of the program fresh.

- Feedback that celebrates achievements of individuals and groups.

- Continuous training to prepare the people involved for each forward step in the program.

A company cannot create a reengineering and reuse program in an instant. It will not spring up by fiat. It must grow from strong roots. If you begin planning in May, you could hope to start small, that is, to set up the first organizational units of the program, in January next year. Focus initially on domain-specific architected reuse. Develop reusable components for product lines or application families where reuse will have high impact.

Work towards the organization pattern that we have elaborated in other chapters: **Application Family Engineering**, **Application System Engineering**, **Component System Engineering**, and **Component Support** teams. Appoint a manager to coordinate this pattern. Do not start from scratch, but instead acquire process and organization frameworks, tools, mentoring, and training.

Plan the training that prepares people to use new tools and methods to carry out the software engineering processes in these new organization units.

A key ingredient of a long-term program is enduring leadership, both by the formal managers and by the change agents or champions. The best way of getting this endurance is to support them, both financially and emotionally. The early years will be full of turmoil.

Then one day, when the organization has achieved steady state, its people will no longer think of reuse as a new program. It will become "the way we do things around here." And you will still be in business!

13.9 Additional reading

The paper by Ted Davis, "Adopting a policy of reuse", *IEEE Spectrum*, pages 44–8, June 1994, provides a crisp and readable introduction to the critical success factors, risk-reduction, maturity models and step-wise reuse adoption process developed at the Software Productivity Consortium.

The paper by Danielle Fafchamps, "Organizational factors and reuse", *IEEE Software*, **11**(5), 31–41, Sept. 1994, provides a careful analysis of 10 different reuse organizations, and how communciation, control, and trust affect the ways these organizations work.

Software Reuse: A Holistic Approach, edited by Karlsson (1995), includes an extensive discussion on how to introduce reuse into an organization. They describe assessments, reuse maturity models, and adoption process and roles, and give several guidelines for determining the reuse business strategy.

Michael Hammer and Steven Stanton, in their book *The Reengineering Revolution: A Handbook*, HarperCollins, New York, 1995, provide numerous pragmatic guidelines for success with business process reengineering, particularly with the role of management leadership, the reengineering team, pilots, and people issues. These provide an excellent complement to the model-driven techniques described in the TOA book.

The book by Geoffrey A. Moore, *Crossing the Chasm: Marketing and Selling Technology Products to Mainstream Customers*, Harper Business, 1991, details the extra effort and techniques needed to move from successful pilots of a technology with early adopters to widespread use by a majority of the organization.

The book by Adele Goldberg and Kenneth Rubin, *Succeeding with Objects, Decision Frameworks for Project Management*, Addison-Wesley, 1995, provides practical advice on establishing reuse and framework organizations, selecting a reuse process, establishing project and organization business objectives, and choosing technology.

MANAGING THE REUSE BUSINESS

14.1 Ongoing management is crucial to RSEB success

In Chapter 13, we established the business motivation, the framework, and the momentum for the transition to a reuse business. We defined an incremental roadmap for change, and created an initial organization for the reuse business. Upper management plays a significant role in getting the transition under way.

But once the transition is under way, upper management cannot simply congratulate itself and turn its attention to other matters. Even with an excellent incremental transition plan and a skilled transition team, management must continue to lead the action and monitor progress. Inevitable business changes will make replanning and directional shifts unavoidable. New actions, adjusted goals and metrics, and changes in process and organization will be needed to keep focused and maintain momentum.

In this ongoing management phase, the various managers of the reuse business have several functions:

- Ensuring continued progress to meet the business goals that first motivated the transition.

- Leading and supporting the transition, and clearing roadblocks so that the transition is accomplished effectively.

- Adjusting the process and organization in response to changes in business conditions, and observed process defects and opportunities for improvement.

- Resolution of conflicts that arise between projects and goals, which are now linked because of the architecture and large-scale reuse.

The good news is that good management *can* make a difference to success, largely using traditional management techniques. However, the nature of the reuse business changes the character and extent of the issues:

- On the one hand, many software project managers and software department managers are unaware that fairly standard organization and project management techniques can be applied to a reuse organization, perhaps with some modification. For example, in several unsuccessful reuse attempts, once a reuse directive was issued and a library created, managers turned to other matters. But by not providing ongoing management leadership to maintain momentum, to resolve conflicts and to ensure that business goals were being met, these efforts failed. On the other hand, many of the decision criteria and trade-offs for a reuse business are different from the intuition that software managers have gained from their experience with previously independent projects. For example, the kind of conflicts that arise, the issues to be faced in legal issues, and the metrics to be used are different.

- The metrics needed to manage the reuse business are more complex. While advanced companies are doing fairly well at measuring traditional software engineering projects, using metrics to run a reuse business is something new that management needs to think about. For example, "How is reuse to be measured?", "How is a reuse measurement to be used to track progress and to estimate costs and time?", and "What other measures should be used?"

- The reuse business will be considerably larger than one-of-a-kind projects, with many interacting projects. Decisions involve more functions, different kinds of jobs, and more managers. The scale of many of the issues often requires the involvement of higher level management for resolution.

- Significant cultural change is needed and will not happen overnight. Most engineers and project managers are unfamiliar with the trade-offs and behavior expected in a reuse business. Most engineers do not learn about systematic reuse or architecture in their normal academic training. Most traditional projects are not accustomed to sharing, or depending on each other. Just-in-time education and ongoing senior management leadership are needed to make such cultural changes.

In this chapter we highlight these management issues, and provide several reuse-oriented guidelines and metrics that managers need.

14.1.1 Ensuring progress towards business goals

The primary function of ongoing reuse business management is to monitor the progress of the roll-out plans towards achieving the business goals, and to adjust expectations and schedule to meet business and organizational realities. Achieving the business goals requires both reuse benefits such as improved costs and time to market, and architecture benefits such as robustness and better control of system evolution.

Day-to-day direction and periodic adjustment of reuse-oriented project management requires focused attention from the **SEB Manager** and sometimes also the **Owners Of The Reuse Business**.

The layered system developed by **Application Family Engineering** may need periodic adjustment. This involves monitoring the application and component system portfolio, and the set of **Component System Engineering** and **Application System Engineering** processes.

Subsequent changes in requirements and customer needs, unexpected project slippage, and third-party vendor delays may result in periodic adjustment of the portfolio and the roll-out plan and schedule. Ideally, we would like to rely only on known working products from third-party vendors, not future products. Likewise, we might prefer to wait until all needed component systems are ready before starting the application systems. But in practice this is not always feasible. Sometimes we must use alpha or beta versions as a base to develop new products to hit a market window. For example, for the next release of Microsoft VB or NT.

Unexpected changes in time-to-market pressures and in requirements increase management work. Processes must execute concurrently. More conflicts will need resolution. We may start work with a release date in mind, but need to adjust to subsequent releases, deal with delays and some changes in features, and so on. The **Software Engineering Business Manager** together with the **Lead Architect** and **Process Leader**s determine engineering trade-offs: time to market vs. functionality vs. quality level.

14.1.2 Ensuring a successful transition

Managers must monitor the transition to the reuse business processes and organization at periodic intervals. They must ensure that the activities covered in Chapter 13 proceed on course. Clear milestones and effective metrics help make problems visible. When problems arise, prompt action must be taken. As the roll-out proceeds, the **SEB Manager** must anticipate and execute strategic changes such as timely changes in architecture, organization, and processes. Several of the issues that RSEB managers will have to confront arise early, and can be dealt with as part of the initial transition. Other issues will require ongoing attention as needs are discovered or become important. Some of these can be anticipated and contingency plans developed. For the others, new plans must be developed to deal with them.

14.1.3 Coordinating multiple teams

By structuring the processes and organization around the layered architecture and component systems as described in Chapter 13, many detailed reuse-oriented management tasks will usually be handled automatically by the processes or by **Process Leader**s who ensure the smooth execution of the processes. Nevertheless, more coordination between projects is required with reuse. This involves several managers, such as the **Process Leader**s, the **Process Owner**s and the **SEB Manager**.

A large-scale reuse program links together many application system engineering projects that would otherwise have been independent. **CSE** projects are now defined as creating component systems that **ASE** projects might use. This increases the opportunity for conflicting objectives between teams, increases the need for clear and continuous communication across the organization, and requires greater care in determining the optimal trade-offs of reuse levels, quality, and time-to-market goals.

The timely resolution of conflicts over resources and incompatible system requirements is very important. While the layered system architecture and well-defined interfaces should minimize surprises, it is inevitable that changing requirements and incremental development will periodically result in less favored surprises that lead to conflict.

SEB Managers have to be actively involved in the problem of sorting out what the architecture ought to be, what components can be built, placating the application people while this is being done, and so forth. The workers involved in **AFE** are trying to capture requirements of the whole field in order to set out an architecture. The component engineers are trying to devise components that meet certain requirements and also fit into the architecture. The application engineers have a threefold task: to fit components, architecture, and unique application requirements into a working whole.

14.2 Measurement is key to managing the reuse business

Detailed measurement is crucial to ensure that overall reuse business goals are met. The **SEB Manager** needs to establish a coherent measurement program to help the various managers assess how well the reuse business is meeting its various goals. Over the years, a variety of measurements have been used to gauge, manage, and predict progress in a reuse program (Poulin, 1996; Malan and Wentzel, 1993; Favaro, 1996).

Some overall measurements are directed at the **Owners Of The Reuse Business** or the **SEB Manager** to track overall performance of the resuse business and progress towards business goals. Some are used by the **SEB Manager**, **Process Owner**s, and **Resource Manager**s to improve the process and organization. Others are used by **Process Leader**s and **Process Owner**s to monitor the progress of individual processes and quality of workproducts.

As Pfleeger (1996) points out, different levels of management and engineers need different types of results. Some managers need convincing "return on investment" measures (ROI), while others are more convinced by an inspiring vision and feasible plan to start. Engineers typically need answers to "How to do it for specific component systems or application systems?" Immediate supervisors, **Process Leader**s, and **Resource Owner**s need to know "How is our project doing?"' and "How much are we doing?" Middle managers, usually the **Process Owner**s, need answers to "Are we doing it efficiently?", "Do we need to improve the process?", while executive managers, the **Owners Of The Reuse Business** and the **SEB Manager**, are concerned with strategy and need answers to "Are we investing the right amount?" and "Will we get the expected long-term benefits?"

Several measurements and estimators are used to gauge resue business progress, support investment decisions, and ensure that the right resources are applied to appropriate parts of the organization. Other measurements are used to support quality and process improvement efforts. The detailed measurements must be designed to expose the key drivers for the chosen business goals. For example:

- Estimates of customer demand are needed to adjust the size and shape of application families and thus to plan the component system portfolio and best roll-out plan. Based on the expected needs and training time, management needs to develop revised hiring and training plans, and so on.

- If time to market is the key business goal, then various architectural and reuse factors that influence time to market must be identified, measured, and tracked. This might include reuse levels, time spent in each step of application engineering, and the number of times an expected component is not ready.

- If improving cost or productivity is the key business issue, then metrics must expose overall and detailed cost drivers, and the number of times a component is developed but not used as heavily as expected.

- If the ability to easily create a larger variety of applications is a key goal, then measures of how easy it is to specialize components and how many ways components can be combined will be useful.

Pfleeger (1996) explains how crucial an effective reuse measurement program is to clarifying and indeed, establishing, the true reuse and business goals of an organization. Her article is a "must read" for managers leading a reuse business.

She provides crucial guidelines and cautions in setting up a reuse measurement program. She explains issues related to setting expectations, and the importance of establishing realistic, measurable reuse goals. Goals should be clearly expressed in priority order. Reuse measurements must clearly reflect these goals and also the different organizational viewpoints that lead to the goals. Participants need this context to understand and analyze progress to the goals. Effective measurement needs to be tied to the detailed process as well as the business needs. Measurements need to be fully integrated into daily activities.

Management should clearly define what is meant by reuse to different parts of the organization, and how to match reuse measurements to business goals of the organization. Reuse measurements must take into account political and organizational realities.

Unresolved stakeholder issues about loss of control or creativity can ultimately block progress. Misunderstandings about the goals and the reuse measurements will lead to significant conflicts later. To avoid conflicts between different parts of the organization, she stresses how important it is to match the reuse measurements to include the different points of view of all participants (particularly the managers) and to the specific reuse process.

For example, the goal "improve productivity" could be interpreted differently by **Application System Engineering** and **Component System Engineering**. This will yield conflicting results. Summing up, the business goals apply to the RSEB as a whole, and need to be broken into compatible sub-goals for the different organizations.

Example

If the XYB is optimizing for time to market, then a key business goal is time to market for application systems. This means that if **ASE** is building a new **Invoicing** system, they need to write the least amount of new software they can. To do this, they need to achieve high levels of reuse, using as many of the components from the **Account Management** and other component systems as possible. To do this, these component systems have to be available, and easy to use. Also, an **ASE** team need to be as efficient as they can in selecting and specializing components. So an **ASE Process Owner** needs to be using longer-term measures of time to market, and shorter-term estimates of reuse levels, component selection, and adaptation time, some sort of requirements mismatch measure, and overall process efficiency.

The **CSE** process helps the **ASE** process succeed, usually not by working faster, but by providing as large a variety of easy to reuse and easy to specialize components as possible. In addition to the **Account Management** component system, they will perhaps create a new facade to the **Bank Customer Management** component system, and develop a specialized **Invoice Management** component system using a new generator. It is critical that a **CSE** team not be judged primarily on how quickly they produce component systems. It is more important to measure how much the design and packaging of their component systems and use of variability mechanisms enable an **ASE** team to work more quickly.

14.2.1 Choosing the measurement goals

When setting up a measurement program we must decide what kind of metrics, or what changes in current metrics, are needed in order to successfully manage a reuse business at the hands-on level. Most of the metrics that software engineering managers use today are aimed at a standalone project group, which does its own estimating, requirements capture, architecting, analysis, design, implementation, and testing.

But a reuse business divides these functions between at least four teams: **Application Family Engineering**, **Application System Engineering**, **Component System Support**, and **Component System Engineering**. Questions to be answered include: Who's going to keep what metrics? Which group is going to use them for what? How can you spread metrics which were designed to measure one project performed by one organization over many projects divided between multiple kinds of organization units?

Reuse measurements are used for several fundamental functions:

- To report results to fund-allocating levels of management, such as the **Owners Of The Reuse Business** or **SEB Manager**. These levels are usually not particularly conversant with software metrics as such. They want measurements presented in their accustomed financial terms, things like return on investment, cost center profit and loss, amount of investment required per time period, and estimated point of crossover into the black. These measures are largely the responsibility of the accounting department. The software department will help on how to treat various details. To the extent that these measurements are favorable, executives are willing to continue funding the reuse business.

- To maintain metrics that enable the immediate management of the reuse business to manage it at all. Different metrics will be needed for different levels of management. If the metrics are well chosen and kept up, one hopes they can manage the software function better. Software managers would like to have metrics that enable them to carry out three important duties: to estimate the effort, schedule time, and defect rate of a forthcoming project; to control the execution of that project; to identify problems as a first step toward correcting them. These are the essential purposes of the major software metrics.

- To provide measures to enable continuous process improvement: to evaluate process improvement from year to year; to compare project teams, not for merit review purposes, but to focus appropriate aid on poorly functioning teams.

To set up an effective measurement program for the reuse business, the **Owners Of The Reuse Business** should decide on which (one or more) business goals to improve. The **SEB Manager** and the **Process Owner**s then decide on which high-level measures most directly indicate progress to these goals.

14.2.2 Customizing measurement for the reuse business

Just as the RSEB architecture, process, and organization models need to be customized to the specific business and organization situation, so too must the measurements be adapted to the specific business goals, architecture, processes, and organization. Poulin (1996), Karlsson (1995), and Pfleeger (1996) discuss some of the issues to be faced in setting up a reuse measurement program.

In the early days of software engineering and reuse measurement, the goal was to find a few standard measurements that all projects could use. Later on, techniques such as Basili's Goal-Question-Metric (GQM) (Basili, 1984) approach have been used to develop optimized and customized metrics for any particular measure. In this approach, we start from the goals and decide on the kinds of questions to answer. Then we devise measures to help answer these questions, ensuring that each measure can be interpreted and presented appropriately to different audiences to make sure the reuse issues are visible.

Measurements are used to determine how the overall program is doing and how well it has met the business objectives by monitoring key business goals of interest to the **SEB Manager** and **Owners Of The Reuse Business**. These measures answer management and prediction questions that the **SEB Manager**, the **Process Leader**s and **Resource Owner**s face as they run a reuse business. Poulin *et al.* (1993) provide a compelling discussion of how such measurements are used to make a business case for reuse.

Some of the measures needed to monitor and control projects to meet business goals can only be obtained late in the project. In order to connect these longer-term measures to shorter-term factors that can be controlled as early as possible, estimation formulas are used (Putnam and Myers, 1996). The longer-term measures include overall costs, time to market, worker effort, and quality of delivered applications. Shorter-term measures include application system size and reuse level, and component size and complexity.

For example, early measures of code size or design complexity are often good predictors of later quality measures, such as defect density. Economic models are used to relate various measures of software size and complexity to resulting cost, team size, and time.

Reuse metrics are different from traditional software engineering metrics. Three points are fairly clear. First, **Component System Engineering** is a project-oriented activity and all the project-oriented metrics are more or less applicable, but there are two provisos. First, since it can take two to three times as much effort and time to develop a reusable component as a project-oriented component, the numbers by which managers evaluate a CSE are going to be different from the established numbers. Second, the defect rate is going to be less, and so application systems will require less maintenance, again suggesting that standard numbers need to change. Furthermore, additional effort will be directed at ensuring components will become defect free, increasing these costs.

The second point is that **Application System Engineering** is also a project-oriented activity and, again, the project-oriented metrics are more or less applicable. In this case, though, their overall metrics are going to be much better, because they are reusing component systems. The theoretical "better" is going to be reduced by some amount by the time spent learning the overall architecture, interface practices, and component systems available.

The third point is that the team for **Application Family Engineering** and the team for **Component Support** are not project-oriented, so traditional project-type metrics will not be of much use. How can their work be measured? For example, new metrics will be needed to assess how robust the architecture is, in terms of how much changing requirements require changes in architecture.

14.2.3 Types of measures to consider

While the exact measures to use should be developed using the GQM method as discussed above, some standard measures have been found to be useful starting points.

At the minimum, collect the recommended SEI software engineering baseline metrics (SEI, 1992), including sizes of various workproducts, staff hours expended, calendar days spent, and software problems and defects detected and fixed.

Direct measures of workproducts are determined by examining or counting items in the workproduct, such as readability, size, or complexity. Indirect measures of the workproduct are process measures that can be associated closely with producing the workproduct, such as time or cost to produce it, or resulting defect density, or changes from a previous version. Indirect measures can typically only be collected when development is done, and the workproduct is in use. Often, we would like estimators of these indirect measures in terms of the direct measures. For example, potential defect density estimators should be expressed in terms of size and complexity. Likewise, an estimator for the development cost could be expressed in terms of size.

Other process metrics include measures of worker productivity, overall process effectiveness in terms of time, cost and rate defects found, and so on.

If a library or repository is used, it is convenient to monitor frequency of access, the size of repository, overall certification costs, and the quality and quantity of components.

Some examples of important architecture, application, and component system measures include:

- Architecture measures: stability, extendability.

- Component system measures: component size, component system size, facade complexity, facade and component system cohesion, facade and component usage level, quality, cost of customizing component systems, difficulties in integrating components.

- Application system measures: reuse level, quality, defect levels and causes, error profiles of old and new code, cost and losses of changing application system requirements to match component systems.

14.2.4 Measuring and estimating size and reuse

Measures (or estimates) of software size and amounts of reuse are used both for tracking the progress of projects directly, and within other estimating formulas to predict and analyze cost, time, effort, or quality. Experience shows that estimators based on a well-chosen metric for size are quite effective in predicting other quantities such as overall and detailed cost, time, effort, defects; for example, COCOMO (Boehm, 1981; Boehm and Papaccio, 1988). Estimated values can be used as early predictors to make decisions that are later validated as more detailed measures are obtained.

Estimating the size of, and reuse in, an application system or component system may seem like a straightforward matter, by simply counting and comparing the lines of code. But for effective management of the reuse business, we must also determine the size and amounts of reuse in non-code components, such as use case models and design models, or other workproducts, such as documents.

Size is some measure of the amount of text or function within a workproduct.

We also usually need to estimate the amount of resulting code reuse and implementation costs while still working on analysis and design.

Many companies have ongoing software measurement programs, and have already confronted the issues of how to measure software size, for example by using the source code counting method recommended by the SEI (Park, 1992). Sometimes they estimate the size of non-code workproducts in terms of equivalent lines of code, or use function points.

Function points are popular as a standard measure of software size because they can be usefully estimated early from requirements and designs. Function points can be defined in terms of measures that do not depend on the final implementation languages. They have been shown to provide a good predictor of later code size (Jones, 1995). One function point typically results in between 50 and 300 lines of code, depending on implementation language.

Some work at Rational has been directed at developing a use-case points measure, similar to function points. These could be used to estimate the size of an application system based on the number and complexity of actors and use cases (Karner, 1993). When these measures and estimators have been validated, they could also be used like function points to estimate cost and effort for the overall project, and later design and code size.

However, companies will need to revisit these decisions on software size for the reuse business. As Poulin indicates, great care has to be taken in deciding what to count as reuse (Poulin *et al.*, 1993; Poulin, 1996). Some things are reused as-is, some are adapted, some are specialized, and some software is just carried over and should not be counted as reuse. Special care has to be taken when using a variability mechanism, such as inheritance, templates, or generators. For example, should one count the generated or specialized code, should one develop an estimator of effective size based on a count of the class or template size, or should one estimate a cost saving, based on the actual work to reuse the component?

The amount of reuse is typically reported in terms of a reuse level or reuse percentage, **R**.

> The **reuse level**, **R**, is defined as the ratio of "size of workproducts derived from reusable component systems" to "total application system size."

Reuse level is used both to monitor reuse and to estimate how much reuse will impact resulting cost, time, or quality measures.

Quality typically goes up because it is easier to amortize the cost of extra testing and inspections, and this can be used to develop a simple estimate of quality improvement in a system with a given reuse level, **R**.

Measures of software *complexity*, determined from a combination of size and structural complexity, can be used to estimate subsequent defect density, error-proneness, and maintainability.

Cohesion and *coupling* measures determine how coherent and independent a component or component system is from other components. These measures relate to the cost of integrating the component, and also to its maintainability.

As an example, Caldiera and Basili (1991) have used a variety of code size and complexity measures to analyze existing applications to identify potentially reusable components that can be subsequently extracted and reengineered. These measures are closely related to the coherence and maintainability of well-designed components.

As another example, given a use case model of a component system, we might use function point and use case point measures to estimate how well the component system will contribute towards business goals. Starting from the component use case models we sketch use case models of future application systems. We then estimate the reuse level, and from there the overall size, development time, and effort. These can then be used to estimate the expected time to market, productivity, and ability to meet new business opportunities.

The key lesson is that each reuse business must agree on a standard way of measuring software size and reuse level. They should use these measures only to track their own progress and improvement, and as input to compatible estimators. These measures should not be used to directly compare one reuse business with another.

14.3 Economic models and reuse investment decisions

In some situations, the decision to become a reuse business is a strategic business decision. As with the Ericsson AXE system and the critical role of architected reuse, the organization simply had to change to be able to build the AXE at all. In other situations, the decision to become a reuse business is part of a goal to decrease time to market or to save money.

Reuse level measures are then used to develop models for estimating the longer-term cost and time savings due to reuse. This helps motivate a move to a reuse business and also to make appropriate investment decisions and trade-offs, related directly to the overall business goals.

To achieve this goal, several models are used to estimate overall quality, cost and time measures in terms of specific process and application and component system measures, such as reuse levels, component size, and complexity.

Favaro (1996) suggests that economic models and investment analyses be arranged in three steps:

1   *Measurement*
    Define and collect raw data, such as size, reuse level, and time spent.

2   Cost/Benefit *Estimation*
    Relate these measurements to each other and to other interesting quantities using models that convert that raw data into effort, cost, or time. For example, a formula that relates cost savings to reuse levels.

3   Reuse *Investment Analysis*
    Analyze the measurements and estimates to determine how the reuse business is doing, and what corrections might be needed.

As Favaro notes, explicitly separating these steps allows one to reason about each activity separately and compare approaches to that step. Some **SEB Manager**s measure well, but make the wrong estimates from their measurements. Other **SEB Manager**s are great at cost estimation, but then draw the wrong conclusions about what it implies in terms of investment analyses.

14.3.1 Paying for reuse

Despite the many strategic and long-term benefits of reuse, a key question to be answered is how and when to recoup the extra costs of component engineering, architecture, and support.

Developing reusable software typically costs more and takes more time than development for one-shot use. Someone has to pay the extra initial costs and account for the extra time spent. Depending on languages and situation, different authors report that developing reusable components costs from 1.0 to 2.5 relative to the cost of developing ordinary software, and also will take correspondingly more time (Poulin, 1996).

The extra initial funding needed to start up the reuse business and create architecture and component systems is expected to be repaid from the later benefits. It is important to have an agreed expectation of the time frame within which the payback will occur, and how.

In the long term, running a reuse business should be a better investment than not running a reuse business. Some benefits will appear early, others later. For example, by using the architecture and reusable component systems, we will have fewer distinct copies of similar software systems to deal with. This will soon reduce the complexity and cost of looking at and maintaining many copies of almost the same piece of software.

The exact payback time is very much dependent on the organization and the business goals that motivated reuse. Usually the additional costs can be recovered within several reuses of a component, but this depends greatly on the type of software being developed, and the explicit business purpose for selecting reuse. If time to market is the goal, then payback appears in terms of greater profits, sooner, not necessarily in reduced costs. One rule of thumb suggests that the payback of the extra effort to develop a component will only start to occur after three uses of a component, or three application engineering cycles. The exact payback period will of course depend on the number of potential reusers of a component, and the specific costs to create, reuse, and maintain the components and the related component systems.

Furthermore, reuse shifts several costs and the time required to do the job from application engineers to component engineers and architects, and this has to be accounted for. The costs can be allocated to different parts of the organization, and may be centralized, or spread in various ways between different application system and component engineering projects. Existing organization accounting procedures may not be able to handle this cost allocation effectively.

There are essentially two approaches. Either the reuse business pays the extra cost of **Component System Engineering** as "overhead," or individual **Application System**

Engineering projects pay some "transfer" cost for the reused components to receive benefits. In either case, an estimate needs to be made of the anticipated costs, and what percentage to charge. Directly allocating costs to application system engineering works best in steady state when there are many available components and costs and benefits are well understood by all. This strategy works less well when initially building up the set of component systems.

In the "overhead" approach, the **SEB Manager** makes funds available to pay for the extra cost of **CSE**, **AFE**, and **Component Support**. The extra cost of **CSE** is added as an overhead charge into the budgets of all **ASE** projects, whether they actually reuse the components or not. A useful comparison can be made with the role of Quality Assurance (QA) in an organization. Both reuse and QA increase development effort and expense. Both reuse and QA appear to lower short-term productivity. The agreed benefits of both reuse and QA are a long-term increase in quality, and hopefully also in productivity. In the case of QA, the approach usually taken has been to establish, by management directive, a separate QA activity which is enforced by the organization as a matter of policy. Similar management backing is needed for the reuse business.

ASE process leaders and resource managers are generally under heavy time and cost pressure to deliver their application systems. They usually will not respond favorably to a request to invest in the reusable component system. A management-imposed "forced" overhead tax may be the only way to get started. It is necessary to convince **ASE** project managers that their reuse-oriented activities will pay off from the inside. The only way to do this is to ensure that the benefits accrue directly to them.

In the "transfer" approach, **ASE** process leaders will need to be shown why it is in their interest to fund a portion of the **CSE**, with confidence of recovering the costs as they go. Logically it would be better to use transfer prices rather than overhead distribution, because it then becomes important for the reuse business to ensure and show a favorable cost–benefit trade-off. Transfer prices are like income taxes; as a taxpayer you feel them, and this can encourage thoughtful financial analysis and trade-offs.

14.3.2 Economic models

Models for software reuse economics try to help us answer the question, "When is it worthwhile to incorporate reusable components into a development and when is custom development without reuse preferable?" These models work closely with lower-level workproduct metrics, which determine the characteristics of components and systems, and process metrics, which measure time, cost, and rate of change. These lower-level metrics become the inputs to the economic models (Favaro, 1996).

Most existing software engineering economic models need to be adjusted to include reuse, and customized to each specific reuse business. Several authors have modified the cost models (such as COCOMO (Boehm, 1988)) that are today used to estimate time and effort and for the development both of components and of applications using components (Malan, 1993; Malan and Wentzel, 1993; Poulin, 1996). These models range from simple but effective spreadsheet models used at HP, IBM, and the Software Productivity Consortium (Gaffney, 1989, 1992) to quite complex estimators using Net Present Value

(NPV) and other factors (Lim, 1994; Malan, 1993) to account for the time value of money and uncertainty in exactly which applications will be developed when.

Because high levels of reuse can reduce the overall cost and time to deliver applications, the extra funding and time can be directed to several alternative projects. The money can be reinvested to produce more components, or used for additional R&D. As Malan and Wentzel (1993) show, releasing some application systems early to the market can increase market share and increase profits dramatically.

Poulin's (1996) book on reuse measurement provides the most comprehensive treatment of all of the issues – what to measure, how to measure, how to establish a reuse metrics program, and how to relate these measurements to economic benefits.

In an early work, Gaffney and Durek (1989) focused on the relationships between **Component System Engineering** costs and overall **Application System Engineering** costs and the number of expected reuses of a component. This study amortized the costs of reuse across many projects, and thereby predicted the number of reuses needed to achieve break-even (positive ROI). Malan and Wentzel (1993) and Poulin (1996) extend the simple Gaffney model to account for maintenance costs, and for the time value of money.

14.3.3 Estimating reuse costs

We will now illustrate how to use a simplified reuse cost and effort model, essentially rephrasing Gaffney and Durek's (1989) analysis and using Poulin's (1996) recommendations for reuse measurement.

We start by imagining we are developing typical application systems without reuse, written in C, C++, Visual Basic, Java, or some other language. The cost of developing a typical application system is:

$$C_{\text{no-reuse}} = \text{Cost of developing typical system without reuse}$$

Now with reuse, we derive some portion, **R**, of the software from a set of component systems.

$$\text{Reuse level, } R = \frac{\text{Total size of reused components}}{\text{Size of application system}}$$

As indicated above, we might measure the software size in function points (FP) or lines of code.

This usually costs less than developing it from scratch.

$$F_{\text{use}} = \text{Relative cost to reuse a component}$$

typically 0.10–0.25, use 0.2 as default.

Now the cost to develop an application system with reuse has two parts. One is the $(1 - R)$ part, developed without reuse at the normal cost. The other is the R part, developed with reuse, at a lower cost. We assume we can simply estimate the costs separately and add.

$$C_{\text{part-with-reuse}} = C_{\text{no-reuse}} * (R * F_{\text{use}})$$
$$C_{\text{part-with-no-reuse}} = C_{\text{no-reuse}} * (1 - R)$$

So the total cost with reuse becomes

$$C_{\text{with-reuse}} = C_{\text{part-with-reuse}} + C_{\text{part-with-no-reuse}}$$
$$C_{\text{with-reuse}} = C_{\text{no-reuse}} * (R * F_{\text{use}} + (1 - R))$$

Example

With $R = 50\%$ and $F_{\text{use}} = 0.2$, the cost to develop with reuse is 60% of the cost of developing an application system without reuse.

Then the cost saving due to reuse is:

$$C_{\text{saved}} = C_{\text{no-reuse}} - C_{\text{with-reuse}}$$
$$= C_{\text{no-reuse}} * (1 - (R * F_{\text{use}} + (1 - R)))$$
$$= C_{\text{no-reuse}} * R * (1 - F_{\text{use}})$$

The relative development cost–benefit (ROI) due to reuse of components is then estimated to be

$$ROI_{\text{saved}} = \frac{C_{\text{saved}}}{C_{\text{no-reuse}}} = R * (1 - F_{\text{use}})$$

Example

With $R = 50\%$ and $F_{\text{use}} = 0.2$, ROI_{saved} is 40%.

Now we account for the cost of developing the set of component systems. It typically costs more to design, implement, test, and document a component system for reuse. The more complex the technology, the more it costs.

$$F_{\text{create}} = \text{Relative cost to create and manage a reusable component system}$$

For simplicity, we assume that all of the developed component systems are used in the reuse part, **R** percent, of any application system. Then the cost to develop the component systems is

$$C_{\text{component-systems}} = \text{Cost to develop enough component systems for } \mathbf{R} \text{ percent}$$
$$= \mathbf{R} * \mathbf{F}_{\text{create}} * \mathbf{C}_{\text{no-reuse}}$$

Since $\mathbf{F}_{\text{create}}$ is typically much greater than $\mathbf{F}_{\text{use}}$, we must reuse each component and component system several times in several application systems, to make this worthwhile from a cost perspective. Different authors suggest different ranges for $\mathbf{F}_{\text{create}}$ and $\mathbf{F}_{\text{use}}$. Values depend on the specific languages, complexity of the problem area, worker experience, and process followed. Poulin (1996) gives about a dozen examples and suggests default values of $\mathbf{F}_{\text{create}} = 1.5$, ranging from 1–2.5, and $\mathbf{F}_{\text{use}} = 0.2$, ranging from 0.03–0.4.

If there are **n** application systems in the family, the cost saving for the application system family is:

$$C_{\text{family-saved}} = \mathbf{n} * \mathbf{C}_{\text{saved}} - \mathbf{C}_{\text{component-systems}}$$
$$= \mathbf{C}_{\text{no-reuse}} * (\mathbf{n} * \mathbf{R} * (1 - \mathbf{F}_{\text{use}}) - \mathbf{R} * \mathbf{F}_{\text{create}})$$

The return on the investment in creating the set of components is then

$$\mathbf{ROI} = \frac{\mathbf{C}_{\text{family-saved}}}{\mathbf{C}_{\text{component-systems}}}$$
$$= \frac{(\mathbf{n} * \mathbf{R} * (1 - \mathbf{F}_{\text{use}}) - \mathbf{R} * \mathbf{F}_{\text{create}})}{\mathbf{R} * \mathbf{F}_{\text{create}}}$$
$$= \frac{(\mathbf{n} * (1 - \mathbf{F}_{\text{use}}) - \mathbf{F}_{\text{create}})}{\mathbf{F}_{\text{create}}}$$

Example

With $\mathbf{F}_{\text{use}} = 0.2$ and $\mathbf{F}_{\text{create}} = 1.5$, we get

$$\mathbf{ROI} = \frac{(\mathbf{n} * 0.8 - 1.5)}{1.5}$$

with breakeven at **n** > 2.

A more complete analysis would allow for a component system "library" containing more component systems than we expect to reuse for any particular application system. This would add a "library utilization factor" to the above equations. We could also allow for some components being more heavily reused than others.

ROI is actually rather ill-defined, meaning many things to many people (Favaro, 1996). We have used what Favaro calls "Benefit/Cost Ratio" or "Profitability Index."

There are several other standard financial estimators that are of interest, such as Net Present Value (NPV), Payback, Book Rate of Return ("depreciation") and Internal Rate of Return. Each helps managers make a different kind of investment decision (Favaro, 1996; Poulin, 1996).

The **SEB Manager** needs to decide how to use these measures in the reuse business decision process. For example, what does an ROI of 3.3 mean? Is it good, bad, or indifferent? Is a 150% ROI good? Better than 125% for a different component? But what if that different component is gigantic and thus the ROI is bigger in absolute terms?

For example, the savings from a reuse investment today may only pay off several years hence. But $1,000 saving this year is not the same as a $1,000 saving next year. At the very least, we could get bank interest on the saved money, or use it for some other purpose sooner. Net Present Value accounts for this cost of money by discounting future savings by some interest rate, **i**. A cost or saving **C** obtained in year **y** becomes effectively

$$C_{today} = \frac{C}{(1+i)^y}$$

to estimate today's value of this saving.

As a more graphic example, consider the scenario shown in Figure 14.1. A set of component systems, CS_1, CS_2, and CS_3, are built over a span of three years, and used to develop an increasing number of application systems, AS_1 to AS_9.... For this scenario, we imagine releasing component systems in one-year increments. In the first year, we start the architecture and develop the first set, CS_1, of component systems. These are reused completely at a reuse level of about 25% to build the first two application systems,

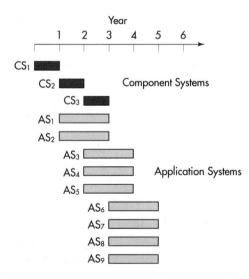

Figure 14.1 *Several years of component system creation and application system development. The maintenance "tail" in later years is not shown.*

AS_1 and AS_2, in the second and third years. In the second year, we also complete additional component systems, CS_2, to yield a reuse level of about 50% to the three application systems, AS_3, AS_4, and AS_5, started in the third year. Finally, in the third year we complete a final set of component systems, CS_3, for a maximum reuse level of about 75%, used in the last four application systems, $AS_6, \ldots AS_9$, started in the fourth year.

For simplicity, we only count a component system if it is complete before the reusing application system starts being developed. In practice, we could start to reuse use case components in the application systems before the design and implementation of the component systems is complete. There is some additional risk with this, but this might help reduce time to market and costs. Note that when there are only a few application systems that depend on a particular component system, it is possible to develop the component systems largely in parallel with the application systems that reuse them. But later, as more application systems come to depend on the component systems, the component systems have to be developed before the application systems, which then reuse from the component systems and suggest improvements on the component systems, and so on.

If this scenario is used with the above estimators, we get the costs and benefits shown in Figure 14.2. We use $F_{use} = 0.25$ and $F_{create} = 2.5$. Component system engineering costs show up in the first three years, and ongoing maintenance and support costs in subsequent years. Application system engineering savings start showing up in year two, growing in later years as more component systems become available.

As shown in Figure 14.3, a net annual benefit shows up in the third year, and the program begins to show a profit by the fourth year. The decline in benefits in years five and six is due to NPV effects and decay in the usefulness of component systems over time.

Estimation gets even more complex if we take into account the fact that incremental development of component systems and application systems happens over time as shown in Figure 14.2. We then have to add separate costs and saving for each year.

The **Software Engineering Business Manager** together with the **Lead Architect** has to make decisions on how much resource to invest in construction of component systems, especially in anticipation of upcoming needs.

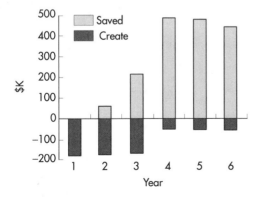

Figure 14.2 *Component system creation costs in the first three years and support in later years are followed by increasing application system savings in years two to five.*

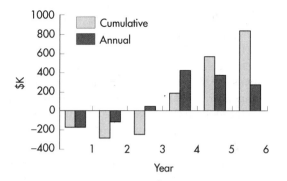

Figure 14.3 *In the first three years, the overall costs of creation and support outweigh the benefits, but in later years the benefits outweigh the costs.*

14.3.4 Estimating time and effort

We can use similar size estimates as input to more complex cost, effort, and time estimators, such as COCOMO (Boehm, 1988, 1994), or Capers Jones (1996) function point estimators. These estimators can be used to relate size and reuse level measures more accurately to estimated project time, costs, and staff size.

Most estimators for time, staff, and quality have the form:

$$\text{Estimated quantity} = C_0 S_0{}^{e_0} + C_1 S_1{}^{e_1} + C_2 S_2{}^{e_2} + \ldots + C_n S_n{}^{e_n}$$

For each estimator, the number of terms, n, the coefficients, C_i and the exponents, e_i, are different, and should be calibrated to the particular situation. S_i is an estimated, measured, or effective size measure, such as lines of code or function points. These can also be combined with Raleigh staffing curves to estimate staff loading across different project phases (Boehm, 1981; Putnam and Myers, 1996). "Standard" values of the coefficients and exponents are provided as a starting point when no experience base is available.

For example, the Basic COCOMO estimators (Boehm, 1981) have the single term form:

$$\text{Development effort, } MM_D = 2.4(KDSI)^{1.05} \quad \text{in person-months}$$

where **KDSI** is delivered system size in 1000s of lines of source instructions, and

$$\text{Development time} = 2.5(MM_D)^{0.38} \quad \text{in months}$$

More precise Intermediate COCOMO estimators adjust C_i and e_i for the complexity of the problem, the target language, the style of development, and the skill and experience of the developers. For more accurate estimates, the specific C_i and e_i and way of computing size, S_i, should also be calibrated to the specific architecture, process, organization, previous metrics baselines, and ongoing experience established in the specific reuse business.

COCOMO partially accounts for maintenance and reuse by defining an effective size, **EKDSI**, to use instead of the delivered size, as some fraction of the actual delivered size

EKDSI = KDSI $*$ AAF

where **AAF** is an adaptation adjustment factor that estimates how much adaptation there was during design, coding, and integration, using factors similar to **R** and F_{use} in spirit.

Notice that the development cost and time are non-linear functions of **EKDSI**, and hence of **R** and F_{use}. This leads to a more complex expression than the simple Gafney and Durek formula for combining costs. Poulin (1996) describes yet another variation of COCOMO due to Balda and Gustafson, which uses three COCOMO-like terms to account for different costs of developing unique code, reused code, and component code. Boehm is developing and validating a new COCOMO 2.0 model (Boehm, 1994), to better account for the costs and benefits of both reuse and architecture.

Capers Jones (1996) provides several simple "back of the envelope" estimators. Using function points (**F**) for software size, the estimates for effort, time, and other costs are found to be relatively independent of the implementation language, though the margin of error for these estimators is higher than more precise (and more complex) estimators:

Development time $= F^{0.4}$ months
Development staff $= F/150$ people (including managers, testers, documenters)
Development effort $= F^{1.4}/150$ person-months
Defect potential $= F^{1.25}$

where defect potential is total life cycle errors in four deliverables, requirements, design, coding, and user documentation. Jones (1995) suggests using a starting estimate of 1 function point $= 60–170$ lines of C code, with a default of 128 non-commented source code statements. For C++ he suggests 30–125, with a suggested default of 53 lines per function point.

While all such estimators summarize experience gained over many different projects of different size, Jones warns us to use these simple estimates cautiously. The rules "are known to have a high margin of error." He warns that "simple rules of thumb are not accurate, and should not be used for contracts, bids, or other serious business purposes." However, such simple rules of thumb are easy to use and can provide a "sanity check" of estimates produced by other, more rigorous methods (Jones, 1996a).

We use these simplified formulas to illustrate how to estimate the consequences of reuse on schedule, quality, effort, and staff. The more complex estimators give similar results.

Example

Consider a 100 function point subsystem, to be implemented in C. We get the following very rough estimates:

Size	= 6000–17 000 lines of C
Development time	= 6.3 calendar months
Development staff	= 0.67 person
Development effort	= 4.2 person-months
Development cost	= $42k, if each person-month costs $10k

Then for a typical 1000 function point application system, without reuse:

Size	= 60 000–170 000 lines of C
Development time	= 15.8 calendar months
Development staff	= 6.7 people
Development effort	= 106 person-months
Development cost	= $1.06M

Note that the non-linearity of the estimation formulas means that the various estimates, such as cost, for the application system is NOT 10 $*$ the equivalent estimate for the subsystem.

To account for reuse, we treat the reuse part and the non-reuse part separately. One way is to "discount" the size of the reused part to produce an effective size, like the COCOMO AAF approach. The other way is compute two separate estimates for the values of interest, and combine them for two separate costs, times, staff, and so on. We would get different results. For simplicity, we compute an estimated size, reducing the size of the reused part by some factor like F_{use}.

Example

With 50% reuse, the 1000 FP application system consists of 500 new FP and 500 reused FP.

We will use an effective $F = 575$ function points (500 new, 75 adaptation and integration).

This now yields:

Development time	= 12.7 calendar months	(saving 3.3 months)
Development staff	= 3.8 people	(saving 3 people)
Development effort	= 48.6 person-months	(saving 57.3 person-months)
Development cost	= $486k	(saving $574k)

> The overall savings would be less than $574k, since at 50% reuse, someone had to pay for at least five 100 FP components, costing between $63k and $105k apiece, perhaps for an overall cost of about $500k. Furthermore, there would be additional costs for Application Family Engineering, training and so on. This cost would be shared across **n** application systems that reuse these components.

Many factors go into the effort of creating components and integrating components into an application system, from locating suitable components all the way to their adaptation and test in the developed system. The **SEB Manager** and the **Process Owner**s are faced with estimating a value for F_{create} and F_{use}. One study shows that the effort involved in integrating a component was closely linked to the complexity of its interface, and to the amount of adaptation needed (Selby, 1989). Selby found that changing less than 10% of the code made the adaptation cost about 14% of the cost of writing the same code. Once about 12% was changed, the cost jumped dramatically to about 50% and more, comprising extra time for significant code understanding, retesting, and redocumenting.

14.4 TRA6: Continuous process improvement

Planned continuous process improvement (CPI) allow us to periodically revisit business goals, organization, process, and metrics. Measurement is a key tool for CPI. Once the initial transition is complete, the structure and processes can be tuned by collecting both appropriate measures and suggestions for improvement.

If business goals change, or if their priorities change, management will adjust funding and revise the processes to better meet these revised objectives. As improved productivity and decreased time to market begin to yield improved profits and reduced costs, this can result in further changes in goals to deliver applications faster, or additional decreases in cost to become even more competitive.

As the business goals and process change, so too will the reuse metrics probably change. Different questions will need to be asked, and will need different metrics. In particular, as the process matures or changes, more detailed questions will be created. New and different people will become an audience for some of the measures as the reuse business grows from pilot to full scale.

Because of the complexity of the processes, an analysis has to be made to determine which factors are affecting performance. We first perform a "root cause analysis" to trace each metrics slip or process defect to the place where it is introduced, or could be most effectively detected and corrected. For example, "Architects did not analyze expected trends well enough," or "**Application System Engineering** changed interfaces without discussion with the **Application Family Engineering** team," or "Requirements changed faster than expected."

We then do a priority analysis to identify the top three to five goals for improvement, ranked in terms of expected ROI (benefit/cost). We create a plan and install those changes, which might require changes in the process, in the organization, in the architecture, in the metrics, or in the training. We then re-measure and re-evaluate to see if the desired improvement was obtained. As an example, Basili describes an incremental improvement process for the Experience Factory reuse projects at Maryland and NASA SEL (Basili, 1993).

14.5 Managing people and organization

SEB Managers and **Process Owner**s must resolve periodic conflicts. **Resource Owner**s and **Process Owner**s must establish and monitor education and training programs, both for newly hired members of competence units and to keep skills up to date as the process, organization, architecture, and technology evolve. As the application system and component system portfolio and the architecture evolve, the organizational structure may need to change, too. The mix of **Component System Engineering** and **Application System Engineering** may have to change, and a separate **Component Support** team may be established. Goals and expectations placed on individual engineers and **Process Leader**s, **Process Owner**s and **Resource Owner**s will change.

   Resource Owners and **Process Leader**s need to continuously monitor motivation, promote awareness, and offer encouragement. Sometimes incentives, rewards, and performance evaluation mechanisms need to be considered and adapted to local organization culture and changing needs.

   The support group are in between the component engineering and application engineering teams; they are a new function and they will be squeezed. Only the **SEB Manager** can resolve most of these issues.

   We recommend that the transition to the reuse program should start with a well-selected RSEB pilot. Even if many others in the emerging reuse business organization are not directly involved in the pilot, it is very important to keep them informed in some way. This increases awareness and readiness for change among people who are not yet part of the reuse business. They see that other people in the organization are moving to reuse, and are succeeding.

14.5.1 Conflict resolution

The most common conflict that arises in a reuse business occurs when a component system does not supply the components expected by an **ASE** team. Either they need more or different components than were promised, or the components provided do not meet their needs. Sometimes when projects start to slip schedule due to unforeseen circumstances, such as changing requirements or technology, **ASE** might request extra resources, or demand new components or component systems. Typically, application system project managers try to get this help from component projects.

   The **Process Owner**s and perhaps even the **SEB Manager** then have to decide what to do. There are several choices:

- Delay the application system until the new functionality can be scheduled and delivered. This may upset customers, leave the **ASE** team idle, and delay revenue.

- Schedule a fast-paced **CSE** team to adapt the component system to the special need, and then merge the changes into a later release of the component system. This may delay other component systems and application systems that depend on them.

- Allow the **ASE** team to develop a work-around, and/or deliver an application system with lesser functionality than initially promised.

- In an extreme case, some **CSE** resources can be redirected to assist the urgent **ASE** projects, but unless carefully handled, doing this can set unfortunate precedents that will make it harder to manage the balance between **ASE** and **CSE** activities in the future.

Some conflicts arise because of the need to meet legal and contractual issues. If delivered application systems do not achieve certain milestones or pass certain tests by key dates, severe financial penalties may be incurred. These factors impact the priority of the above trade-offs. Also, while some contracts permit software developed on one project to be reused on others, some do not.

These and other conflicts can arise because managers and engineers at different levels or associated with different teams might interpret the same reuse business goals (such as to improve productivity) in different ways (Pfleeger, 1996). When these conflicts arise, changes in expectations and agreements can decrease trust and make it easy for the **ASE** team to blame the **CSE** team. The **SEB Manager** may need to initiate activities to help improve trust, such as establishing goals for certification of component systems, additional training, or team building.

14.5.2 Certify component systems to build trust and ensure quality

Since most application engineers initially seem to distrust the idea of reuse, and the loss of control and creativity, it is important that their first experience with the component systems be very positive. Components should be easy to use, not promise too much, and be very reliable. A simple economic calculation shows that in most cases it is worth getting software from a component system library even if it requires some work. But most application engineers underestimate the cost of developing their own code, particularly in terms of debugging, maintaining, and documenting it, and overestimate the difficulties of reusing code from a library (Woodfield, 1986, 1987). Education, publication of success stories, and good experiences can help overcome this.

A simple, well-publicized certification program can do a lot to increase reuser confidence in components. The important thing is to establish and enforce a set of standards, including inspections and metrics. Standards and well-structured documents and indexes can aid the reuser in finding and understanding the components. See also the discussion of component packaging in Chapter 11. Certification inspections and packaging reviews ensure that all the pieces of a complete component system are present and have been tested. Some metrics can be gathered on submitted components to expose the complexity, size, quality, and performance of candidate components.

14.5.3 Education and training

In the course of planning the transition to a reuse business, just-in-time training specific to the reuse business should be a key part of the plan. The **SEB Manager**, **Transition Driver**, **Resource Owner**, and the **Process Owner**s must decide how many workers the reuse business needs and what skills they should have. While skills are similar to those in ordinary software organizations, many skills are unique to the RSEB or take on a different character. The plan should include the use of short start-up courses, on-the-job training, and experienced mentors to ease the transition. Mentors are often trained as members of the reuse business pilots. They are then rotated into new projects as leaders or trainers.

Most software engineers are not "naturally" effective at software reuse (Woodfield, 1987; Frakes *et al.*, 1995). Some training should focus on following the specific reuse business processes.

Component engineers need to learn new skills to develop and test components and component systems. Variability, conformance to the architecture, and the need for much higher quality in a broader range of uses of components introduce substantial new demands.

Application engineers should learn how to develop with reuse. In particular, they can no longer do a design from scratch, but must start from the architecture and models supplied by component systems. For instance, application developers now have to learn what component systems are available, how they interface to each other, what they have to do to build new models and code that fit into the architecture and interface successfully with reusable component systems. They must be familiar with the architecture and available component systems. Since we have designed for reuse, in most cases, the component systems to reuse are obvious. But in some other cases, application engineers will need to choose carefully between several alternative component systems. Some of these might need considerable specialization or even adaptation.

Key concepts and needed skills might be transferred using a comprehensive RSEB training program with courses or seminars such as the following.

Introduction to the RSEB   This provides a first look at the principles of reuse-oriented architecture, process and organization of the RSEB, at about the level of Chapter 2. Summarizes motivation for reuse and RSEB. Everyone involved in the reuse business should take this course.

Application Family Engineering   This provides principles of business-model-driven layered system architecture. Teaches incremental, risk-aversive engineering of an architecture. Describes variability analysis and other techniques suitable for large-scale reuse.

Component System Engineering, introduction   This course provides general design and implementation guidelines aimed at producing reusable software.

Component System Engineering, advanced implementation techniques   This provides more language-specific techniques and guidelines. For Ada, this includes the use of generics, and several related areas, described in great detail in Booch (1987). For C++, this includes effective use of inheritance, templates, and abstract base classes. If the choice of programming language is Java, Visual Basic, or some other language, then their particular techniques have to be taught.

Application System Engineering This provides guidelines on how to develop application systems with substantial reuse of component systems. This course provides familiarization with the existing set of component systems and layered architecture.

Library and Component Support If a central repository and certification is established, librarians and component supporters will need training in classification and library maintenance, certification, documentation, maintenance, packaging, and so on.

Transition to a Reuse Business This teaches the basics of writing the reengineering directive and developing transition plans and provides guidance in customizing the generic RSEB. Some introduction to business engineering and key activities.

Managing a Reuse Business This provides overall guidelines on economic models and reuse estimators. Provides process improvement guidelines, organizational heuristics, and management guidelines. Shows how to use and extend project management techniques.

With so much material there is considerable risk that key people will not attend the courses. Management must stress the importance of this training, remove obstacles that prevent participation, and ensure that the training is optimized for the participants and delivered in short "just in time" segments.

People working in the reuse business must have a common terminology to allow clear communication and unambiguous measurement. Since the reuse business will be fairly new to the organization, the precise meaning of terms such as reuse, reuse level, component, component system, and so on will be unfamiliar.

14.5.4 Increase motivation through rewards and incentives

There are new expectations and new roles for people in the reuse business. Some people now create component systems, rather than applications. Application engineers will be constrained to live within the space defined by the architects and component engineers, rather than having the freedom to create software as they desire. Others are component system supporters, sometimes viewed as less important than those who develop component systems or application systems.

SEB Managers, **Resource Owner**s, and **Process Owner**s must stress that each role in the reuse business has its own excitement and rewards, and select people to match. Some people prefer to work on application systems, with customers. Others prefer technology and component development.

Some organizations will use some kind of explicit financial or job incentives to keep motivation for change high as the reuse business grows (for example, GTE (Prieto-Diaz and Arango, 1991)). Some organizations offer more substantial royalties for heavily used components. Most such financial incentives do not change behavior as much or for as long as hoped. Such incentives need to be periodically revisited and adjusted or removed if no longer effective. They always need to be adapted to the local culture and tied to the overall business goals to be effective.

It is important that rewards should be team-oriented enough to foster team cooperation, trust, and creativity. Rewards have to be adapted so that "really" innovative ideas do not get lost because engineers are so focused on short-term reuse level incentives that they do not have time to experiment or take some risks.

For example, component engineers should have goals that tie in to the improved business value that their components have helped the application engineers achieve. Component engineers should get a bonus that reflects application system savings or increased profits due to shorter time to market, as well as to reduced **Component System Engineering** costs. Unfortunately, many of the RSEB business goals can only be tested in the longer term, and so rewards, like measurement, need to be tied to other estimates of progress to these goals, such as reuse levels. Some part of the rewards can be short term, and others tied to the longer-term financial results.

In general, we do not recommend reuse-oriented financial incentives for the RSEB. It is best to establish explicit business and reuse goals as a standard part of the job description (Malan, 1993). These are reinforced by the regular performance review process, bonuses, and other standard organizational rewards.

14.6 Summary

Once the **Owners Of The Reuse Business** and the **Software Engineering Business Manager**s have enabled the transition to a reuse business, there are a number of management tasks. **Process Owner**- and **SEB Manager**-led activities are needed to ensure the continued growth and success of the reuse business. These include conflict resolution, training, measuring economic performance, and continuous adjustment and tuning of process and organization to optimize the business. **Process Owner**s and **SEB Manager**s need to deal with changing goals, requirements, and expectations that often lead to conflicts between teams.

Successful monitoring and control of the progress towards the business goals and of day-to-day performance needs an effective measurement program. A variety of people, process, and product measurements are gathered, and used both directly and via estimation formulas and economic models to ensure that resources are used correctly, and that the processes are being followed.

Typically, it takes more time and effort to develop the architecture and reusable component systems than to develop non-reusable software, and this effort must be directed towards the components that most help to achieve the business goals. Appropriate measurements of reuse by the **Application System Engineering** projects, and careful attention to the design of the architecture and components, will ensure that overall business goals of time to market, cost, or other business drivers are met.

The management tasks are distributed among several different workers, such as the **SEB Manager**, **Process Owner**, **Process Leader**s, **Resource Owner**s, and the **Lead Architect**.

14.7 Additional reading

The paper by Shari Lawrence Pfleeger, "Measuring reuse: A cautionary tale," *IEEE Software*, NY, July 1996, 118–27, should be read carefully before embarking on a reuse measurement program. She provides key insights, warnings, and guidelines as to how a reuse metrics program must be carefully adapted to the specific reuse processes.

Comprehensive discussions of reuse metrics, economic models, and management guidelines can be found in the excellent and thorough book by Jeff Poulin, *Measuring Software Reuse: Principles, Practices and Economic Models*, Addison-Wesley, 1996. The survey by William Frakes and Carol Terry, "Software Reuse Metrics and Models," *ACM Computing Surveys*, 1996, **28**(2), 415–35, defines a variety of reuse-related measurements, and includes discussions of reuse-level measurements, reuse maturity models, and several economic models. Lim provides a detailed analysis of many previous economic models in a common format (Lim, 1996c).

There are numerous pragmatic reuse project management guidelines, as well as some reuse metrics, in the books by Karlsson, *Software Reuse: A Holistic Approach*, Wiley, 1995, and Adele Goldberg and Kenneth Rubin, *Succeeding with Objects: Decision Frameworks for Project Management*, Addison-Wesley, 1995. See also the books by Bassett (1996) and Hooper and Chester (1991).

The chapter by Martin Griss, John Favaro, and Paul Walton, "Managerial and Organizational Issues – Starting and Running a Software Reuse Program," in the book *Software Reusability*, pp. 51–78, Ellis Horwood, Chichester, 1993, provides an extensive discussion of management pragmatics, additional case studies, and some reuse economics.

Grady Booch's book *Object Solutions: Managing the Object-Oriented Project*, Addison-Wesley, 1996, also provides useful pragmatics on structuring and managing object reuse.

AFTERWORD: MAKING THE REUSE BUSINESS WORK

15.1 Putting it all together

Reuse technology is ready now. In fact, as we saw in Chapter 1, enough companies have demonstrated substantial improvement, often as much as 90 percent reuse, to assure us that it can be achieved. If we take 15 percent as an approximation of the current rate of "passive" reuse that individual engineers achieve anyway and 90 percent as the figure that more than a few organizations are achieving, that is a gain of six times. With this level of reuse, the overall cost savings are dramatic. Moreover, these organizations are achieving comparable gains in development time. They are getting a system into operation in months, instead of years.

The third great component of software system development (after cost of development and time to market) is quality. "Quality" implies a host of factors. Many of them are hard to quantify or, at least, have not been quantified by most organizations. However, participants in successful reuse invariably believe that "quality," however they define it, has improved. Certainly, freedom from defects, flexibility, and robustness in the face of system evolution are important aspects of quality to many organizations.

One aspect of quality, defect rate, has been measured by many companies. For instance, on applications of reuse to two Hewlett-Packard projects, as reported in Chapter 1, the defect density of the reused code was less than a quarter of the defect density of new code.

15.2 Reuse improves the performance of your business processes

Increasing the productivity of your software development, shortening the time to market, and reducing the number of defects in the software product are all very nice. They are certainly worth seeking, but they are only the first installment of the prospective gains. The second installment is the improvement of the business processes that this software supports. Even though you are not consciously applying the methods of business engineering, the act of redoing the software that operates your business processes will result in some incremental improvement of those processes.

In Charles Dickens' day, clerks sat on high stools in poor light and scratched out the payroll with quill pens. They stopped scratching every few seconds to wet the quills with ink and rather often to resharpen the point. Now a computer program does most of this work. Every year since computers appeared in business in the 1950s, improved programs have incrementally improved the payroll process.

The third installment is the gain that the conscious application of business engineering offers. Instead of automating the business model that the business currently follows, business engineering straightens out these processes and takes advantage of the coordination capabilities that information systems provide.

First, however, let's clear the decks. A number of misconceptions stand in the way of achieving these gains.

15.3 Common misconceptions

Software reuse is a field replete with misunderstandings. We list some of the common misconceptions and our responses:

Instituting software reuse is primarily a matter of introducing the appropriate technology It is not. It is that and everything else — management, organization, architecture, processes, investment, and persistence.

Reuse does not work Put that in the past tense. Some companies have failed to make it work. Many companies are making it work.

It may work, but it is too expensive True, it does cost money up front, but it coins money down the trail. How far do you want to follow the trail?

The changes reuse asks us to make are too risky Take out the "too." Change is "risky" in the near term, but failure to change is "too" risky in the long term.

You should defer a systematic reuse program until your organization reaches SEI Capability Maturity Level 3   You should not. Start one now. Achieving reuse takes the same kind of steps that bettering your maturity level does.

Architecture does not have to be addressed as a specific task   Oh, yes, it does. It is the technical plan that leads to effective reuse across an application family.

Adopting object-oriented languages will lead to systematic reuse   No, it won't. Not all by itself. There are all those factors listed under the first misconception. Moreover, most successful reuse has been in COBOL, Fortran, C, and even Ada, because that is where much of the existing code is.

Limit reuse to code components   Don't. Just writing code is usually down in the 10–20 percent range of total development costs.

Developers will select the components they will reuse from tens of thousands of small components   No, they won't. They are human; their brains are adapted by evolution to hold in contemplation only seven, plus or minus two, items at a time. (And those seven have to include lunch and a few other pressing matters.)

Reused code components are too slow   They may be, but then that is a design flaw. Components should be developed under even more rigorous requirements than "ordinary" classes, which includes requirements on performance, size, and quality.

Setting up a library of reusable components will itself induce developers to reuse them   It does not work. There is the little matter of trust, for instance.

Paying application developers to contribute components to the repository will build up the library   This sortie has not worked in practice.

Paying application developers to use components from the repository will encourage reuse   This bribe, too, has been ineffectual.

Well, have we offended everyone in sight? Have we missed your favorite misconception? Possibly, just possibly, we have been a bit more blunt than the history of reuse efforts justifies. Still, suffice it to say that all these misconceptions together have blinded management and greatly delayed the coming of systematic reuse and the reuse business (Figure 15.1).

Figure 15.1   *Some managers, still blinded by misconceptions, fail to see that reuse is rising over the horizon.*

15.4 Doing reuse is difficult

In addition to the role that misconceptions have played in delaying the arrival of systematic reuse, the plain fact is that it is hard. It is hard primarily because at least five factors have to be interwoven and mastered:

- Vision

- Architecture

- Organization, and the management of it

- Financing

- Software engineering process.

In addition, if a company chooses to employ object-oriented requirements capture, analysis, design, and implementation, that is a new technology for its people to master. It is a paradigm shift from the structured-design approaches that many developers have employed for several decades. Furthermore, if an organization decides to reengineer its business processes, that effort is another complicating factor to integrate into the entire picture.

A single developer can reuse a little of what he or she has done before — on the order of 10–20 percent. If the manager of a single project can establish some machinery to encourage sharing within the project, he or she can add another 10–20 percent. At the level of a group of similar projects, such as a line of instruments, systematic reuse can get under way. At this level, of course, the five factors appear and the reuse task becomes complicated.

An entire worldwide corporation of 50 divisions need not embark all together on a reuse program. Probably a single division should, or at a minimum a group of related application development projects within a division. Based on this first-hand experience, the program can spread.

The conclusion: Systematic reuse cannot be adopted piecemeal. An occasional forward-looking developer can keep some experience and some code in his hip pocket, but he is not in an organizational position to carry through a systematic reuse program. At best, he is in a position to talk about the need for reuse, providing the organizational culture does not choke him off. In fact, such a person can sometimes become the champion a systematic program needs.

The integration that a systematic reuse program involves means that only management can lead it, which means that the upper management (division head and department directors) of a division has to understand what reuse can accomplish and how to go about it. They also have to be in a position to back a fairly expensive and long-running effort. It takes several years for the funds invested in reuse to begin coming back from:

- the reduction in time-to-market,

- the savings in effort and cost of developing application systems, and

- improved quality.

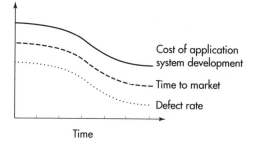

Time

Figure 15.2 *Cost or effort, time to market, and defect rate all start at a fairly high level. At first, as the reuse effort is in the planning stage, they remain steady. As reuse begins to make a difference, they drop rapidly. Eventually, when reuse reaches 80 or 90 percent, the rate of decline flattens out.*

Typical reductions are diagrammed in Figure 15.2.

A marginal company may not be able to afford the several-year-long initial investment. Its executives may be fully occupied just in keeping the company afloat. That seems to have been the case with the FoxMeyer Drug Company, then the fourth largest drug wholesaler in the United States, as reported in the *Wall Street Journal* of 18 November, 1996. In 1994 its chief information officer proudly announced, "We are betting the company on this [$65 million computerized system]." Two years later, having lost a major customer (a large chain of drug stores) to bankruptcy, and having underbid a hoped-for replacement (a chain of hospitals), FoxMeyer itself was forced into bankruptcy. The "happy" ending came a few months later. The system, though late, did work, most of it, though under a new, financially stronger, owner.

15.5 Without vision, the people perish

Wolves hunt in packs. They seem to have a vision of what cooperative hunting can do for the pack — in spite of lacking language in which to communicate that vision. We humans do have language; we have also abused that facility to the point where we hardly know any more whom to trust to set out a common vision. The problem in business organizations is how to carry it out in an atmosphere that may be laden with mistrust.

The past generation has seen a score of promising initiatives held forth. Our personal favorite is "TGM" – Total Good Management! (Don't search the literature for it; it's our own little joke!). Their number, probably, is limited only by the number of three-letter combinations the alphabet provides. Only a few succeed. What characterizes them? Can we pick out those features and apply them to a systematic reuse program – SRP. There, we have used up one of the remaining letter combinations! (But we are not going to use that three-letter acronym again.)

The first requisite is: Does the company have a problem that its management (both executives and middle management) can agree on and that reuse can solve, such as too many defects in the software? Is there a family of applications in which there are exploitable reuse opportunities?

Second: Is the company prepared to make a long-term commitment? Can it commit the investment funds necessary? Is it prepared to change its organization structure to meet the needs of reuse? Can it finance the training that underlies a complex effort? Lower-level managers and employees tend to have a sense of such matters, deriving from the manner in which the company has handled previous three-letter programs.

Third: Will the company have some sort of measure of the degree to which the program is working? This measure may be established based on the obtained return on investment, the reduction in product cycle time, or even something as simple as a count of the number of component systems reused in each new project. Having a metric to measure success is both an indication of seriousness and a guide to whether the program is on the right track.

Fourth is the promise of persistence. Executives often have to multiplex between many issues each day. Appointments may be scheduled at 15-minute intervals. Can component management spend the time and provide the focus a program takes? This short-run pattern sometimes makes it difficult to pay attention to such major change effort.

What, then, can they do? The fact of persistence has to show up in more than posters on the walls. Rather, it is better to maintain a continuing interest in the reuse metrics. Get them every week or every month and comment on them. Even more important, take the actions that they suggest: commit more investment capital; assign training funds where needed; correct deficiencies. The words in company-wide communications — or on those wall posters — matter little. It is action appropriate to the situation that people rack up on their mental score cards.

Fifth comes feedback. Of course, the taking of action is a form of feedback. Here, however, we refer to letting people immersed in the bowels of some activity know how it turned out. There is specific feedback to the group involved — a particular detail worked out. There is general feedback, perhaps to the entire division — the program flew. Everyone is interested in word of how the program first worked out in the field. For instance, Lockheed Aircraft used to mail a colored photograph of each new airplane model to employees' homes at about the time it went into operation. "See what Daddy worked on," was a powerful motivator. Similar software development success stories need to be shared in as graphic a form with all participants.

15.6 Reuse depends on architecture

As recently as one hundred years ago in rural United States, farm neighbors used to get together and raise a barn. They all knew what a barn looked like. It was simple enough to build without architectural plans. About the same time in US cities large contractors were building the first skyscrapers. They worked from architectural plans. There appeared to be a difference between small, well-understood buildings on the plentiful acres of a farm and tall steel-framed structures on city lots.

Similarly, there is a difference between a small, well-understood software application being coded by one or two programmers and a system of hundreds of thousands of source lines of code being attacked by groups of teams. There is another step-up in complexity when we go from a single system, however large, to a family of application systems. There is a further step-up when we make component systems that are reusable throughout the family. And again, complexity increases when we add variability mechanisms to the components to enable them to be employed satisfactorily within a greater family range. Finally, a time frame extending into the future increases complexity still further. The entire reuse operation has to endure through time — through changes in the application environment or in the operating systems or machines on which the systems run.

This ever-increasing complexity is inherent in large-scale reusable systems. It cannot be sidestepped. It requires a plan. This plan is called the architecture. It is analogous to the architectural plan that a contractor follows to build a skyscraper. The software architecture, first of all, defines a structure. Software components have to fit into some kind of design. The lowest layer of components, for example, rests on the operating system. It is the most general layer. Successively more specialized layers build on it, up to the application systems themselves, as expounded in Chapter 7.

Second, the architecture defines the interfaces between components. It defines the patterns by which information is passed back and forth through these interfaces. With this kind of architectural plan, component engineers can develop components that work for application systems developed by different groups or at different locations.

Frankly, we have encountered some resistance to the concept of software architecture. This resistance may arise from lack of experience with architecture. Many systems in the past have been small and developers worked from some mental plans that may never have been formalized. Even larger systems were built without formal acknowledgment of the need for architecture. That is, architecture was not recognized as a separate function. When an organization plans a family of large systems and expects substantial software reuse, it will need component systems reusable in dozens of systems for years to come. This requires coming to terms with significant planning, and specifically, with architecture.

Coming to terms implies a string of obligations. It requires a separate team headed by a broadly experienced developer, assisted by the best people available. The reason: Developing architecture for a family is more difficult than developing it for a single system.

It requires time. The application family engineering team has to gather information not just on a single system's requirements, but on the requirements of a whole group of systems, now and into the future, preferably by looking at a business model of the organization to support with information systems. It has to analyze this information as a basis for defining a layered architecture. In the course of preparing this architecture, the team will often find that its analysis is incomplete. It will have to gather and analyze additional information. That takes more time. The time frame can be speeded up only at the expense of an incomplete or incorrect architecture. A weak architecture would lead to poor application systems later on. That, of course, would take time (and cost money) at that point. Getting the architecture right is one of the reasons it takes several years to move a reuse business into the black.

On the plus side, however, the main part of the architectural task is a one-time-only assignment. Once completed, it is good for a period of years. Of course, during its lifetime, a smaller team has to monitor its relevance and make such modifications as experience and changing circumstances dictate.

Getting the architecture right provides many advantages. It ensures that many organization units, scattered in space and time, can work on different components and rest assured that they will come together successfully. It ensures that a system put together in this manner will have integrity and a robust structure. It enables maintainers later to modify local parts of it without disrupting other parts. This ability to modify the system successfully enables it to evolve, as its environment changes. In turn, successful evolution extends the life of the system.

Perhaps not the least of the merits of a good architecture is that the underlying design of the scores of component and application systems based on it can be understood. On the one hand, no one but the original programmer can understand the code, if that is all there is, and he or she may forget in time. On the other hand, an architecture, explained with use cases and an analysis model, can be understood, not only by the original developers but also by new recruits and the later maintainers. A layered architecture is furthermore intuitive enough to be relevant to several layers of management, customers, and end users. This understanding enhances everyone's ability to manage the work.

15.7 Management works through organization

Management itself is not going to reuse software. Its task, rather, is to establish an organization structure and operating procedures that enable software to be reused. Up until recently there has been a tendency to assume that the existing organization structure, given a few statistics on the benefits of reuse to motivate it and given some technical training on the mechanics of it, could go forth and practice reuse.

This approach has not been successful. One of the reasons is that existing software development is organized on a project basis. Projects focus on getting out a "good enough" product within the time and cost budgeted. Producing reusable components takes longer and costs more, as those parts of the industry practicing reuse have found by experience. This experience runs counter to project motivation. Systematic reuse rests on an organization structure adapted to its needs.

What are these needs? There are four principal functions. First is an organization unit to capture the requirements of a family of applications and to construct an architecture, as we outlined in the preceding section. This architecture leads to an indication of what components and component systems are reusable. Creating these reusable components is the province of the second function: component system engineering. The third function is application system engineering, roughly comparable to the older project engineering groups. People in these groups capture the requirements on their particular application, perhaps by studying the particular business process that the application supports, and then combine reusable component systems with new work to meet the requirements.

After studying a variety of software reuse organizations at Hewlett-Packard, Danielle Fafchamps observed that the most effective one was the team-producer model. This model consists of a component system engineering team, separate from the application system engineering teams, but all reporting to the same manager. Our experience leads us to add a further function to her model. This fourth function is a component support group under a support manager. Its function is to relieve the component system engineering team of housekeeping chores and project-support activities, so that it can concentrate on its creative tasks.

These four functions report to a single manager, the software engineering business manager. Some organizations use the alternative title, reuse manager. That title in itself emphasizes that the whole organization – architects, component engineers, application engineers, and component support people – are coordinating their work to achieve systematic, architected reuse.

This overall structure of architects, component system engineering team, component support group, application system engineering teams, and software engineering business manager then becomes a Reuse-driven Software Engineering Business. We call it a "business" because it exists in an economic environment. It has to make its way in this environment, a subject to which we turn next.

15.8 The reuse business must earn a return on its investment

Setting up a reuse business costs money. Over a period of time, it should more than return that money and also meet the strategic business goals that motivate establishing the reuse business. The overall business in which the reuse business is embedded has to advance that money and measure the resulting savings and other benefits. Doing this is a fairly tall order for a company that has been accustomed to project financing: Bid, accumulate project costs, add overhead, and note profit or loss.

However, cost recovery is not necessarily the most important reason to mount a large-scale, architected reuse effort. In many cases, without an architected reuse effort it would not be possible to meet the business objectives at all. For example, in the case of Ericsson the telecommunications company, it was critical to invest in architected reuse for its AXE telecommunications switching systems – without architected reuse it would simply not have been feasible to develop the 1000s of customized AXE installations.

In the case of the reuse business, the company has to provide funds – partly investment and partly operational to:

- analyze the family of applications to build with reuse,

- define an architecture,

- create components and component systems,

- reorganize,

- communicate the use of component systems through the support group to reusers, and

- train all types of teams in the pertinent technology.

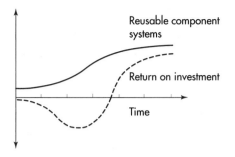

Figure 15.3 *In the first months of the reuse program the investment is small, as only a few people are working on the planning stage. Then, for several years the investment is heavy as architects develop architecture and component engineers generate component systems. When component systems become available in quantity, as the Reusable component systems curve shows, the reuse business begins to return its investment. Eventually, when reuse reaches 90 percent or so, ROI, too, approaches a ceiling. In time, it may decline as competition erodes the advantages of reuse.*

The pattern that this flow of investment funds follows is charted in Figure 15.3. In the early years, as the reuse program is getting under way, the outgo is negative. In later years, when application engineers can draw component systems from a substantial stock, the investment pays off.

Typically, it costs several times as much to create a component for reuse as it does to develop it within one project for a single application. Not until a component has been reused several times does this investment begin to pay off.

A rather lackadaisical reuse program in which a few indifferent creators provide a few components that developers don't much care for is not going to pay off. Reuse is not a "faith" that one wishes to spread to the benighted. It is a business in which the company wishes to make money. Financial people who have tried to place money values on the factors involved in ROI (return on investment) programs know that it is difficult to evaluate all these factors. For example, how do you place a monetary value on seizing the market window a few months sooner? How do you place a value on the increased competitiveness and new opportunities that the reduced time to market and flexible architecture enable? Nevertheless, making a return on investment is what keeps the reuse business in business.

For the component engineers and support people, having a positive ROI is a program plus. There is no better way to maintain the support — to buck up the persistence — of the executives at levels responsible for allocating funds. Without this financial feedback, the reuse program has to depend on enthusiasm, plus the general view that reuse is a good thing. In the competition within the company for scarce funds, this view is a thin reed.

"Clearly stating the potential benefits of reuse in financial terms has proven to be a powerful motivator," Jeffrey S. Poulin told the 5th Annual Workshop on Software Reuse, held at Hewlett-Packard in Palo Alto, California in 1992. At the time Poulin was responsible for reuse standards and metrics at IBM. "Establishing a realistic return on investment in a reuse program is essential to inserting reuse into a corporate software development process," he said.

In addition to ROI, Poulin went on to enumerate six sources of reuse data that the reuse business itself can collect:

- Source lines of code

- Number of lines, not written, but reused, included in a source file

- Number of lines reused by other products

- Software development cost

- Software development error rate

- Error repair cost.

From these observable data elements, he derives three further metrics:

- Percentage of reuse in a product

- Cost avoidance resulting from reuse

- Reuse value added – a productivity ratio comparing a reusing organization with one that is not.

These metrics enable the reuse business to focus in on specific areas that need attention. For example, the percentage of reuse in a product enables management and others concerned to compare the extent to which different application system engineering teams are utilizing reusable component systems. Teams with low percentages may need more support to find and use the existing components. Contrariwise, the component system engineering team may not be producing reusable component systems appropriate to some applications.

The cost-avoidance metric reflects the reduction in product costs resulting from reuse. The reuse value-added productivity ratio measures the leverage provided by practicing reuse and contributing to the reuse practiced by others.

In general, metrics derived directly from reuse measures are available sooner than cost or ROI figures provided by accounting. Often they act as early indicators of specific process problems, and can do so more precisely than overall accounting results can. For example, these detailed metrics can help determine if problems are due to an inadequate supply of components, if application engineers are not reusing enough components, or if some other process problem is the source of difficulty. These measures enable management to investigate troublesome projects and processes more quickly and to take action more pointedly.

15.9 Software engineering depends on process

Software systems have become large and complex. Even a single system is difficult to understand. From this difficulty stems the large number of errors and the resulting lack of reliability and usability that characterize much modern software. How much more acute, then, must be the problems faced by reuse engineers. They are trying to analyze, architect, design, implement, test, and maintain not just one system, but a family of systems — an application domain. They are trying to sort out components that can be reused repeatedly. They are trying to design components capable of the variation demanded by different systems. They are trying to devise components that can be grouped in component systems so as to reduce the load imposed on application engineers by thousands of tiny components. It is a tall order.

An example is Ericsson's AXE telecommunications switching system, which has been specialized for use in more than one hundred countries. Each application system in the family is different from the others in various degrees. Each system may be configured, packaged, or installed in a different way from the others.

Still, all telephone switching systems have much in common. They are complex. They are very large, in the past requiring thousands of programmers. Subscribers expect high reliability; even short down-times get in the newspapers. More seriously, life and death hang on the availability of a telephone connection. Subscribers also expect response times on the order of milliseconds. There are tens of thousands of subscribers depending on each switching system. So there is much going on concurrently and very rapidly.

Behind the scenes there is still more for the developers to keep in mind. At installation time, for example, installers must load tens of thousands of customization parameters for incoming subscriber lines and outgoing trunk lines. During operation, engineers must be able to install changes with little disturbance of ongoing traffic.

Adding to this complexity is the reality that systems in different countries or companies have considerable elements of difference. Ericsson has been accommodating these differences since 1978 by specialization mechanisms that were the forerunners of those described in this book. Its ability to adapt its switching system rapidly to different requirements gave it a competitive advantage that led one worldwide competitor, ITT, to withdraw from the telecommunications business. It reduced others (GTE, Phillips, GEC, Plessey) to much smaller market shares.

One reason for these difficulties is that developers have trouble visualizing the whole software engineering process. The software community has been aware of this trouble all along. It has developed many diagrammatic ways of representing the stages of analysis and design leading up to the code. "If one superimposes all the diagrams generated by the many relevant views," Fred Brooks noted more than a decade ago, "it is difficult to extract any global overview" (Brooks, 1987).

Nevertheless, difficult as it may be, we have no choice but to try. The first step is to accept the likelihood that there are a number of stages between the fuzzy reality of the world as it is and the precision of the 0's and 1's that finally reside deep in the computer's transistors. Through these stages the component engineers and the reusers make this transition. The best way for them to think through this series of stages is by means of models.

Each stage is a "model" at its own level of development of the eventual software system. There are at least five models and stages, discussed at length earlier in this book:

- Use case model

- Analysis model

- Design model

- Implementation (code and documentation)

- Test model.

The intent of this model sequence is to divide the entire task of going from requirements to code into "thinking" steps. In the case of a very small program, a programmer might be able to visualize what he or she needs and write code to represent it without going through this series of stages. The experience of the software community with large systems, however, indicates that people need to think through these steps. Using this five-stage modeling process, a reuse business can successfully control the process of developing software. It can thrive on complexity and win out over competitors. Note that these stages do not form a waterfall, instead there are numerous iterations over them, where for instance the use case model gets revisited as new requirements are discovered.

15.10 Object technology aids process

Object-oriented analysis and design, followed by the use of an object-oriented programming language at the implementation stage, do not, by themselves, guarantee a high level of reuse. The fact that some characteristics of object-oriented languages, such as inheritance, make it possible to reuse code have been emphasized far too much. There is much more to reuse than object orientation, as our earlier discussion of vision, architecture, organization, financing, and software engineering processes suggest.

At the same time object-oriented ways of thinking can be a great aid to carrying through the software engineering processes that enable reuse to take place. The reason lies all the way back in the physical world and in the way that human beings have evolved to view that world. The world consists of objects that (1) have properties and (2) can act. For instance, a dog has four movable feet and runs.

The first step in requirements capture, the creation of use cases, focuses on value added. After that, object orientation is often an aid in thinking through the analysis model, the design model, and the remaining development stages. The "object" concept represents the elements in this series, enabling engineers to move smoothly from high-level abstractions in the early stages to concrete code in the construction phase.

Object-oriented development methods have come into prominence in the past decade, but the concept dates back to Simula, developed in Norway in 1967. Ericsson began to develop a computerized telecommunications switch even earlier, in the early 1960s. By 1967 it had completed a comprehensive field test of the prototype. It began development of the switch as a product.

Ivar Jacobson joined the project at this point, having just put in four years developing electromechanical systems. This experience had taught him to think in terms of complete systems as well as implementing them in terms of building blocks. The building block approach has since matured and come to be what we call object-oriented. After a couple of months on the switch project, he realized that the system would not be manageable. But a novel approach, which objects was at that time, would be risky.

Indeed, the 13-person steering group realized that, but at the same time they grasped that the traditional approach gave little promise of success. After six months of what seemed, at the time, to be endless discussion, it was time to make a decision. Emotions ran high. The entire steering group, except two, voted "no." Lars-Olof Noren was one of the two, but he was the manager with overall responsibility for the technical organization for computerized switching systems. He asked the group to accept the "yes" decision and they did. The other "yes" vote, of course, was that of Jacobson.

The concept was in its infancy and the means to carry it out were meager. The implementation environment was late 60s. Programming was in assembly language. The proposed software architecture matched the operating system and the underlying hardware architecture poorly. There was no support for managing objects and message communication was supported only by awkward macro instructions.

In spite of these difficulties, the product did work and it was at least as good as competitive products. Ten countries bought it, enabling Ericsson to proceed to the next step. Internally, the engineering group realized that the system would be hard to manage at large sales volumes. The costs would be astronomical. Ericsson decided in the early 1970s to develop a new and more manageable version, which became the AXE 10. Gradually the deficiencies were overcome. The engineers developed a long series of innovations, enabling Ericsson to achieve prominence in switching systems.

15.11 Business engineering: Overhauling the business model

Software engineering is, at its core, model building. Changing a business also requires building models — be it traditional hierarchical organization charts, or process-oriented diagrams as in business engineering. A business, however, is not a model; it is a rather woolly slice of reality. The people down in the ranks who make it work may have to twist its formal procedures (that is, the business models) almost beyond recognition to make things come out. When software engineers implement support for a business's procedures in code, they often find, as the code operates, that the implemented support does not support the true business needs. The reason, of course, is undocumented twisting of the formal procedures. This twisting leads to complications, and complications spell inefficiency. As a result of this gap between formal procedures and twisted operations, a current model of the existing business is difficult to lay hands on, that is, to express as use cases, the first of our model stages. Then, when the existing business is being reengineered, the complications mount.

Still, improving processes is not new. Businessmen have been engineering processes at least since the days of Adam Smith's pin factory. Then they took the labor of making a pin from one worker and divided it into many steps, each performed by a different worker. It was the principle of "division of labor." Put that way, it sounds very efficient.

As work became ever more finely divided into hundreds of operations in factories or service operations employing thousands of workers, the information content of keeping all these jobs in play became formidably large. We know it under such names as receiving, receiving inspection, stockroom, material control, production control, mainten-ance, and many more. We also know it — and decry it — as overhead.

Moreover, all these people in overhead, as well as the direct labor force, the purchasing people extending out to suppliers, and the marketing force reaching out into the world, have to be kept on track by a substantial structure of supervisors, managers, executives, and their clerical assistants. Some observers have characterized this adminis-trative structure as a series of "stovepipes." Each stovepipe works fairly well within its stack. Needed information passes up and down through supervisory levels within a stovepipe, that is, a department. One stovepipe, however, doesn't pass information very well to and from the other stovepipes.

Keeping track of the information needed to control the flow of work through a series of stovepipe departments is something that computer programs can do. By now it is evident that forward-looking businesses can substitute information systems for at least part of the information coordination formerly done in the stovepipe structure and make some coordination obsolete by instead reorganizing to perform the business processes directly. To the extent that a business can accomplish this transformation, it could put its emphasis on the process that is going on at the bottom level of this series of stovepipes. It could de-emphasize — or even "downsize" — the upper levels of the stovepipes, as shown in Figure 15.4.

That is business engineering. It is the use of information systems, rather than an administrative (stovepipe) structure, to coordinate a business process. The point for us to note especially is that the creation of this coordinating information system is an integral part of business engineering. The information system is not just "something nice to have." Without it, you have to have the stovepipes. With the stovepipes comes the discontinuity from one pipe to the next, that is, the difficulty of focusing on the user. That user, of course, is the customer at the output end of the business process.

It has taken about 40 years to build up the 100 billion lines of code that now operate the stovepipe structure of business. If we were to redo that code in the same way to operate the business-process approach, it might take another 40 years. If we could reduce cycle time by 70 percent through reuse, as Netron's sample projects did (Bassett, 1996), we might reengineer business processes in a decade or so. That is a goal that is within reach with presently known methods.

One of the companies in Netron's sample is very large, over $10 billion a year in revenue. It operates its worldwide business with only 40 software people, where comparable businesses would have several thousand. These 40 people process over 28 000 change requests each year. That is an average of three per working day, each. When this company acquires a subsidiary, a small team of software engineers adapts the standard software to the new division's operations. "It took only three of them," Bassett reports, "to implement a network of VAXes that supports their entire European operations."

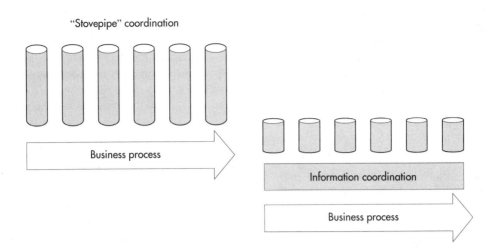

"Stovepipe" coordination

Business process

Information coordination

Business process

Figure 15.4   *The division-of-labor principle made a large management structure necessary to coordinate the actual process of turning raw materials into a finished product. If information systems can take over part of the coordination task and remove some when organizing to support the business processes, a company can reduce administrative overhead and at the same time improve the coordination of its business processes. With business engineering and information coordination, stovepipes become competence units.*

Under this scenario, the gains can be enormous. First, it greatly enhances the business process itself. Second, it thins out the cost of the existing administrative structure. Third, of course, a high level of software reuse reduces the cost of the needed software and brings it into operation much sooner. Fourth, the improved reliability of the software enables the business process to run more smoothly.

These gains sound wonderful! No doubt everyone is getting into business engineering. No doubt they are gearing up to support it with high levels of reuse. Well, if you look around a bit, you see that they are not. In fact, 50–70 percent of business engineering attempts fail, largely due to insufficient attention to the "soft" factors. In our approach we try to address these risks with a systematic transition process that emphasizes vision, organization building focused on competence units, and suitable models of financing.

Despite the many challenges, business engineering, software modeling, and systematic reuse mark the path business is to follow in the future. In fact, the pioneers are already following it. Their success establishes that it can be done.

15.12   Summing up

Once a senior executive has decided that software reuse is a promising way of organizing software development and a basis for expediting business engineering, his or her first action might well be to select a small planning team. After all, the rest of the executive team, too, has to appreciate its merit if they are to support it through thick and thin for the several years it takes to establish it. The planning team gets together the case to persuade management. Its work culminates in the vision directive (reengineering directive), which explains to all the company's people the direction the company is going to take.

As we have seen earlier in this chapter, as well as in the book as a whole, inaugurating a reuse business requires integrating:

- an overall vision of where the company is heading;

- an architecture that sets the pattern for sorting out components, grouping them in component systems, and fitting them into application systems;

- a compatible organization with distinct processes and teams for application family engineering, component system engineering, application system engineering, a unit for component support, and reuse management;

- the financing arrangements that, first, make the up-front investments and, second, make the measurements that show the reuse business to be operating in the black;

- the software engineering processes — the five-stage modeling sequence — that enables engineers in both component and application system engineering teams to think through development in communicable steps from requirements to code.

Further, the software engineering processes have to be carried out under some guiding principles. It is possible to do so with the structured-design approach, but it is preferable to use object-oriented technology.

Finally, software reuse makes business engineering feasible, particularly in terms of three factors:

- By reducing the time to complete the software that supports reengineered business processes, reuse brings the software online in the same time frame as the reengineering takes, and increases market agility.

- By reducing the cost of this software, reuse makes a major contribution to the execution of business reengineering.

- By improving the quality and reliability of this software, reuse makes the business process run more smoothly. As a result customers are happy. They get quality and reliability sooner at less cost.

Now, we have just gone through quite a string of new activities of which your people will not exactly be masters. We'll just list education, training, in-house conferences, consultants, mentors, and so on. Getting these aids to the right people at the time they need them is another factor to be integrated into the mix.

Without these aids and, in particular, without being continuously filled in on what is going on, people become edgy. With the issuance of the reengineering directive, they begin to wonder "How does this new stuff affect me?" As Figure 15.5 indicates, tension

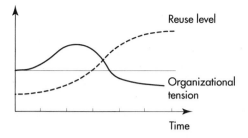

Reuse level

Organizational
tension

Time

Figure 15.5 *During the transition to a reuse business, tension among the people may rise and stay high during the period of change. As the reuse business becomes fully established, tension drops, eventually to a level lower than that at the start.*

tends to rise as the reuse business gets under way. Some rise is probably inevitable, but good communication can hold it within bounds. As the reuse business demonstrates its effectiveness, tension falls off. If the reuse business is fully successful, the tension falls to a level below that at the start.

There is one "little" issue yet to consider. How do we get to the point where a senior executive (a chief executive officer, chief operating officer, division head) is ready to kick off the steps leading to a reuse business? We might cast that question in slightly different terms. What help does a senior executive need to get to that point?

A company of some size has professionals in the fields that lead to its future. It sends these professionals to conferences, short courses, and university programs where they are exposed to the latest ideas in each field. They read the latest books. They may themselves be advancing the state of the art. As a result of these efforts, they become well informed.

The next step is sometimes neglected. Senior professionals also have to have some knowledge of the business in which they work. Ultimately it is their task, not just to know a lot about their field, but to know how their field affects the company. Some companies invite senior professionals to sit in on meetings that explore the company's problems or look to the company's future. As an outcome of this two-way knowledge acquisition (business and new ideas), professionals are likely to generate some ideas about how future developments in their field will affect the company.

The third step is difficult. How does a valid idea get into practice? Well, it has to get to an executive with the organizational position necessary to take action. In the case of reuse, the professional is probably several levels below that executive. That means the idea has to move through several levels. Those levels exist because the senior executive is already overburdened. The intervening executives try, quite rightly, to reduce that burden.

Many companies have become aware of the need for good ideas to move up. Several arrangements are in use. One is that the less senior executives also look for what Andrew Grove, Intel's CEO, calls "10x" factors, that is, developments that may have a significant effect on the company. Another is that the senior executives reach out to senior professionals in such events as all-day retreats.

A third is practiced by Bill Gates of Microsoft. He goes off to his mountain cabin for a week at a time, several times a year, to "think." He carries with him books and reports with which he believes he ought to be familiar. Some have been suggested to him by colleagues. It takes time to "think," when you put it in quotation marks. It also takes material to "think" with.

A fourth arrangement is the divisional organization structure. It was probably instituted for reasons other than the nourishing of new ideas, but one or another division often has an idea and makes it work. The challenge then is for other divisions or the company as a whole to notice the step forward.

Once a senior executive "notices" a valid idea, he or she can kick off the planning process to flesh it out, as we outlined at the beginning of this section.

We hope you enjoyed the journey through this book. We hope that you "enjoy" the journey to a reuse business, and we put it in quotation marks because at times you might not feel that way. You will find that the end result is worth the effort.

15.13 Additional reading

Will Tracz's book, *Confessions of a Used Program Salesman – Institutionalizing Software Reuse*, Addison-Wesley, 1995, is an amusing and insightful description of the many misconceptions and truths of bringing effective software reuse to corporate practicality.

PART V
APPENDICES

Appendix A provides a complete glossary of terms.

Appendix B provides an annotated reading list.

Appendix C provides a summary of UML and RSEB modeling notation.

Appendix D provides a complete list of references.

A

GLOSSARY

In this appendix, we summarize key terms and definitions used in this book. Related and additional definitions may be found in the OOSE book (Jacobson *et al.*, 1992), the TOA book (Jacobson *et al.*, 1994), the STARS CFRP (STARS, 1993) definition, and the WISR lexicon (Ogush, 1992). We include both RSEB specific terms, and key related terms from the UML (Booch *et al.*, 1997a), and the systematic reuse and software engineering literature.

Abstract   Used as an adjective to qualify a class or type that cannot be directly instantiated (antonym: concrete). An abstract class or type needs to be specialized.

Acquaintance association   An association that indicates that instances of one class or type hold a reference to instances of some other class or type. Represented by the «acquaintance» stereotype.

ActiveX   Microsoft OLE and Internet Explorer components. Defines a fairly complete framework for reusable components that are easy to use in WWW applets, support distributed object computing and adhere to more open standards. Previously called OLE Controls (OCX).

Actor type   An actor is anything that interacts, that is, exchanges data and events, with the system or business. An actor type defines a set of actor instances, where each actor instance plays the same role in relation to the system or business.

Actor instance   An instance of an actor type.

AFE   Application Family Engineering

Aggregation   A whole/part relationship, represented by a «consists-of» association.

Analysis type   A type of analysis objects.

Analysis model   A model of the system design at a high level, ignoring the specific low-level details of the target implementation environment. The analysis model consists of analysis types and subsystems plus their relationships, defining the architectural structure of the system.

Analysis object   Analysis objects are imagined executing objects in an ideal system, where many (implementation) factors such as database management system, distribution, specific programming language, existing products, performance, and storage specifications have not been addressed.

API   Application Programming Interface

Applet   A small application or application fragment, meant to be used within a task-oriented environment, such as Microsoft Windows, Microsoft Office, or from within WWW browsers.

Application family   See Application system family.

Application Family Engineering (AFE)   A business use case (process) or SEP. Application Family Engineering develops the product plan and engineers the layered system.

Application objects   In CORBA application objects are objects specific to particular industries or end-user applications. These correspond to objects in the business-specific and application layer.

Application System (AS)   An application system is a system product delivered outside of the Reuse Business. When installed, application systems offer a coherent set of use cases to an end user.

Application System Engineering (ASE)   A business use case (process) or SEP. Application System Engineering develops new versions of application systems by reusing component systems, as requested by a Customer.

Application system family   A set of related applications that can be usefully implemented from a common set of reusable components, or from a customizable application system.

Application System Layer   The Application System Layer of the layered architecture should contain one application system for each software system that offers a coherent set of use cases to some end users.

Application system suite   An application system suite is a set of different application systems that are intended to work together to add value to some actors.

Application system variants   Variants of essentially the same application system are useful when a system needs to be configured, packaged, and installed differently for different users.

Architect One or more persons in charge of defining and maintaining the architecture of a system, that is, the essential part of the use case, analysis, design, implementation, and test models; the architect decides on most architectural patterns to use in the system.

Architectural style Systems that share a similar high-level structure and key mechanisms are said to have a similar architectural style.

Architecture Describes the static organization of software into subsystems interconnected through interfaces and defines at a significant level how nodes executing those software subsystems interact with each other. An architecture conforms to one or several architectural styles.

Architecture Unit The Architecture Unit is a competence unit containing the workers needed for defining the architecture of the layered system, an application, or a component system.

AS Application System

ASE Application System Engineering

Asset Valuable, high-quality software workproducts (such as code, designs, architectures, interfaces, tests), documents, tools, processes, and compiled knowledge (guidelines, models, formulas, . . .). This term is sometimes used instead of component or workproduct.

Association An association is a relationship used to show that object A can access or refer to object B, perhaps to express communication between the objects, or that B is "part" of object A, or that A has a pointer to object B.

ATM Automatic Teller Machine

Attribute An attribute represents a property of the object. Attributes are owned by the object and are local to it, that is, they are not shared with other objects, but they may be public so that other objects may read or set them. An attribute has a type that defines the type of its instances.

Attribute type The type of an attribute.

Baseline *(noun)* A reviewed and approved release of artifacts that constitutes an agreed basis for further evolution or development and that can be changed only through a formal procedure, that is, a release that is subject to change management and configuration control.

Also, baseline metrics, a starting point for developing reuse business metrics.

BE Business Engineering

Boundary type Boundary types constitute the presentation-dependent part of the system, whereas control and entity types are surroundings-independent. Windows, communication protocols, sensors and printer interfaces are all examples of boundary types. Represented by the «boundary» stereotype.

BPR Business Process Reengineering

Business actor A business actor represents a role that someone or something in the environment can play in relation to the business.

Business Engineering See Object-oriented business engineering.

Business entity object   A business entity object represents a "thing" that is handled or used in the business. In a software engineering business these would be use case classes, object models, subsystems, and so on.

Business model   A business model clarifies an organization's function in the world and its internal structure. It shows what the company's environment is, how the company acts in relation to this environment, and how things happen within the organization. It is a use case or an object model of the business system.

Business object   A business object represents something concrete and significant in the business – a type of competence within the business (worker) or "some thing" handled or used by people in the business (business entity object).

Business Process Reengineering (BPR)   The fundamental rethinking and radical redesign of business processes to achieve dramatic improvements in critical, contemporary measures of performance, such as cost, quality, service, and speed, also called Business Engineering.

Business Specific Layer   The Business Specific Layer contains a number of component systems specific to the type of business.

Business system   A business system is used to represent an organization unit that we want to understand better in order to make it more competitive.

Business use case   Short form of business use case type.

Business use case instance   A business use case instance is a sequence of work steps performed in a business system that produces a result of perceived and measurable value to an individual actor of the business. The purpose of each business use case is to offer each customer the right product or service (that is, the right deliverable), with a high degree of performance measured against cost, longevity, service, and quality.

Business use case type   A business use case type defines a set of business use case instances.

Capability Maturity Model (CMM)   A five-level model developed by the Software Engineering Institute (SEI), used to assess software engineering process maturity. See Humphrey (1989).

CASE   Computer Aided Software Engineering

Case worker   A business worker primarily dealing with actors.

CATV   Cable Television

CEO   Chief Executive Officer

Class   A class defines a set of objects that share the same characteristics. A class is a realization of a type.

Client   The requester of a service.

CM   Configuration Management

CMM   Capability Maturity Model (developed by SEI)

COCOMO   COnstructive COst MOdeling, developed by Boehm (1981).

Collaboration   A collaboration defines how instances of classes or types participate, most often to perform a use case. The behavior involved in a collaboration can be described using collaboration diagrams or sequence diagrams, collectively called interaction diagrams, various textual documents, and trace links.

Collaboration diagram   A collaboration diagram is a special type of diagram whose purpose is to illustrate the classes or types whose objects participate, typically in a use case.

COM   Component Object Model

Commonality   The set of features or properties of a component, component system, or application system that are the same, or common, between systems.

Communicates association   An association between two classes or types that indicates that their objects interact. The direction of the association is the same as the direction of the message or stimulus. Represented by the «communicates» stereotype.

Communicates association   An association that indicates that workers interact with each other, or with business entity objects, or that business actors and use cases interact with each other. Represented by the «communicates» stereotype.

Competence unit   A competence unit contains workers with similar competencies and types of business entity objects that these workers are responsible for. The purpose of a competence unit is to maintain and develop a certain type of competence within the business and also to improve the types of material (that is, the business entity objects) and documentation used.

Component   A component is a high-quality type, class, or other UML workproduct, designed, documented, and packaged to be reusable. A component is cohesive and has a stable interface. Components include interfaces; subsystems; use cases, types, actors, or classes; and attribute types. Components also include other workproducts, such as templates, or test case specifications. Note that this is different from the UML definition of the term.

Component Engineering Unit   The Component Engineering Unit is a competence unit containing some specialized workers required when developing a component system, in addition to requirements capturers, architects, designers, and testers.

Component Object Model (COM)   Microsoft's Component Object Model used with OLE and ActiveX. OLE/COM defines an architectural style for components. That is, the component definition model provides several services such as compound document objects, structured storage, uniform data transfer, and OLE automation and scripting.

Component Support Unit   The Component Support Unit is a competence unit containing workers skilled at packaging and facilitating the reuse of component systems. They are mostly concerned with maintaining the facades, and distributing the component systems, so that the reusers can get at the desired components.

Component System (CS)   A component system exports a well-packaged and certified set of components, via one or more facades, and is generally not delivered outside the Reuse Business. A component system is a system product and may be accompanied by closely related SEP and SEPSE systems.

Component System Engineering (CSE)   A business use case or SEP. Component System Engineering develops component systems to be reused by application engineers.

Conceptual Framework for Reuse Processes (CFRP)   A general model of standard reuse process descriptions and terminology proposed by a consortium of companies working under the STARS umbrella. Introduces the notion of Creator and Utilizer, Reuse Management, Reuse Engineering, and Cascading processes. See STARS (1993).

Concrete   Used as an adjective to qualify a class, type or a use case that can be instantiated (antonym: abstract). A concrete class or type does not need to be specialized.

Concurrency model   The concurrency model captures concurrency, processes, and synchronization aspects.

Configuration   1. A configuration consists of particular versions of configuration items.
   2. The requirements, design, and implementation that define a particular version of a system or system component. (See Configuration management.) Represented by a package, «configuration».

Configuration item   A configuration item is a segment of a model that may be subject to version control, such as a use case type, a service package containing analysis types, or some code modules. Represented by a package, «configuration item».
   An entity is a configuration that satisfies an end-user function and that can be uniquely identified at given reference points.

Configuration management   A supporting process whose purpose is to identify, define, and baseline items; control modifications and releases of these items; report and record status of the items and modification requests; ensure completeness, consistency, and correctness of the items; control storage, handling, and delivery of the items.

Consists of association   An association that is used to represent object aggregation. Represented by the «consists of» stereotype.

Control type   A control object performs use case specific behavior. Control objects often control or coordinate other objects. A control type offers behavior that does not belong to an entity or interface type. Represented by the «control» stereotype.

CORBA   The Common Object Request Broker Architecture (CORBA) is a vendor interoperability standard designed to allow interoperability between components regardless of the platform, language, author, or vendor infrastructure. (See also IDL, OMG.)

CORBAfacilities   A collection of common facilities and objects that provide a set of generic application functions that can be configured to the specific requirements of a particular installation. These are facilities such as printing, document management, database, and electronic mail facilities.

CORBAservices   A collection of services (interfaces and objects) that support functions common in distributed systems. These components standardize the life-cycle management of objects. Interfaces are provided to create objects, to control access to objects, to keep track of relocated objects, and to control the relationship between styles of objects (class management).

COTS   Commercial Off The Shelf

CPI   Continuous Process Improvement

Creator   A systematic reuse term for the people or organization(s) that produce a component system. Also, the term producer is sometimes used.

CS   Component System

CSE   Component System Engineering

Customer   Customers request application systems, place requirements on them, and usually pay for the systems. Customers also interact when deciding on needed features, priorities, and roll-out plans when developing new versions of component systems and the layered system as a whole. Customers can be both internal, such as a business process owner, or external, such as another company.

DBMS   Database Management System

DCOM   Distributed Component Object Model, see COM.

Deliverable   An output from a process that has a value – material or immaterial – to a customer.

Dependency   A relationship between two modeling elements, in which a change to one modeling element (the independent element) will affect the other modeling element (the dependent element). A dependency is for instance used to show that type A has some historical, implementation, or other connection to type B. For example, A «imports» from B. We can also use this to show how subsystems are dependent on other subsystems – «depends on».

Deployment model   The deployment model describes the mapping(s) of the software onto the hardware and reflects its distributed aspect.

Design *(noun)*   The result of the design activity. See Design model.

Design *(verb)*   During design, the *designers* develop the *design model* that expresses how to implement the system.

Design class   A design class is an abstraction of a class in the system's implementation. A design class defines a set of design objects with attributes, associations, and methods.

Design guidelines   General design and implementation guidelines, regarding issues such as: detecting, handling, and reporting faults, memory management, and fault-tolerance.

Coding standards, regarding code layouts, commenting, naming, and so on.

Design model   The design model serves as a higher-level view of the source code – a "blueprint" of how the source code is organized, and some of its key features. The design model consists of design classes and types and design subsystems.

Design object   A design object represents an abstraction in the system's implementation. A design object is an instance of a design class and type.

Design type   A design type can be used to specify objects without deciding on which class should implement them. A design type defines a set of design objects with attributes, associations, and operations.

Design Unit   The Design Unit contains the workers needed for doing robustness analysis and designing and implementing the layered system, an application, or a component system.

Diagram   A diagram is a pictorial (graphical) view of some part of a model or of models.

Domain   A systematic reuse term that refers to the conceptual space of applications or subsystems that will be "covered" by a collection of reusable assets, and as they are engineered, particularly the applications in an application family in the domain.

Domain analysis   A systematic reuse term that describes a part of domain engineering activities, used to model an appropriate range of commonality and variability of an application or subsystem domain.

Domain dictionary   A systematic reuse term that describes a collection of the key terms used to describe the domain model. See Glossary.

Domain engineering   A systematic reuse term that describes a systematic way of identifying a domain model, commonality and variability, potentially reusable assets, and an architecture to enable their reuse.

Domain-specific architecture   An architecture specialized for a given domain, but general enough to construct a range of systems across the domain.

Domain-specific language   A problem or task oriented modeling language, used to simplify the process of assembling, customizing, generating, or configuring a system or component.

Domain-specific kit   A packaged set of compatible, reusable parts that work well together. These are a framework, components, languages, tools (SEPSE), and procedures (SEP).

End user   The person who will use a delivered application system.

Entity type   An entity type is a generic type, reused in many use cases, often with persistent characteristics. An entity type defines a set of entity objects, which participate in several use cases and typically survive those use cases. Represented by the «entity» stereotype.

Envisioning   In business engineering, envisioning is the use of knowledge about the existing business to try new ideas and new technologies in order to envision the new business. This vision is formulated in terms of goals, objectives, and high-level descriptions of future business processes.

Evolution   The life of the software after its initial development cycle; any subsequent cycle, where the product evolves.

Export   Each component system exports a set of reusable components; that is, makes them publicly accessible for reuse. Only those classes and types that application engineers need to "connect to" directly are exported via a facade. The other classes and types are considered component system internals and are hidden as private elements.

Extends generalization   An relationship from a use case B to a use case A that indicates that an instance obeying the use case A may at some time discontinue obeying that use case and instead begin obeying use case B. When the instance has finished obeying B it will return again to obey A. Thus A and B together act as a specialization of the use case A. Represented by the «extends» stereotype. Also used with types.

Extension   A small type-like attachment that extends another type or use case.

Extension point   A type of variation point suitable for extensions. An extension point may be implicit which means that it is not directly visible at all in the type or use case itself, or explicit, which means that it is explicitly visible and documented in the type or use case.

Facade   A facade is a packaged subset of components, or references to components, selected from the component system. Each facade provides public access to only those parts of the component system that have been chosen to be available for reuse. Represented by «facade».

Feature   In this book we mostly talk of features related to use cases and requirements. A *feature* is a use case, part of a use case or a responsibility of a use case.

FODA   Feature Oriented Domain Analysis, a style of systematic reuse domain analysis.

Forward engineering   In business engineering, forward engineering the new business incrementally develops and describes the new business, and develops the information systems that will support it. The results define what the business will do in terms of business processes and how the business will be organized internally in order to perform the processes, and also instructions for the people in the new business.

FP   Function Points

Framework   A micro-architecture that provides an incomplete template for systems within a specific domain. In RSEB, defined as abstract subsystems.

Function points   A software engineering metric used to estimate the size of any workproduct. Function points may be computed from lines of code, or computed from other observable features of a workproduct.

GE   General Electric

Generalization   A taxonomic relationship between a more general element and a more specific element. The more specific element is fully consistent with the more general element and contains additional information. An instance of the more specific element may be used where the more general element is allowed. The most common form of generalization is inheritance, «inherits».

Generator   A generator creates derived components and various relationships from languages or templates. The generator is often a conversational or language-driven tool.

Glossary   A common and consistent set of problem space and solution space terminology developed during modeling. Used as a catalog and thesaurus during systematic reuse domain engineering to describe the key concepts. Sometimes also called domain dictionary in systematic reuse.

Goal-Question-Metric (GQM)   A software engineering metrics approach developed by Basili to systematically associate a metric with a goal and a question to be asked about it.

GTE   General Telephone and Electric

GUI   Graphical User Interface

Ideal implementation environment   When factors such as database management system, distribution, specific programming language, existing products, performance, storage requirements, and so on are not taken into consideration.

Implementation (of a reengineered business)   A process step in the business engineering process, with the purpose of installing the processes, competence units, and tools.

Implementation (of software)   A process step in the software engineering process, with the purpose of implementing and unit testing the classes.

Implementation model   The implementation model consists of the source code, classes, and also necessary documents and annotations to make the code readable. It also includes scripts and instructions to produce the final code and supporting files.

Import   A system may import components which means that they become available for reuse in models of that system.

Imports dependency   Systems reuse common components by importing reusable components from component systems. The «imports» dependency is used to show the reuse relationships. Notated by «imports» dependency.

Increment   The difference (delta) between two releases at the end of two subsequent iterations.

Incremental, iterative development   Instead of producing the complete system as a single, monolithic release, the approach is to build up the complete functionality of the system by deliberately developing the system as a series of smaller increments, or releases.

Inheritance   The mechanism by which more specific elements incorporate structure and behavior of more general elements related by behavior, see also «inherits» generalization.

Inheritance generalization (between actors)   A generalization from an actor type (descendant) to another actor type (ancestor) that indicates that the descendant inherits the role the ancestor can play in a use case. Represented by the «inheritance» stereotype.

Inheritance generalization (between types or classes)   A generalization from a type (or class), the descendant, to another type (or class), the ancestor, that indicates that an instance of the descendant has all the attributes, operations (or methods) and associations defined in both the descendant and the ancestor types (or classes). Represented by the «inherits» stereotype.

Inspection   A formal software engineering evaluation technique in which some artifact (a model, a document, the software) is examined by a person or group other than the originator to detect faults, violations of development standards, and other problems. Specific guidelines on preparation, facilitating scope and exact inspection steps are defined. See also Review.

Instance   An instance is a concrete manifestation of a type.

Integration testing   A step in the testing process to validate that various units work together.

Interaction diagram   An interaction diagram is used to show the collaboration between objects, typically during the performance of a use case instance; see also Collaboration.

Interface   The use of a type to describe the externally visible behavior of a class, object, or other entity. In the case of a class or object, the interface includes the signatures of the operations. Each client conforms to the interface implemented by a supplying class.

Interface Definition Language (IDL)   IDL gives a precise description of types and exceptions and is similar to C++ interface and type declarations but permits multiple language bindings. CORBA objects can have multiple interfaces, perhaps composed or inherited from other interfaces. Microsoft COM uses a different IDL.

Internal worker   A business worker primarily dealing with or controlling internal processes.

Interoperable   Application systems are said to be interoperable if they are able to exchange data and have some control over each other using some mechanisms or interfaces. Often implemented on top of some interoperation middleware.

Iteration   A distinct sequence of activities with a baselined plan and evaluation criteria. We mostly use the term to signify one pass through all the development steps: requirements capture, robustness analysis, design, implementation, and testing.

JAVA   Sun's C++-like interpreted language used for writing hardware and operating system independent applets.

Kit   A set of compatible, reusable parts that work well together. These are a framework, components, languages, and tools. Typically, a domain-specific kit.

Layer   A layer can loosely be defined as a set of (sub)systems with the same degree of application specificity, and typically only reference each other or (sub)systems in a lower layer.

Layered architecture   A layered architecture is a software architecture that organizes software in layers, where each layer is built on top of another more general layer. By software organization we mean that the layering addresses how static constructs such as modules depend on each other at compile and link time, but not the run-time "organization" of the software.

Layered system   A layered system is fashioned after a layered architecture and is composed of application systems at the top and component systems underneath.

Layered system architecture   See Layered architecture.

Legacy system   A legacy system is a pre-existing system that was created using other design methods and technology.

Management   In the RSEB context, management is a group of people (SEB Managers, Process Owners, Resource Owners and Leaders) responsible for ensuring progress, leading activities, monitoring goals, adjusting the process and organization, making funding decisions, and resolving conflicts.

Manufacturer   The people or organization(s) that receive a new version of an application system when developed, and then customize, configure, produce, and deliver complete applications to Customers.

Message   Objects can interact by sending messages or signals to one another.

Method   1. A regular and systematic way of accomplishing something, the detailed, logically ordered plans or procedures followed to accomplish a task or attain a goal.

   2. The implementation of an operation. The algorithm or procedure that effects the results of an operation. The behavior of an object is performed via its methods, which may affect the attributes and the associations the object holds, and cause methods on other objects to be performed.

Microsoft Foundation Classes (MFC)   A set of utility and interface classes in C++ that provide access to several services of the Windows or NT operating systems, such as OLE, DCOM, user interface, and so on.

Middleware   System software that provides interoperability services for applications, such as distributed object computing, and conceals some aspects of hardware and operating system differences in a heterogeneous, distributed environment.

Middleware Layer   The Middleware Layer offers component systems for utility classes and platform-independent services for things like distributed object computing and interoperability in heterogeneous environments.

Milestone   A software process or life-cycle event held to formally initiate and/or conclude an iteration.

Model   A semantically closed abstraction of a system. Each model defines a specific aspect of the system. Each model is described using several diagrams and documents with a prescribed format. Each model is examined or manipulated by different people with different specific interests, roles, or tasks.

Modeling element   The basic elements from which UML models are constructed.

Modeling language   The set of symbols, model elements, connectors, and combination rules used to describe models. For example, UML.

Module   A software unit of storage and manipulation. Modules include source code modules, binary code modules, and executable code modules.

MVC   Model View Controller, a pattern or framework used for GUI construction.

Node   A node is used to describe one node type, for example a computer or a device, in a physical network that executes the system's functionality.

NPV   Net Present Value

Object   An entity with a well-defined boundary and identity that encapsulates state and behavior. State is represented by attributes and relationships, behavior is represented by operations and methods. An object is an instance of a type (and a class).

Object Linking and Embedding (OLE)   Microsoft's Object Linking and Embedding standard (OLE) is a set of services and mechanisms that define a component-oriented application architecture, implemented using [D]COM, Microsoft Foundation Classes, and OCXs or ActiveXs. See also [D]COM.

Object Management Group (OMG)   A consortium engaged in developing standards for distributed object computing. See http://www.omg.org.

Object model   An object model is an abstraction of a system design, consisting of many related objects.

Object Request Broker (ORB)   An Object Request Broker enables objects to transparently make and receive requests and responses in a distributed heterogeneous environment. An object request broker is an implementation of the CORBA standard.

Object-oriented business engineering   Business engineering is a process where the current organization is analyzed, envisioned, and designed. Also the required information systems are identified and developed in parallel with the business engineering.

OCX   OLE Custom Control, see also ActiveX.

ODM   Organizational Domain Modeling

OFC   Open Financial Connection, Microsoft

OLE   Object Linking and Embedding, Microsoft

OLE Custom Control (OCX)   Microsoft term; OCX is a module that provides a collection of functions (sometimes called methods or member functions) that reusers can connect their software to. Newer term is ActiveX.

OMG   Object Management Group

OOSE   Object-Oriented Software Engineering

OpenDoc   OpenDoc is a compound document architecture, implemented as a set of compound document components and services, aimed at development of rich user interfaces and document-oriented applications.

Operation   In UML an operation is implemented by a method. A service that can be requested from an object to effect behavior. An operation has a signature, which may restrict the actual parameters that are possible.

ORB   Object Request Broker

Owners Of The Reuse Business   The executives that control the reuse business and that the Software Engineering Business Manager reports to. They are responsible for giving direction and funding during the setup and execution of the reuse business.

Package   A general purpose mechanism for organizing elements into groups. Packages may be nested within other packages. A system may be thought of as a single high-level package, with everything else in the system contained in it. Packages typically contain packages, types, and classes that belong together according to some criterion, perhaps because they offer a particular service, or should be used together, or will be implemented for execution on a particular machine.

Packaging *(verb)*   Grouping of types and classes and the like into packages, facades, and configuration items.

Parameter (in template)   A component is parameterized by inserting unbound parameters or macro expressions at appropriate variation points within a component. The parameterized component can then be specialized by binding or macro-expanding the parameters with actual parameter values.

Pattern   Standard object-oriented designs for standard problems, described in a standard way. A pattern is a template collaboration.

Process   A process is used to represent a single "advancing computation" in most computing environments. That is, a thread of control in a computing environment that can be carried out concurrently with the threads of control represented by other processes, a stereotype of «active class».

Process (Business)   Corresponds to what is called a business use case.

Process Leader   There is a Process Leader appointed for each individual (instance of a) business use case. The Process Leader reports to the Process Owner and is responsible for supervising the execution of an instance of a process and may in many ways be compared with a project leader or project manager.

Process Owner   There is an Process Owner appointed for each business use case type, such as for Application System Engineering. A Process Owner is responsible for the design, improvement, and appropriate configurations of the business process description.

Product plan   Here, a plan of the evolution of the application and component systems.

QA   Quality Assurance

REBOOT   An ESPRIT III project, #7808 REBOOT ("Reuse Based on Object-Oriented Techniques").

Reengineering Directive (Business)   The reengineering directive clearly and effectively tells the entire organization that top management has looked ahead and determined the direction in which the company must go.

Relationship   A semantic connection among model elements. Relationships include associations, generalizations, and dependencies.

Release   A subset of the end product at a major milestone (see: Prototype, Baseline).

Repository   A database or distributed storage service for making common components, models, and system definitions available to developers. Typically used for a distributed development environment or larger development team.

Requirements capture   A process step in the software engineering process, with the purpose of defining *what* the system should do. The most significant activity is to develop a use case model.

Requirements Capture Unit   The Requirements Capture Unit contains the workers needed to capture the requirements on the layered system, an application, or a component system.

Resource   We can think of people and information systems as resources that enact the workers as they participate in the business processes.

Resource Owner   A Resource Owner is responsible for staffing and funding, training individuals as reuse workers and for solving problems in resource allocation.

Resource unit   Individual persons and tools such as information systems are organized in resource units and may enact many workers – almost always within one competence unit. A resource unit is managed by a Resource Owner.

Responsibility   A contract or obligation of a type or class. A responsibility is typically something that an object or a use case instance needs to do or keep track of as the system is used.

Reuse   Further use or repeated use of an artifact. Typically, software artifacts are designed for use outside of their original context to create new systems.

Reuse Business (RSEB)   Our process and organization framework for systematic reuse. Full name Reuse-driven Software Engineering Business. We abbreviate it as RSEB. For short, we call it the Reuse Business. We use the lowercase "reuse business" to refer to an "instance" of the Reuse Business, a custom installation of the Reuse Business in a particular software organization.

Reuse Manager   A synonymous term used when we want to emphasize the "reuse orientation" of a SEB Manager. See also RSEB Manager.

Reuser   Someone who reuses components.

Reverse engineering   In business engineering, reverse engineering of the existing organization is done to get an accepted common picture of the existing business. Also, in software engineering, done to recover the design and architecture of a system.

Review   An informal or formal examination of a software artifact (a model, a document, or code) applied at various points in the development process to detect faults, ensure compliance with standards, or determine status. See also Inspection.

Risk   An ongoing or upcoming concern which has a significant probability of adversely affecting the success of major milestones. Risk management is a systematic approach to dealing with software risks.

ROI   Return On Investment

RSEB   Reuse Driven Software Engineering Business

RSEB Manager   A synonymous term used when we want to emphasize the "reuse orientation" of a SEB Manager. See also Reuse Manager.

Scenario   A description of a use case instance.

SCM   Source Code Management

SEB   Software Engineering Business

SEB Manager   Software Engineering Business Manager. See also Reuse Manager and RSEB Manager.

SEI   Software Engineering Institute (at Carnegie Mellon University)

SEP   Software Engineering Process

SEPSE   Software Engineering Process Support Environment

Sequence diagram   A sequence diagram is a particularly detailed version of an interaction diagram, that shows in what time-order stimuli are sent between objects to perform a specific flow of events of a use case.

Service package   Service packages contain types or classes and variants that together make up an optional or mandatory set of functionality.

Software architecture   See Architecture.

Software Engineering Business Manager (SEB Manager)   The Software Engineering Business Manager is responsible for the (Reuse-Driven) SEB organization, reporting to the Owners Of The Reuse Business. The Software Engineering Business Manager is responsible for the evolution of the application and component system roll-out plan.

Software Engineering Process (SEP)   A complete software engineering process describes in detail which workproducts to build, what steps to follow in order to build them, who should build them, and what sort of standards and tests should be used to control quality and system correctness. More precisely, software engineering is a process of building several related models.

Software Engineering Process Support Environment (SEPSE)   A set of tools integrated to support one or more SEP, targeted to specific workers.

Software Technology for Adaptable and Reliable Systems (STARS)   A United States Department of Defense (DoD) program aimed at developing improved software technology for mission-critical systems. Funded and inspired a lot of work on systematic reuse, software process, and software architecture.

State A condition or situation during the life of an object during which it satisfies some condition, performs some activity, or waits for some event. The cumulative results of the behavior of an object; one of the possible conditions in which an object may exist.

Stereotype A new type of modeling element that extends the semantics of the metamodel. Stereotypes must be based on certain existing types or classes in the metamodel. Stereotypes may extend the semantics, but not the structure of pre-existing types and classes. Shown by guillemots « ».

Stimulus A generic term for communication primitives like signal and message.

Subordinate system Each individual application and component system in a system of interoperating systems is a subordinate system.

Subscribes to association The publish-subscribe pattern is represented using a «subscribes to» association, similar to the Observer pattern (Gamma *et al.*, 1994).

Subsystem A subsystem is a stereotype of package used to divide the system into smaller parts. Subsystems may in turn contain other subsystems.

Superordinate model The models of the superordinate system are called superordinate models and the constructs defined in them are called superordinate use cases, superordinate subsystems, and so on.

Superordinate subsystem A subsystem defined in a model of a superordinate system.

Superordinate system The superordinate system − with its models − is used to represent both the static and dynamic aspects of the layered system as a whole.

Superordinate use case A use case defined in a use case model of a superordinate system.

Supplier A class or subsystem that is responsible for implementing an interface.

System A collection of connected units that are organized to accomplish a specific purpose. A system can be described by one or more models, possibly from different viewpoints. A system instance is an executable configuration of a software application, or software application family.

A system type is a particular software application, or software application family, that can be configured and installed on some hardware platform.

The word System by itself denotes an arbitrary system instance.

System Object Model (SOM) IBM's CORBA-compliant system object model.

System of Interoperating Systems (SIS) A system that is composed of other systems. In the context of the RSEB − the whole layered system thought of as one system − a system of interoperating application and component systems.

System Software Layer The System Software Layer contains the software for the computing and networking infrastructure, such as operating systems, interfaces to specific hardware, and so on.

System test To test an entire system (often when the use cases have been tested individually).

Systematic reuse Systematic software reuse is the purposeful creation, management, and application of reusable assets.

Target organization(s) The organization(s) for which the application systems are developed. Contains the end users.

Team A group of people who staff a process. Usually drawn from several distinct competence units.

Template A software workproduct with unbound parameters or slots that can be used to create (generate) a complete workproduct. For example, in C++, a template has types as parameters, and can be used to create a C++ class.

Testing A work step in the software engineering process, aimed at uncovering defects by executing specialized programs and test cases. See Inspection and Review for other ways of uncovering defects. See Unit testing, Integration testing and Use case testing.

Testing Unit The Testing Unit is a competence unit which contains the workers needed for testing the layered system, an application, or a component system.

Third-party vendor A person or organization that supplies component systems to an RSEB, either pre-existing or developed under contract.

Thread A single path of execution through a program, a dynamic model, or some other representation of control flow. A thread is a stereotype of the UML active class construct.

TRA Transition to a reuse business.

Trace The different models, and the elements defined in the different models, are seamlessly connected with each other by «trace» dependencies.

Transaction A transaction consists of a set of actions performed by a system. A transaction is invoked by a stimulus from an actor to the system, or by a timed trigger within the system.

Transition to a reuse business The process of customizing and installing a reuse business in one software development organization.

TTM Time To Market

Type A description of a set of instances that share the same operations, abstract attributes, and relationships, and semantics. A type may define an operation specification (such as a signature) but not an operation implementation (such as a method).

UML Unified Modeling Language, version 1.0. A set of semantics and notation for precisely describing system and business models.

Unit testing Testing that a unit matches its specification. By unit we mean either an individual class, a group of classes, or other subprograms, such as member functions in C++. See Testing.

Use case Short for use case type.

Use case instance A use case instance is a sequence of transactions performed by a system, which yields an observable result of values to a particular actor. See also scenario.

Use case model The main purposes of the use case model is to define *what* the system should do, and to allow software engineers and customers to agree on this. The use case model is used to drive the rest of the development work where the object modeling activities are performed with the use case model as a starting point. The model consists of actor types, use cases, and relations between them.

Use case testing   Testing that a use case does what it should for the actor (black-box) and testing of the collaboration between the classes (white-box).

Use case type   A use case type defines a set of use case instances.

Uses generalization   A generalization from a use case type A to a use case type B that indicates that the use case A inherits the use case B. Represented by the «uses» stereotype.

Variability mechanisms   Abstract components can be specialized using a wide range of variability mechanisms, such as inheritance, parametrization, and extension.

Variant   A type-like construct, typically use case or object type or class, intended to be inserted at an appropriate variation point to specialize an abstract type or class.

Variation point   A variation point identifies one or more locations at which variation will occur within a class, type or use case.

VBScript   Microsoft scripting language for use primarily in WWW browsers, but can be used as a simple customization language for other purposes.

Version   A generation of some workproduct; typically, later versions expand upon earlier versions of a workproduct.

Visual Basic (VB)   Microsoft's application implementation language and environment, built on an interpreted, event-extended Basic, with visual forms and controls.

Visual Basic for Applications (VBA)   A subset of Microsoft's Visual Basic, embedded as a customization or business rule language in many application systems, such as Microsoft Word or Microsoft Excel.

Work step   A work step is a piece of work a worker can perform.

Worker   A (business) worker represents people with a certain competence that work within the business. See Internal worker and Case worker.

Workproduct   A workproduct is a unit of software model, code, or document that can be independently managed within a software engineering organization. Individual types and classes from different models, diagrams, and related documents are typical workproducts. Complete models, subsystems, and test models are also workproducts.

Wrapper   A wrapper is a piece of object-oriented software that encapsulates something and manages the interaction with it.

WWW   World Wide Web

XYB   A symbol standing for our hypothetical banking consortium.

XYBsoft   XYB's software development subsidiary

ANNOTATED BIBLIOGRAPHY

This appendix provides an annotated bibliography of selected readings and some online resources. While this is not a comprehensive list, it includes many books and articles we find useful and often recommend to others. We have included many of the articles and books we suggested at the end of each chapter.

B.1 Systematic software reuse

The September 1994 *IEEE Software* special issue on software reuse, edited by Frakes and Isoda (1994), provides a superb starting point for more information on systematic reuse. It includes a literature survey, a brief history of reuse, and several articles describing a variety of reuse programs.

Several books provide excellent discussions of systematic reuse history, principles, and practice. Of particular note are *Software Reusability*, edited by Schaefer, Prieto-Diaz, and Matsumoto (1994) and *Software Reuse: A Holistic Approach*, edited by Karlsson (1995).

B.1.1 Systematic reuse books

Hooper and Chester's (1991) book, *Software Reuse – Guidelines and Methods*, provides a readable and comprehensive introduction to the reuse literature and especially many pragmatic technical and non-technical guidelines.

The book, *Software Reusability*, edited by Schaefer *et al.* (1994) was produced by several attendees at the "First International Workshop on Software Reusability," Dortmund, Germany, July 1991. Six chapters provide a historical overview, a summary of domain analysis methods, discussion of managerial and organizational issues in starting and running a software reuse program, a discussion of formal methods, a summary of tools and environments, and a survey of software reuse empirical studies. Each chapter includes extensive references.

The book, *Software Reuse: A Holistic Approach* (ed. Karlsson, 1995), contains many detailed design and implementation guidelines for the use of C++ to create reusable components and frameworks. They discuss many aspects of modifying the normal software life cycle to support "design for reuse" and "design with reuse." They include an extensive discussion on how to introduce reuse into an organization. They describe assessments, reuse maturity models, and adoption process and roles, and several guidelines for determining the reuse business strategy. They provide a good introduction to reuse metrics.

The excellent and thorough book by Poulin (1996), *Measuring Software Reuse: Principles, Practices and Economic Models*, provides a comprehensive discussion of reuse metrics, and related process and management guidelines on how to start a reuse measurement program.

Tracz's (1995b) book, *Confessions of a Used Program Salesman — Institutionalizing Software Reuse*, is an amusing and insightful description of the many misconceptions and truths of bringing effective software reuse to corporate practicality.

Bassett's (1996) book, *Framing Software Reuse: Lessons from the Real World*, describes an approach to large-scale reuse based on frames, which combine the concepts of both generators and object-like inheritance and encapsulation. The book describes technology and management issues, as well as several detailed case studies and success stories using NETRON/CAP, the product based on the frame technology. This work is characterized by a very thorough set of reuse and productivity metrics.

Prieto-Diaz and Arango's (1991) tutorial book, *Domain Analysis: Acquisition of Reusable Information for Software Construction*, provides an excellent model and summary material prefacing an extensive compilation of papers on different approaches and goals for domain analysis.

Cusumano's (1991) book, *Japan's Software Factories*, describes the organizational aspects and economics of running reuse-based industrial software development organizations.

Biggerstaff and Perlis' (1989) two-volume book, *Software Reusability*, and Tracz's (1988a) IEEE tutorial, *Software Reuse: Emerging Technology*, bring together many useful papers, with additional explanatory material.

B.1.2 Systematic reuse papers

Several papers in the September 1994 *IEEE Software* special issue on "Systematic Reuse" discuss reuse impediments (Frakes and Isoda, 1994), reuse metrics and economics (Lim, 1994), reuse organization structure (Fafchamps, 1994) and generative reuse (Batory *et al.*, 1994). Fafchamp's paper, "Organizational factors and reuse" (Fafchamps, 1994) provides a careful analysis of 10 different reuse organizations, and how communication, control, and trust affect the ways these organizations work.

The November 1993 *IBM Systems Journal* is a special issue on reuse. It includes several papers on IBM's reuse program, such as Poulin *et al.*'s (1993) paper on reuse metrics, and Wasmund's paper on critical factors for reuse success. Several articles discuss reuse experiments, metrics and economics, such as Lewis *et al.* (1991) (comparing OO and non-OO reuse), Stevens (1992) and Poulin *et al.* (1993), including tables, formulas, and practical experience.

Barnes and Bollinger's (1991) paper, "Making Reuse Cost-Effective," stresses that software reuse has the same cost and risk features as any financial investment, and suggests analytical approaches for making good reuse investments. Their "broad spectrum" view of reuse is more than reuse of software (especially not just code). It is reuse of human problem solving (a scarce resource). They suggest that a reuse mindset is one of the fundamentals of proper software development, not just a technology or methodology.

A series of papers by Basili and colleagues on the Experience Factory and the Component Factory provide additional insight on the reuse process and organizing for reuse. "A Reference Architecture for the Component Factory" (Basili *et al.*, 1992) and "The experience factory and its relationship to other improvement paradigms" (Basili, 1993). Basili, Brand and Melo (1996) also describe a carefully constructed and measured experiment, aimed at seeing how reuse influences productivity in OO systems.

The paper by Pfleeger (1996), "Measuring reuse: A cautionary tale," provides insights, warnings, and guidelines as to how a reuse metrics program must be carefully adapted to the specific reuse processes. It has to match the participants' needs and interest in order to be effective.

Comprehensive discussions of reuse metrics, economic models, and management guidelines can be found in the survey by Frakes and Terry (1996), "Software Reuse Metrics and Models".

The paper by Cornwell (1996) describes HP's Domain Engineering process and reuse organization model. See also Arango (1994) and Lung and Urban (1995) for more on domain modeling.

Wegner's (1984) comprehensive four-part paper on "Capital-Intensive Software Technology" fills most of the *IEEE Software* July 1984 issue and was one of the first studies to thoroughly cover many aspects of components and life cycles associated with systematic reuse and a components industry.

Prieto-Diaz's (1991) paper "Making Software Reuse Work: An Implementation Model" suggests that an incremental introduction of reuse is needed. In this paper he stresses the importance of both technical and non-technical issues, and provides a model for implementing a successful software reuse program. This paper gives an excellent view of how to start and run a reuse program, and summarizes many of the issues.

The paper by Davis (1994b), "Adopting a policy of reuse," provides a crisp and readable introduction to the critical success factors, risk-reduction, maturity models, and step-wise reuse adoption process developed at the Software Productivity Consortium. Navarro (1993) also describes an incremental reuse adoption process developed at Hewlett-Packard.

Krueger's (1992) survey, "Software Reuse," analyzes many papers to develop a taxonomy for reuse approaches. He believes that any effective method of doing reuse of any software artifact (such as code, documents, designs, and tests) is closely tied to a method of raising the level of abstraction for that approach. The survey starts with general discussion of abstraction techniques, and ties it to the process of "selection," "specialization," and "integration" needed to reuse the artifact. He then surveys several areas using this framework.

The STARS (1993) *Conceptual Framework for Reuse Processes* (CFRP) has been developed as a concensus reuse macro-process. It defines in two volumes a reuse management process (plan, enact, learn) and a reuse engineering process (create, manage, utilize). It includes a comprehensive glossary, several case studies, and carefully discusses process elements, roles, and issues relevant to initiating and running a reuse program.

The Seybold report on "Component Software: A Market Perspective on the Coming Revolution in Software Development" (Lavoie *et al.*, 1993) gives an economic/market perspective on the forces and scenarios leading to a software components industry. The report covers the driving forces, such as the need to produce ever more complex software at decreasing costs, the role of modularity and new technologies in managing complexity and change, and the issues of investment, management and coordination of creators and users, market growth and segmentation, and modes of selling to various marketplaces.

The "Economics of Software Reuse" panel at OOPSLA'91 (Griss *et al.*, 1991) explored several scenarios of how and whether a components industry would arise. See also the paper on reuse economics by Jones (1994), and Kain's (1994b) paper on reuse ROI and metrics.

Griss's (1993) paper, "Software reuse: From library to factory," discusses many of the non-technical issues, and describes how to move incrementally from a repository-centered view, through the purposeful design and construction of reusable software kits, to a fully systematic reuse process-driven software factory. This paper describes the early history of reuse at HP, the concepts of domain-specific kits, and provides an extensive set of references to other reuse experiences.

The book chapter by Griss, Favaro and Walton (1994), "Managerial and Organizational Issues – Starting and Running a Software Reuse Program," provides an extensive discussion of management pragmatics, additional case studies, and some reuse economics. It describes many managerial issues in starting and running a reuse program.

Several *Object Magazine* columns by Griss and colleagues describe reuse adoption and processes at HP (Griss, 1995a, 1995b; Griss and Collins, 1995), experience with domain-specific kits (Griss, 1995c; Griss and Kessler, 1996), and how application domain commonality and variability are represented (Griss, 1996). Reuse process and reuse organization for significant software reuse, based on HP experience, are discussed in Griss (1995b). Several connect these reuse issues to OO reuse and to Visual Basic component-based software (Griss, 1995c, 1995d, 1996). A short paper by Griss and Wosser (1995) discusses common myths about software reuse and HP's experience with reuse. Papers by Griss and Wentzel discuss domain-specific kits in more detail (Griss and Wentzel, 1994; Griss, 1995c; Griss and Wentzel, 1995) and how variability and domain-specificity are allocated across components with different kinds of variability mechanism.

B.1.3 Systematic reuse journals and conferences

Many reuse workshops have been held since Wegner's survey in 1984. For more detail, see the history chapter in Schaefer *et al.* (1994). Several of the workshops have been summarized in accessible newsletters and journals, and have their proceedings online: WISR'92 (Griss and Tracz, 1992, 1993), WISR'93 (Poulin and Tracz, 1994), WISR'95. International workshops were held in Dortmund, Germany (IWSR'91) (Schaefer *et al.*, 1994), Lucca, Italy (IWSR'93) (Prieto-Diaz and Frakes, 1993; Tracz, 1993) and Rio, Brazil (Tracz, 1995a), the latter of which became the Third International Conference on Software Reusability (ICSR'94), and was held 1–4 November, 1994, in Rio, Brazil. Most of these conferences have introductory reuse tutorials as part of the program. WISR'95 was held in August 1995, in St. Charles Illinois. See the WWW page: http://www.umcs.maine.edu:80/~ftp/wisr/wisr.html for online copies of the WISR proceedings and other reuse events.

American Programmer (Yourdon, 1991a, 1993, 1995), and *IEEE Software* (Tracz, 1987; Reilly and Shriver, 1987) have special issues on reuse and component-software. *IEEE Software* had a special issue on Systematic reuse in September 1994. The *Journal of Systems and Software* had a special software reuse issue in September 1995. The *Application Development Strategies* Newsletter has periodic articles on reuse and component-based development. The February 1997 issue (Yourdon, 1997) discusses several recent books, the IBM "San Francisco" project, the importance of process and organization, Netron and others.

Software Engineering Notes has many issues containing good reuse and OO articles, such as reuse fundamentals (Tracz, 1988a), how to start and run a reuse program (Tracz, 1990; Prieto-Diaz, 1991a), on mega-programming and DSSA (Tracz, 1991; Tracz *et al.*, 1993), reuse conference reports (Griss and Tracz, 1993; Poulin and Tracz, 1994), OO patterns (Gamma *et al.*, 1993; Lea, 1994; Anderson, 1994), and domain-analysis (Prieto-Diaz, 1990). Recent copies of this newsletter are online at http://www.acm.org/sigsoft/SEN/index.html.

The journal of defense software engineering, *CrossTalk*, has numerous short articles on DARPA, DoD, and STARS reuse programs, as well as other reuse-related articles and workshop reports (Piper-Arnett, 1992; Mettala and Graham, 1992; Riggs, 1992; Wallnau, 1992; Ogush, 1992; Stevens, 1992; Hovell, 1994). The STARS Technology Center publishes a periodic newsletter. The STARS ASSET program produces numerous reports, see http://www.asset.com/.

B.2 Object-oriented technology

There are many OO books, and a large number of competing OOA and OOD methods, many complete with tools and training. Although most of these books assert that OO methods support reuse well, only a few go into much detail about reuse, and what it takes to succeed with object-oriented reuse. Only a few of these books provide a well-found software engineering approach based on object technology.

Taylor's (1990) book, *Object-Oriented Technology: A Manager's Guide*, is a concise introduction to the concepts of objects and their importance to software engineering.

This describes for managers how to evaluate OO technology, and succinctly tabulates the benefits and risks, highlighting the role that objects play in obtaining industrial strength reuse. He also includes an excellent glossary.

B.2.1 Object-oriented technology books

Berard (1993), *Essays on Object-Oriented Software Engineering*, covers many items relevant to systematic OO reuse, including a recursive/parallel life cycle, cohesion and coupling, large OO entities and kits, OO domain analysis, OO and reuse mindset, and testing.

Meyer's (1994) book, *Reusable Software: The Base Object-Oriented Component Libraries*, provides many guidelines and patterns for reusable library construction, focusing on key OO techniques and methods, as well as identifying a library taxonomy and illustrating useful and reusable components. His preface discusses the importance and process of reuse. He makes the assertion that "Reuse is a required condition of any progress in software. Not by any means a sufficient condition, but one without which the others — better methods, new development tools, faster hardware, more formal approaches, improved management techniques — cannot fulfill their promises."

Jacobson *et al.*'s (1992) book, *Object-Oriented Software Engineering: A Use Case Driven Approach* (OOSE), extensively discusses techniques based on use cases and factoring of the object model (into three kinds of objects) to support reuse and an incremental, evolutionary process. It provides sections on component development and use. The authors discuss criteria for writing good use case models and provide extensive examples. The book also includes more information on extensions and their role for variability, and provides extensive discussion of analysis and design models, and the use and mapping of various relationships, as well as some programming language issues and guidelines.

Lorenz, in his book *Object-Oriented Software Development: A Practical Guide* (1993b), combines an incremental, iterative process with an OO development model. He highlights the importance of (and difference between) incremental and iterative life cycles in support of OO reuse. He gives numerous practical suggestions, templates, and guidelines for both Smalltalk and C++ programming. In his book *Rapid Software Development with Smalltalk* (1995) he gives practical advice on how to organize a software team for Smalltalk development.

Booch, in the second edition of his book *Object-Oriented Analysis and Design* (1994) has adapted his method to be more consistent with OMT (Rumbaugh *et al.*, 1991) and OOSE (Jacobson *et al.*, 1992), with some examples more oriented to C++ than Ada. He describes a reuse-oriented macro-process and object-oriented micro-process, highlighting the importance of architecture and a well-managed iterative and incremental life cycle. He describes the reuse of components, frameworks, and patterns. He provides pragmatic guidance regarding what can be reused, reuse metrics, and organizational issues. He has a good chapter on frameworks, discussing both vertical (domain specific) and horizontal (general purpose) frameworks applied to the design and construction of the C++ Booch Components, a foundation class library.

Coleman *et al.*, in their book, *Object-Oriented Development: The Fusion Method* (1994), describe an OOA/OOD method that combines features from several methods: object model and process from OMT (Rumbaugh *et al.*, 1991), object interaction from CRC (Wirfs-Brock *et al.*, 1990), object visibility from Booch (1994) and pre- and post-conditions from formal methods. This produces a method that requires a strong commitment to being systematic and rigorous. The book also includes a very well written reuse chapter, summarizing key ideas in systematic reuse, and some of the implications on how OO methods should be adapted and employed to support a reuse organization. However, it does not link reuse closely with the other parts of the OO method. Another book contains several Fusion case studies by Coleman and others (1995), and includes several experience reports describing OO reuse and OO platforms.

Wirfs-Brock *et al.*, in their book *Designing Object-Oriented Software* (1990), describe the CRC method (Class-Responsibility-Collaborations). They make the point that OO programming tools do not, by themselves, guarantee reusable, maintainable, extensible software. Nor are they absolutely necessary. Their role is to make it easier for a team to spend the time to design for reuse. They suggest that it is possible to reuse components, frameworks, subsystems, and complete applications. Applications are built by combining components, frameworks, and application-specific entities. They introduce the notion of clients and servers, and the concept of contracts, which they see as an important feature for reuse.

Goldberg and Rubin's book, *Succeeding with Objects: Decision Frameworks for Project Management* (1995), involves an analysis of several large case studies. The book covers the entire OO development process, including organization, reuse, training, process improvement, tools, and technology. It provides numerous guidelines and models for selecting between alternative approaches. Reuse is one of the dominant motivators for selecting OT and structuring a development. They provide practical advice on establishing reuse and framework organizations, selecting a reuse process, establishing project and organization business objectives, and choosing technology.

The book by McGregor and Sykes, *Object-Oriented Software Development: Engineering Software for Reuse* (1992), describes a complete OO development process, with a process model, component guidelines, material on testing, metrics, frameworks, and component libraries. They provide an excellent discussion of the technical criteria to be used in evaluating object-oriented libraries, and many other guidelines related to a fractal, incremental, iterative, component-based software development process. Also contains many useful component development and testing guidelines.

Booch's book, *Object Solutions: Managing the Object-Oriented Project* (1996), provides useful pragmatics on structuring and managing an incremental, iterative software life cycle for object-oriented development.

The excellent book *The Essential Distributed Objects Survival Guide*, by Orfali, Harkey and Edwards (1996), provides a comprehensive discussion and comparison of several distributed computing systems, such as CORBA, OLE/COM, and several others.

B.2.2 Object-oriented technology papers

Several of Jacobson's *Object Magazine* columns describe the development of Ericsson's AXE (Jacobson, 1996a, 1996b). The papers provide compelling details on the strategic importance and technical details of the Ericsson AXE experience, and how OO architecture, process, and reuse were key to success. They explain the principles of architecture, process, and organization change needed for success.

Several papers by Jacobson, colleagues and students give detail on early industrial experience with OOSE (Jacobson, 1987), how it can be used to describe large object-oriented systems (Koistinen, 1994), introducing pluggable architectures (Jacobson et al., 1995a). System of interoperating systems and superordinate systems are discussed in detail in the "Systems of Interconnected Systems" article by Ivar Jacobson, Karin Palmkvist, Susanne Dyrhage, *ROAD* (Jacobson et al., 1995b).

Cox's (1990a, 1990b) papers, "Planning the software industrial revolution" and "There is a silver bullet," suggest using a hardware analogy of "Software ICs" and software buses, and addresses how large-scale reuse should be pursued. An earlier paper by Meyer (1987), "Reusability: The Case for Object-Oriented Design," gives many guidelines.

Lorenz's (1993a) paper "Facilitating reuse using OO technology" explains how naive use of OT will not enhance reuse. Overuse of inheritance is cited as an example.

Pittman's (1993) paper, "Lessons learned in managing object-oriented development," discusses the issues involved in managing OT, and provides guidelines and an incremental, iterative process to enhance reuse and increase changes of success. He stresses that reuse happens by design, not by accident. In a sidebar, "Managing Reuse: Exposing the hidden agenda," he explains that choosing OO does not automatically guarantee reuse. Despite several technical and standards issues, a carefully managed, reuse-oriented iterative and incremental process is the most critical element necessary to achieve significant levels of OO reuse.

Johnson and Foote (1988) and Johnson and Russo (1991) carefully define and distinguish reuse achieved from (abstract) base classes, and that achieved from frameworks.

Neirstrasz, Gibbs, and Tsichritzis (1992) suggest that modifications to OOP, OO frameworks, and OO tools will be needed before true component-oriented software development will arise. While the confluence of the need for open applications and the advent of OO technology is creating the drive, the current focus on OO programming languages and tools, rather than reuse-oriented composition, is delaying progress. They see the need to augment OO inheritance and encapsulation technology with additional guidelines and mechanisms to enhance reuse, support finding, composition, and adaptation of components, and guidelines for reusable framework design.

Several papers explain how inheritance can be severely misused, leading to lots of non-local connection between methods (so-called "yo-yo" problem) (Taenzer et al., 1989a, 1989b). Multiple inheritance is particularly troublesome (McGregor and Korson, 1992). Both lead to software that is hard to debug and trace, though tools might help (Lorenz, 1991, 1993a). Even though object-oriented software is easier to understand, inheritance and polymorphism often make many OO systems much harder to maintain (Wilde et al., 1993).

Information on the Unified Modeling Language, UML, can be obtained from the UML Report, issued by Rational Software Corporation (Booch et al., 1997a) and several papers and books by Jacobson, Rumbaugh, and Booch (Booch et al., 1998; Jacobson et al., 1998; Rumbaugh et al., 1998). See the WWW page, http://www.rational.com/.

B.2.3 Object-oriented journals and conferences

American Programmer (Yourdon, 1991b, 1992), *IEEE Software* (Kozaczynski and Kuntzman-Combules, 1993), *CACM* (McGregor and Korson, 1990; Korson *et al.*, 1992; Meyer and Lambert, 1993) and *IEEE Computer* (Rine and Bhargava, 1992) have periodic special issues on OO software including many articles on OO analysis and design, and OO reuse.

Object-Oriented Strategies, provides frequent discussion of object components, tools, frameworks and methods. See Harmon (1994a, b, c; 1995a, b) and the various WWW pages: http://www.yourdon.com, http://www.cutter.com, http://www.acm.org and http://www.ieee.org.

Object Magazine, the *Journal of Object-Oriented Programming*, and *Byte* have periodic columns and short articles on issues related to commercial production of software components (Taylor, 1992a, 1992b, 1994; Udell, 1994), object-oriented reuse methods and management (Taylor, 1993; Kain, 1994a), economics and metrics (Kain, 1994b), class, library, and framework design (Firesmith, 1994; Chen and Chen, 1994; Koenig, 1994), and improved OO methods (Henderson-Sellers and Edwards, 1994).

Several articles by Jacobson and colleagues on use case engineering and System of Interconnected Systems appear in *ROAD* (Jacobson, 1994a, 1994b, 1994c).

The OMG publishes a newsletter, and also has several publications on the Common Object Request Broker Architecture (CORBA), the Common Object Services Specification (COSS), and several OO method descriptions and analysis (Hutt, 1994). A list of publications, a packet of material describing the OMG, and the newsletter can be obtained from the OMG, 492 Old Connecticut Path, Framingham, MA 01701, USA (Fax 508–820–4303, email: pubs@omg.org). See the WWW pages at http://www.omg.org.

Berard's (1989) seminar, "Object-Oriented Domain Analysis," and material in his book (1993) describe the connections between OOA/D and domain analysis, and motivates an OODA process to enhance reuse.

The OOPSLA, ECOOP, TOOLS, and Object World conferences have many papers, panels, workshops, and tutorials on OO reuse, as do many other ACM and IEEE conferences. See the WWW http://www.acm.org/sigplan/ and http://www.acm.org/sigsoft/.

The Internet *comp.object newsgroup* often has discussions on OO and its relation to software reuse.

B.3 Architecture and patterns

Of growing significance to the understanding of successful software systems and software reuse is software architecture. Associated with the architecture of software systems are the notions of architectural style, architecture catalogs, architectural modeling systems, frameworks, and patterns.

The paper by Kruchten (1995) illustrates how important it is to take multiple views of an architecture in order to understand and develop it. Physical, process, logical, and development views reveal different aspects of a system to different stakeholders. He also shows how use cases can be used as scenarios to illustrate and derive these views.

The concept of a pattern language was developed originally by Christopher Alexander (1977, 1979), an architect and town planner who has attempted to unify sets of interacting rules, used for living space designs, ranging in scope from kitchens and porches to complete towns. In the OO software engineering community, a standard style of documenting patterns has emerged, describing a standard solution to a standard design problem, and the forces that act to make this pattern. Lea's (1994) paper, "Christopher Alexander: An introduction for object-oriented designers," describes how the essential ideas apply to software.

B.3.1 Architecture and patterns books

The book, *Software Architecture: Perspectives on an Emerging Discipline*, by Shaw and Garlan (1996) tries to define carefully what an architecture is and provides a detailed look at the concept of architectural style, summarizing a variety of standard styles, such as pipes and filters, layered systems, object-oriented systems, and event-based implicit invocation. They provide numerous case studies, and include several articles by others on specific architectural design guidance. They also discuss how architects should be educated, and describe tools and formal models of architecture.

The book, *Design Patterns – Elements of Reusable Object-Oriented Software*, by Gamma, Helm, Johnson, and Vlissides (1994) shows how the concept of pattern languages and pattern catalogs can be applied to object-oriented software. A pattern is a description of a common software problem that can be solved by a relatively standard set of connected objects. They describe some standard design patterns, and how these should be implemented as a society of collaborating objects. This set of objects is typically viewed as a small architecture or set of mechanisms. It can be represented as a class or a composite object, and instantiated informally by following the pattern guidelines. Sometimes, use cases, collaborations, and more formal object models can be used to describe patterns, and perhaps lead to more formal generation of systems from patterns. They also discuss how OO techniques such as inheritance, delegation, and aggregation can best be exploited to produce reusable components.

The book edited by Coplien and Schmidt (1995), *Pattern Languages of Program Design*, includes numerous short papers that describe patterns for frameworks and components, systems and distributed processing, business objects, architecture, and events. They also include some "non-technical" patterns describing software engineering processes, management guidelines, and techniques to organization patterns.

The book, *A System of Patterns*, by Buschman, Meurier, Rohnert, Sommerland and Stal (1996) provides a useful catalog of architectural patterns that can be combined into a suitable architecture. They provide advice on implementing the patterns and discussions of the pros and cons of the individual patterns. See also the book by Pree (1995), *Design Patterns for Object-Oriented Software*.

B.3.1 Architecture and patterns papers

Several papers in the *IEEE Software* special issue on software architecture edited by Boasson (1995), suggest that architecture is a key element of ensuring success with reuse.

The paper by Garlan, Allen and Ockerbloom (1995) shows how different architectural assumptions make it almost impossible to integrate independent components that initially seem to be compatible and worth using. They also summarize several other issues, related to domain-specific architectures and reuse.

Papers by Shaw (1995), Garlan (1995) and Garlan and Shaw (1993), describe the issue of architectural style, and the importance of catalogs of styles and standard architectures. They relate the use of standard styles and standard architectures to successful reuse. Such styles include "pipes and filters," "objects," "data-centered," "blackboard" and "layered." More formally, if an architecture is viewed as a set of Components and Connections, these should be drawn from a legal architectural style of allowed Components, Connectors, and Connection rules.

Several groups are collecting reusable designs, frameworks, and patterns in "architecture handbooks." See papers by Anderson (1994), Lea (1994) and Johnson (1994) discussing the application of architecture pattern language to software architecture, particularly to mechanisms and frameworks. Coad's (1992) paper discusses object-oriented patterns, gives examples of seven basic patterns, and shows how to apply these in a simple design. See also the set of OO reuse guidelines compiled by Lea and Frakes (1993) at WISR'92 (Griss and Tracz, 1993) and WISR'93 (Poulin and Tracz, 1994). Beck (1994) describes object patterns, and Betz (1995) describes frameworks in an interesting way.

See the WWW http://st-www.cs.uiuc.edu/users/patterns/patterns.html for extensive pattern information.

B.4   Software engineering

The short and extremely cogent book, *Controlling Software Development*, by Putnam and Myers (1996) describes at an executive briefing level, the essence of how to use software metrics to manage software development.

Pressman's (1997) software engineering textbook, *Software Engineering: A practitioner's approach*, is a recently revised, very readable and comprehensive survey of a large number of key topics in software engineering, covering life cycles, software processes, managing software projects, metrics, risk management, configuration management, architecture, analysis and design, object technology, and reuse. He includes extensive references, and many useful WWW pointers.

B.4.1   Software engineering books

Watts Humphrey's (1995) book, *A Discipline for Software Engineering*, describes a personal software process (PSP). This combines the incremental process improvement ideas pioneered in the Software Engineering Institute (SEI) Capability Maturity Model (CMM) and his previous book (1989), with a systematic reuse-oriented, C++-based design and implementation strategy. There is a lot of material on design methods, inspections, metrics, cyclic processes, project planning, process and quality management, and reuse.

Boehm's classic book, *Software Engineering Economics* (1981), provides an extensive and comprehensive discussion of software process and software metrics, with details on the Constructive Cost Modeling (COCOMO) approach to estimating costs and effort.

Grady, in two books, describes HP's extensive experience with establishing a company-wide software metrics program (Grady and Caswell, 1987) and how software metrics can be used as a pragmatic tool for project management and process improvement (Grady, 1992). He provides numerous guidelines as to how company metrics standards should be established and how a measurement program should be introduced.

The book by Gilb, *Principles of Software Engineering Management* (1988), defines in great detail various incremental life cycles, and how these are used to control development in various situations.

B.4.2 Software engineering papers

Boehm describes the spiral model of Software Development and Enhancement (Boehm, 1988). This is an incremental life-cycle model, aimed as a replacement for the older waterfall life cycle. Each increment is focused on identifying and controlling specific risks in an environment with changing requirements, technology, and other uncertainty. The spiral model and other techniques help in a systematic approach to management of software risk (Boehm, 1991).

Additional details on COCOMO can be found in a paper describing how to control software costs (Boehm and Papaccio, 1988). New work on an updated COCOMO 2.0 model can be found in a USC technical report (Boehm *et al.*, 1994).

Basili and Weiss's (1984) paper on software metrics describes the essence of the goal-question-metric (GQM) method of gathering process improvement specific measurements.

The paper, "Beyond methods and CASE: The software engineering process with its integral support environment" by Jacobson and Jacobson, *Object Magazine* (1995) presents the idea of comprehensive tools support for a software engineering process.

B.4.3 Software engineering journals and conferences

The *IEEE Computer* has several articles by Jones, discussing the economics of software reuse (1994), function points (1995) and software estimations (1996). Most issues of *IEEE Software* and *IEEE Transactions on Software Methods* carry numerous articles on metrics, life cycles, and process.

Software Engineering Notes (SEN) has numerous articles on software process, software metrics, software reuse, and objects. *American Programmer* is another excellent resource, covering technical issues, and opinions of industry experts.

The Software Engineering Institute at CMU publishes a variety of reports on various aspects of software engineering, including architecture and reuse. Their WWW page http://www.sei.cmu.edu/ describes their courses and technical reports.

B.5 Business Process Reengineering and Organizational Change Management

Business process reengineering deals with a systematic restructuring of the organization, management, and technology of companies to optimize work around key business processes.

The object-oriented business engineering approach used in this book is described in the book, *The Object Advantage: Business Process Reengineering with Object Technology*, (TOA) by Jacobson and colleagues (1994). The book describes how the use case approach can be used to analyze the business processes of an enterprise, and from there to develop information systems and business objects.

Organizational change management is focused on systematically managing the people issues during organization changes, providing guidance on directly addressing concerns such as fear and uncertainty.

Hammer and Stanton, in their book *The Reengineering Revolution: A Handbook* (1995), provide numerous pragmatic guidelines for success with Business Process Reengineering (BPR), particularly with the role of management leadership, the reengineering team, pilots, and people issues. They provide many pragmatic guidelines on how to succeed with BPR. The basic concepts of BPR are described in an earlier book (Hammer and Champy, 1993).

Another perspective on using objects to model business processes can be found in Taylor's book, *Business Engineering with Object Technology* (1995a), which describes a BPR process, called Convergent Engineering, which uses object modeling and a set of business objects as the basis of a systematic merger of business engineering and software engineering. Reuse of the models and business objects is an important part of this work.

The book by Moore, *Crossing the Chasm: Marketing and Selling Technology Products to Mainstream Customers* (1991), details the extra effort and techniques needed to move from successful pilots of a technology with early adopters to widespread use by a majority of the organization.

Systematic organization change management offers specific guidance in dealing with people issues during changes. Techniques include identifying the needs and issues of key stakeholders, assessing the readiness of an organization to change, developing a staged communication plan, and monitoring stages of change, such as "denial," "anger," "unfreezing," and "transition." Many companies have their own change management processes, such as that used by the Hewlett-Packard Professional Services Organization (HP PSO Americas, 1995) or Price-Waterhouse (Price-Waterhouse Change Integration Team, 1995). Tutorials and consulting such as that by Fiman (1992) provide change management workshops.

USE OF THE UNIFIED MODELING LANGUAGE IN THE RSEB

C.1 Using the Unified Modeling Language

The modeling language and the notation used in the RSEB are based on the Unified Modeling Language (UML) (Booch and Rumbaugh, 1995; Booch *et al.*, 1996, 1997, 1998; Jacobson, 1998; Rumbaugh, 1998). A few constructs have been adapted to the needs of the RSEB and several new constructs have been added. The UML concept of stereotypes has been used extensively to both add new constructs and specialize existing ones.

"A stereotype represents the metaclassification of an element." (Booch *et al.*, 1996)

Moreover,

"Stereotypes have semantic implications which may be specified for every specific stereotype value." (Booch *et al.*, 1996)

This leaves the UML very flexible; almost any new "modeling element type" can be added by introducing the corresponding stereotype, together with its "semantic implications."

Below we list the UML stereotypes used in the RSEB for each model together with additional and specialized constructs.

C.2 UML types, classes and stereotypes

A type or class is shown in general by a bold rectangular shape, with several variations showing more details, as indicated in Figure C.1 for an **Account** type.

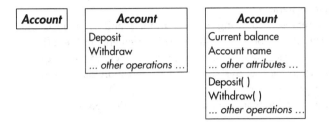

Figure C.1 *Three alternative notations for a type (or class). The first shows only the type name. The second shows the type name and a list of operations. The third shows type, list of attributes, and list of operations.*

The stereotype is a "tag," or symbol, used to mark the type (or meta-classification) of an object or other construct so that it can be distinguished and treated differently from other types of types, classes or other elements. The stereotype is sometimes shown on the type/class rectangle using the «*stereotype*» notation, or may instead be shown by a distinguished icon on the type rectangle, or by a different shape or notation for the type instead of the rectangle when using a more collapsed notation. As an example, Figure C.2 shows a *boundary type*, indicated by the stereotype «*boundary*», a particular kind of type used in analysis models.

Figure C.2 *The standard, the expanded, and the collapsed view of a «boundary» stereotype of a type.*

The name of a UML construct can be shown in several ways; in the tag, within the "main symbol," or underneath the symbol, as illustrated in Figure C.3.

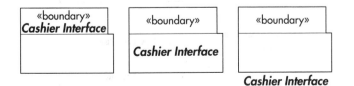

Figure C.3 *Different ways to show the name of an element.*

C.3 General RSEB constructs

The reuse business relies heavily on the notion of interoperating systems of different kinds. There is the superordinate system that is used to represent the layered system itself. Then there are the individual application and component systems, each a system that is subordinate to the superordinate system.

Each of these systems is represented using several models and is divided into configuration items to allow easy adaptation at installation time. Elements in the different models may be connected with trace links. Each component system may export components by including them in its facade. Systems, models, and individual types and classes may import from component systems.

Each type, class or use case may have an arbitrary set of variation points.

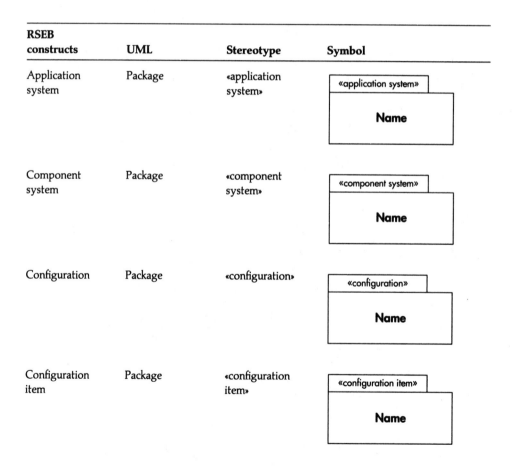

RSEB constructs	UML	Stereotype	Symbol
Application system	Package	«application system»	«application system» Name
Component system	Package	«component system»	«component system» Name
Configuration	Package	«configuration»	«configuration» Name
Configuration item	Package	«configuration item»	«configuration item» Name

RSEB constructs	UML	Stereotype	Symbol
Facade	Package	«facade»	
Imports (an import in UML)	Dependency	«imports»	
Model	Package	«model»	
Subordinate system	Package	«subordinate system»	
Superordinate system	Package	«superordinate system»	
System	Package	«system»	
Traceability link or trace	Dependency	«trace»	

RSEB constructs	UML	Stereotype	Symbol
Variation point		«variation point»	•

C.4 The use case model of an information system

The main purposes of the use case model are to define *what* the system should do, and to allow the software engineers and the customers to agree on this (Jacobson, 1994a). The use case model consists of *«actor»* and *«use case»* types.

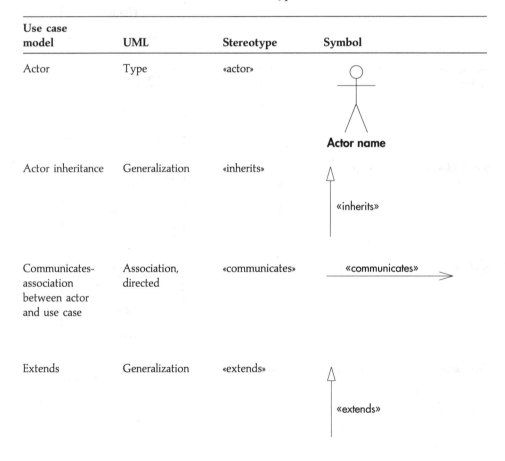

Use case model	UML	Stereotype	Symbol
Actor	Type	«actor»	**Actor name**
Actor inheritance	Generalization	«inherits»	«inherits»
Communicates-association between actor and use case	Association, directed	«communicates»	«communicates»
Extends	Generalization	«extends»	«extends»

Use case model	UML	Stereotype	Symbol
Use case	Use case		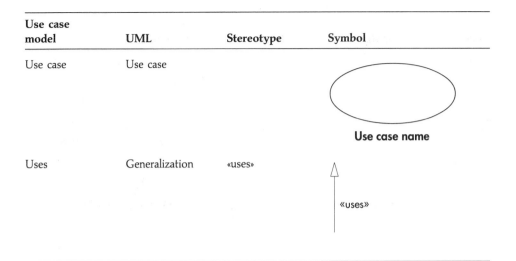
			Use case name
Uses	Generalization	«uses»	«uses»

C.5 The analysis model of an information system

The *analysis model* is a model of the system design at a high level, ignoring the specific low-level details of the target implementation environment.

Analysis model	UML	Stereotype	Symbol
Acquaintance-association	Association, directed	«acquaintance»	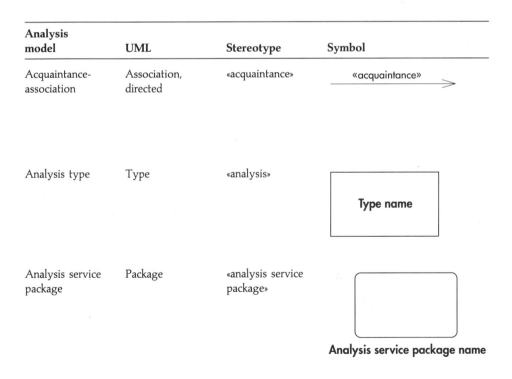 «acquaintance»
Analysis type	Type	«analysis»	**Type name**
Analysis service package	Package	«analysis service package»	
			Analysis service package name

Analysis model	UML	Stereotype	Symbol
Analysis subsystem	Package	«analysis subsystem»	 **Analysis subsystem name**
Boundary type	Type	«boundary»	**Boundary type name**
Collaboration	Collaboration		**Collaboration name**
Communicates-association	Association, directed	«communicates»	«communicates»
Consists of-association	Association, directed, aggregation	«consists of»	«consists of»
Control type	Type	«control»	**Control type name**
Depends on-relationship	Dependency	«depends on»	«depends on»

Analysis model	UML	Stereotype	Symbol
Entity type	Type	«entity»	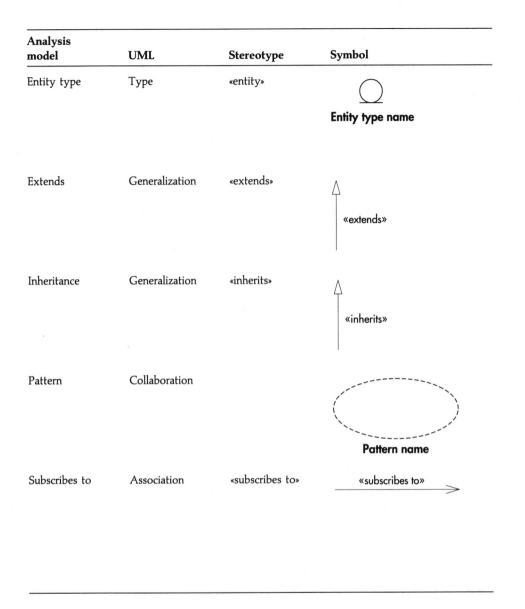
Extends	Generalization	«extends»	
Inheritance	Generalization	«inherits»	
Pattern	Collaboration		
Subscribes to	Association	«subscribes to»	

C.6 The design model of an information system

The *design model* serves as a "blueprint" of how the source code is organized, and some of its key features. Similar to the analysis model, the design model consists of design classes (and types) and design subsystems.

Design model	UML	Stereotype	Symbol
Acquaintance-association	Association, directed	«acquaintance»	«acquaintance» ⟶
Collaboration	Collaboration		(dashed ellipse) **Collaboration name**
Communicates-association	Association, directed	«communicates»	«communicates» ⟶
Consists of-association	Association, directed, aggregation	«consists of»	«consists of» ⟶
Depends on-association	Dependency	«depends on»	«depends on» ⤍
Design class	Class	«design»	(box) **Design class name**
Design type	Type	«design type», or «control», «entity», «boundary»	(box) **Design type name**

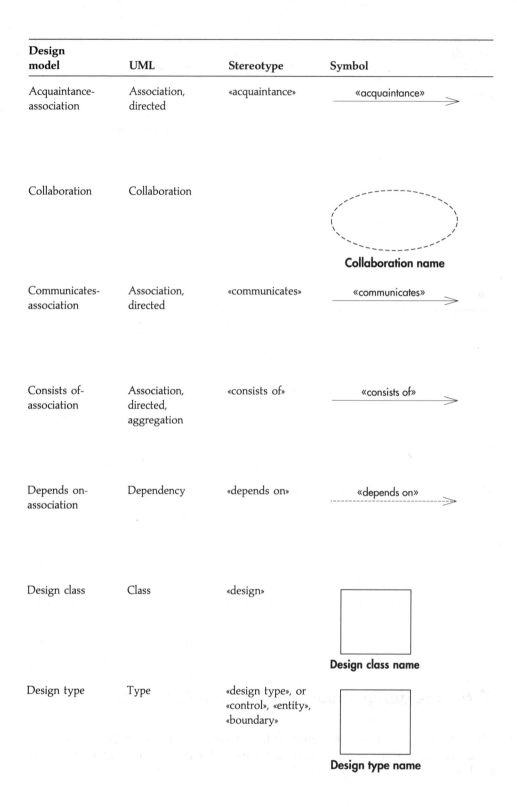

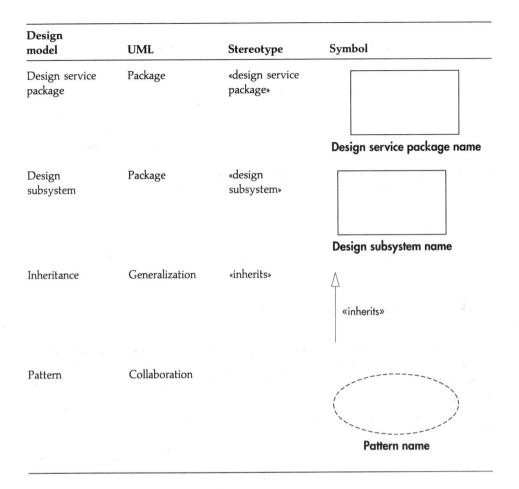

Design model	UML	Stereotype	Symbol
Design service package	Package	«design service package»	**Design service package name**
Design subsystem	Package	«design subsystem»	**Design subsystem name**
Inheritance	Generalization	«inherits»	«inherits»
Pattern	Collaboration		**Pattern name**

C.7   The business use case model

The use cases and actors in the *business use case model* provide a *usability view* of the business, that is, how the business adds value to customers and partners.

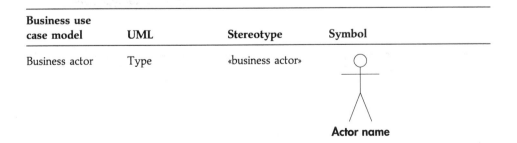

Business use case model	UML	Stereotype	Symbol
Business actor	Type	«business actor»	**Actor name**

Business use case model	UML	Stereotype	Symbol
Business use case	Use case	«business use case»	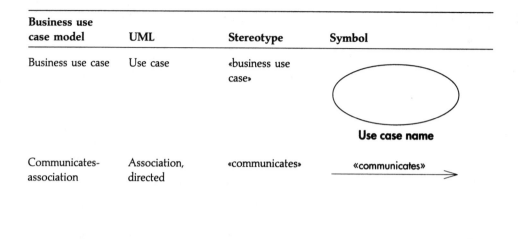 Use case name
Communicates-association	Association, directed	«communicates»	«communicates»

C.8   The business object model

In order to organize a business it is necessary to identify the competencies required by the employees, the roles they need to play and the "things" that one or several of the employees use or handle as they perform the business use cases. This is done in terms of the *business object model*.

Business object model	UML	Stereotype	Symbol
Business entity type	Type	«entity»	Business entity type name
Case worker type	Type	«case worker»	Case worker type name
Communicates-association	Association, directed	«communicates»	«communicates»

Business object model	UML	Stereotype	Symbol
Competence unit	Package	«competence unit»	**Competence unit name**
Internal worker type	Type	«internal worker»	**Internal worker type name**

REFERENCES

This appendix lists all references used in the book.

Alexander C. *et al.* (1977). *A Pattern Language: Towns, Buildings, Construction.* New York: Oxford University Press

Alexander C. (1979). *The Timeless Way of Building.* New York: Oxford University Press

Anderson B. (1994). Patterns: Building blocks for object-oriented architectures. *Software Engineering Notes*, **19**(1), 47–9

Arango G. (1994). Domain analysis methods. In *Software Reusability*, Ellis Horwood

Asker B. (1994). Att bygga produkter med köpt programvara – nya möjligheter och nya krav, Sveriges Verkstadsindustrier, Report, on information technology, No. 4, November (Order no. V040024)

Barnes B. and Bollinger T.B. (1991). Making reuse cost-effective. *IEEE Software*, **8**(1), 13–24

Basili V.R. (1993). The experience factory and its relationship to other improvement paradigms. In *Fourth European Software Engineering Conference Proceedings* (Sommerville I. and Paul M., eds), September, pp. 68–83. Berlin, Germany: Springer-Verlag

Basili V.R. and Weiss D.R. (1984). A method for collecting valid software engineering data. *IEEE Transactions of Software Engineering*, November, 728−38

Basili V.R., Caldiera G. and Cantone G. (1992). A reference architecture for the component factory. *ACM Transactions on Software Engineering and Methodology*, **1**(1), 53−80

Basili V.R., Brand L.C. and Melo W. (1996). How reuse influences productivity in object-oriented systems. *CACM*, **39**(10), pp. 104−36

Bassett P.G. (1991). Software engineering for softness. *American Programmer*, **4**(3), 24−38

Bassett P.G. (1995). To make or buy? There is a third alternative. *American Programmer*, November

Bassett P.G. (1996). *Framing Software Reuse: Lessons from the Real World*. NJ: Yourdon Press, Prentice Hall

Batory D. *et al.* (1993). Scalable software libraries. *Proc. Sigsoft*, pp. 191−9. ACM Press, New York

Batory D. *et al.* (1994). The GenVoca model of software-system generators. *IEEE Software*, **11**(5), 89−94

Beck R.P., Ryan D.R. *et al.* (1992). Architectures for large scale reuse. *AT&T Technical Journal*, **71**(6), 34−45

Beck K. (1994). Patterns and software engineering. *Dr Dobb's Journal*, February

Berard Software Engineering (1989). *Object-oriented domain analysis* (OODA), June

Berard E.V. (1993). *Essays on Object-Oriented Software Engineering*, Vol. 1. Englewood Cliffs, NJ: Prentice Hall

Betz M. (1995). Enterprise object frameworks: Foundations of reuse. *American Programmer*, **8**(11)

Biggerstaff T. and Perlis A. (1989). *Software Reusability*, Vols 1 & 2. NY: ACM Press

Boasson M., ed. (1995). Special issue: Architecture. *IEEE Software*, November, **12**(6)

Boehm B.W. (1981). *Software Engineering Economics*. Englewood Cliffs, NJ: Prentice Hall

Boehm B.W. (1988). A Spiral Model of Software Development and Enhancement. *IEEE Communications*, **21**(5), 61−72

Boehm B.W. and Papaccio P.N. (1988). Understanding and controlling software costs. *IEEE Transactions on Software Engineering*, **14**(10), 1462−77

Boehm B.W. (1991). Software risk management: Principles and practices. *IEEE Software*, **8**(1), 32−4

Boehm B.W., Clark B. *et al.* (1994). Cost Models for Future Software Life Cycle Processes: Cocomo 2.0. Technical Report 2.2, USC and UC Irvine, October

Booch G. (1987). *Software Components with Ada*. Menlo Park, CA: Benjamin/Cummings

Booch G. (1994). *Object-Oriented Analysis and Design, with Applications* 2nd edn. Redwood City, CA: The Benjamin/Cummins Publishing Company

Booch G. (1996). *Object Solutions, Managing the Object-Oriented Project*. Menlo Park, CA: Addison-Wesley

Booch G. and Rumbaugh J. (1995). *Unified Method for Object-Oriented Development*, Documentation set, version 0.8. Rational Software Corporation

Booch G., Jacobson I. and Rumbaugh J. (1996). *The Unified Modeling Language for Object-Oriented Development*, Documentation set, version 0.9 Addendum. Rational Software Corporation

Booch G., Jacobson I. and Rumbaugh J. (1997). *The Unified Modeling Language for Object-Oriented Development*, Documentation set, version 1.0. Rational Software Corporation

Booch G., Jacobson I. and Rumbaugh J. (1998 [expected Spring]). *Unified Modeling Language User Guide*. Menlo Park, CA: Addison-Wesley

Bowles A. (1995). Modeling business abstractions. *Object Magazine*, July–August

Brändemar M. (1996). Pilotprojekt, Workshops och Boot Camps. *Object Computing*, February, 20–22. Stockholm, Sweden

Brockschmidt K. (1995). *Inside OLE 2* 2nd edn. Microsoft Press

Brooks F.P. Jr (1987). No silver bullet: Essence and accidents of software engineering. *Computer*, April, pp. 10–19

Buschmann F., Meurier R., Rohnert H., Sommerlad P. and Stal M. (1996). *A System of Patterns*. Wiley

Caldiera G. and Basili V.R. (1991). Identifying and qualifying reusable software components. *IEEE Computer*, February

Chen D.J. and Chen D.T.K. (1994). An experimental study of using reusable software design frameworks to achieve software reuse. *Journal of Object-Oriented Programming*, 7(2), 56–66

Coad P. (1992). Object-oriented patterns. *Communications of the ACM*, **35**(9)

Coleman D., Arnold P., Bodoff S., Dolin C., Hayes F. and Jeremaes P. (1994). *Object-Oriented Development: The Fusion Method*. Englewood Cliffs, NJ: Prentice Hall

Coleman D., Letsinger R. and Malan R. (1995). *Object-oriented Development at Work: The Fusion Method in the Real World*. Englewood Cliffs, NJ: Prentice Hall

Cooley J. (1993). SynverVision task objects. *Softbench Insights*, Hewlett-Packard, May

Coplien J.O. and Schmidt D.C. (1995). *Pattern Languages of Program Design*. Reading, MA: Addison-Wesley

Cornwell P.C. (1996). HP Domain Analysis: Producing useful models for reusable software. *Hewlett-Packard Journal*, **47**(4), pp. 46–55

Cox B.J. (1990a). Planning the software industrial revolution. *IEEE Software*, 7(6), 25–33

Cox B.J. (1990b). There is a silver bullet. *BYTE*, October, pp. 209–18

Cusumano M.A. (1991). *Japan's Software Factories: A Challenge to US Management*. New York: Oxford University Press

Cusumano M.A. and Selby R.W. (1995). *Microsoft Secrets*. New York: The Free Press, a division of Simon & Schuster

Davis T. (1992). Toward a reuse maturity model. In *Proceedings of the 5th Annual Workshop on Software Reuse* (Griss M. and Latour L., eds), pp. Davis/t-1:7. University of Maine, Department of Computer Science, October

Davis M.J. (1992). Stars reuse maturity model: Guidelines for reuse strategy formulation. In *Proceedings of the 5th Annual Workshop on Software Reuse* (Griss M. and Latour L., eds), pp. Davis/M-1:7. Department of Computer Science, University of Maine, October

Davis J. and Morgan T. (1993). Object-oriented development at Brooklyn Union Gas. *IEEE Software*, **10**(1), 67−74

Davis T. (1994a). The reuse capability model. *CrossTalk*, March, pp. 5−9

Davis T. (1994b). Adopting a policy of reuse. *IEEE Spectrum*, June, pp. 44−8

Deloitte & Touche Consulting Group (1996). 7th Annual Survey of North American Telecommunications

DeMarco T. (1982). *Controlling Software Projects*. New York: Yourdon Press

Fafchamps D. (1994). Organizational factors and reuse. *IEEE Software*, **11**(5), 31−41

Favaro J. (1996). A comparison of approaches to reuse investment analysis. *Fourth International Conference of Software Reuse*, April, pp. 136−45. Orlando, FL: IEEE

Fiman B. (1992). *Managing Change*. IMA

Firesmith D.G. (1994). Using parameterized classes to achieve reusability while maintaining the coupling of application-specific objects. *Journal of Object-Oriented Programming*, **7**(3), 41−4

Frakes W.B. and Fox C.J. (1995). Sixteen questions about software reuse. *CACM*, **38**(6), 75−87, 112

Frakes W.B. and Fox C.J. (1996). Quality improvement using a software reuse failure modes model. *IEEE Transactions on Software Engineering*, **22**(4), 274−9

Frakes W.B. and Isoda S. (1994). Success factors of systematic reuse. *IEEE Software*, **11**(5), 15−19

Frakes W.B. and Pol T. (1992). An empirical study of representation methods for reusable software components. *Technical Report*. Herndon VA: Software Productivity Consortium

Frakes W.B. and Terry C. (1996). Software reuse metrics and models. *ACM Computing Surveys*, **28**(2), 415−35

Gaffney J.E. Jr and Cruikshank R.D. (1992). A general economics model of software reuse. *Proceeedings of 14th ICSE*, May, 327−37

Gaffney J.E. Jr and Durek T.A. (1989). Software reuse-key to enhanced productivity: Some quantitative models. *Inf. Softw. Technol.* (UK), **31**(5), 258−67

Gamma E., Helm R., Johnson R. and Vlissides J. (1993). *Design Patterns: Abstraction and Reuse of Object-Oriented Design*. ECOOP, Springer-Verlag, July, pp. 406−31

Gamma E., Helm R., Johnson R. and Vlissides J. (1994). *Design Patterns − Elements of Reusable Object-Oriented Software*. Reading, MA: Addison-Wesley

Garlan D. (1995). Research directions in software architecture. *ACM Computing Surveys*, **27**(2), 257−61

Garlan D. and Shaw M. (1993). *An Introduction to Software Architecture, Advances in Software Engineering and Knowledge Engineering* Volume I. World Scientific Publishing Company

Garlan D., Allen R. and Ockerbloom J. (1995). Architectural mismatch: Why reuse is so hard. *IEEE Software*, November, pp. 17–26

Gilb T. (1988). *Principles of Software Engineering Management*. Addison-Wesley

Goldberg A. and Rubin K. (1995). *Succeeding with Objects – Decision Frameworks for Project Management*. Reading, MA: Addison-Wesley

Grady R.B. (1995). *Practical Software Metrics for Project Management and Process Improvement*. Prentice Hall

Grady R.B. and Caswell D. (1987). *Software Metrics: Establishing a Company Wide Program*. Prentice Hall

Gregory P. (1995). CARDS support for systematic reuse technology transfer. *CrossTalk*, July

Griss M.L. (1993). Software reuse: From library to factory. *IBM Systems Journal*, **32**(4), 548–66

Griss M.L. (1995a). Software reuse: Objects and frameworks are not enough. *Object Magazine*, February

Griss M.L. (1995b). Software reuse: A process of getting organized. *Object Magazine*, May

Griss M.L. (1995c). Packaging software reuse technologies as kits. *Object Magazine*, July

Griss M.L. (1995d). Software reuse – We are making progress. *Object Magazine*, December

Griss M.L. (1996). Domain engineering and variability in the reuse-driven software engineering business. *Object Magazine*, December

Griss M.L. and Collins P. (1995). Pilot projects in incremental adoption of reuse. *Object Magazine*, July

Griss M.L. and Kessler R.R. (1996). Building OO instrument kits. *Object Magazine*, April

Griss M.L. and Tracz W. (1993). WISR'92: 5th annual workshop on software reuse working groups report. *Software Engineering Notes*, **18**(2), 74–85

Griss M.L. and Wentzel K. (1994). Hybrid domain-specific kits for a flexible software factory. In *Proceedings of SAC'94*, March, pp. 47–52, New York: ACM

Griss M.L. and Wentzel K. (1995). Hybrid domain-specific kits. *Journal of Software and Systems*, **30**, 213–30

Griss M.L. and Wosser M. (1995). Making reuse work at Hewlett-Packard. *IEEE Software*, **12**(1), 105–7

Griss M.L., Adams S.S., Baetjer H. Jr, Cox B.J and Goldberg A. (1991). The economics of software reuse (panel). In *Proceedings of OOPSLA'91*, Phoenix, Arizona, 6–11 October, pp. 264–70, November. (Also as *SIGPLAN Notices*, **26**(1))

Griss M.L., Favaro J. and Walton P. (1994). Managerial and organizational issues – Starting and running a software reuse program. In *Software Reusability*, pp. 51–78. Chichester, UK: Ellis Horwood

Hammer M. and Champy J. (1993). *Reengineering the Corporation*. New York: HarperCollins

Hammer M. and Stanton S. (1995). *The Reengineering Revolution: A Handbook*. New York: HarperCollins

Harmon P. (1994a). *Object-Oriented Application Development Tools — Part I*. Object-Oriented Strategies, Cutter Information Corp., **4**(8)

Harmon P. (1994b). *Object-Oriented Application Development Tools — Part II*. Object-Oriented Strategies, Cutter Information Corp., **4**(9)

Harmon P. (1994c). *Object-Oriented Application Development Tools — Part 3*. Object-Oriented Strategies, Cutter Information Corp., **4**(10)

Harmon P. (1995a). *Objects and Components*. Oriented Strategies, Cutter Information Corp., **5**(5)

Harmon P. (1995b). *Objects and Components — Part II*. Oriented Strategies, Cutter Information Corp., **5**(6)

Henderson-Sellers B. and Edwards J.M. (1994). MOSES: A second generation object-oriented methodology. *Object Magazine*, **4**(3), 68−71

Hooper J.W. and Chester R. (1991). *Software Reuse — Guidelines and Methods*. New York: Plenum Press

Hovell J. (1994). Software reuse training. *CrossTalk*, January, pp. 26−7

HP PSO Americas (1995). *Change Management*

Humphrey W.S. (1989). *Managing the Software Process*. Reading, MA: Addison-Wesley

Humphrey W.S. (1995). *A Discipline for Software Engineering*. SEI Series in Software Engineering. Reading, MA: Addison-Wesley

Hutt A.T.F., ed. (1994). *Object Analysis and Design: Description of Methods*. OMG series. Wiley-QED. NY: Wiley

Isoda S. (1994). Progress in reuse in Japan. *IEEE Software*, September, p. 18

Jacobson I. (1987). Object-oriented development in an industrial environment. In *Proceedings of OOPSLA'87, SIGPLAN Notices*, **22**(12), 183−91

Jacobson I. (1994a). Basic use case modeling. *ROAD*, **1**(2)

Jacobson I. (1994b). Basic use case modeling (continued). *ROAD*, **1**(3)

Jacobson I. (1994c). Use cases and objects. *ROAD*, **1**(4)

Jacobson I. (1996a). A large commercial success story based on objects. *Object Magazine*, May

Jacobson I. (1996b). Succeeding with objects: Reuse in reality. *Object Magazine*, July

Jacobson I. and Jacobson S. (1995). Beyond methods and CASE: The software engineering process with its integral support environment. *Object Magazine*, January

Jacobson I. and Lindström F. (1991). Re-engineering of old systems to an object-oriented architecture. OOPSLA '91, pp. 340−50. ACM Press

Jacobson I., Christerson M., Jonsson P. and Övergaard G. (1992). *Object-Oriented Software Engineering: A Use Case Driven Approach*. Addison-Wesley. (Revised 4th printing, 1993)

Jacobson I., Ericsson M. and Jacobson A. (1994). *The Object Advantage – Business Process Reengineering with Object Technology*. Menlo Park, CA: Addison-Wesley

Jacobson I., Bylund S., Jonsson P. and Ehnebom S. (1995a). Using contracts and use cases to build pluggable architectures. *Journal of Object-Oriented Programming*, **8**(2)

Jacobson I., Palmkvist K. and Dyrhage S. (1995b). Systems of interconnected systems. *ROAD*, May–June

Jacobson I., Booch G. and Rumbaugh J. (1998 [expected Spring]). *The Objectory Software Development Process*. Menlo Park, CA: Addison-Wesley

Jandorek E. (1996). A model for platform development. *Hewlett-Packard Journal*, **47**(4), 56–71

Johnson R.E. (1994). Why a conference on pattern languages? *Software Engineering Notes*, **19**(1), 50–2

Johnson R.E. and Foote B. (1988). Designing reusable classes. *Journal of Object-Oriented Programming*, June, pp. 22–30, 35

Johnson R.E. and Russo V. (1991). Reusing Object-Oriented Designs. *Technical report*, University of Illinois and Purdue, April

Jones C. (1994). Economics of software reuse. *IEEE Computer*, **27**(7), 106–7

Jones C. (1995). Backfiring: Converting lines of code to function points. *IEEE Computer*, **28**(11), 87–8

Jones C. (1996a). Software estimating rules of thumb. *IEEE Computer*, **29**(3), 116–18

Jones C. (1996b). The pragmatics of software process improvement. *Software Process Newsletter*, No. 5 (Winter), pp. 1–4

Joos R. (1994). Software reuse at Motorola. *IEEE Software*, September, pp. 42–7

Kain J.B. (1994a). Pragmatics of reuse in the enterprise. *Object Magazine*, **3**(6), 55–8

Kain J.B. (1994b). Measuring the ROI of reuse. *Object Magazine*, **4**(3), 49–54

Kang K.C. (1990). Feature-based domain analysis methodology. In *Third Annual Workshop: Methods & Tools for Reuse* (Latour L., ed.), June. CASE Center, Syracuse University, University of Maine

Kang K., Cohen S., Hess J., Novak W. and Peterson S. (1990). Feature-Oriented Domain Analysis (FODA). Feasability Study. *Technical Report, CMU/SEI-90-TR-21*, November. Software Engineering Institute, Pittsburgh, PA 15213

Karlsson E.-A., ed. (1995). *Software Reuse: A Holistic Approach*. Chichester: Wiley

Karner G. (1993). Metrics for Objectory. *Master Thesis Report*, LiTH-IDA-Ex-9344. Linköping, Sweden

Koenig A. (1994). Templates and generic algorithms. *Journal of Object-Oriented Programming*, **7**(3), 45–7

Koistinen J. (1994). Large-grained modularization of object-oriented software. *Licentiate Thesis*, Report no. 94–015, May. Royal Institute of Technology and Stokholm University

Korson T. and McGregor J.D. (1991). Technical Criteria for the Specification and Evaluation of Object-Oriented Libraries. *Technical Report TR91–112*. Department of Computer Science, Clemson University

Korson T., Vaishnavi V. and Lambert T., eds (1992). Special issue: Analysis and modeling in software development. *Communications of the ACM*, September, **35**(9). ACM

Kozaczynski W. and Kunztman-Combelles A., eds (1993). Special issue: Making O-O work. *IEEE Software*, January, **10**(1)

Krasner G.E. and Pope S.T. (1988). *A Cookbook for Using the Model-View-Controller User Interface Paradigm in Smalltalk-80*. ParcPlace Systems

Kruchten P. (1995). The 4 + 1 view model of architecture. *IEEE Software*, **12**(6), 42–50

Kruchten P. (1996). A Rational development process. *Crosstalk*, **9**(7), July, Hill AFB, UT: STSC, pp. 11–16

Kruchten P.B. and Thompson C. (1994). An object-oriented, distributed architecture for large scale Ada systems. In *Proc. of the Tri-Ada '94 Conference*, 6–11 November, pp. 262–71. Baltimore: ACM

Krueger C. (1992). Software reuse. *ACM Computing Surveys*, **24**(2), 131–83

Laubsch J. (1996). A beginner's guide to developing with the Taligent application frameworks. *JOOP*, November–December

Lavoie D., Baetjer H., Tulloh W. and Langlois R. (1993). *Component Software: A Market Perspective on the Coming Revolution in Software Development*. Patricia Seybold Group, April

Lea D. (1994). Christopher Alexander: An introduction for object-oriented designers. *Software Engineering Notes*, **19**(1), 39–45

Lea D. and Frakes B. (1993). WISR'93 design for reuse working group report. Copy of slides prepared for WISR'93, November 1993. (See also WISR'93 report by Poulin and Tracz)

Lewis J., Henry S., Kafura D. and Schulmann R. (1991) An empirical study of the object-oriented paradigm and software reuse. In *OOPSLA'91 Proceedings*, October, pp. 184–96. ACM

Lim W.C. (1994). Effects of reuse on quality, productivity and economics. *IEEE Software*, **11**(5), 23–30

Lim W.C. (1996a). Tutorial: "Does Your Reuse Program Measure Up?: Reuse Assessment, Economics, and Metrics." *The 4th International Conference of Software Reuse*, April. Orlando, FL

Lim W.C. (1996b). *Managing Software Reuse*. Prentice Hall

Lim W.C. (1996c). Reuse Economics: A comparison of seventeen models and directions for future research. *Proceeedings of ICSR4*, pp. 41–51. Orlando, FL: IEEE

Lorenz M. (1991). Real-world reuse. *Journal of Object-Oriented Programming*, **4**(7), 35–9

Lorenz M. (1993a). Facilitating reuse using OO technology. *American Programmer*, August, pp. 44–9

Lorenz M. (1993b). *Object-Oriented Software Development: A Practical Guide*, Object-Oriented Series. Englewood Cliffs, NJ: Prentice Hall

Lorenz M. (1995). *Rapid Software Development with Smalltalk*. New York, NY: SIGS Books

Lung C.-H. and Urban J.E. (1995). An Approach to the Classification of Domain Models in Support of Analogical Reuse. In *Proceedings of the ACM SIGSOFT Symposium on Software Reusability* (SSR'95), Seattle, Washington, 28–30 April, pp. 169–78. (*Software Engineering Notes*, Special issue, August.)

Macala R.R., Stuckey L.D. Jr and Gross D.C. (1996). Managing domain-specific, product-line development. *IEEE Software*, May, pp. 57–67

Malan R. (1993). Motivating software reuse. In *WISR Proceedings*, November, pp. m1–6

Malan R. and Dicolen T. (1996). Risk management in an HP reuse project. *Fusion Newsletter*, April. (See http://www.hpl.hp.com/fusion)

Malan R. and Wentzel K. (1993b). Economics of software reuse revisited. *Proceedings of the 3rd Irvine Software Symposium* (Richardson D. and Taylor R., eds), 30 April, pp. 109–21. University of California, Irvine

McGregor J.D. and Korson T., eds (1990). Introduction to Special Issue: Object-oriented design. *Communications of the ACM*, September, **33**(9)

McGregor J. and Korson T. (1992). Supporting Dimensions of Classification in Object-Oriented Design. *Technical report*, February. Clemson University, Clemson, South Carolina

McGregor J.D. and Sykes D.A. (1992). *Object-Oriented Software Development: Engineering Software for Reuse*. New York: Van Nostrand Reinhold

McIlroy D. (1969). Mass produced software components. *1968 NATO Conf. on Software Engineering*, pp. 138–55

Mettala E. and Graham M. (1992). The domain-specific software architecture program. *CrossTalk*, **37**, 19–21

Meyer B. (1987). Reusability: The case for object-oriented design. *IEEE Software*, **4**(2), 50–64

Meyer B. (1994). *Reusable Software: The Base Object-Oriented Component Libraries*. Prentice Hall

Meyer B. and Lambert T., eds (1993). Special issue: Concurrent object-oriented programming. *Communications of the ACM*, September

Microsoft Corporation and Digital Equipment Corporation (1994). *Common Object Model Specification*, Draft ver. 0.2, October

Moore G.A. (1991). *Crossing the Chasm: Marketing and Selling Technology Products to Mainstream Customers*. Harper Business

Morel J.-M. and Faget J. (1993). The REBOOT environment. In *Proceedings of the Second International Workshop on Software Reuse*, March, pp. 80–8. IEEE Computer Society Press

Myers I. (1962). *The Myers-Briggs Type Indicator*. Palo Alto, CA: Consulting Psychologists Press

Navarro J.J. (1993). Organization design-based software reuse adoption strategy. In *WISR'93* (Latour L., ed.), November, pp. Navarro-1:9

Nierstrasz O., Gibbs S. and Tschritzis D. (1992). Component-oriented software development. *Communications of the ACM*, **35**(9), 160–5

Ogush M. (1992). Terms in transition: A software reuse lexicon. *CrossTalk*, **39**, 41–5

OMG and X/Open (1991). *The Common Object Request Broker: Architecture and Specification*, rev. 1.1

OMG (1996). *The Object Management Architecture Guide* (OMA Guide), contains the central design guideline (the Reference Model) used by OMG to create a distributed object computing environment

OMG (1996a). Common Facilities RFP-4, Common Business Objects and Business Object Facility. *OMG TC Document CF/96-01-04*

OMG (1996b). *The Common Object Request Broker: Architecture and Specification* (CORBA). Framingham, MA: OMG

OMG (1996c). *CORBAservices*. Framingham, MA: OMG

OMG (1996d). *CORBAfacilities*. Framingham, MA: OMG

Orfali R., Harkey D. and Edwards J. (1996). *The Essential Distributed Objects Survival Guide*. NY: Wiley

Park R.E. (1992). Software Size Measurement: A Framework for Counting Source Statements. *Software Engineering Institute Technical Report, CMU/SEI-92-TR-20*, September

Pfleeger S.L. (1996). Measuring reuse: A cautionary tale. *IEEE Software*, July, pp. 118–27. NY

Piper-Arnett J. (1992). DoD software reuse vision and strategy. *CrossTalk*, **37**, 2–8

Pittman M. (1993). Lessons learned in managing object-oriented development. *IEEE Software*, **10**(1), 43–53

Potel M. and Cotter S. (1995). *Inside Taligent Technology*. Addison-Wesley

Poulin J.S. (1996). *Measuring Software Reuse: Principles, Practices, and Economic Models*. Addison-Wesley

Poulin J.S. and Tracz W. (1994). WISR'93: 6th annual workshop on software reuse, summary and working group reports. *Software Engineering Notes*, January, **19**(1), 55–71

Poulin J.S. and Werkman K.J. (1995). Melding structured abstracts and the World Wide Web for retrieval of reusable components. *Proceedings of the ACM SIGSOFT Symposium on Software Reusability* (SSR'95), April, pp. 160–8. Seattle, WA. See also http://pooh.unl.edu/~scotth/ssr95/poulin/poulin.html

Poulin J.S, Caruso J.M. and Hancock D.R. (1993). The business case for software reuse. *IBM Systems Journal*, **4**(32), 567–94

Pree W. (1995). *Design Patterns for Object-Oriented Software Engineering*. Addison-Wesley

Pressman R. (1997). *Software Engineering: A Practitioner's Approach* 4th edn. McGraw-Hill

Price Waterhouse Change Integration Team (1995). *Better Change – Best Practices for Transforming your Organization*. Irwin Professional Publishing

Prieto-Diaz R. (1990). Domain analysis: An introduction. *Software Engineering Notes*, **15**(2), 47–54

Prieto-Diaz R. (1991). Making software reuse work: An implementation model. *Software Engineering Notes*, **16**(3), 61–8

Prieto-Diaz R. and Arango G. (1991). *Domain Analysis: Acquisition of Reusable Information for Software Construction*. IEEE Computer Society Press Tutorial, New York

Prieto-Diaz R. and Frakes W.B., eds (1993). *Advances in Software Reuse*: Selected papers from the Second International Workshop on Software Reusability, Los Alamitos, California, March. IEEE Computer Society Press

Purtilo J.M. (1994). The PolyLith Software Bus, *TOPLAS*, **16**(1), 151–74

Putnam L.H. and Myers W. (1996). *Executive Briefing: Controlling Software Development*. Los Alamitos, CA: IEEE Computer Society Press

Rational (1995). Software architecture and iterative development, Version 3.2. Training course material. Santa Clara: Rational

Reilly A. and Shriver B.D., eds (1987). Special issue: Reusing software. *IEEE Software*, January, **4**(1), NY

Riggs M.H. (1992). Army reuse center services. *CrossTalk*, December, p. 30

Rine D.C. and Bhargava B., eds (1992). Special issue: Object-oriented computing. *IEEE Computer*, **25**(10). New York

Rumbaugh J., Blaha M., Remerlani W., Eddy F. and Lorensen W. (1991). *Object-Oriented Modeling and Design*. Englewood Cliffs, NJ: Prentice Hall

Rumbaugh J., Jacobson I. and Booch G. (1998 [expected Spring]). *Unified Modeling Language Reference Manual*. Menlo Park, CA: Addison-Wesley

Ryan D. (1991). Software reuse: A competitive advantage. AT&T Bell Laboratories, November. Software Technology Center, slides

Schaefer W., Prieto-Diaz R. and Matsumoto M., eds (1994). *Software Reusability*. Chichester, UK: Ellis Horwood

Schmucker K.J. (1986). *Object-Oriented Programming for the Macintosh*. Hayden Book Company

SEI (1992). Software Measurement for DoD Systems: Recommendations for Initial Core Measure. *Proceedings of the Software Engineering Symposium*, September, SEI, CMU. Pittsburg, PA. (See brief description in *IEEE Software*, November, pp. 111–12)

Selby R.W. (1989). Quantitative studies of software reuse. In *Software Reusability* Vol. II (Biggerstaff T.J. and Perlis A.J., eds), pp. 213–33. ACM Press, Addison-Wesley

Shaw M. (1995). Comparing architectural design styles. *IEEE Software*, **12**(6), 27–41

Shaw M. and Garlan D. (1996). *Software Architecture – Perspectives on an Emerging Discipline*. Englewood Cliffs, NJ: Prentice Hall

Shelton R.E. (1995). Business object frameworks and patterns business object. *Data Management Review*, May

Simos M.A. (1995a). Comparing domain analysis method. *Proceedings of WISR*

Simos M.A. (1995b). Organization Domain Modelling (ODM): Formalizing the core domain modeling life cycle. *Proceedings of SSR'95*. Seattle, WA

Sims O. (1994). *Business Objects: Delivering Cooperative Objects for Client/Server*. McGraw-Hill

STARS (1993). STARS Conceptual Framework for Reuse Processes (CFRP). *Technical Report STARS-VC-A018/001/00*, Paramax, October. (Version 3.0 Vols I & II)

STARS (1995). Software Technology for Adaptable Reliable Systems, Organization Domain Modeling (ODM) Guidebook, version 1.0. *STARS-VC-A023/011/00*, 17 March

Stevens B.J. (1992). Linking software re-engineering and reuse: An economic motivation. *CrossTalk*, **35**, 13–20

Taenzer D., Ganti M. and Podar S. (1989a). Problems in object-oriented software reuse. In *ECOOP'89 – Proceedings of the 1989 European Conference on Object-Oriented Programming*, July, pp. 25–38. Cambridge, UK: Cambridge Univ. Press

Taenzer D., Ganti M. and Podar S. (1989b). Object-oriented software reuse: the "yoyo" problem. *Journal of Object-Oriented Programming*, **2**, 30–5

Taligent (1994). *Taligent's Guide to Designing Programs*. Addison-Wesley

Taligent (1995). *The Power of Frameworks*. Addison-Wesley

Taylor D. (1990). *Object Oriented Technology: A Manager's Guide*. Reading, MA: Addison-Wesley

Taylor D.A. (1992a). Easing into objects: Whatever happened to the object components industry? *Object Magazine*, **1**(6), 17–18

Taylor D.A. (1992b). Easing into objects: Developing the object components industry. *Object Magazine*, **1**(6), 19–21

Taylor D.A. (1993). Easing into objects: A development lifecycle for object technology. *Object Magazine*, **2**(5), 18–24

Taylor D.A. (1994). Easing into objects: SOM is the key to integrating objects. *Object Magazine*, **3**(6), 16–18

Taylor D.A. (1995a). *Business Engineering with Object Technology*. New York: Wiley

Teknekron (1994). Enterprise Toolkit. White paper. Teknekron Software Systems Inc., 530 Lytton Ave, Palo Alto, CA

Tirso J.R. (1991a). Establishing a software reuse support structure. In *IEEE International Conference on Communications*, June, pp. 1500–4. IEEE

Tirso J.R. (1991b). The IBM reuse program. In *Proceedings of the 4th Annual Workshop on Software Reuse*, November, pp. 1–5. 222 Neville Hall, Orono, Maine 04469. Department of Computer Science, University of Maine

Tirso J.R. (1992). Championing the cause: Making reuse stick. In *Proceedings of the 5th Annual Workshop on Software Reuse* (Griss M. and Latour L., eds), October, pp. Tirso-1:6. Department of Computer Science, University of Maine

Tracz W., ed. (1987). Special issue: Making reuse a reality. *IEEE Software*, July, **4**(4)

Tracz W. (1988a). Software Reuse Maxims. *ACM SIGSOFT: Software Engineering Notes*, **13**(4), pp. 28–31

Tracz W. (1988b). *Tutorial: Software Reuse: Emerging Technology*. IEEE Computer Society Press, IEEE Catalog Number EH0278-2

Tracz W. (1990). Where does reuse start? *Software Engineering Notes*, **15**(2)

Tracz W. (1991). A conceptual model for megaprogramming. *Software Engineering Notes,* July, pp. 1–10

Tracz W. (1992). Software Reuse Technical Opportunities. *Technical report,* June. IBM Corporation, Federal Systems Company

Tracz W. (1993). Second international workshop on software reusability. *CrossTalk,* pp. [26–9]

Tracz W. (1995a). Third international conference on software reusability. *Software Engineering Notes,* **20**(2), 23–7

Tracz W. (1995b). *Confessions of a Used Program Salesman – Institutionalizing Software Reuse.* Addison-Wesley

Tracz W., Coglianese L. and Young P. (1993). Domain-specific SW architecture engineering. *Software Engineering Notes,* **18**(2), 40–9

Udell J. (1994). Component software. *BYTE,* **19**(5), 46–55

Wallnau K. (1992). An introduction to CARDS. *CrossTalk,* **36**, 30–1

Wasmund M. (1993). Implementing critical success factors in software reuse. *IBM Systems Journal,* **4**(32), 595–611

Wegner P. (1984). Capital intensive software technology. *IEEE Software,* **1**(3), 7–46

Wilde N. *et al.* (1993). Maintaining object-oriented software. *IEEE Software,* January, pp. 75–80

Wirfs-Brock R., Wilkerson B. and Wiener L. (1990). *Designing Object-Oriented Software.* Englewood Cliffs, NJ: Prentice Hall

Wirfs-Brock R. (1993). Characterizing your objects. *Smalltalk Report,* February

Woodfield S.N., Embley D.W., Stokes G.L. and Zhang K. (1986). Assumptions and issues of software reusability. Fifth Annual International Phoenix Conference on Computers and Communications (PCCC'86. *1986 Conference Proceedings*), March, pp. 450–4. Washington DC: Computer Society Press

Woodfield S.N., Embley D.W. and Scott D.T. (1987). Can programs reuse software? *IEEE Software,* **4**(July), 52–9

Yourdon E., ed. (1991a). Reusability. *American Programmer.* New York, March. (Special issue, **4**(9))

Yourdon E., ed. (1991b). Object-orientation. *American Programmer.* New York, October. (Special issue, **4**(10))

Yourdon E., ed. (1992). Object orientation update. *American Programmer.* New York, October. (Special issue, **5**(8))

Yourdon E., ed. (1993). Reusability. *American Programmer.* New York, August. (Special issue, **6**(9))

Yourdon E. (1994). Software reuse. *Application Development Strategies,* **VI**(12), 1–5

Yourdon E. (1995). Component-based software development. *American Programmer.* New York, November. (Special issue, **8**(11)). (See: http://www.yourdon.com)

Yourdon E. (1996a). Visual Basic 4. *Application Development Strategies,* **VIII**(2), 1–16

Yourdon E. (1996b). *Rise and Resurrection of the American Programmer.* Upper Saddle River, NJ: Yourdon Press, Prentice Hall

Yourdon E. (1996c). CASE Update. *Application Development Strategies.* **VIII**(10), 1–16

Yourdon E. (1997). Software reuse, revisited. *Application Development Strategies,* Cutter, **IX**(2), February

INDEX

in layered architecture   194, 202, 204, 208, 210
in object components   134, 136, 139, 141, 143, 150–1, 153, 167
in UML notation   456
in use case components   122, 130
Component System Engineering (CSE)   297–320
and AFE   266, 295
and ASE   321, 322
and CSE   319
definition   297, 427
designing component system   299, 310–11
education in RSEB   398–9
flexible systems   297–9
implementing component system   299, 312–14
in C++   312–13
in packaging   313–14
in Smalltalk   313
in managing the reuse business   376–8, 380–1, 385–7, 396–7
in OOBE   231
packaging
actor and use case components   304
for reuse   299, 315–18
requirements capture   298, 299–304
actor and use case components   304
business models   300–1
main inputs   301–2
other inputs   302–3
superordinate systems   300–1
use case models   303
in reuse business   40, 41, 43, 48, 236–7
in reuse business transition   346, 347, 348, 355, 362, 369–71
robustness analysis   298–9, 305–10
analysis model   309–10
analysis types for reuse   309
variability, structuring   306–9
and RSEB   233–5, 235–9, 247–8, 253
in RSEB   400
testing component system   299, 314–15
and workers   318–19
Component System Librarian   250
education in RSEB   399
in reuse business transition   366, 369
Component System Supporter   249, 250, 304, 316, 319
in ASE   334
in managing the reuse business   380, 386
in reuse business transition   366, 369
Component System Trainer   249, 250, 256
in ASE   334
in reuse business transition   366
Component Systems   81–113
in AFE, acquiring   285–6
facades in   89–90
export of components   93–5
as special packages   90–2
group components in   86–9

reusable components in   85–6
in reuse business   38–9, 48
reuse of OOSE components   81–3
packaging and documentation   110–13
specialization of   95–8
significant reuse of   83–4
variability in   95, 98–100
mechanisms for   96, 100–5
reuse of   106–10
Component Use Case Engineer   235, 365
components   50
reusable   85
Conceptual Framework for Reuse Process (CFRP)   25, 300
definition   428
concrete
components   97
definition   428
use case components   120–3
in OOSE   68
ConcreteStrategy in CSE   307
concurrency model
definition   428
in layered architecture   191
configurable testing in CSE   314–15
configuration
in component systems   101, 102, 110–13
management   110
definition   428
management   110
definition   428
in UML notation   456
in use case components   129
configuration item
in component systems   102, 110–13
definition   428
in object components   166–7
in UML notation   456
in use case components   129–30
conflict resolution in managing the reuse business   396–7
conforms in object components   155
consists of   312–13
consists of association
definition   428
in UML notation   460, 462
Constructive Cost Modelling (COCOMO)   382, 386, 392–4
definition   426
constructs   51
contains, in object components   150
Context in CSE   307
continuous process improvement
definition   428
managing the reuse business   395–6
control type
definition   428
in object components   147
in OOSE   69, 72
in UML notation   460
copied dependency   91

education in the reuse business 398–9
effectiveness in use case components 117
embedded software in reuse business 46
encapsulating data 59
end users 56
    in ASE 331, 334
    in ASE, inputs 325–6
    in business engineering 235, 240, 249
    in CSE, inputs 301–2
    definition 430
    in reuse business 42
    in SEP 233
engineering deficiencies in reuse 8
engineering discipline in reuse business 36
engineering orientation of RSEB 32
entity object, in OOBE 229
entity type
    in application systems 85–6
    definition 430
    in object components 146, 147
    in OOBE 222–4
    in OOSE 69, 71
    in UML notation 461
    in use case components 124
envisioning 430
Ericsson 6
    acquiring component systems 286
    application system variants 83
    architected reuse 34–5
    reuse experience 10–11, 23, 46
    variability of components 97
error-detection
    in object components 145
    in use case components 124
ESS5 (telephone switch) 46
evolution, defined 430
explicit extensions 104
explicit techniques 231
exports
    in component systems 93–5
    definition 430
Extended Intelligence RPM 364
extends
    generalization, defined 430
    in object components 158
    in UML notation 458, 461
    in use case components 129
extends facility
    in AFE 269, 277
    in CSE 303, 306
    definition 68
    in object components 141, 146, 148
    in OOSE 67–8, 110
    in use case components 123
extension points 102, 104, 108, 110
    definition 430–1
    specification 104
extensions
    in component systems 101, 102
        using 104–5

definition 430
    in object components 160–2
    in use case components 128

Facade Engineer 247
    in CSE 318, 319
    in reuse business transition 365
facades
    in AFE 290
    in application systems 87, 89–90, 90–3, 94, 96,
        100, 107–9, 111–12
        export of components 93–5
        as special packages 90–3
    in business engineering 252–3
    definition 89, 431
    designing in AFE 289–90
    in layered architecture 190, 199, 202, 203, 204,
        208, 210
    in object components 136, 143, 167
    in reuse business 39
    in UML notation 457
    in use case components 122, 130
Feature Engineer 359
Feature Oriented Domain Analysis (FODA) 25, 98,
    268, 300
    definition 431
features
    in component systems 98
    definition 98
file scope 168
Fixing Defects in Application Systems 251
FODA (Feature Oriented Domain Analysis) 25, 98,
    268, 300, 431
Forté 211
Fortran 7
forward engineering
    definition 431
    of transition to reuse business 361–6
        designing processes and workers 361–3
        tools for workers 364–6
frame technology 14, 97, 129, 164
frameworks
    in AFE 284
    definition 154, 431
    in layered architecture 186
    in object components groups 152–4
function points, defined 431

generalizations 100
    definition 431
    in OOSE 61, 62
generation
    in component systems 101, 102
    definition 431
    in object components 162–5
Globally Unique Identifiers 183
glossary
    definition 431
    of use case components 118